Cynical Therapies
Perspectives on the Antitherapeutic Nature of Critical Social Justice

EDITED BY DR VAL THOMAS

ISBN: 978-1-922956-48-4 (paperback)
          978-1-922956-56-9 (eBook)

 A catalogue record for this book is available from the National Library of Australia

Edited by Marisa Parker
Cover image designed by Christopher Barr
Printed in Australia by Ocean Reeve Publishing
www.oceanreevepublishing.com
Published by Dr Val Thomas and Ocean Reeve Publishing

REEVE
PUBLISHING

Contents

CRITICAL SOCIAL JUSTICE THEORIES IN APPLICATION

PROFESSIONAL MATTERS

THE FUTURE

Acknowledgments

Many people have made helpful contributions to the authors' chapters contained within this edited book. Although they are not identified by name here, they know who they are. The authors are very grateful for their input.

There is one person, though, for whom all of us have reason to be especially grateful, and that is Helen Pluckrose. In the middle of a very heavy workload, Helen made time to review all the chapters in the light of Critical Social Justice theories. Her comments and observations helped us all refine and develop the arguments and perspectives presented here on the antitherapeutic nature of Critical Social Justice and the existential threat this ideology poses to traditional therapy.

Author Biographies

Bret Alderman, PhD, graduated from the Pacifica Graduate Institute in 2013, where he studied Depth Psychology. He is a life coach and writer based in Oakland, California. His book *Symptom, Symbol, and the Other of Language: A Jungian interpretation of the linguistic turn* (2016) was published by Routledge in the series *Research in Analytical Psychology and Jungian Studies*.

Sasha Ayad, M.Ed (Counseling Psychology) is a Licensed Professional Counselor based in Houston, Texas, USA who has worked with adolescents for over thirteen years. Her current work is focused on adolescent-onset gender identity issues. She discovered, through working with hundreds of families, that teens were developing gender dysphoria only *after* adopting a trans identity. She is the co-host of the *Gender: A Wider Lens* podcast.

John Barry, PhD, is a Chartered Psychologist and Associate Fellow of the British Psychological Society and past Chair of the Male Psychology Section of the BPS. He is also an Honorary Lecturer in Psychology at University College London, a clinical hypnotherapist with around twenty years experience, and the author of around seventy peer-reviewed papers and books, mostly on the psychological aspects of polycystic ovary syndrome (PCOS) and men's mental health.

Tim Courtois, MA, is a Licensed Professional Counselor based in Michigan, USA. He has been practising since 2006 and has received a certificate in Narrative-Focused Trauma Therapy from The Allender Center and a Sexual Health Certificate from the University of Michigan. His work has specialized in issues relating to sexuality, including sexual abuse, trauma, and sexual identity.

Birgit Ewald, FirstTheolExam (German qualification comparable to MA), is a UK-based counsellor, clinical supervisor, and lecturer in counselling. She has worked with adults, adolescents, and families in diverse settings, as well as having her own private practice. She has a longstanding interest in psycho-spiritual development, the interface between psychology and spirituality, and the nature of relationships. For her PhD, in 2022, she is currently researching the therapist's experience of therapeutic presence, in particular the transpersonal/spiritual dimension of presence.

Ben Harris, MA (Integrative Psychotherapy), is a psychotherapist practising privately in London, the Channel Islands, and online. He read Philosophy, Politics, and Economics at Oxford University before pursuing a career in the city (London) as a corporate analyst and lawyer. An exploration of suffering and meaning in his own life later drew him into the world of psychotherapy. His practice draws from psychoanalytic, Jungian, and existentialist insights.

Lisa Marchiano, LCSW. (Licensed Clinical Social Worker), is a writer and Jungian analyst in private practice in Philadelphia, Pennsylvania, USA. She is the co-host and creator of the popular podcast, *This Jungian Life.* She teaches at the C.G. Jung Institute of Philadelphia and lectures widely on Jungian topics. Her writings have appeared in *Quillette, The Journal of Analytical Psychology,* and *Psychological Perspectives,* among other publications. She is the author of the book *Motherhood: Facing and Finding Yourself,* published by Sounds True.

Robert D. Mather, PhD, is the CEO and Founder of Mather Professional Services, LLC. A behavioral scientist with expertise in social cognition, attitudes, persuasion, stereotypes, prejudice, and discrimination, he earned his doctorate in experimental psychology from Texas Tech University, USA. He has authored over forty peer-reviewed journal articles and four books, including *Implicit Biases and the Unconscious: Liberal Biases, Racial Prejudice, and Politics* (2020).

Dina McMillan, PhD, is an American social psychologist and academic currently based in Brisbane, Australia. She specialises in domestic abuse prevention and effective bias reduction, with an education program, podcast series, and TEDx talk called *Unmasking the Abuser*. She has published a book with Allen & Unwin on abuse prevention titled *But He Says He Loves Me: How to Avoid Being Trapped in a Manipulative Relationship*. In 2020, she developed a unique program called *Healing the Rift* designed to reduce racism and other types of bias without using blame-and-shame methods that may increase divisions and exacerbate intolerance.

Kirsty Miller, PhD, is a lecturer based in Scotland. After completing a Doctor of Philosophy in social and clinical psychology, her interests turned to investigating the dangers of groupthink and ideological conformity within academia. She is committed to open enquiry in science, is a member of The Heterodox Academy and the Society for Open Inquiry in the Behavioural Sciences, and is working towards protecting psychology and academia from the excesses of Critical Social Justice.

Piers Newman, MSc (Family Therapy), is a Systemic Family Psychotherapist working in private practice and the National Health Service (NHS) in England. He supervises, teaches, and trains family therapists as both a tutor on an intermediate-level course and as a 'live-supervisor' of training clinics. His professional interests are working with parents with traumatic childhoods and families in crisis.

Stella O'Malley, MA (Cognitive Behavioural Therapy) is a psychotherapist, bestselling author, and public speaker based in Ireland. She has written three bestselling books, *Cotton Wool Kids*, *Bully-Proof Kids*, and *Fragile*. In 2018, she was the writer and presenter of the Channel 4 documentary *Trans Kids: It's Time to Talk*. She is the founder and director of Genspect and the co-host of the *Gender: A Wider Lens* podcast. Stella is currently studying for a PhD and is researching gender-related distress in childhood.

Nicholas Opyrchal, MA (Transpersonal Psychology) is a psychotherapist in private practice in the UK and a doctoral student researching the meeting of transpersonal psychotherapy and identity politics. He has previously researched the theoretical similarities and differences between transpersonal psychotherapy and Lacanian (and post-Lacanian) psychoanalysis. Before working as a psychotherapist, he was a professional Thai boxer and martial arts instructor. He is developing an interest in ecotherapy.

Philip J. Pellegrino, PsyD (Doctor of Psychology), is a Licensed Psychologist in solo practice in the United States. He specializes in Cognitive Behavioral Therapy (CBT) and is board certified in Behavioral and Cognitive Psychology by the American Board of Professional Psychology (ABPP). He is a co-author of a book chapter on CBT for insomnia in *The Handbook of Cognitive-Behavioral Therapy in Primary Care* by DiTomasso, Golden, and Morris (Springer, 2010).

Dennis Relojo-Howell, MSc, is the founder of *Psychreg*, a digital publication that focuses on psychology, mental health, and wellness. His doctoral research project at the University of Edinburgh, Scotland, examines the viability of a blog-based resilience intervention.

Christine Sefein, MA, LMFT (Licensed Marriage and Family Therapist), specialises in grief and trauma work and has held positions such as Clinical Director of OUR HOUSE Grief Support Center and Clinical Supervisor of the Interpersonal Violence programs at California Lutheran University. She was a former full-time teaching faculty in the Master of Arts in Clinical Psychology program at Antioch University, Los Angeles. She currently works with clients in a group private practice setting.

Carole Sherwood, DClinPsy (Doctor of Clinical Psychology), is a retired UK clinical psychologist. She previously worked for the National Health Service at St Mary's Hospital in London, providing psychological care for patients and supervision and training for health professionals. She specialised in HIV, trauma, chronic pain, cancer, and palliative care. She held the role of Consultant Clinical Psychologist for Cancer Services at Imperial College Healthcare NHS Trust before retiring in 2013.

Nina C. Silander, PsyD (Doctor of Psychology), is a clinical psychologist who earned her doctorate at Regent University in Virginia, USA, and specializes in health, medical, and trauma psychology services. Since becoming increasingly concerned with ideological bias in psychology, she seeks to shed light on its effects on research, professional roles, and especially clinical practice through peer-reviewed publications and blog articles.

Val Thomas, DPsych (Professional Doctorate in Psychotherapy), is a UK-based psychotherapist, writer, and formerly a counsellor educator. She has specialised in developing applications of mental imagery and has published two books for Routledge titled *Using Mental Imagery in Counselling and Psychotherapy* and *Using Mental Imagery to Enhance Creative and Work-Related Processes*.

In 2020, she co-founded *Critical Therapy Antidote*, a platform for therapists concerned by the encroachments of Critical Social Justice in the therapy field.

Note: Nineteen authors from the United Kingdom and the United States have contributed to this important publication. With some different approaches to the English language (spelling and punctuation), the global use of descriptions for degrees has been applied. Throughout the book content, however, British and American English have been used depending on the author of that chapter.

Introduction

by Val Thomas

Why this book is needed

At the beginning of the third decade of the 21st century, there can be no one who remains unaffected by the great changes sweeping through society. On the physical level, people are reeling from an experience of a global pandemic accompanied by economic uncertainty and climate disturbances while immersed in a digital technology that has revolutionised communication and social interaction. Meanwhile, a new worldview labelled Critical Social Justice (or wokeness in common parlance) has increasing purchase on the culture—a collectivist ideology that is antithetical to the principles informing Western liberal democracies. The old certainties have eroded away, and people find themselves unsettled and disturbed. They can no longer rely on the wider containment offered by a stable and secure culture: indeed, there are indications that society itself is descending into a trough of collective depression and anxiety.[1] During periods of unrest and great change, people have historically looked outside of themselves for sources of help. Authority figures who could provide solace and wisdom in the past were priests, doctors, and wise elders. But now, in the West, it is far more likely that therapists would come to the fore at times like these.

Yet, these professional helpers have a complex relationship with the wider society. It is one that we need to be acutely aware of, as nowadays, they help individuals with the difficulties they face in life. Sometimes, these difficulties are the universal conditions of life itself, such as illness, grief, and loss; sometimes these problems may have their origins in social conditions, for example, poverty. But it is important to bear in mind that professional helpers also operate as agents of their society and re-enforce its moral code and values.

An extreme example from recent times is the way that the Soviet Russian state used psychiatrists to diagnose dissidents as mentally disordered—during the 1970s and 80s—as one-third of political prisoners were locked up in psychiatric hospitals.[2]

Consequently, as a new way of understanding the world is gaining ground in our institutions and social systems, and culture more generally, it is important to think about how therapy is being affected by these changes. To what extent is therapy changing to accommodate itself to new ideas in society, and if it is, what are the consequences for the vulnerable people seeking help?

One would presume that big questions such as these would have evoked considerable public discussion and debate. Yet the therapy field has been almost completely silent. This silence should not be taken as meaning that this new ideology has not gained much ground in the therapy field—one glance at the websites of professional bodies such as the American Psychological Association would make it clear that the status quo now is Critical Social Justice (CSJ).[3] Look at the syllabi for professional counselling trainings in universities and note how the focus is on advocacy and reframing clients' problems as the result of oppressive power structures. No, it is my opinion and that of my esteemed colleagues in this publication that instead, the extraordinary lack of public debate is due to the hold that social justice activists now have over the therapy professions. Behind closed walls, in committee rooms, and in newly formed task forces, therapy is being co-opted for political purposes.

The first step in countering this alarming transformation—that is happening silently behind the scenes—is to make it public. People need to know that when they look for help, the potential helper might have a political agenda that will be imposed upon them. People who have a vocation to be a therapist need to know that many professional training programmes are now designed to produce activists rather than effective healers and helpers.

The professions need to answer questions about the claim that Critical Social Justice-driven practice is actually therapy—how does it work? Is it effective? Particularly important questions would be: How does it help a client to re-enforce their sense of victimhood? What happens when the therapist diagnoses the client's problems as the inevitable consequences of an oppressive society? Who benefits when the client's personal agency is weakened?[4] Where is the evidence that making the client's identity the most important factor is in any way therapeutic? How are the obvious human deficits of woke activists—the refusal of dialogue, lack of humour and forgiveness—likely to deaden therapeutic relationships?

This book is a response to the urgent need to defend the healing ethos of therapy and resist the campaign to turn it into a practice of moral re-education that serves the political interests of an authoritarian elite. It is a warning to those seeking therapy that they have a right to a functionally apolitical therapist rather than one who has a hidden potentially antitherapeutic agenda.

Aim and scope

At the end of 2020, a group of therapists, academics, clinical theorists, researchers, and educators assembled in order to articulate the existential threat that Critical Social Justice poses to traditional and well-established therapeutic approaches.

All of these concerned professionals had noted, with alarm, the uniform response of the therapy field in the wake of George Floyd's death: professional bodies and institutions issued statements aligning themselves with political groups such as Black Lives Matter. No principled critique of these positions would be countenanced. The natural revulsion that people felt concerning the death of an unarmed black man at the hands of the police was easily exploited by activists with a political agenda. Who could object to the wholescale commitment of therapy institutions to anti-racism without being characterised as a bigot?

Almost overnight, the CSJ project—many years in the making—appeared to be complete: therapy would no longer be focused on helping individuals; instead, it would be reframed as a political practice, a means of dismantling systems of power believed to be oppressive.

All members of this group cast around to find different avenues to engage the therapy professions from within. All to no avail. Colleagues close their doors and shut down collaborative ventures. No academic journal will publish any paper that does not accept the status quo. No professional body journal will countenance any debate, even within its letters page. Political activists hound professionals who attempt to counter this narrative, organising social media campaigns to defame professional reputations. Mainstream academic publishing houses serve the same narrative.

And so, finding the professional therapy field sealing itself up inside heavily fortified defences, the group looked outwards. The most important people in the therapeutic enterprise are the clients, the consumers of therapy. Clients have a right to a therapist who suspends their political preoccupations and who gives the client's own agenda their full attention. So, we are walking out of the professional city walls in order to address the general public. Standing on soap boxes around its perimeter, we are all delivering the same message: Beware! Political activists are turning therapy into an antitherapeutic practice, one that weakens the individual, nurtures resentment, and encourages victimhood.

Our voices are gathered together in this book in a collection of chapters. It is a diverse international group of people with different voices.

This is not a systemised overview; this is not a political position; this is not a reactionary move. We have particular areas of expertise, different perspectives, and sometimes, disagreements, but we all have one thing in common: we will not accept the imposition of an authoritarian ideology that prevents free and open debate about the nature of therapy.

Every chapter delivers one piece of the story that is happening inside the professions of counselling and psychotherapy—a story that everyone with an interest or stake in therapy needs to understand.

Our hopes for this book

We believe that this book represents one of the first steps in what must become a concerted effort to expose how political activists are driving therapy down a non-therapeutic path. We hope that it begins to make the wider public aware that they need to select a therapist very carefully lest they find themselves with a professional who is intent on their moral re-education.

We also want to inform people who are feeling called to a healing vocation that they must ask questions about the training institution syllabus—are they going to be trained as activists rather than therapists?

Further, we also want to address practitioners and trainees, many of whom feel beleaguered and under pressure to conform to an ideology that they do not subscribe to.

We hope that reading this publication will assist them in developing and articulating their own critique of the direction that therapy is moving in. We would also hope that it will encourage professionals within the therapy field to challenge the orthodoxy in public.

Both academia and the professional therapy world are numerically dominated by leftist-sympathising personnel, a bias that makes it extremely difficult to challenge the woke narrative. For too long, the 'speaking truth to power' chant has enraptured professionals influenced by CSJ, who assume they speak as and to the oppressed; but by stealth, it is the CSJ lobby itself that has seized ideological power in our institutions, and we hope to encourage the silent minority of independent-minded students and therapists to speak out. The more of us who can stand our ground and tell the truth of our experience, the more that the integrity of therapy can be preserved. We owe this to the clients our professions serve and to the future generations of people who will be training as therapists.

Contents

The introduction includes an extended glossary and a brief explanation of the tenets of CSJ, which will assist the reader in following the arguments presented in the book. It is recommended that each chapter is read in conjunction with this glossary.

The book opens by setting its contents in the wider historical context of the development of the disciplines of counselling and psychotherapy. Val Thomas provides an account of how the therapy field arrived at this critical point where it has opened itself up to a takeover by a political ideology. Counselling and psychotherapy were born out of the Western liberal and enlightenment tradition with a focus on the individual. But, by the turn of the millennium, these disciplines had evolved into a pluralistic field that was able to integrate postmodern perspectives and include the collective dimension of the self in a productive way.

However, during the first two decades of the 21st century, this promising expansion pivoted into a narrow focus on the collective to the exclusion of all other aspects of the self, the individual and universal dimensions of human experience being pushed to one side. The chapter identifies how political activists informed by applied postmodernism (aka CSJ) gained control over the institutions of therapy, its professional bodies, and training institutions, and the field was primed for the re-engineering of therapy as a political practice.

The first section on wider perspectives—Critical Perspectives on Critical Social Justice—starts with Nick Opyrchal's chapter, which explores the factors implicated in the psychotherapy profession's eagerness to align itself with a political ideology promulgated by the cultural elite. He argues that over recent decades there has been a fusion between politics and therapy. Therapeutic concepts and language have been imported into mainstream society, and this language is then put to use for political purposes. He also argues that the whole-scale adoption of CSJ and identity politics by the institutions of therapy leads inevitably to an authoritarian mindset, one that constrains the subjectivity of its practitioners and limits their ability to help their clients.

Ben Harris draws on theories produced within the therapy disciplines to critique CSJ in action. In this chapter, he considers how existential psychotherapy and psychodynamic theory are particularly illuminating concerning the limitations of this new collectivist ideological worldview. Existential perspectives argue for an acceptance of the universal conditions of human existence which counter the utopian and unachievable dreams of CSJ. Psychodynamic theories such as "splitting" can help to explain why people caught up in this ideology are prone to identifying themselves as the "good" who can then treat nonbelievers as objects only worthy of hate.

Kirsty Miller's chapter is next. It issues a challenge to psychologists to draw on the theory from within their own discipline to critique the uncontested take-up of CSJ within the profession. She identifies some key concepts from within social identity theory that can help to explain the polarising nature of CSJ. It is suggested that one model, the five-step social identity model of the development of collective hate, sheds light on the way that CSJ exacerbates the human tendency to produce in-groups and out-groups. Kirsty goes on to make the case that therapeutic practices informed by CSJ are priming clients for a concerning increase in hate-filled and destructive interpersonal relations.

This first section ends with Bret Alderman's chapter discussing the religious character of CSJ. He draws on the theory and insights of Carl Jung, the founder of archetypal psychology, to shed light on the intoxicating nature of ideologies and the zealotry exhibited by its believers. Jung noted that in the absence of formal religion, the religious tendencies in human beings will attach themselves to secular belief systems. In particular, he draws attention to one of Jung's key ideas, the notion of archetypal possession, which offers a persuasive explanation of how CSJ has gained such a hold over the culture.

The next section deals with the ramifications of particular CSJ theories and ideas for therapeutic practice. The topic of the first three chapters is arguably one that has attracted the most ire from activists: gender ideology—the title of this segment—that has particular reference to Rapid-Onset Gender Dysphoria (ROGD). This subject is highly controversial, and any clinician who speaks out and questions the ideologically informed treatment approach is subjected to cancelling and online harassment.

Furthermore, changes to the law in various countries, as well as the US states, increasingly criminalises therapists who seek to explore their young client's expressed desire to transition rather than automatically affirm it. The first three of the six chapters in this section are a determined attempt to open up this important topic for public debate. The first two chapters by Sasha Ayad and Stella O'Malley lay out a thorough and authoritative background to the current crisis of increasing numbers of young people seeking to transition. They identify the various factors involved in this sudden increase and discuss how therapists are being hampered in their attempts to help their clients.

In the third chapter, Lisa Marchiano focuses on two applied postmodern themes—the blurring of boundaries and the loss of the individual and the universal—and examines how they play a role in cutting people off from inner resources that can help to address suffering. She argues that therapy approaches which strengthen the client's resilience are much more suitable than the identity affirmation model which has been generally adopted.

Tim Courtois expands the discussion on gender ideology to consider its implications for how therapists work with clients' sexual issues. He explains how the treatment of this fundamental dimension of human life has become influenced by Queer Theory. This CSJ theory takes the position that sexual preferences and predilections are not things we do rather, they are the things we are. This view insists that heteronormative sex practices need to be challenged as they are merely expressions of a dominant power system. This identity-based understanding of sex is now being taught in post-qualification training programmes. Tim considers the implications for therapeutic practice.

The two remaining chapters in this section are discussions of the related matter of how CSJ takes a dim view of the masculine. John Barry considers the implications for men's mental health of new ideas that traditional masculinity, with its emphasis on hierarchy, competitiveness, and stoicism, is toxic. He discusses how the concept of patriarchy with its negative connotations has been accepted uncritically into the therapy field. John presents findings from his own research that suggest a therapist's views on patriarchy and masculinity have a direct bearing on how they work with male clients. Finally, suggestions for a more male-friendly approach, one based on evidence for the psychological needs of male clients rather than socio-political theory, are described.

Dennis Relojo-Howell's chapter expands on the previous chapter by looking, in particular, at the higher rate of suicides in males as compared with females. He makes the case that CSJ concepts of "toxic masculinity" and "patriarchy" promote emasculation; consequently, they are very unhelpful in terms of working therapeutically with stressed and depressed male clients. New waves in resilience research have emphasised the role of social support and a sense of belonging as vital protective factors against suicidal behaviour. In line with this, his chapter also discusses how resilience intervention—instead of emasculation—can prevent the onset or exacerbation of suicide ideation among male clients.

The third section—Critical Social Justice Theories in Application—broadens out and considers the incompatibility of CSJ with counselling and psychotherapy theory and approaches. The first three chapters in this section reflect on the implications of Critical Race Theory (CRT) for therapy—a particularly significant area of concern given its increasing prominence in the therapy field.

An introduction and overview of the theory are given in the first of these chapters. Then, the two authors, Carole Sherwood and Dina McMillan, take a novel and creative approach in their individual chapters by personifying CRT as a client who has arrived at the counsellor's clinic. Both of them elucidate some of the key tenets of CRT and link them to key concepts in Cognitive Behavioural Therapy. The main thrust of their argument is that CRT encourages people to think in ways that are potentially detrimental to mental health. Reference will be made to various thinking styles, such as emotional reasoning, labelling, etc.

The first author, Carole Sherwood, considers how she, as a white therapist, would work with CRT presenting itself in a clinical space. The second author, Dina McMillan, discusses the different challenges faced by a black therapist responding to clients who have taken on the beliefs of CRT.

Philip Pellegrino then makes the case that CSJ is fundamentally incompatible with the enlightenment values and scientific worldview of Cognitive Behavioral Therapy (CBT). This therapeutic approach is evidence-based and has been the leader in identifying specific mechanisms of change in the treatment of specific clinical conditions. The author will discuss the threat posed by CSJ to empirically based approaches to therapy and consider its rhetorical claims that CBT is an expression of colonialism and white supremacy.

Val Thomas' chapter then reflects on the therapeutic relationship universally accepted as fundamentally important to the healing enterprise. She argues that contemporary attempts to insert CSJ into the therapy field are misguided: its worldview is antithetical to the therapeutic potential of relationship, and furthermore, this ideology actively undermines what is, in fact, the ground of counselling and psychotherapy. The relational implications of this worldview will be discussed, including the likely consequence that the relationship between therapist and client will be a transactional one harnessed to political rather than therapeutic ends.

The following chapter takes another complementary perspective on the threat that CSJ poses to the relationship between therapist and client. Birgit Ewald discusses the view taken by humanistic/transpersonal therapy approaches to the therapeutic relationship, in particular the concept of the therapist's presence. She then explores Buber's notion of the I-thou relationship which offers the possibility of a deep healing encounter between therapist and client. This is contrasted with the I-it type of relationship—a merely transactional type of relationship which is the only possibility afforded by CSJ and its understanding that relationships operate between two identities rather than two people.

She makes the case that it is the I-thou relationship that is truly inclusive.

In the final chapter of this section, Piers Newman examines the contradictions between CSJ and a group-oriented approach, Systemic Family Therapy (SFT). On the surface, it might appear that SFT with its focus on membership within a system would be more compatible with CSJ and its collective worldview. The author explains why this is not the case and, instead, how the political agenda of CSJ distorts the primary objective of SFT, which is the productive resolution of the family system's negative internal dynamics.

The fourth section opens out to consider some wider professional issues in counselling and psychotherapy and is titled Professional Matters. The first chapter by Nina Silander and Robert Mather examines the politicisation of the therapy professions. The chapter reviews the relevant historical context for politicisation and the lack of ideological diversity in the American Psychological Association (APA). It gives examples of and commentary about critical and postmodern theories in the mental health profession, such as implicit biases and race-related constructs. The authors flag the implications for the provision of psychotherapeutic services in the American context, such as the risks to therapeutic rapport and the growing subculture of political minority-identifying therapists.

The following chapter discusses the issues raised for professional therapy training in an institutional context that is increasingly captured by CSJ ideology. Christine Sefein draws on her experience of graduating from a traditional professional therapy training programme and then returning several years later as a professor. During her time as a teacher, she observed how CSJ became established as the main lens for therapeutic practice and how this move made the teaching of traditional psychotherapy untenable. She identifies and discusses the main drivers of CSJ ideology in the training programme, which include the "woke" administrative university context and the recruitment of activist students into professional trainings. Christine considers how these drivers result in classroom conditions that are counterproductive to learning to become therapists. Her chapter ends with some thoughts about how to respond to this detrimental direction in therapy training.

The contents of the book are completed with a final chapter by Val Thomas, who discusses ways in which the therapy professions can move through this crisis—The Future. One rhetorical strategy would be to insist on the differentiation between generic, traditional, and established counselling approaches and one that is informed by a radically different worldview. She explores ways in which heterodox practitioners, educators, and academics can build a moral and ethical case for naming this politicised approach as a CSJ-driven therapeutic modality. She acknowledges that the encroachment of CSJ into the field may be so far advanced that a likely outcome would be a chaotic fracturing of the field into a politicised official therapy field with traditional approaches pushed to the edges. Nevertheless, this chapter concludes on a hopeful note that challenging times provide an opportunity for a revisioning of therapy in the contemporary world. Traditional therapy, split off from a politicised mainstream, can develop new institutions and practices, ones that are informed by a true healing ethos.

The complete account ends with a short afterword by the editor that situates the issues facing the therapy field in a wider professional landscape. It focuses on lessons that can be learned by considering how the fields of education and medicine have engaged with CSJ.

A note on terms and definitions

The term, Critical Social Justice (CSJ), is used throughout the book as the umbrella term for the collection of applied postmodern Critical Theories often referred to as "wokeness" in common parlance.

Sometimes, the authors will want to discuss one particular CSJ theory. When they do, the theory will be identified as such by using initial capital letters e.g., Critical Race Theory or Queer Theory.

If the authors use the term Critical Theory itself, then this means they are specifically referring to the set of political/cultural ideas developed in the mid-20th century by the Frankfurt School.

All of these terms are explained in more detail in the glossary, which the reader is encouraged to read in conjunction with the chapters in the book.

It should be noted that views are provided by a mixture of British and American authors. Consequently, both British spelling and American English spelling are used.

Endnotes

[1] An analysis of books published in English, German, and Spanish indicates depression is on the rise. Johan Bollen, Marijn ten Thij, Fritz Breithaupt, Alexander T. J. Barron, Lauren A. Rutter, Lorenzo Lorenzo-Luaces, and Marten Scheffer, "Historical language records indicate a surge in cognitive distortions in recent decades", *Proceedings of the National Academy of Sciences (PNAS)* 118, no. 30 e2102061118, July 23, 2021, https://www.pnas.org/doi/10.1073/pnas.2102061118.

[2] See the overview given by Robert van Voren, "Political Abuse of Psychiatry—An Historical Overview", *Schizophrenia Bulletin*, Vol 36, Issue 1, January 2010 pp. 33–35, https://academic.oup.com/schizophreniabulletin/article/36/1/33/1871265.

[3] *American Psychological Association*, https://www.apa.org/.

[4] For an analysis of the detrimental effects of CSJ-driven therapy see Val Thomas, " 'Woke' Therapy Weakens the Client", *Critical Therapy Antidote*, February 5, 2022, https://criticaltherapyantidote.org/2022/02/05/woke-therapy-weakens-the-client/.

Glossary of Terms

Some of the terms used in this book are technical and may be unfamiliar to some readers. Some differences between the USA, the UK, and other parts of the English-speaking world may be confusing. Scholarly, popular, culturally prized, and slang terms can overlap. Many terms are contentious, and we cannot claim this list, although compiled in good faith, to be wholly accurate or acceptable to all. Also included are some abbreviated titles of relevant major therapy organisations.

Ableism. The idea that people with disabilities are oppressed or disadvantaged by society's privileging of able-bodied norms.

ACA. American Counseling Association.

Ally. One who is actively committed to supporting Critical Social Justice while having an oppressor identity.

Antiracism. The argument and practice of finding the stance of "non-racism" insufficient. Only by continuously educating oneself, working on one's own racism, and vigorously challenging one's white peers, for example, does one effectively stand against racism.

Authoritarianism. Holding dogmatic views and exercising power dictatorially, such as Nazism, Maoism, and Stalinism—clearly extremely authoritarian.

AMA. American Medical Association.

APA. American Psychological Association.

BACP. British Association for Counselling and Psychotherapy.

Black Lives Matter (commonly abbreviated as **BLM)**. Originally an American organisation, BLM was founded in 2013 as a social justice and liberation movement after Trayvon Martin's death. As well as opposing racism, it embraces the movement against homophobia and transphobia, endorses the abolition of police and prisons, and has a Marxist affiliation.

BPS. British Psychological Society.

Cancel culture. Refers to the practice of removing people with "non-woke" views (refer to "woke" definition below) from the public square. Charges of racism, misogyny, homophobia, trans-phobia, antisemitism, and Islamophobia are common tactics used to damage peoples' reputations and harm their careers and public standing.

Cisgender. The match between one's biological natal sex and one's subjective feeling of one's gender.

Conversion therapy. Any therapy that seeks to change a person's sexuality (mainly from homosexuality to heterosexuality) without informed consent, and sometimes with recourse to aversive methods.

Critical consciousness. A mindset that is able to perceive the workings of systems of oppressive power and to take action to expose and correct them. See Critical Pedagogy and Critical Theory below.

Critical Pedagogy. With roots in the 1960s work of Paulo Freire, Critical Pedagogy is a Marxist-linked educational ideology whose remit is the liberation of groups perceived as oppressed. It takes education as a vehicle for social change above the transmission of knowledge. The focus of this approach to education is to inculcate critical consciousness in school pupils and students more generally.

Critical Race Theory (commonly abbreviated as **CRT**, aka **Critical Theories of Race**). Originating in Critical Legal Studies during the 1980s/1990s, CRT takes as axiomatic that Western culture is structured along racist lines by white supremacy. CRT does not ask if racism takes place; instead, it asks how. This particular Critical Theory is openly hostile to the Western Liberal position which advocates for colour blindness.

Critical Social Justice (abbreviated in the text as **CSJ**). CSJ serves as an umbrella term for the set of contemporary Critical Theories and was originally formalised by Robin DiAngelo and Özlem Sensoy. CSJ (or "wokeness" in common parlance) is shorthand for a particularly radical political approach to achieving social justice. Its goal is to uncover the systems of power that are believed to structure society and, by so doing, create the opportunity for a revolutionary transformation into an idealised state. CSJ is characterised by activism that aims to find problems, disrupt and dismantle societal norms, centre the marginalised, privilege subjective over objective truth, and control speech.

Critical Theory (sometimes abbreviated in the text as **CT**). In its original form, CT refers to the post-Marxist analysis of society in terms of systems of power developed by the Frankfurt School. CT is different from traditional theories which attempt to understand society; its purpose is to change society. Consequently, it has a strong focus on criticising how current conditions deviate from the ideal (see "problematising"). Over the last three decades, CT has broadened by incorporating postmodern perspectives on the nature of truth and the power of language. This has resulted in a set of distinct but connected Critical Theories such as Queer Theory, Critical Race Theory, Gender Theory, etc.

Decolonisation. Raising awareness of and purging victims of the effects of colonialism. "Decolonising the curriculum" is a project which involves radical changes to Western education, reducing

Western texts and theories, and replacing them with literature from the Global South.

Equity. Often confused with the broader term "equality". Equity refers to a particular kind of equality; in this case, equality of outcome. A commitment to equity lends itself to calls for the redistribution of resources, sometimes framed as recompense for historic injustices.

Gender dysphoria. This is a notion that even from an early age, some people feel a distressing conflict between their natal sex classification and their subjective gender identity. The American Psychiatric Association recognises "clinically significant distress" of this kind. Gender dysphoria is taken to be valid grounds for seeking a change in gender identity, often entailing diagnosis, certification, and hormonal and surgical treatments.

Gender Theory. Drawing initially from anthropology, Gender Theory has critiqued traditional notions of masculinity and femininity. It challenges biological definitions and stereotypes and proposes fluid, individualised behaviours.

Heteronormativity. The longstanding traditional assumption that everyone is heterosexual, or should be so, and cultural reinforcement of that view.

Homophobia. Hatred of same-sex attracted people.

Identity politics. Politics focusing primarily on identity groups and their grievances rather than on traditional concerns with economics, prosperity, law and order, and so on.

Ideology. A system of ideas applied to large social issues, often containing views on power relations and often insisted upon as truth. They may be seen as positive or negative, as explicit or implicit. Capitalism, for example, may be presented as an inevitable good in no need of critique.

Implicit (or unconscious) bias. This is the idea that individuals hold prejudices and act on these without awareness. Implicit bias is commonly attributed to members of oppressor groups in their dealings with people with oppressed identities.

Intersectionality. An influential concept from Kimberlé Crenshaw outlines multiple intersecting forms of oppression which can be found in individuals. Straight white female feminists had assumed their experiences and perceptions were valid for all, but this did not take into account the experiences of other oppressions in addition such as being a person of colour, disabled, or gay.

Liberalism. A broad political philosophy that has been the mainstay of Western democracies. Some of its key features include individualism, freedom of speech, equality, rationalism, universality, tolerance, the rule of law, and pluralism. There can be confusion regarding the use of the term "liberal": in the US, this term indicates left-wing policies, whereas in the UK and Australia it indicates a right-of-centre political position (the equivalent of "libertarian" in the US).

Lived experience. The subjective account of one's personal (usually negative) life experience.

Microaggression. Any everyday interpersonal interaction in which one person feels hurt, stereotyped, or diminished by another's words, looks, or actions, or lack of expected affirmative behaviours. From a CSJ perspective, microaggressions are committed by oppressors against members of oppressed groups and not the other way around.

Misandry. Hatred of men.

Misogyny. Hatred of women.

Multicultural counselling. Offered as a corrective to Eurocentric theory and practice in counselling, multicultural counselling is well established in the USA as a set of competencies recognising and working with many ethnic groups, challenging stereotypes, and examining linguistic issues.

Non-binary sexuality. A Queer Theory notion argues that the traditional, oppressive heteronormative scheme must give way to sexual and gender fluidity, whereby individuals decide their own sexual identity and preferences.

Oppressor–oppressed. The system in which all human institutions and behaviour are interpreted as dominant and dominated groups.

Otherness/othering. Dehumanising attitudes displayed by members of oppressor groups towards members of oppressed groups.

Patriarchy. Rule by patriarchs, fathers, or men.

Postcolonialism. The legacy of colonialism and imperialism that is critiqued academically.

Postmodernism. An intellectual movement critiquing modernism and the notion of objective truth, and seen in academia, the arts, architecture, etc. It regards knowledge as traditionally concocted by Western assumptions and thought systems. Postmodernism is particularly focused on the power of language, and it rejects grand narratives.

Problematics/problematising. The practice of finding fault with current conditions, particularly concerning how these conditions depart from an imagined ideal state.

Progressive. Political progressivism implies a deliberate, engineered movement of large-scale social changes towards something like socialism or utopia. It suggests revolutionary transformation and upheaval rather than cautious, evolved, and measured changes.

Psychotherapy. All talking therapies, however so labelled, e.g. psychoanalysis, clinical psychology, counselling psychology, clinical social work, couple and family therapy, etc. The psycho-therapy (or simply "therapy") field is pluralistic, containing dozens of named schools of theory and practice. Psychotherapy is usually said to originate with Freud and undeniably has European and American roots.

Queer Theory. Drawing on "queer" as a homophobic slur, Queer Theory extends LGBT and Gender Ideology to suggest unprece-dented new ways of perceiving the world, not only in sexual and gender terms but organisationally, technologically, and politically. The "celebration of transgression" would radicalize the arts, cul-ture, and human behaviour generally.

Racism/racist. This always refers to white racism and has usually been framed by CSJ proponents as prejudice plus power.

Rapid-Onset Gender Dysphoria (ROGD). A term originally coined by Lisa Littman for a subset of adolescents and young adults who suddenly manifest symptoms of gender dysphoria and identify as transgender.

Social constructionism. In contrast to social Darwinism, and genetic and religious views, this view insists that human behaviour is created by human society and its prevailing ideologies and that these are open to change.

Systemic racism. Also known as structural or institutional racism, in this view, racism is regarded as permeating entire systems, largely unconsciously, and usually as a way of holding on to power and denying rights to non-whites.

TERF. Trans-exclusionary radical feminists, also known as gen-der-critical feminists who defend biological sex differences.

Transgenderism. Either due to gender dysphoria or in some cases free choice, individuals who identify as the gender opposite to their natal sex are now known as transwomen or transmen.

Transphobia. Prejudice against transgender people. This ranges from actual violence against trans people through misgendering and deadnaming (using the person's pre-transition name) to disagreeing about any aspect of transgender claims.

UKCP. United Kingdom Council for Psychotherapy.

Viewpoint diversity. This term is used to point out that the CSJ usage of the term "diversity" does not include the holding of different perspectives.

White fragility. Coined by Robin DiAngelo (a white American woman), this term suggests that whites are systemically (not necessarily individually) racist, but because this is largely unconscious, when challenged, whites often become very uncomfortable and defensive.

Whiteness. Increasingly, whiteness is portrayed as an essential negative characteristic of European, American, and Western majority populations. After criticising whites for being oblivious to their own race, critics have proceeded to name so-called white psychosis, white pathology, white privilege, and supremacy as facts and as impediments to racial justice. Critical Whiteness studies aim to dismantle white dominance and its assumptions.

White privilege. This is the idea that all whites, regardless of their social and economic position, benefit from the perceived automatic societal advantages of being white.

White supremacy. This is the notion that all whites regardless of social position feel superior to blacks and act accordingly, and that the West is structured to the advantage of whites and white history and culture. This has thus expanded in meaning since its application to the KKK.

Woke. Officially added to the dictionary in 2017, this term means that a person has been or is marked by an active (Critical Social Justice-informed) awareness of systemic injustices and prejudices, especially those involving the treatment of ethnic, racial, or sexual minorities. "Non-woke" is the opposite of this.

Chapter 1:

How Did We Get Here?

by Val Thomas

Behind the scenes, a quiet revolution is underway in the therapy field. Although there are still many therapists in private practice working in the same way as they always have, professional therapy institutions are promoting a new way of thinking about therapeutic practice. It would appear that counselling and psychotherapy are starting to be repurposed: instead of helping people focus on how to make changes in their individual lives, these professional institutions are increasingly concerned with changing society as a whole. If this trajectory continues uninterrupted, therapy will soon look different from the established practices of today.

In the near future, your counsellor will be increasingly likely to diagnose your problem primarily through the lens of societal oppression. Your condition will be unreservedly affirmed, and you will be encouraged to identify yourself as a victim. The treatment will then consist of advocacy and encouraging you to take action against oppressive societal forces. *Why have the therapy professions uncritically and passively allowed a political ideology to gain such a strong hold on their field? And even more significantly, why is no one talking about this?*

1

Background

In order to answer these questions, it is helpful to look at the bigger picture. At their inception, psychotherapy and counselling introduced radical ideas into 20th-century Western culture such as Freud's concept of the unconscious and its influence on human behaviour and Rogers' insights into the healing power of a real relationship that provided empathy, congruence, and unconditional positive regard.[1,2] It would be hard to overstate these contributions which offered a corrective to a historical overemphasis on the role of conscious, rational thought processes in bringing about constructive changes in human behaviour.

But approaches to the task of healing inevitably bear the imprint of their times. Three of the main types of therapeutic approaches (these big umbrella categories are usually termed "forces"—the psychodynamic; behaviourist, later Cognitive Behavioural Therapy; and humanistic-existential schools)— have their origins in the first half of the 20th century.[3] These three forces were therefore inevitably informed by the perspectives of modernity with its focus on individualism and an acceptance of the universality of human nature. A salient characteristic of all these approaches would be the situating of the person's difficulties within the self (intrapsychic) and the resultant emphasis on fostering self-insight, self-responsibility, and individual agency.[4]

However, over the last couple of decades of the 20th century, wider intellectual currents in Western thought accompanied by material social changes began to challenge the exclusively individual focus of therapeutic theory and practice. In particular, factors such as postmodernism, systems theories, and the establishment of multicultural societies prompted concern with understanding the individual within a wider context.[5,6] New therapeutic methods developed during this time include a whole category of approaches grouped under the rubric of systemic/contextual approaches—retrospectively identified as a fourth "force" in therapy.[7,8]

The postmodern turn during the final decades of the 20th century is particularly significant as it helped to lay the ground for a later infiltration of the therapy field by Critical Social Justice (CSJ), a political ideology informed by postmodern philosophical tenets. Postmodernism brought with it the highly influential theory of social constructionism—the idea that the person's identity or self is shaped by contemporary cultural conditions and beliefs.[9] This understanding of the nature of the self, combined with its focus on the power of language, generated some productive new therapeutic approaches, e.g. narrative therapy.[10] In addition, the postmodern distrust of "grand narratives"—overarching explanations or theories of the human condition—led to an increasing critique of the practice of therapy itself; it became problematised as a product of, and therefore limited by, the Western intellectual tradition. By the turn of the millennium, the disciplines of counselling and psychotherapy had matured into a stable pluralistic field able to apply a range of perspectives to the task of developing effective therapeutic practices for a rapidly changing world. Overall, there was an acceptance of multiple factors implicated in the problems that clients bring to therapy.

In essence, postmodern perspectives had been assimilated, which meant that earlier modern perspectives on the individual and universal dimensions of the self were expanded by paying attention to the way that context shapes human experience. New frameworks were adopted, such as the biopsychosocial model, that could accommodate this wider view.[11] Overall, despite the multiplicity of approaches, the professions were grounded in a recognisable Western intellectual tradition, one that is committed to developing knowledge about effective practice through an incremental process based on cumulative clinical observations and research. Not perfect—but on a journey towards integrating ever-wider dimensions of human nature and experience into the healing enterprise.

Yet, two decades on, this balanced expansion has not materialised. Instead, a lopsided, reductive view of human nature is being promoted, which has serious ramifications for therapeutic practice. The following section focuses on the critical period when the therapy professions, mirroring the wider culture, began to embrace a new worldview.

The turning point

At the turn of the millennium, the original postmodern ideas about the influence of power dynamics on what we consider knowledge, and how this is perpetuated through language, had been a useful additional perspective on the human condition. But this perspective soon began to harden into a simplistic identity-based understanding of power dynamics and socialisation. This shift happened with the advent of certain fields of cultural studies which used Postcolonial and Decolonial Theory, Queer Theory, Critical Race Theory, and intersectional feminism; this then further solidified into the framework known simply as Critical Social Justice (CSJ).

An examination of two versions of the American Psychology Association's (APA) guidelines for multicultural practice will serve to illustrate this process at work in the therapy field.[12] These detailed documents are intended to serve an unarguable moral good; their purpose is to provide psychologists with a framework for working with an increasingly diverse population and to help them in providing effective services. However, despite this common aim, the second set of guidelines, issued little more than a decade later, reveals that psychology (and its application to clinical practice) has been fully captured by a particular political ideology.

In 2003, the guidelines commenced with an uncontroversial standard definition of multiculturalism and diversity.[13] It is important to note that an acceptance of viewpoint diversity can also be inferred by the fact that the guidelines proffer a range of potentially helpful theoretical perspectives such as social categorisation and intersectionality. There is also evidence for supporting classic liberal principles of individual rights and free speech, for example, when it is stated that psychologists in their role as educators about diversity issues need to "be prepared to understand and facilitate respectful discussion and disagreement".[14] The advice being dispensed seems reasonable and uncontroversial, stating that "psychologists are encouraged to be aware of their attitudes and work to increase their contact with members of other racial/ethnic groups, building trust in others and increasing their tolerance for others".[15]

In summary, these guidelines issued at the beginning of the millennium reflect the state of the therapy field at that time, one grounded in a Western worldview informed by modernity that is assimilating postmodern perspectives on the importance of social and cultural contexts. The document bows out by positioning the guidelines on a historical and corrective trajectory, stating that "Psychology has been traditionally defined by and based upon Western, Eurocentric, and biological perspectives and assumptions. These traditional premises in psychological education, research, practice, and organizational change, and have not always considered the influence and impact of racial and cultural socialization".[16]

Moving forward to 2017, a new set of guidelines was released, and these were "conceptualised from a need to reconsider diversity and multicultural practice within professional psychology *at a different period in time*" (italics added).[17]

The tone, framing, and language of this document go on to support the inference that can be drawn from this opening statement that the task force which produced these guidelines has a missionary zeal. The nascent political tendency, evident in the earlier guidelines, has now become a fully fledged determining ideology.[18] It appears that it is no longer open to a range of theoretical frameworks, as the guidelines declare "intersectionality as its primary purview".[19] Adopting this idea "that an individual's identity is derived from interacting systemic effects" then leads the authors to assert that "psychologists strive to understand associated human biases informed by systems of power, privilege, oppression, social dictates, constraints, values, and negative perceptions of marginalized societies."[20]

Other perspectives that were grudgingly acceptable in 2003 are now completely frowned upon, as "psychologists are encouraged to challenge their color-blind racial attitudes and beliefs that the world is just and fair".[21] Alongside this, the universalism of human experience, a fundamentally important tenet of modern therapeutic approaches, is given short shrift and quickly dismissed.[22] Throughout the document, concepts that have established themselves in the mainstream, such as micro-aggressions, privilege, and cultural humility, are presented uncritically as uncontested facts.

Further, psychologists are viewed as agents of wider social change who "seek to address institutional barriers and related inequities, disproportionalities, and disparities of law enforcement, administration of criminal justice, educational, mental health, and other systems as they seek to promote justice, human rights, and access to quality and equitable mental and behavioral health services".[23] In fact, the guidelines go on to promote a new type of activist practitioner termed the "citizen psychologist".[24]

Therefore, by 2017, the trajectory announced in 2003—of correcting a historical minimisation of the importance of context—has clearly overshot its mark. These APA guidelines are emblematic of the shift happening across the rest of the field.

Within fourteen years, psychology and its clinical applications appear to be pivoting from one worldview to another: social and cultural context is now viewed as the most important dimension of human experience and the therapist's role is now to *facilitate collective rather than individual change*. Furthermore, this shift is accompanied by a new certainty and moral conviction, a particularly concerning development in a field that until recently respected the irreducible complexity of human nature.

How Critical Social Justice tactics have been used to infiltrate therapy

How could such a radical change be brought about in disciplines that have always focused on healing the individual? A short answer is that the therapy field is passively reflecting much wider trends in Western culture wherein CSJ is becoming the cultural hegemony. The tactics used by this ideology to capture the mainstream are being deployed across all cultural practices, including therapy.

It is important to bear in mind that CSJ is informed by Critical Theory, which is an explicitly political enterprise and highly strategic, playing a long game—readers will no doubt be familiar with the trope of "the long march through the institutions".[25] This long-term tactical approach has been effectively deployed in education and across the applied social science professions. The methods include using academia to change the narrative of the disciplines, infiltrating the bureaucratic institutions (professional bodies/institutions/service providers, etc.), gaining control over professional education, and aggressively shutting down any opposition in the form of public critique and debate.

These moves can be observed in the therapy professions. Activists have targeted the professional bodies and are now able to use these institutions as a base for changing the profession (an example being the APA practice guidelines discussed earlier).

A significant tactical goal would be to change the ethical requirements for practice in order to repurpose therapy as a type of social activism.[26] Once this move has been achieved, then compliance to a particular worldview can be enforced through real-world sanctions such as withdrawal of a licence to practice. But the long-term aim is to capture the education of future therapists. Once CSJ is fully instantiated in the professional education trainings, then the established therapy approaches can be dismantled; characterised as reactionary and/or oppressive, and consigned to the dustbin of history. A previous generation of therapists retires, and new indoctrinated cohorts of practitioners take their place. The job is done.

The reason for the success so far, of this strategy, is that early on very few people in the therapy field, apart from the activist scholars and a couple of perceptive critics, realised what they were dealing with. CSJ theories combine postmodern deconstructionism with Critical Theory's revolutionary political aim to devastating effect. And, crucially, this ideology has a particular view of the creation of knowledge that would be unfamiliar to most therapists. In the established traditions of therapy, new understandings of practice have evolved out of a combination of clinical observations, research, and new ideas about how to help people and their responses to social change. It has been a slow, incremental, hard-won endeavour, new ideas and concepts are continuously subjected to critical debate in the public domain.

However, in the CSJ worldview, knowledge is grounded in discourses—the way we talk about things. To change social reality, it is necessary to focus on language. The genius of CSJ lies not in its contents or theories but in its rhetorical strategies. And three, in particular, have been applied with devasting effects to counselling and psychotherapy. First, the generally accepted lay definition of the term "social justice" was replaced by a new political one and imported into the professional literature.

Second, on the back of this, a new story of therapy was inserted into textbooks. And third, all opposition is recast as reactionary. These strategies will be discussed in more detail in the following sections.

Changing the definition of social justice in therapy

It is not surprising that issues of social justice would be important in professions whose main aim is to relieve distress and improve the capacity of individuals to live productive and fulfilling lives. At the time of the 2003 guidelines, the contribution of the therapy profession to achieving social justice would have been expressed through developing well-formulated cultural competencies for clinicians working in multicultural contexts and anti-oppressive practice guidelines with marginalised sexual minorities.

However, over the next few years, activist scholars and clinical theorists were successful in replacing this traditional lay understanding of social justice with a collectivist political one: injustice is caused by systems of power that have to be identified and dismantled.[27] As this new meaning was also becoming established across mainstream culture, it was easily imported into applied social sciences.

A good example of this sleight-of-hand rhetorical strategy is provided by a description given in an American counselling textbook (published halfway between the two versions of the APA multicultural practice guidelines discussed earlier) of an association titled Counselors for Social Justice.[28] It states that this association "promotes embracing and endorsing a new perspective by acknowledging cultural oppression—such as heterosexism, racism, sexism, ageism, and ablism, and, by providing culturally sensitive counseling while working towards eradicating these types of oppression in the wider society".[29] Note how both definitions of social justice are elided together here; the activist agenda which denotes Critical Social Justice being tacked on at the end.

Over the next few years, this new definition of social justice has effectively replaced the previous one and is accompanied by a push to repurpose therapy as a political practice. These moves are uncritically promoted in the academic literature, for example, the Canadian Counselling Journal's special issue on counselling and social justice highlights in its abstract: "the importance of expanding professional focus and counsellor roles *to engage in system-level change, with and on behalf of our client. ...* In turn, counsellors have to be willing to do more than notice injustices; professional roles as counsellors require a stance of action" (italics added for emphasis).[30]

Changing the story of therapy

This recasting of the therapist's role has been bolstered by other rhetorical strategies such as changing the story of therapy.[31] From the perspective of CSJ, professional discourses determine and legitimise the "truth" of that particular practice. Therefore, scholar–activists have focused their efforts on reshaping the foundational narrative of talking therapies, announcing early on "that social justice counseling is the 'fifth force' and 'a new paradigm' .... emerging in the counseling profession".[32] For anyone familiar with the counselling and psychotherapy field, this is a bold claim. These "forces" (touched on earlier) refer to the overarching categories of therapy approaches identified in retrospect that define the contours of the field. This new "social justice fifth force" has not been identified in the usual way but instead inserted into the field prospectively.

Yet, within a few years, it has been accepted as a matter of fact.[33] The extraordinary success of this strategy can be seen in the way that some therapy scholars now appear to accept this fifth force as part of the bedrock of the field—one example being a recent attempt to go further and identify a possible "sixth force" overlying the social justice stratum.[34]

Infiltrating professional therapy training through the diversity module

CSJ has also been able to establish itself in professional therapy training, mainly through the Trojan Horse of the obligatory diversity module. At the turn of the millennium, all professional courses required a component of the training syllabus to be explicitly dedicated to issues of working with diversity. The sleight-of-hand shift of the meaning of the term "social justice" described earlier started to allow a new worldview to become established within one part of the training. Textbooks on multicultural practice, containing this new understanding of social justice and consequent politicised therapist role, would now become standard fare for the new generations of therapy trainees.

Furthermore, the diversity module also creates an opportunity for Critical Pedagogy specialists—theorists who have been radically changing school and college education practices—to infiltrate professional counselling training.[35] Historically, therapy training has always made significant use of experiential teaching methods: these have been used to help develop the required authentic self-awareness necessary for working with clients. Critical Pedagogy approaches have been able to harness self-reflective/interactive methods such as open group dialogues to very different ends. Instead of facilitating deeper self-inquiry, these methods are used to encourage "critical consciousness".[36] The end result is enforced compliance with a particular ideology. Any resistance to the CSJ worldview is pathologised. The student counsellors are required, if they are not already on board, to accept as fact the dominant collectivist ideology.

In general, once CSJ gains a foothold, it will then start to target the rest of the territory; it is a political ideology and consequently motivated by power. Therapy training is no exception. Once CSJ is established in the diversity module, it will employ tactics to take over the whole of the programme.[37] These dismantling moves include calls for decolonising the curriculum, which involves ampli-fying the voices of indigenous people and people of colour as well as reducing reliance on "white" clinical theory.[38] I do not doubt that other established therapeutic approaches will be attacked as the products of "oppressive" groups and the pluralistic inclusive nature of therapy will be dismantled.

Bad ideas can be imported without any challenge, such as recasting attempts to help people recover from or manage chronic disabling conditions as 'ableist'—the consequence being that the only acceptable therapeutic response would be unreservedly affirming the client's perception of their condition.[39] When this takeover is complete, the professional training programme will be harnessed into a politicised practice focused on social justice activism and advocacy.[40]

We now come to the biggest question of all. *Why has there been no defence of the field and its well-established and effective healing practices?*

Silencing critics

Probably the most significant factor that is allowing CSJ to become the status quo in counselling and psychotherapy is the almost complete lack of public critique of its tenets concerning therapeu-tic practice. The tactics used by social justice activists to silence opposition in mainstream culture have been applied with equal success in the therapy field—perhaps even greater success, as which therapy professional could withstand publicly being slurred with any of the usual labels: racist, transphobe, misogynist, homo-phobe, etc.?[41] Public arenas with the potential for debate are unavailable to nonconformists; academic and professional jour-nals do not support viewpoint diversity, and critics are harshly and unfairly dealt with.[42] Opposition to the accepted CSJ narrative is either pathologised ("white fragility") or dismissed as a reaction-ary backlash.[43] And, in some cases, ideologues have completely hijacked particular arenas of therapeutic practice and have been able to force out non-compliant therapists; one particularly pernicious example is the treatment of trans-identified children.[44]

Conclusion

This silence is deeply concerning. Authoritarian ideologies are by their very nature antitherapeutic. It is time to stand together with the authors of the work included in this book and insist on open public debate and critique. If this does not happen, then counselling and psychotherapy will cease to be therapeutic practices. At the turn of the millennium, the therapy field was on a journey towards integrating ever-wider dimensions of human nature and experience into the healing enterprise—we need to reclaim that vision; otherwise, professional therapy will be harnessed to narrow political ends.

Endnotes

1   S. Freud, *The Unconscious* (Standard Edition, vol. 14), (London: Hogarth, 1915), 159-190.

2   See Carl Rogers' now classic paper, "The Necessary and Sufficient Conditions for Therapeutic Personality Change," *Journal of Consulting Psychology*, 21, (1957): 95–103.

3   The term "forces"—sometimes identified as paradigms—in talking therapies refers to overarching categories of therapeutic approaches. These "forces", comprising theoretically compatible approaches and methods, are groupings that have been recognised in retrospect. They are generally accepted as defining the contours of the whole of the field as they have withstood long processes of rigorous testing including cumulative clinical observations, research, the refining of theory and ideas, the resolving of internal contradictions, and, most importantly, in the long run, they proved therapeutically efficacious. See the overview provided by Windy Dryden and Jill Mytton: *Four Approaches to Counselling and Psychotherapy (Routledge Mental Health Classic Editions),* London and New York: Routledge, 2016).

4   It is worth noting that humanistic approaches did include some emphasis on social forces and political influences from the 1960s onwards. Examples would include Re-evaluation Co-counselling, developed in 1950s by Harvey Jackins, which became increasingly concerned with liberating people from their internalised oppression; and Reichian Therapy, a type of bodywork developed by Wilhelm Reich that focuses on loosening 'bodily armour' believed to be caused by negative societal conditions.

5   Postmodern thought is a difficult-to-define philosophical movement that could be very broadly characterised by radical scepticism, subjectivism and relativism. See the overview by Helen Pluckrose and James Lindsay: "Postmodernism", in *Cynical Theories,* (Durham, NC: Pitchstone, 2020), 21-43.

6   Systems theory was originally conceptualised in the 1940s by the Austrian biologist von Bertalanffy (1901–72) and refers to the interdisciplinary study of systems comprising interacting components. Systems theory proved to be an influential approach in the applied social sciences because it provides a way of understanding human behaviour within larger complex contexts ranging from families through to organisational structures.

7   Examples of such approaches would be family systems therapy, originally developed by the American psychiatrist Murray Bowen (1913–90) based

on the premise that what happens to one member of the family also affects everyone in the family system. Another example would be feminist therapy, an approach that seeks to empower clients and help them understand how social factors have contributed to shaping their sense of self.

8   By the turn of the millennium, there were other contenders for the "fourth force" in therapy, including transpersonal psychology. See A. J. Sutich, "Transpersonal psychology: An emerging force," *Journal of Humanistic Psychology*, 8, (1968): 77-78. And multiculturalism—see P. B. Pedersen, (1990). "The multicultural perspective as a fourth force in counselling," *Journal of Mental Health Counseling*, 12, (19900: 93-95.

9   A particularly influential text in therapy was Kenneth Gergen and Keith E. Davis, *The Social Construction of the Person* (New York: Springer-Verlag, 1985).

10   Narrative therapy is based on the premise that people's sense of self arises out of the stories that they tell about themselves—some of which are shaped by the wider culture. Identifying and making changes to their stories can bring about positive changes in people's lives. See M. White, and D. Epston, *Narrative Means to Therapeutic Ends* (New York: W. W. Norton, 1990).

11   The biopsychosocial model was originally proposed by the American psychiatrist George Engel (1913–1990) to provide a more holistic framework (than the clinical medical model) which included other factors both subjective and societal implicated in the patient's condition.

12   These documents have been selected because the APA, due to its size of membership, reach, and influence, can be taken as a reliable indicator of the mainstream position on talking therapy practice more generally.

13   It is worth noting that diversity here refers to individuals' social identities including age, sexual orientation, physical disability, socioeconomic status, race/ethnicity, workplace role/position, religious and spiritual orientation, and work/family concerns. See American Psychological Association, *Guidelines on Multicultural Education, Training, Research, Practice, and Organizational Change for Psychologists (2003)*. https://www.apa.org/about/policy/multicultural-guidelines-archived.pdf, p.11.

14   Ibid, p. 36.

15   Ibid, p. 26.

16   Ibid, p. 63.

17   See American Psychological Association, *Multicultural Guidelines: An Ecological Approach to Context, Identity, and Intersectionality* (2017), 6. http://www.apa.org/about/policy/multicultural-guidelines.pdf.

[18] One of the principles in the 2003 version states that "Psychologists are uniquely able to promote racial equity and social justice," and this is used to support a case for psychologists as agents of social change.

[19] APA guidelines, 2017, p. 6.

[20] Ibid, p. 20-21.

[21] Ibid, p. 28.

[22] Ibid, p. 28.

[23] Ibid, p. 4.

[24] Ibid, p. 46.

[25] This phrase is attributed to the Italian communist Antonio Gramsci (1891–1937), who advocated for subverting society by co-opting society's chief institutions—education, criminal justice system, corporations, media, and religion.

[26] Some American State Licensure Boards are beginning to insert CSJ-driven commitments into their requirements for maintaining a license to practise therapy. See the State of Michigan's new requirement for counsellors to attend yearly implicit bias training. https://www.nasw-michigan.org/news/567811/LARA-Announce-Adopted-Training-Requirement-to-Improve-Equity-Across-MI.htm.

[27] At the turn of the millennium, a small group of influential clinical theorists were pushing for an increased commitment to social justice, arguing that not paying attention to contextual factors could be clinically harmful. Over the next decade, they helped to centre this new political understanding of social justice and were responsible for producing the now standard textbooks used in counselling training. See, for example, D. W. Sue & D. Sue, *Counseling the culturally diverse: Theory and practice* (6th ed.) (Hoboken, NJ: John Wiley, 2013). And P. B. Pederson, J. G. Draguns, W. J. Lonner, & J. E. Trimble, (eds.) *Counseling across cultures* (6th ed.) (Thousand Oaks, CA: Sage, 2008).

[28] Counselors for Social Justice (CSJ) was founded in 1999 and accepted within the American Psychological Association as an official division in 2000. See its website: https://www.counseling-csj.org/.

[29] R. C. Chung and F. P. Bernak, *Social Justice Counseling: The next steps beyond multiculturalism.* (Thousand Oaks, CA: Sage, 2012), 42.

[30] Nancy Arthur and Sandra Collins, "Counsellors, Counselling, and Social Justice: The Professional Is Political", *Canadian Journal of Counselling and Psychotherapy* 48 (3) Fall 2014, 171.

[31] An example of a narrative revision project in mainstream culture is the 1619 project, which is an attempt to change the foundational story of America. https://pulitzercenter.org/lesson-plan-grouping/1619-project-curriculum.

[32] C. Fleuridas and D. Krafcik, "Beyond Four Forces: The Evolution of Psychotherapy", *SAGE Open*. 2019, 7. https://doi.org/10.1177/2158244 018824492.

[33] An illustration of this can be found in a reputable counselling textbook published in 2012 which has a chapter titled *Social Justice as the fifth force: Theories and concepts.* See R. C. Chung and F. P. Bernak, *Social Justice Counseling,* 2012.

[34] Fleuridas and Krafcik propose a sixth force (above and beyond the fifth force of social justice) which they identify as integrative, integral, and comprehensive holistic approaches. Fleuridas and Krafcik, "Beyond Four Forces:", 2019.

[35] Critical Pedagogy is a philosophy of education that applies Critical Theory to teaching. Developed by Paulo Freire (1921–1997), it is designed to help students develop "critical consciousness" that is the ability to identify and then challenge societal structures of oppression.

[36] For further discussion of CSJ-driven pedagogic strategies being applied to counsellor education programmes, see an analysis of one paper written by a specialist in intersectionality and pedagogy titled *White practitioners in therapeutic ally-ance: An Intersectional Privilege Awareness Training Model* (Case, 2015) (unorthodox spelling is used in the original title). https://criticaltherapyantidote.org/2020/09/28/disingenuous-pedagogy-in-professional-counselling-training-turning-an-intersectional-lens-into-an-ideological-straitjacket/.

[37] Examples of full take over can be detected in the mission statements of training institutions. For example, The University of Vermont states under the rubric of Core Beliefs, "We also believe that our role of counseling in the community is to identify and *redress processes of oppression* in order to promote equity and justice" (italics added). See https://www.uvm.edu/cess/dlds/counseling_program_about_us.

[38] Decolonising the curriculum is already established policy in professional bodies. For example, see the British Psychological Society's webinar, which states, "it's about creating space and introducing multiple voices set to enrich and empower the curriculum as well as continue the long journey of decolonising the mind." See https://learn.bps.org.uk/local/intellicart/view.php?id=13.

[39] Ableism views disability, in whatever form, as an identity first and foremost. See the explanation given by Özlem Sensoy & Robin DiAngelo in *Is everyone really equal?: an introduction to key concepts in social justice education.* (2nd ed), (New York: Teachers College Press, 2017), 94. "Disability isn't a condition external to a person that can be discarded with a cure and left behind." And, "People with disabilities must navigate structures of privilege, definitions of normalcy, and the internalised superiority of the able-bodied everyday." These "ableist" notions are being applied to mental health conditions such as depression.

[40] An independent inquiry using Freedom of Information requests provides empirical evidence for the political capture of clinical psychology training in the UK. Carole Sherwood and Kirsty Miller, "The Politicisation of Clinical Psychology Training Courses in the UK. " See https://save-mental-health.com/training-courses/.

[41] Intense pressure is brought to bear on academics who publicly express counter-narratives. See the recent example of the philosopher Kathleen Stock, who resigned from her academic post at Sussex University. https://www.theguardian.com/education/2021/nov/03/kathleen-stock-says-she-quit-university-post-over-medieval-ostracism.

[42] See the account of how the British Psychology Society first published Dr Kirsty Miller's resignation letter and then retracted it from publication. Accessed on August 10 2022 at https://drkirsty.medium.com/the-now-cancelled-letter-to-the-british-psychological-society-3b4582334bc7.

[43] First coined by Robin DiAngelo in an article titled "White Fragility," in *International Journal of Critical Pedagogy*, Vol 3, no 3, (Fall 2011), 54-70. Subsequently characterised as a "Kafka trap", which is any attempt to refute an accusation that is then used as evidence for its truth. See David Burke's critique of DiAngelo's work in https://newdiscourses.com/2020/06/intellectual-fraud-robin-diangelos-white-fragility/.

[44] Concerns raised by whistle blowers about the damaging effects of gender ideology at the Tavistock GID clinic were ignored for years. Bernard Lane, "Shuttering the Tavistock." *Quillette,* August 5, 2022, https://quillette.com/2022/08/05/closing-the-tavistock-is-an-important-step/.

Chapter 2:

Psychotherapy, Ideology, and the New Aristocracy

by Nick Opyrchal

Introduction

This chapter will make an argument that might not be popular with the partisans of the ongoing culture war. What might particularly offend the belligerents is that I aim to upend a narrative which is both epic and universally popular: this being the belief that we are going through an apocalyptic revolution of the down-trodden, a great "awokening" which is sweeping away the old Western order like a biblical deluge. This is the story that the followers of Critical Social Justice (CSJ) use to prop up a grandiose image of themselves as revolutionary heroes, and which those on the political right whisper around campfires in order to justify themselves as equally grandiose defenders of order against monstrous evil.

Instead, I am going to argue a perhaps more deflated and pessimistic viewpoint: that the revolutionaries *already are* Western elites, *already are* firmly entrenched in power, and their "revolution" is largely a *smoke-and-mirrors show* employed in the service of getting a tighter grip on it, albeit undemocratically. Here I will show what part psychotherapy plays in this process, especially with regard to so-called "critical" psychotherapies and therapeutic politics, and I will be exploring the profession's political–ideological role, which has grown in parallel.

To provide clarity on this, I will first look at the term "critical" and how this has been appropriated by movements such as "Critical Social Justice". Forlornly, I will attempt to rehabilitate this much-abused word in this chapter, but I ask for the reader's forbearance for some of the more academic language in doing so. Unfortunately, as the term "critical" has become so associated with these particular political viewpoints it needs a bit of unpacking.

Next, drawing on various sociological theorists who describe this new ideology and its relationship to the new elite, I argue in more detail that CSJ, despite its rhetoric, is not genuinely critical or revolutionary in theory or practice. Rather it is ideological, a case of revolutionary imagery and rhetoric being used to reinforce the interests of an already dominant class: think the political equivalent of Jeff Bezos wearing a Che Guevara t-shirt. Following this, I will then explore how psychotherapy and this elite ideology have begun to merge together. Political psychotherapy and psychotherapeutic politics create a chimaera that threatens to undermine the integrity of both the political system and profession.

"Critical" credulity

Firstly, an essential question: *What separates "critical" forms of psychotherapy from "ideological" psychotherapy?* This question is important for the thesis of this chapter. It is also perhaps less easy to answer than one might first think. When faced with the motley assortment of self-appointed critical psychotherapists, it may seem easy to identify practitioners who take a critical approach to theory and practice owing to this label.[1] However, the word "critical" here misleads; it functions merely as an ideological–tribal marker such as in "Critical" Theory or "Critical" Social Justice.

The more naive use of the word "critical" suggests instead the attempt to raise questions, move past first appearances, and evolve through a concentrated analysis, producing more nuanced and accurate understandings of a problem.[2] Ideological modes of interpreting the world in contrast represent "closed loops"; systems of self-replication in which the answer to any question (and the questions themselves) are predetermined in advance. The aim of an ideology is not to openly question but actually to *prohibit asking the wrong questions,* those which might cause undue disturbance to an established system through threatening the capacity of the thinker to match the emerging evidence comfortably to their pre-ordained, ideologically prescribed answers.[3,4]

I distinguish here between critical and ideological orientations because so-called "critical" therapies and practices have been adopted so hurriedly by many psychotherapeutic institutions. I am making the unpopular argument that these are actually not *authentically* critical but are instead explicitly ideological, comfortable, and self-congratulatory. They are "closed loops", providing predictable answers which only reinforce those who find themselves already in a decidedly beneficial position in society.

Worse still, they often do this by deflecting guilt and responsibility onto both the working- and lower-middle-class ethnic majority and injustices of the past while ignoring the elitism of the present. Whilst on a rhetorical level, these paradigms call loudly for a revolution, it is on closer critical inspection a pseudo-revolution serving the status quo.[5] The justification given for cementing the cultural power of these already-dominant elites is by presenting it in the guise of a radical change.

As discussed by other authors within this book, psychotherapy has become an important arm of enforcement within this ideological apparatus. Psychotherapy and psychotherapists are becoming willing and enthusiastic enforcers of this pseudo-critical, pseudo-revolutionary ideology of the elites.

Psychotherapy: propaganda arm of the new aristocracy?

Within scathing, near-prophetic works such as *The Culture of Narcissism, The Minimal Self*, and *Revolt of the Elites*, the noted politico-psychoanalytic theorist Cristopher Lasch made an astute observation on modern revolutionary movements.[6] He noted that these movements (and the social programs they promoted) were only adopted wholesale by the dominant orders and pre-established institutions of a society when they secretly served an *ideological* purpose. Their adoption was essentially "two-faced", reinforcing the existing order of society whilst at the same time claiming to overthrow it. Lasch observed that these "revolutions" of the elite consolidated the interests of the already powerful and often acted (in practical terms) in direct contradiction to the revolutionary rhetoric, aims, and ideals that they subscribed to in theory ... that of overthrowing established order, imposing justice, and uplifting the powerless.

Political philosopher Michael Lind's more contemporary work, *The New Class War – Saving Democracy from the Metropolitan Elite*, strongly supports Lasch's earlier analysis concerning this point.[7] Applying a similar lens to our current political moment, Lind highlights many ways in which the policies which are pushed by CSJ "revolutionaries" converge with the interests of giant technocratic oligarchies. These oligarchies are situated unmistakably within the highest levels of society, both in terms of economic and cultural power. In a similar mode to Lasch, Lind argues that the interests of these two groups—the academic supporters of CSJ on one hand, and oligarchic multinational tech corporations such as Google, Facebook, etc. on the other—significantly overlap.[8]

Lind and Lasch, along with a growing number of other political theorists from both the "old" left, such as Mark Lilla and Joel Kotkin, and the right, such as Patrick Deneen, often refer to this combined alliance of academics and technocratic oligarchy as forming almost a new aristocracy.[9,10,11]

This aristocracy justifies its ever-strengthening social dominance on the basis of an implicit belief in meritocracy. This is the idea that this new elite finds themselves in their dominant position in society through having rightly "earned it"; being the most worthy, high-achieving, and educated.[12] Although the political rhetoric of this elite expresses pipe dreams of equality, the aristocracy's supposedly left-leaning cultural values are contrasted uneasily with the (somewhat embarrassing) reality of their growing economic and cultural dominance. Their members are largely wealthy, university-educated cosmopolitans dwelling within expensive "hub" cities such as London, Los Angeles, or New York.[13] Their deployment of specialised academic concepts in everyday situations (e.g., privilege, microaggressions, and pronouns) function largely as symbols of exclusivity. They position the speaker as part of a university-educated, meritocratic high society in the same way that knowledge of formal etiquette (such as knowing exactly which piece of cutlery to eat your dessert with) did for the old hereditary aristocracy in the days of yore.

The academic and ideological wing of the new aristocracy is equivalent to what this book terms "Critical Social Justice". The theorists named above (broadly) argue that whilst this movement positions itself in its own rhetoric as opposed to established elites and hierarchies within society, this is deceptive. It actually functions in practical terms analogously to how the church operated in feudal times, providing a valuable function for the aristocracy.[14] Essentially a propaganda arm, it pays lip service to eradicating inequality and increasing representation whilst in real terms it actually adds powerful ideological support to the culture and policies of already-dominant elites, enforcing these through increasingly undemocratic means (cancelling, de-platforming, etc.).

As the sociologist Erik Kaufmann notes, the ideological role of the CSJ movement is also to provide an interpretation of the cause of social ills which deflect psychological responsibility away from the metropolitan elite.[15] Through the scapegoating and "other-ing" of the culture, interests, and identity of the more traditional, provincial, working- and lower-middle-class ethnic majorities, there is a shift and deferral of guilt away from the cosmopolitan elite classes which truly benefit from the status quo. The culpa-bility and guilt that this class (perhaps) deserves for the system they largely benefit from are instead invariably projected onto the culture of the white working and lower-middle classes—the "deplorables", if you will.

This struggling demographic, in turn, increasingly adopts a populist politics of rejection.[16] Partly as a defensive response, they spurn the elites who scapegoat them.[17] This *is* therefore a "systemic" problem, but not in the hugely simplified, ideological, "black-or-white" sense that we are continually confronted with through the works of Robin Diangelo, Ibram X. Kendi, and other luminaries of the CSJ movement.[18]

An increasingly therapeutic politics

It is notable that both Lind and Lasch highlight the growing rela-tionship that psychotherapy (or rather a pseudo-therapeutic popular culture) has with the ideology of the new aristocracy.[19] Although writing decades before the current explosion in Criti-cal Social Justice, Lasch demonstrates an almost paranormal abil-ity to predict our current situation. He noted that the preferred policies of the emergent upper-middle class (who he dubbed the "managerial elite") were increasingly being framed in the mode of therapeutic decisions. Refusal to obey authority was being reframed as pathology, signifying the existence of emotional or psychological disturbance. What were essentially political and moral decisions were increasingly reinterpreted as public health issues, with opposition to these positions framed as pathological and threatening to the psychological and physical health of indi-viduals and social groups.

These observations found a strange postmodern bedfellow in that they mirrored comments made by Michel Foucault in his work on "psychiatric power".[20] Foucault identified a shift in the form in which power is expressed: rather than power being expressed as enforcing the will of an authority (such as a king, president, nation, etc.), power is instead increasingly expressed in a bureaucratic, psychiatric form, supposedly on behalf of benevolent therapeutic interests, such as defending public "health" or preventing "harm". Although the target of this repressive power has changed since Foucault first described it, the bureaucratic–psychiatric method of delivery has become increasingly popular.

Highlighting just how popular, Michael Lind identifies this trend as growing exponentially as CSJ took hold of mainstream culture. Especially noticeable were the increasing varieties of pathologising terminology which were deployed following the explosion of populist political sentiment in both the run-up to the 2016 US election and the Brexit vote in the UK. During this time, a repertoire of ever-increasing variations on psychological "phobias" emerged into the public sphere. These were applied liberally in increasingly spurious circumstances, gaining prominence during periods when the tide of rising populist discontent threatened the established political system. Diagnoses of irrational phobias, psychological disorders, and pathology became leveraged enthusiastically by the dominant culture against disfavoured political decision-making.

As a result, the psyches of those adopting political positions outside of those preferred by the managerial elite of university-educated, left-wing, upper-middle-class city dwellers were increasingly pathologised. The desire for more control over borders or immigration (for example) was interpreted as an act of psychological racism or xenophobia, and it was immaterial whether the motivation for that came from concern for protecting existent working-class wages or a genuinely racist impulse.[21] Not voting for Hilary Clinton became an act of pathological sexism. Voting for a conservative (or even centrist) party over a progressive one is interpreted as an act of internalised white supremacy.

Similarly, choosing to reject CSJ as an ideology is pathologised even when a rational argument is presented demonstrating why the assumptions of the paradigm are suspect. Rejection or questioning of the movement is re-framed in pseudo-psychotherapeutic terminology as being the result of the rejecter's unconscious racism, privilege, sexism, or (increasingly) "white fragility".

Often, the suggestion is made that to openly oppose the penetration of CSJ into psychology is equivalent to causing minorities psychological harm or violence. This makes patronising assumptions that this ideology is directly equivalent to minorities and their interests, and to oppose it constitutes an attack on their personhood and identity.[22] In these cases, what is glaringly evident is that the language of psychological pathology and pseudo-psychotherapeutic terminology is deployed in a brutal and blatantly ideological fashion. It is leveraged by a dominant intellectual class to prevent private citizens from legitimately adopting political choices which contradict those preferred by the technocratic aristocracy.

The catchphrase "the personal is political" is a favourite aphorism deployed vacuously by "critical" psychotherapists to justify the increasing movement of psychotherapy towards adopting a politics of identity.[23] The obvious flip side to this is that the political is personal; politics becomes increasingly reduced to a purely personal, identarian, and psychotherapeutic process. Differing politics from the interests of the dominant class are de-legitimised, not by political or moral argument but increasingly by reference to this hybrid of psychotherapy and ideology. Either of the interpretations is made of pathology in the person expressing the view (e.g., "white fragility", "toxic masculinity", even (bizarrely) "internalised whiteness" of conservative minorities), or psychological injury is taken to be a risk to listeners ("trauma"), or potential psychological damage is hypothesised to occur to vulnerable minorities should it be taken seriously.[24,25]

The use of psychological and psychotherapeutic power in this hybridised, ideological way has (of course) a grim precedent—this being the "sluggish schizophrenia" of Soviet psychiatry. Those who opposed Soviet Communism were diagnosed with a degenerative and incurable psychological disorder and sectioned to suppress and reduce the impact of their dissent.[26] We have not yet reached the moment where one can be sectioned for opposing intersectionality, and I do not wish to encourage hysteria through this comparison, but as the next section will show we are perhaps creating our own (admittedly much more limp and tepid) postmodern parallel.

An increasingly political psychotherapy

Alongside disguising political and moral decisions with a deceptively therapeutic cloak, there exists a burgeoning movement within psychotherapy that attempts to merge clinical practice and political ideology entirely. One of the more insidious ways this is enacted is through various practitioners and academics attempting to "politicise" ethical codes. These form the institutional frameworks on which psychotherapeutic practices are unavoidably built. Leading CSJ theorists such DiAngelo, Crenshaw, Hill Collins & Bilge, and Kendi promote the world-view that almost all institutions (even if claiming to be politically neutral) are already incorrigibly corrupted by a Western "white supremacist" ideology that feigns neutrality in order to enact brutal racism.[27] It is therefore legitimate and justified, in the eyes of these theorists (and the CSJ paradigm which they influence), to re-engineer *all* of our social institutions which profess neutrality along *explicitly politicised*, non-neutral lines to conform with their preferred political orientation. Psychotherapy is, evidently, one of these institutions marked for re-engineering.

The journey toward this assimilation process was gathering steam before the summer of 2020, a pivotal cultural point when the Western world's "Black Lives Matter" protests led to the reflexive and widespread adoption of intersectional theory and CSJ ideology by the largest psychotherapeutic organisations.[28] In the months following the protests, psychotherapeutic and counselling institutions within the UK, such as the British Association for Counselling and Psychotherapy (BACP) and the British Psychological Society (BPS), followed the (perhaps more radical) example of the American Psychological Association (APA) (whose embrace of CSJ is highlighted in the opening chapter).[29]

Foreshadowing this "crossing of the Rubicon" for the political direction of Western psychotherapeutic organisations, many theorists had pre-emptively argued that psychotherapy should enshrine itself in the "radical" cultural politics favoured by the oligarchy and academy. As an example, the counselling psychologist Grzanka, and other authors, published a detailed paper suggesting that therapy should be entirely transformed in aim, becoming instead "A site of resistance and intersectional conscious raising amongst white people".[30] Enthusiastically employing the same "for-us-or-against-us" moral binaries beloved by the most prominent theorists of CSJ, Grzanka (following Ibram X. Kendi) states that even "non-racist" psychotherapists are unacceptably complicit in systemic global white supremacy. One must instead be "anti-racist". Dismissing the waning orthodoxy of therapists who adopt a politically neutral, non-coercive stance concerning clients, Grzanka argues that practitioners must instead adopt an explicitly "activist" position. Clients must also be pushed unbidden by the psychotherapist within the psychotherapeutic process to become "antiracist" activists themselves. The unmistakably dogmatic and moralistic instruction is given to therapists to address issues of white supremacy in psychotherapy, even if this is entirely unrelated to the therapeutic material causing the client to seek help in the first place. Psychotherapy becomes an arena for ideological conversion; clients are reduced to merely potential converts.

In their 2018 paper, psychologists Dodd and Alan extend even further than Grzanka's messianic politicising of the psychotherapeutic process within the clinic. These theorists argue for imposing ethical injunctions upon the public expressions and persona of the psychotherapist or psychologist—*outside* their clinical role. They suggest that not only the clinical but also the *public* expression of politics by psychological professionals should be regulated by ethical codes, such as those of the APA.[31] They object to the public work of psychologist Jordan Peterson explicitly on these grounds. Whereas Peterson's work is debated by some psychology professionals, these theorists go beyond debate; instead, they want to prohibit his *public* expression. This is justified under the increasingly familiar therapeutic–ideological grounds; these views expressed by a psychology professional cause "harm". Again, we witness the ideological hybrid of politics and psychotherapy.

These are merely two examples of many which illustrate the attempt to create an intentional hybrid of therapy and political ideology before 2020. Both seek to alter ethical codes, turning psychotherapy into the psychological arm of a political–ideological movement (essentially reducing the therapeutic process to ideological imprinting). The client material, the therapeutic process, the therapist in the clinic, and even the expressed political views of the therapist outside of the clinic are prescribed according to CSJ. Theorists such as these laid the groundwork for the quick changes that came into force following the global 2020 protests. Although these changes were identified as spontaneous reactions to global protests, in truth, they were built upon well-established foundations. The zeitgeist behind the protests merely allowed them to be implemented in the clinic without being slowed by the need for critical analysis as to whether they were appropriate for psychotherapy.

Conclusion: a systemic problem?

As illustrated within this short chapter, therapy and political ideology have begun to form a mutually reinforcing system. The ideology of the day consists of the use of pseudo-psychotherapeutic and pseudo-psychoanalytic terminology as a means of protecting elites in positions of political, economic, and cultural dominance from threats—all done in the name of mental health, social justice, and well-being. The total lack of serious threat that this "revolution" poses to the status quo is best demonstrated by the farcical spectacle of Coca-Cola, Facebook, Google, and Lockheed Martin enthusiastically adopting pop-therapy catchphrases and pseudo-therapeutic workshops promoting Critical Social Justice, thrusting these upon their long-suffering employees.[32]

These measures offer next to no danger to the power or profits of these companies or the others situated within powerful positions in society who often most enthusiastically adopt them. Their implementation makes very little meaningful change to the dominance of established elites, and yet simultaneously, the act of adopting them affords these powerful groups a great ideological defence. They become reframed as members of (in their own language) "the resistance". When Prince Harry, Ivy League and Oxbridge universities, the CIA, and the US military align their public image with this pseudo-therapeutic worldview of CSJ and resistance, we should not shy away from using our supposedly powerful analytical skills as psychotherapists to raise uncomfortable questions: "Who" it is they are actually "resisting"? How legitimate is it to really see this paradigm as "revolutionary"?[33]

Unfortunately, this critical interrogation from psychotherapists seldom occurs. Instead, at the same time as this "therapeutic" politics undermines the potential for genuinely radical political change, "critical" psychotherapy also undermines its potential for genuine personal change by throwing in its lot with this ideology of the new aristocracy. Rather than practitioners using their finely honed psychotherapeutic tools to create a genuinely critical and politically informed practice (which could engage with all political orientations and populations), it instead narrows itself, adopting the favoured views of elite American universities which ideologically support the interests of their largely university educated, wealthy, upper-middle class, left-wing, cosmopolitan populations. This is (of course) the same population which constitutes the majority of practising psychotherapists and psychotherapy institutes.

As the reader will gather, I stubbornly remain a "critical" psychotherapist, someone with an interest in helping people who experience oppression and separating ideological demands from best therapeutic practice. My argument here is that "Critical Social Justice" in psychotherapy is offering something deceptive; it is ideological rather than analytical. Dogmatic rather than critical. It supports elites, but in the name of the dispossessed. Whereas psychoanalysis and psychotherapy have historically attempted to maintain some distance from ideological dogmas and therefore have been (in their best moments) a genuinely critical force, there is a real danger here of the profession becoming the most zealous members of a new inquisition.

Endnotes

1   Some examples of "critical psychotherapy": Pamela LiVecchi and Mayowa Obasaju, "Utilizing an Ecological Framework to Integrate Social Identities and Sociopolitical Analysis in Psychotherapy," *Journal of Clinical Psychology* 74, no 5 (March 2018): 755-765, https://doi.org/10.1002/jclp.22606; Arianne E. Miller and Lawrence Josephs, "Whiteness as Pathological Narcissism," *Contemporary Psychoanalysis* 45, no 1, (Spring 2009): 93-119; Martin Milton, *The Personal is Political – Stories of Difference in Psychotherapy* (1st edn.) (London: Palgrave Publishing, 2018); Dwight Turner, "Fight the Power: A Heuristic *Exploration* of Systemic Racism Through Dreams," *Counselling and Psychotherapy Research* 21, no 3 (June 2020), retrieved from: https://onlinelibrary.wiley.com/doi/abs/10.1002/capr.12329.

2   To paraphrase the political philosopher Eric Voegelin, truly "critical" thinking raises an additional question in the face of every (supposedly) final answer. For other definitions of "critical", see https://counterweight-support.com/2021/02/17/what-do-we-mean-by-critical-social-justice/.

3   Eric Voegelin, *Science, Politics and Gnosticism* (Delaware: ISI Books, 2005).

4   Although there are different conceptions of ideology—Marx, Weber, Voegelin, etc.—they share the phenomenological quality of a closed, self-replicating system in consciousness. Whether the purpose of this system is to maintain the existing power relations regarding access to means of production or an alternative explanation is not addressed here.

5   Apart from the work of Christopher Lasch, the Italian Catholic philosopher Augusto Del Noce's work is the best exposition of why this ideology is neither authentically revolutionary or Marxist despite theoretical roots in this tradition. Del Noce points out that this ideology is profoundly conservative in the sense that it alters Marxist epistemology—emphasising historical materialism whilst downplaying the dialectical aspect. In this respect, there is no movement towards an eschatological end point nor emphasis on universality as there is with Marxism. Sandra Harding later tried to remedy this epistemological issue by adopting "strong objectivity" (see below). However, this makes standpoint theory self-contradictory—emphasising both difference and universality. This explains why the dissident historian of Marxism Leszek Kolakowski described the "new left" as having almost no real relation to Marxism and expressing instead the "spoiled whims of middle-class children".

See: Augusto Del Noce. *The Age of Secularization* (1st edn.) (Montreal, Canada: McGill-Queens University Press, 2017) and *The Crisis of Modernity*

(1st edn.) (Montreal, Canada; McGill-Queens University Press, 2014). Sarah Harding, "Rethinking Standpoint Epistemology: What is "Strong Objectivity?" *The Centennial Review* 36, no. 3 (Fall 1992): 437-470.

6   Cristopher Lasch, *The Culture of Narcissism: American Life in an Age of Diminishing Expectations* (new edn.) (London: W.W. Norton, 2018).

   Cristopher Lasch, *The Minimal Self: Psychic Survival in Troubled Times* (London: W.W. Norton,1984).

   Cristopher Lasch, *The Revolt of the Elites: and the Betrayal of Democracy* (London: W.W. Norton, 1994).

7   Michael Lind, *The New Class War: Saving Democracy from the Managerial Elite* (New York: Portfolio/Penguin, 2020).

8   Lind observes that the dissolution of national boundaries and open borders uncritically applauded by Critical Social Justice is exploited by larger companies via outsourcing of staff, attempts at tax evasion, and the employment of cheap labour below minimum wage. This is at the expense of the majority of working-class populations, so fuelling populist discontent. This discontent is framed by the ideology of CSJ as xenophobic and seen as a psychological issue rather than having an economic basis.

9   Mark Lila, *The Once and Future Liberal – After Identity Politics* (Glasgow, UK: Bell and Bain Publishing, 2018).

10 Joel Kotkin, *The Coming of Neo Feudalism: A Warning to the Global Middle Class* (New York: Encounter Books, 2020).

11 Patrick Deneen, *Why Liberalism Failed* (New Haven, Connecticut: Yale University Press, 2018). A nuanced conservative theorist, Deneen sees the political crisis in the West, and Critical Social Justice itself, as being a development of Liberal ideology towards its logical conclusion rather than an outright rejection and deviation from it, as some other theorists (such as James Lindsay and Helen Pluckrose) have proposed. Deneen makes a convincing argument that we cannot escape this crisis by reverting back to liberal universalism, as the ideological injunction promoted by CSJ, that we should (in essence) live a life of total self-affirmation of desire and lack of obligation to existing conservative traditions and structures, is itself a sort of extremist liberalism. This political analysis has similarities with psychological analysis on narcissism by Cristopher Lasch and the social psychoanalytic work on the "pristine self" of Howard Schwartz.

12 Michael Sandel, *The Tyranny of Merit: What's Become of the Common Good?* (New York: Farrar, Strauss and Giroux, 2021); and Lasch, *The Revolt of the Elites.*

13 Lind, *The New Class War,* for a description of shifting class lines in accordance with our current social context, and the importance of "hub" cities in this restructure. These new class lines include the following categories: those able to live in hub cities and own assets there (the managerial elite/oligarchy); those unable to live in hub cities and who instead live and own property in the suburbs, rural, and ex-urb communities around them (the working and lower-middle class); and a service class to the elite comprising mainly minority and migrant workers who work and sometimes rent in the city but will never own assets (essentially an underclass). Kotkin names similar categorical designations but adds the category of middle-class artists and academics who live in the city but do not own assets, yet their politics align with the technocratic oligarchy (these form a large portion of supporters of Critical Social Justice) before city life exhausts them and they retire to the suburbs. Lind and Kotkin highlight the lack of social mobility between these classes (Kotkin describes this as akin to feudalism) in comparison to earlier time periods during the previous century.

14 Kotkin, *The Coming of Neo Feudalism.*

15 Erik Kaufmann, *Whiteshift: Populism, Immigration and the Future of White Majorities* (New York: Penguin Random House Publishing, 2019).

16 Sandel, *The Tyranny of Merit,* for information on the increase of "deaths of despair" amongst this demographic.

17 Kaufmann writes extensively on how the culture of the working-class ethnic majority is used within the ideology of the upper-middle-class elite as a means to compare and define itself through contrast. Kaufmann identifies that prohibition on expressing ethno-nationalist interests on behalf of the ethnic majority is one of the strongest signals of membership into this elite class. The ideology which underpins this class he names "Left-modernism". See also Kotkin and Deneen in this regard.

18 See the following: Robin DiAngelo, *White Fragility: Why It is so Hard for White People to Talk about Racism* (Boston: Beacon Press, 2018); Patricia Hill Collins and Simone Bilge, *Intersectionality* (2nd edn.) (Cambridge, UK: Polity Press, 2018); Ibram X. Kendi, *How To Be An Antiracist* (New York: Vintage, 2019); Kimberlé Crenshaw, Charles Harris, Daniel Martinez Hosang, and George Lipsitz, eds., *Seeing Race Again: Countering Colorblindness Across the Disciplines* (Oakland, CA: University of California Press, 2019); R. Delgado and R. and J. Stefancic, *Critical Race Theory: An Introduction* (New York: New York University Press, 2017).

The adoption of the standpoint epistemology of Sandra Harding by these theorists (or assumptions close to these, in the case of Kendi) means that supposedly systemic analyses are predetermined along particular lines.

"Systemic" is equated with the conclusion that systems are dominated by white, straight, male populations, and that their dominance ideologically restricts consciousness—preventing a restructuring of society to afford equal access to the means of production. The "dialectical" aspect of standpoint epistemology sees the world progressing via the perspective of the "marginal" eventually negating this system. Harding talks about strong objectivity, the belief that there is a special type of objectivity distinct to "scientific" objectivity which is held by those at distance from the perspective of the "centre" of privilege and power. This strong objectivity will negate perspectives which ideologically reinforce the status quo of white male privilege and supposedly lead us into a more "objective" mode of social organisation. This perspective is therefore Marxo-Hegelian in terms of origin. However, its emphasis on both an imminent relativism and dialectical universalism make it self-contradictory.

19 Lasch, *The Culture of Narcissism* and Lind, *The New Class War.*

20 Michel Foucault, *Psychiatric Power: Lectures at the College De France 1973 – 1974* (London: Palgrave Macmillan, 2003). Foucault uses the example of the psychological treatment of King George III as the archetypal example of psychiatric power. Foucault observes that King George's royal, patriarchal status was not enough to stop him from being subjected to a number of torturous treatments nominally intended to improve his mental health. That the King was subject to this alternative, managerial, and bureaucratic structure of power in the name of "mental health" was for Foucault a "changing of the guard" away from the old, patriarchal, top-down form of power which Critical Social Justice theorists often identify as entirely dominant.

21 Lind, *The New Class War.* See also Dwight Turner, *Intersections of Privilege and Otherness in Counselling and Psychotherapy: Mockingbird* (Abingdon, UK: Routledge, 2021) for a current author within counselling and psychotherapy who deploys these diagnoses as explanation for these events.

22 In regard to these tactics being employed towards psychologist Kirsty Miller, who was denounced for citing a need for objectivity within psychology, see N. Opyrchal, "The Ideological Takeover of British Psychotherapy," February 9, 2020, at *Merion West,* https://merionwest. com/2020/09/02/the-ideological-takeover-of-british-psychotherapy/.

23 Milton, *The Personal is Political,* who describes intersectionality in obscurantist quasi-religious terms.

24 DiAngelo, *White Fragility* and Turner, *Intersections of Privilege and Otherness in Counselling and Psychotherapy.*

25 Opyrchal, *The Ideological Takeover of British Psychotherapy.*

26 Also described by Lind in *The New Class War.*

27 DiAngelo, *White Fragility;* Hill Collins and Bilge, *Intersectionality;* Kendi, *How To Be An Antiracist;* and Crenshaw et al, *Seeing Race Again.*

28 Larry Buchanan, Quoctrung Bui, and Jugal K. Patel, "Black Lives Matter May Be the Largest Movement in U.S. History," The New York Times, July 3, 2020. https://www.nytimes.com/interactive/2020/07/03/us/george-floyd-protests-crowd-size.html.

29 *British Psychological Society*, "The Psychologist September 2020", August 18, 2020, https://issuu.com/thepsychologist/docs/psy0920shoppreview. Also, *American Psychological Association*, "APA calls for true systemic change in U.S. culture", Zarah Abrams, September 1, 2020, https://www.apa.org/monitor/2020/09/systemic-change. Also, *American Psychological Association*, "Harmful masculinity and violence", September 2018, https://www.apa.org/pi/about/newsletter/2018/09/harmful-masculinity.

30 P. Grzanka, K. Gonzalez and L. Spanierman, "White Supremacy and Counseling Psychology: A Critical–Conceptual Framework," *The Counseling Psychologist,* Vol. 47, no.4, November 27, 2019, 478-529. https://doi.org/10.1177/0011000019880843.

31 L. R. Allen and C. G. Dodd, "Psychologists' responsibility to society: Public policy and the ethics of political action", *Journal of Theoretical and Philosophical Psychology,* 38, no.1, Spring 2018, 42–53, https://doi.org/10.1037/teo0000077.

32 See the 'training' of Lockheed Martin and Coca-Cola. Liz George, "1,000+ Lockheed Martin employees forced to take anti-white race training allegedly forcing execs to call white men 'racist,' 'KKK,' 'privileged', " *American Military News,* June 8, 2021, https://americanmilitarynews.com/2021/06/1000-lockheed-martin-employees-forced-to-take-anti-white-race-training-allegedly-forcing-execs-to-call-white-men-racist-kkk-privileged/.

Also, Lia Eustachewich, "Coca-Cola slammed for diversity training that urged workers to be 'less white', " *New York Post,* February 23, 2021, https://nypost.com/2021/02/23/coca-cola-diversity-training-urged-workers-to-be-less-white/.

33 Julia Borger, "CIA forges unity in diversity: everybody hates their 'woke' recruitment ad," *Guardian*, May 4, 2021, https://www.theguardian.com/us-news/2021/may/04/cia-woke-recruitment-ad.

Also, Liz George, "Here's the new US Army ad drawing controversy as 'woke' or 'great to see' – you decide," *American Military News*, May 12, 2021, https://americanmilitarynews.com/2021/05/heres-the-new-us-army-ad-drawing-controversy-as-woke-or-great-to-see-you-decide/.

Chapter 3:

Viewing Critical Social Justice From a Psychotherapeutic Perspective

by Ben Harris

Before we begin, I have a confession: I think post-modernist philosophy has useful insights. In my view, one of the primary problems of Critical Social Justice (CSJ) theory is that despite it being inspired by the post-modern turn, it contradicts the most useful insight of post-modernism—that all knowledge is contextual and partial.[1]

Psychotherapy draws upon numerous perspectives that illuminate, complement, and critique one another. This invites the production of new knowledge in creative tension with that already established. Critical Social Justice evaluates other fields through its own lens, "problematising" and "deconstructing" the knowledge and knowledge-production methods of the examined field.

As CSJ becomes more influential in the field, psychotherapy, with its intellectually flexible nature and enquiry into the human condition, is well placed to "return the favour" by undertaking an analysis of CSJ using therapeutic insights. Thus, greater contextual understanding emerges. Psychotherapy encourages introspection. Examining Critical Theory from a therapeutic perspective involves moving from a sociological or political mindset focussed on external phenomena to a psychological mindset where inner

37

experience is foundational. Second-wave feminists used to say, "The personal is political."[2] Indeed. But the political is also deeply personal.

Psychoanalysis operates within "the hermeneutics of suspicion"—we ask what is *really* going on, including of ourselves.[3] I am a clinician contributing to a timely critique of an intellectual phenomenon whose urgent demands and narrow mindset I believe may do damage to my profession and the people it serves. True. But I also have a mortgage to pay—so, you may ponder whether my contribution is to do with an attempt to gain a new stream of clients. Or perhaps it is because I like to think of myself as rather clever, so shouldn't a wider segment of people be given the opportunity to think of me as rather clever too? I was once a grim young radical seeing sexism, racism, and homophobia everywhere in a fallen imperialist world (none of this dynamic is a new one—merely it is mainstreaming). Perhaps I'm offering advice to my young self but am wary of his resentful rage also. Of competing virtues, I'm temperamentally and philosophically more inclined towards freedom and responsibility than equality these days.

The late analyst Peter Lomas pointed out that the therapist who believes they have access to the truth and commits to bringing their client to that understanding is one who coerces and uses force.[4] He contrasts coercion with the therapist offering an honest account of their own perspective whilst leaving space for the other to find their own understanding of life and their place in it.[5] I have a perspective, but it is mine—necessarily partial. Our "critical" friends demanding that therapy should be conducted from within their own sense of cognitive certainty might want to think about the implications of this. For people who are interested in how narratives legitimate power, they seem to be rather uninterested in examining their own.

There are many approaches within a pluralistic psychotherapy field to analysing psychological phenomena. In this chapter, we'll examine Critical Social Justice from two perspectives—the existentialist approach and the psychoanalytic school. These distinct approaches are complementary: existentialist therapy offers insights into the human condition—the conditions of the external world that we must learn to navigate—whilst psychoanalysis examines how our inner world reacts to these conditions and how the psyche in turn shapes our experience of the external world.

The doctrine of Critical Social Justice

This ideology maintains that the West operates under oppressive social structures designed to conserve the power of dominant groups, those who are male, able, white, heterosexual, cisgender, etc.[6] The institutions of Western societies are therefore largely corrupt power structures that exist to offer preferment to powerful identity groups. Any difference between groups is considered a function of discrimination. As Ibram X. Kendi states, "As an anti-racist, when I see racial disparities, I see racism."[7] This is the aspect of the belief structure that describes the material conditions of reality.

Secondly, there are a series of applied ethical calls to action:

- the moral requirement for an individual to believe the world is like this
- to acknowledge how the individual benefits from oppression
- to accept culpability for the continuation of oppression
- to act to disrupt the structures of oppression.

I have some sympathy with aspects of the descriptive analysis of reality, as it applies to race, at least. People throughout history have had a tribal in-group bias, often racial, and race is often a meaningfully felt attribute of self or other.[8] But experiences of race are subjective, varying, and individual. Intergenerational trauma may be common. Most of humanity has experienced grinding poverty within the last few generations; attendant trauma may impact us

39

all variably, and descendants of those historically oppressed may be impacted in specific ways.[9]

The material and ethical assertions of CSJ are controversial. Most people with apparently oppressed identities don't think about the world through this ideological lens—it is an artifact of academia. To bring a psychotherapeutic perspective to bear on the controversy, it will be useful to think about the nature of the world we live in (the human condition from an existentialist perspective) and the response of the human mind to the nature of that world (human nature from a psychoanalytic perspective).

What does existentialism say about our existence?

Existentialism is an enquiry into the human experience of being alive which centres around core questions of meaning, freedom, isolation, responsibility, and death.[10] Existentialists recognise the tragic aspect of life, bound up as it is with our suffering. Because therapy is about life and how to live it, philosophical perspectives inevitably impinge on the therapy room.[11] Reactions to the concerns of existentialism underpin many of our actions over a lifetime. R.D. Laing, the existentialist-minded psychiatrist, said that life was about despair, terror, and boredom.[12] Many don't acknowledge that life is naturally a hard grind. Dependent on stripe, politicians prosper by offering a return to an untroubled time of tradition and harmony before the grim demands of modernity, or by selling what Jung called the "big myth ... the time-hallowed archetypal dream of a Golden Age where everything is provided in abundance for everyone".[13] Jung was discussing communism but commented that in the West there is equally a great desire to produce the "Kingdom of God on Earth".[14]

Is life really so terrible, then? Any economist can tell you that life is limited—limited resources yet unlimited desires. We compete and cooperate in the face of an impassive universe, building lives that will be washed away by the sands of time. We are cruel to one another. Competition produces winners and losers— the guilty and the shamed. Cooperation stultifies and controls, the necessary oppressions of group life and civilisation gnawing away at the spark of individuality. We love and are rejected, or betrayed. In turn, we hate, reject, and betray. All in the lonely solitude of our own singular mind. Our bodies inevitably decline into ill health, and, after decrepitude, death. Life is bounded by death—a perhaps inescapable conscious or unconscious fear, the full embodied weight of which we spend considerable psychic resources keeping at bay.[15]

Existentialists say that despite this, we have freedom. Not the freedom to defy existential laws or circumstances of birth, but real freedom nonetheless.[16] To choose, to act, to struggle, to become—we are, in Sartre's words, "condemned to be free".[17]

There is another side to the life of equal weight. Life is exhil- arating. It contains love, compassion, the erotic, creativity, excite- ment, deep tranquillity, transcendent beauty, humour, discov- ery, wonder—and an enormous amount of mystery. Jung told us that humans face a universe of "inexorable opposites" which we cannot extinguish because this is the nature of existence itself.[18] We know how much being human encompasses—magnificent, terrible, and mundane by turns—and how little of this squeezes through into the realm of public discussion.

Reactions to a suffering existence

So, notwithstanding its richness, life is hard. It's a losing streak. The slot machine is rigged, and the house always wins … in the long run, we are all dead. This is not palatable, but we do under- stand it; hence people may react by both ruminating on the evils and disappointments of life (human and natural) and by denying them, *sometimes at exactly the same time*. Critical Social Justice is a symptom that results from the simultaneous fixation on *and*

41

denial of the tragic aspects of life. The pain is real and inevitable; we know this tragedy, but we don't want to face it.

Existentialism emphasises our desire to create meaning that sustains us in the face of the frustrations and suffering of existence. CSJ is an example of this. If we can only overturn the established order of our societies we can create fairness, end suffering, and all be happy. A small price to pay, no? If only it were possible. This is a key motivation—the belief that life does not have to be how it is. The "vale of tears" may be transformed into the sunlit uplands of the Kingdom of Heaven. Religions restricted themselves to offering salvation after death, but from the 19th century, left and right totalitarian ideologies emerged to offer salvation in *this* life. Like these ideologies, this is what CSJ does, serving as a secular religion.[19] Freud understood religion as a delusion operating as a defence to deny "the crushingly superior force of nature".[20] Secular totalising ideologies are even more effective at denying this superior force, instilling hope by denying the necessity of suffering in this life.

There are consequences, in life and the psyche, to our psychological commitments. We must pay the piper. The cost in this case seems high. A believer is invited to swing between two mental constructs—the dark dystopian reality as it exists and the wonderful utopian reality as it could be if we "do the work" of Critical Social Justice. With this understanding, the nightmare and the dream can never be brought together through the healing of integration—a psychic process of bringing the extremes together which would allow the understanding that life, as it stands, is not so bad, and life, as it could be, is not perfect.

The CSJ worldview brings its own brand of distress. The denial of the elementary but often unvoiced tragic truths can lead people to feel that struggling is abnormal. If you deny the necessity of suffering but are keenly aware that you do suffer, you may flee to one of two psychic extremes in your response. Simply put, you may be overcome by a sense of shame, inadequacy, and self-loathing at your perceived failure, or you might be captured by what Nietzsche calls "ressentiment", a type of resentment embodying envious hostility towards the source (real or perceived) of your frustration.[21] This results in envious attacks on others aimed at the destruction of something good that is denied to you.[22]

Many of the acolytes of CSJ are themselves thought of by the ideology as being part of the "oppressor classes"—white, male, or heterosexual, for instance. Why would the privileged support a movement that highlights their privilege and their guilt in maintaining it? A key motivation is to deny their own suffering. Commonly, people who come to therapy at first minimise the magnitude and importance of their own pain. They may feel they are being strong, or thoughtful toward others' suffering. There is a cogent—though long-term dysfunctional—self-interest at play. We want to maintain that everything is fine to ourselves and to others to reduce psychic pain. There is a certain reassurance and flattery to thinking oneself privileged. CSJ offers a conveniently avoidant buttress to the desire to repress one's own pain: "You have it easy, not like these oppressed people," the ideology says.[23] Gnawing doubts can be pushed back; the rising sense of panic attendant on things not being alright is repressed.

The ideology in the abstract denies the *necessity* of suffering whilst magnifying the suffering of groups it defines as oppressed. The so-called privileged who support the movement are claiming in agreement, "We do not suffer; the oppressed do."

Then one may say, "Not only am I not suffering, but I am also a considerate and virtuous person—see, I put others' interests before my own!"

There are many benefits and costs to this gambit. This psychic denial of necessary self-interest keeps us from confronting the darker elements of the self that we find unacceptable. There may be practical as well as psychological benefits to this—the person may be judged virtuous and their power in the social hierarchy legitimised. We might think of CSJ as an elaborate linguistic and behavioural code operating as a new guild beginning to restrict competition for desirable employment.[24] The cost of lying to preserve your position is that you feel more divorced from your "true self" whilst if one is a genuine believer one may find oneself confronting real guilt at one's—apparently—easier life.[25] This inevitably leads to a growing sense of unconscious resentment towards the recipients for whom the "ally" sacrifices. Service to others enriches us, but to do so it must come from desire, not guilt.

As the privileged rescuer says, "I do not suffer," so the oppressed victim says, "I suffer."[26] Most suffering is lonely, specific to the individual. But it may be that some drawn to CSJ have little experience of being listened to in their daily lives. Their real subjective suffering is validated and made meaningful for them when understood by the ideology as oppression and held aloft as such. Through being shared with others who make similar meaning of their pain, it becomes an objective yet superficial truth rather than a genuine subjective experience. This understanding is then buttressed by the guilty, pious cries of the privileged flagellants.

Those who identify as oppressed are also saying that they experience themselves as weak. To be oppressed, you must feel that the other has a dominant position over you. You might feel inferior, or "not worth it". It seems there is an implicit conflation of being victimised with being virtuous—what Bertrand Russell termed "the superior virtue of the oppressed".[27] This may result in receiving moral plaudits and greater assistance. The ideology is a megaphone; the cost may be that it is not an expression of personal pain, but distorted pain mediated through an ideological lens.

Why might you want to see the world as full of powerful enemies? It excuses the pain of facing up to one's disappointment in oneself if failure can be ascribed externally. Sartre said that an essential aspect of the human condition is *mauvaise foi*, or bad faith—the desire to evade the responsibility of freedom.[28] Freedom is an anxiety-inducing burden as well as being the golden route by which we develop a more authentic version of ourselves. If you deny freedom, you won't have to examine your shame, fear, and self-justifications for inaction. The cost is a life unlived, reproached by a failure to maintain a compassionate balance of acknowledgment between the inexorable opposites of our capacities and our limitations.

A psychoanalytic perspective: light inside, dark outside

Freud saw humanity as a house divided against itself, with consciousness underpinned by powerful unconscious processes. The purpose of the defence mechanisms he articulated is to protect us from fully knowing ourselves. Darker motivations like malice, aggression, envy, and ravening desire initially lead to painful concomitant feelings like guilt, shame, fear, and anger. We construct our understanding of self and world to reduce psychic discomfort. This always has a cost, because everything does.

Post-Freud, object relations psychoanalysts focused on relationality—both between different aspects of the self and with other "objects", primarily individual people but also other things of human importance such as families, groups, races, nations, art, churches, political parties, and places. Object Relations Theory conceives of us as being in a feedback relationship whereby the external world influences our attitudes to self and others in the inner world of the psyche, which in turn influences our understanding and positioning of objects in the external world.[29] The crucial point is that our inner world radically affects how we perceive and act in the outer world.

Critical Social Justice is predisposed to seeing the evil that dwells in all human hearts in some more than in others. Melanie Klein outlined a developmental model widely used for its explanatory power.[30] The paranoid-schizoid position is conceptualised as our original mental state. A baby's desire to make sense of the privations and disruptions of early life leads the infant to split the experience into good (e.g. warmth, being fed) and bad (e.g. hunger, tiredness). There is no nuance at this developmental stage. Good and bad are experienced as entirely distinct. This allows love and trust for the good to develop, but the price of this is "persecutory anxiety" that the infant experiences concerning the purely bad—existentially threatening and thus hated and feared.[31]

It is only as infants reliably enter the depressive position that they become aware that they have been dividing their experience into two unreal categories. The good and the bad become more integrated—the good less good and the bad less bad. This is a mournful loss as well as a gain. Everything becomes shades of grey. The infant realises their own mixed nature. The despised figure when neglecting the child was the mother as much as the loved figure when she tended to the infant in blissful rapport. The anger, hatred, and envy we recognise in ourselves represent the key difficulty of the depressive position. As we become aware that we harbour these potentially aggressive and destructive emotions in response to inevitable frustrations in our upbringing, we start to develop a sense of fear and guilt at what we might do with them. It is this position that allows us to make reparations to the world for our badness and which also promotes a sense of gratitude for, and creativity inspired by, the good that we have experienced.

The splits of the paranoid-schizoid are not exactly transcended, according to Klein. As we gradually develop the capacity to tolerate ambivalence and ambiguity in ourselves and others, we become better able to inhabit the depressive position. Nonetheless, this is a matter of relative dominance. There is a certain forceful power to the paranoid-schizoid as the position is concerned with threat and survival. It has its uses for the psyche. So, throughout life, we flit between these two positions, particularly when stressed. The positions are infant developmental experiences but also adult states of mind.

An incapacity to sufficiently integrate the ambivalent attitudes towards self and others—characteristic of the depressive position—is often associated with a heightened sense of persecutory anxiety and enviousness; these are characteristics we can see in the energetic field surrounding the rise of CSJ.[32]

Despite the language of CSJ ostensibly coming from the guilt of the depressive position (discussion of reparations comes to mind), the energy of its advance comes from the paranoid-schizoid—the rage at and fear of those who don't identify with the same perspectives, the accusations of harm and oppressive behaviour. A philosophical disagreement could be experienced as a brutal personal attack: it threatens to disrupt the ideological structure which the person has chosen to order their experience around. This structure justifies splitting into all-good and all-bad, which in turn sustains the fragmentation of self and "other" the subject has engaged in so as to avoid the psychic discomfort of integrating their mixed nature. The reckoning with and integration of your will to power, will to pleasure, narrow-mindedness, aggression, and self-interest can all be avoided by seeing them in the oppressive other.

Followers of CSJ claim a mantle of psychological sophistication when they talk about examining racism, misogyny, etc. in their "shadow", as Jung would call it—the unacceptable part of the self.[33] Yet the recognition operates as a device to evade processing feelings that pain the psychic structure. We are all prejudiced in various ways. A person is a mixture of attributes, some more admirable and some more regrettable. This understanding of our ambivalent nature cannot be comfortable enough held in the psyche prone to operating from the paranoid-schizoid. So, an evasive gambit is undertaken: the declaration "I am racist" operates not as a real reflection on self but as a defence to evade the psychic discomfort of guilt. What is meant in many cases is "I am racist, but more importantly, I am less racist than others who don't acknowledge this about themselves. Therefore, I am good, and will communicate my goodness through these beliefs". This is an evasion of the genuine (but contextual and measured) guilt of the depressive.

It is also a demand that others share the weight of one's own partial conceptualisation of self, real or otherwise. This is a form of what psychoanalysts call projection. Projection occurs when someone has a feeling, thought, or motivation that is unacceptable to them. The unacceptable nature of the internal experience leads a person to project it onto another's psyche. In this case, the individual projects their own sense of badness— being an unaware oppressor—onto those who do not publicly offer the same mea culpa as the believer. The believer is aware of and has mitigated their oppressive tendencies, whereas the other has not.

In this way, announcing one's own negative tendencies becomes a device to advertise one's "self-awareness" whilst shifting the badness of culpability to the other who has not done so. This is intellectually sophisticated but psychologically naïve. The terror of bearing guilt within the self leads to the subject vesting it in others *whilst appearing to do the exact opposite*.

CSJ fixates on extremes of perfection and imperfection. Life is bleakly oppressive, but believers talk about kindness as the perfect moral good. The definition of harm is expanded to cover ever more ambiguous scenarios. Oppression is manufactured so splitting can continue as a way of being. Consider microaggressions: proponents of this behavioural interpretation see profound imperfection shot through every engagement and aim for perfection, to wrap themselves and all interactions in smothering cotton wool.[34] Thoughtless comments causing material harm to people are supposedly an endemic problem, but they aim to have no negative impact by navigating social interactions with tortuous and perhaps saintly care. *What does this do to people's sense of self and sense of the other?* Both are imperfect entities that receive and enact some harm through the rough and tumble of living—but both are also reasonably robust. We would not be alive if this was not so, because life is hard. The benefit of avoiding this awareness is a clear conscience, the sense of being a "harmless good person" rather than a "harmful bad person". The cost of this split between the dismal outer world and the pristine inner one is the cost of denying one's own resilience, which exists precisely because we know we're not harmless and can give as good as we get.

When we understand that the world is like us and we are like the world, this leads to chagrin and guilt, but also a stronger sense of resilience and safety. The evil that CSJ sees in the culture is also evil that resides within ... but it cannot be genuinely acknowledged. Superficially acknowledged, it is split off and projected into other objects. Safely outside the self, the subject who is hate-filled can justly hate the "hate-full" other. The hateful object may or may not be acting hatefully, but they have been imbued with the subject's own hatred. The subject may then unconsciously seek to vanquish their own hatred externally. This is merely a trick of the mind, however, as it is our subject who is expressing hatred, energetically fashioning it into a powerful weapon with which to smite the unjust (as the subject sees it).

Ironically, this will add ballast to the subject's idealised sense of their own moral righteousness. But, contrary to the firm avowal "no place for hate", there are many places for hate, including every human heart. The cost of this way of being is profound: you can keep your own false innocence and the power of your righteous rage but must endure a shallow, fragmented experience of self and world. The outside world becomes a terrifying and dread-filled hell because that is where you locate all the evil. You paint the inside as light and the outside as dark as night.

The sadness that abides

Critical Social Justice is a movement ignorant of its own ignorance about human beings and existence itself. It provides a mechanism for people in pain to demand obeisance to a reductionist and psychically fragmented fantasy reality. It is as if the rich traditions of psychoanalysis have been redrawn in crayon. Such arrogant certainty cannot stand; it must be invited to "check its privilege".

We clinicians who have brought our expertise to bear on this precocious ideology will be accused by some, though not all of its followers, of all manner of extraordinary evils for doing so. Perhaps we are simply blind to our own bigotry—misogynistic, racist, and homophobic. Or perhaps we are gaslighters revelling in our evil and the harm we may cause? Each reader will make their own judgment.

But what is the *real* threat we pose? It is quite profound. The narcissistic moral–ideological certainty masks a fearful rigidity. Beneath the bright fire of moral conviction lies ashen disappointment. Allowing questioning would mean allowing the failures of the world (which are many, I do not deny) and the disappointments of life to be lodged closer to home in personal relationships. Anguish would become experienced internally rather than acted out externally. The performative political pain, so enthusiastically rehearsed, would lose its meaning. The fortress-like defences against one's own real yearning, relational pain would start to crack and fail.

The dynamics discussed here are not essentially about CSJ; they are about human beings. We all split and project, but the simplistic object relations of this ideology can easily become a powerful cover for the flight from self-realisation. I myself have lived this. Growing up, I was a good comrade, intoxicated by righteous fury, projecting my own bitterness and resentment outwards, trying to tear at the imperfect world to make it heal me. It is a difficult state of affairs, and only by finding a way to listen to the part of yourself that is committed to your growth can you sustain the shifts necessary for a better life. I cannot tell you love is the answer because we cannot love each other all of the time. Conflict is part of life within the psyche and between psyches.

But there is a path, one which all travellers fall off at times. A path of responsibility, integration, acceptance, and the struggle to find a balance between the tug of opposites. If not love, this engenders a kind of existential respect for all, even those we hate. As Kant said, "Out of the crooked timber of humanity, no straight thing was ever made."[35]

But we can make crooked things with accents of beauty and majesty. We are all human, sublime, and terrible. We are different. But we are also the same. We cannot allow this hard-won insight into the existential paradox to perish before the assault of bright, energetic, fragmenting, and ignorant certainty. We must master the tension between the dystopian and the utopian. Oscillating wildly between extremes of collapsed fear and repressive judgment will bring only individual and collective misery. The truth is always in-between. We must dance in the gaps. This is where we can encounter reality and our own authenticity, creativity, and compassion, not to mention fun. I firmly believe that our future depends on the understanding that *this* human condition and *this* human nature—all of it—that we all share, is all that there is.

Endnotes

[1] For a useful overview of how post-modern perspectives concretised into the applied moral perspectives of Critical Social Justice theory, see Helen Pluckrose and James Lindsay, *Cynical Theories* (Durham, NC: Pitchstone, 2020), 45-66.

[2] Carol Hanisch, "The Personal is Political," in *Notes from the Second Year: Women's Liberation*, eds. Shulasmith Firestone and Anne Koedt (New York: Radical Feminism, 1970).

[3] Paul Ricoeur, *Freud and Philosophy: An Essay on Interpretation*, trans. Denis Savage (Delhi: Motilal Banarsidass, 2008 [1965]), 33,35.

[4] Peter Lomas, *The Limits of Interpretation* (London: Penguin, 1987), 95.

[5] Ibid.

[6] For an extended expostulation of this position from within the intellectual antecedents of Critical Social Justice, see Michel Foucault, *Power/Knowledge: Selected Interviews and Other Writings, 1972-1977* (New York: Pantheon, 1980).

[7] Claire Cain Miller et al, "'When I See Racial Disparities, I See Racism.' Discussing Race, Gender and Mobility," *New York Times*, March 27, 2012, https://www.nytimes.com/interactive/2018/03/27/upshot/reader-questions-about-race-gender-and-mobility.html.

[8] Feng Fu et al., "Evolution of in-group favoritism," *Scientific Reports* 2 (June 2012): 460, DOI: 10.1038/srep00460.

[9] R Yehuda and A Lehrner, "Intergenerational transmission of trauma effects: putative role of epigenetic mechanisms," *World Psychiatry* 17, (3) (October 2018): 243–257, https://doi.org/10.1002/wps.20568. This article contains a review of possible mechanisms of transmission. It should be noted that the scope of intergenerational trauma is subject to considerable debate and waters are muddied by political contestation.

[10] Irvin Yalom, *Existentialist Psychotherapy* (New York: Basic Books, 1980), p. 8.

[11] Hans W. Cohn, *Heidegger and the Roots of Existential Therapy* (London: Continuum, 2002), p. 113.

[12] Ronald D. Laing, *The Divided Self* (London: Penguin, 1990 [1960]), p. 41.

[13] Carl G. Jung et al., *Man and His Symbols* (New York: Doubleday, 1964), p. 85.

[14] Ibid.

[15] Irvin Yalom, *Existentialist Psychotherapy* (New York: Basic Books, 1980), p. 41.

[16] Cohn, *Heidegger and the Roots of Existential Therapy*, p. 96.

[17] Jean-Paul Sartre, *Existentialism and Humanism*, trans. Philip Mairet (London: Eyre Methuen, 1948), p. 34.

[18] Jung et al., *Man and His Symbols*, p. 85.

[19] Many commentators, including Jonathan Haidt, John McWhorter, and Andrew Sullivan, have resorted to a religious analogy in respect of the dynamics of Critical Social Justice over the last five years, or so. For a detailed statement of the case, see James Lindsay and Mike Naynor, "Postmodern Religion and the Faith of Social Justice", *Areo Magazine*, December 18, 2018, https://areomagazine.com/2018/12/18/postmodern-religion-and-the-faith-of-social-justice/.

[20] Sigmund Freud, *The future of an illusion*, trans. James Strachey (New York: Norton, 1961 [1927]), p. 21.

[21] Friedrich Nietzsche, *On the Genealogy of Morals*, trans. Michael Scarpitti (London: Penguin, 2013 [1887]), pp. 10–11.

[22] Melanie Klein, *Envy and Gratitude*, ed. M. Masud Khan (London: Vintage, 1975), p. 181.

[23] John Bowlby, *Attachment* (New York: Basic Books, 1999 [1969]).

[24] Oliver Traldi, "The Left Has Turned Into a Guild Hall", *The Bellows*, July 11, 2020, https://www.thebellows.org/the-left-has-become-a-guild/.

[25] Donald Winnicott, "Ego distortion in terms of true and false self", *The Maturational Process and the Facilitating Environment: Studies in the Theory of Emotional Development*, (New York: International Universities Press 1960), pp. 140–57.

[26] For a "drama triangle" model of victim/rescuer/persecutor dynamics, see Stephen Karpman, "Fairy tales and script drama analysis". *Transactional Analysis Bulletin*. 26 (7) (1968): 39–43, https://karpmandramatriangle.com/pdf/DramaTriangle.pdf.

[27] Bertrand Russell, "The Superior Virtue of the Oppressed," In *Unpopular Essays* (London: Routledge, 1950) pp. 56-62.

[28] Jean-Paul Sartre, *Nausea, trans. Robert Baldick (*London: Penguin, 1979 [1938]).

[29] For a clear introduction to the varying perspectives within object relations see Lavinia Gomez, *An Introduction to Object Relations* (London: Free Association Books, 1997).

[30] Klein, *Envy and Gratitude*, pp. 1-16.

[31] Ibid, p. 2.

[32] For a thorough discussion in greater depth of the Kleinian dynamics surrounding the Critical Social Justice movement, see Jaco van Zyl, *The Psychology of Critical Social Justice,* accessed September 5, 2021, https://merion-west.com/2021/09/02/the-psychology-of-critical-social-justice/ (2021).

[33] Carl G. Jung, (1969). *Psychology and Religion: West and East*, eds. Herbert Read, Michael Fordham, Gerhard Adler. Executive ed. W. McGuire, trans. R.F.C. Hull (Princeton NJ: Princeton University Press, 1969), para 132.

[34] D. W. Sue et al., "Racial microaggressions in everyday life: implications for clinical practice," *The American Psychologist* 62, no.4 (May-June 2007): 271-286, https://doi.org/10.1037/0003-066X.62.4.271.

[35] Immanuel Kant, "Idea for a Universal History with a Cosmopolitan Purpose" in *Kant's Political Writings,* ed. H. Reiss, trans. H. Nisbet (Cambridge: Cambridge University Press, 1970 [1784]), p. 46.

Chapter 4:

From Helping to Hating—Critical Social Justice From a Social Psychological Perspective

by Kirsty Miller

Instead of wondering how people can ignore the evil that they do, research needs to be aimed at explaining how people [...] come to celebrate acts of inhumanity as acts of virtue.[1]

When I first introduce my students to the topic of social psychology, I show them footage from Nazi Germany. We see thousands marching, signalling allegiance to Hitler, and we see hopeless figures standing in the streets, adorned with their identifying labels as they await deportation. Finally, we see carriages full of people being wheeled to their "final destination", and emaciated, lifeless bodies of men, women, and children being piled high.[2]

The reason I show this footage is because I think it gets to the root of why many of us want to become psychologists—we want to understand why people think, and behave, the way they do, especially when they behave in ways that horrify us. From the social psychological perspective, the influence of people (and groups) is particularly important. Considering the role of others can help us to understand what leads people to try to prevent, participate in, or stand back and allow the atrocities of the kind we saw in Nazi Germany (or indeed Stalin's Soviet Union, Mao's China, or Pol Pot's Cambodia).

When faced with events such as these, our focus tends to be on their enormity. However, as historians will tell us, atrocities rarely come out of nowhere—they are often a culmination of many smaller events and processes, building and combining to lead to the unimaginable horrors on the scale we saw in Germany, Russia, China, and Cambodia. Indeed, this is the argument of a group of social psychologists who provided a critique of the "Banality of Evil" hypothesis.[3,4]

They argued that instead of atrocities being committed by mindless, evil people, the reality was perhaps even more chilling—the atrocities were committed by people who genuinely believed that what they were doing was right. From this theory, they developed "The five-step social identity model of the development of collective hate" (SIMDCH), which proposes that people can cause harm and even come to celebrate this harm when they genuinely believe that causing it is an act of virtue.[5]

In this chapter, the SIMDCH (referred to from now on as the *Steps to Hate* model) developed in social psychology will be used to explain how we can come from viewing the world in terms of groups to justifying hatred, or even harm, towards others.[6] We will then look at Critical Social Justice (CSJ) in light of this model, arguing that CSJ actually encourages this movement toward hate. Real-world examples from psychology will then be discussed, as will implications for therapy. Finally, and most importantly, we will reflect on ways to prevent the carving of the road to hatred.

Critical Social Justice and Social Identity Theory

The definition of social justice used in this chapter is that employed by authors such as Sensoy and DiAngelo.[7] Note the use of the word "critical" in relation to the term "social justice". While it has its origins in neo-Marxist thought, CSJ draws heavily upon identity power dynamics and the notion that inequality is embedded in the very fabric of society.[8] These inequalities are drawn across social group lines, which means that in order to address this injustice, one has to be aware of one's own group's positions within society and actively challenge the inequalities associated with these group memberships.

CSJ, therefore, encourages seeing the world in terms of groups, and according to the *Steps to Hate* model, this is the start of the process that can lead to us legitimising hatred towards others. This means that, according to the model, therapists who endorse CSJ, and, therefore, group thinking, are actually directing clients down a path that could lead to hatred.

However, before we look at this pathway, we need to understand a little about the background theory on which the model is based. The *Steps to Hate* model draws upon Social Identity Theory (SIT)—a well-established theory from social psychology.[9] SIT teaches us that as well as having a sense of individual identity, we can derive a sense of self or self-definition from the groups that we are part of.

To the extent that we view these groups as important to us and part of "who we are", they are considered to be our "in-groups". We start to view ourselves in terms of the collective "us" instead of our individual identity, "me". Our in-groups are defined in part by their distinction from the groups that they are not—or the "out-groups". To illustrate, if my identity as a woman is important to me and I view myself in terms of this group membership, then I will consider women as my in-group, as opposed to "men", who would be considered the out-group. In other words, our in-groups are the groups that matter to our sense of self-definition, and the out-groups are those that are differentiated from them.

It is this sense of group identity and the demarcation of in-groups and out-groups that the "model to hate" builds upon.

The model follows a five-step process consisting of the following steps:

1. 'Identification': the construction of an in-group
2. 'Exclusion' or identification of targets that are not part of the in-group (i.e. they are in the out-group)
3. 'Threat': presentation of the out-group as a threat or as endangering the in-group identity
4. 'Virtue': championing the in-group as uniquely good (or virtuous)
5. 'Celebration' in the destruction of the out-group (because destruction involves defending the virtue of the in-group).

Each of these steps will be explained in more detail in order to highlight how they are paralleled in CSJ and how they can ultimately lead to hatred (and a celebration of this hatred) toward other groups. However, it is worth noting, at this stage, some similarities and differences between SIT and CSJ.

To the extent that both theories centre around group memberships, they are similar—they both highlight the importance of groups in our lives. However, SIT doesn't pre-empt which groups people use to draw their sense of self—any groups that are important to the individual will be adopted into one's self-definition (and as a result, they are chosen by the individual). In contrast, CSJ tells us which groups are important—they are predefined and usually based on immutable characteristics such as sex, race, place of birth, sexuality, etc. Crucially, the individual is told that these group memberships have an impact on their life—whether or not they, themselves, believe that they do.

Since the *Steps to Hate* model draws upon SIT, it speaks in terms of in-groups and out-groups, but it can be applied equally to any "us" and "them" categories, including those portrayed in terms of power differentials where (for example) "we" are oppressed—or "we" align ourselves with those who are oppressed. Indeed, to the extent that CSJ already defines the world in terms of groups (regardless of whether individuals want to be viewed this way or not), it has already fulfilled the first steps in the model to hate for us—it tells us which groups we are part of, and therefore which groups we are not part of (in SIT terms, it creates an in-group and an out-group).

Critical Social Justice and the five steps to hate as demonstrated through the SIMDCH

Let us now look at the implications of the *Steps to Hate* model (SIMDCH). As we have seen from the preceding discussion, without our explicit permission, CSJ has pigeonholed us into several groups. To this extent, it has given us both in-groups and out-groups, creating a mindset that is divisive from the outset, encouraging us to see ourselves as "different" and "separate from" those not in our groups.

For example, because I'm female, according to CSJ, I'm part of an oppressed group (as opposed to men, who are the oppressors). To this extent, CSJ has again fulfilled the next two steps towards hatred according to the model: it has presented the out-group of men as a threat (trying to maintain their power and privilege over women) and the in-group of women as virtuous ("nobly" struggling against their unjustified oppression).

This is relevant because by presenting the out-group as a threat, we are setting it up as something that we need to work to protect ourselves against. By painting men as oppressors who want to dominate and benefit from all the privileges that come with this group membership, it makes sense that women would want to fight back against this injustice. Coinciding with this process, the in-group (of women in this case—we see the same process regardless of the power groups in question) is presented as being virtuous, partly because of their fight against injustice, and partly also through comparison with the out-group.[10]

In this way, we can see a situation arising where women (or the oppressed group) would be justified in retaliating in order to protect themselves or their rights and values. Not only this, but should a group be presented as having virtuous qualities, then we can see that there would almost be a duty to protect it from being destroyed. "Good" must not be destroyed by "bad", and we must protect it at all costs.

We can therefore see how the process of setting the in-group up as "good" and the out-group as "bad" creates a situation where it could be seen as acceptable, or even necessary, to act to protect and defend the in-group. It doesn't take much to imagine a situation where the "threat" against the in-group is considered (or portrayed) to be sufficient to justify using more extreme (and possibly unnecessary) measures to "protect" it.

This brings us to the final stage in the process, where it is possible for in-group members to actively celebrate or embrace the destruction of the out-group.[11] It is possible because the destruction is (considered) necessary in order to defend the virtue of the in-group. Indeed, we can all think of events from history where we may have felt horrified to witness people celebrating the death of others. However, when we think of these people as actually celebrating the death of those who (they perceive) pose a mortal threat to them or their way of life, their joy makes more sense.

To recap, the *Steps to Hate* model highlights how it can be a relatively simple process from identifying oneself as being in one group (as opposed to another), to assigning meanings to these group memberships (threat vs virtue), and, finally, to celebrating the destruction of a group that is perceived as being an active threat to our own.

As we have seen, CSJ encourages and hastens this process by pre-defining our in-groups and out-groups, and additionally by assigning a meaning to them which automatically portrays one group as positive and another as negative (thus fulfilling the first four steps in the process). To this extent, it is natural for those in the "oppressed" group to want to seek justice from their oppressors, and from here, it is not difficult to see how the oppressors would be demonised and any harm to them celebrated. Indeed, there have been examples of this in the real world, and the next section will go on to see examples of this process in action in psychology.

On the road to hatred within psychology

Other chapters in this book discuss how psychology has increasingly adopted a CSJ approach—an approach that has been increasingly promoted since 2020. There are many consequences of this, but in this chapter, we will focus predominantly on manifestations of the *Steps to Hate* model.

Indeed, in psychology, it is now commonplace for us to see attempts to split people into groups alongside selective demonisation of certain groups (often being announced in official statements). For example, after the death of George Floyd, in 2020, the British Psychological Society (the governing body for British Psychology: the BPS), like many other organisations, released several statements regarding his death and the Black Lives Matter (BLM) movement.[12] In these, a clear division was drawn between whites and non-whites, and the suffering experienced by the latter group, at the hands of the former, was emphasised.

For example, on the webpage of the Division of Clinical Psychology, there was a link to a statement where support is pledged to "the BLM movement".[13,14] In this statement, the distress and upset felt by black people (as a homogenous group) was strongly emphasised, as was the role of white people. Statements included "this is not a black problem, but a structural issue built on centuries of racism"; "we need to be committed to doing better"; and "those of us in the white majority need to listen to and validate the feelings and experiences of our marginalised colleagues whilst accepting that it is not their role to educate us".

Since virtue is assigned to the oppressed group (the non-whites) and threat or negativity to the white group, it would not be surprising for us to see attempts to justify mistreatment of or attacks on the group that is perceived to be a threat.

Indeed, these justifications follow: the innocence, victimhood, and virtuousness of black people are emphasised, as is the "harm" that white people have caused. We then see the final step to hatred—"destruction" of the out-group as a goal: "it is our task to [...] eradicate the ways we allow [...] whiteness to perpetuate."

The picture presented in this document is that in order to stop this harm, white people need to change, and ultimately "whiteness" needs to be eradicated. The language used throughout the statement leads to justification and legitimisation (including emphasising the centuries of suffering, the marginalisation and oppression, and the "everyday" occurrence of racism), and indeed, in other statements, we see phrases such as "righteous anger"—crucially, justifying any consequences of this anger.[15] When couched in these terms, of course, the grief, anger, and emotional strain suffered by the "victims" are understandable, and any extreme actions taken could almost seem justifiable.

While whites have been the primary focus of explicit animosity in the last year or so, other so-called "privileged" groups have also been targeted, with men being a similarly vilified group.[16] Again, we see men being presented as a threat to women, with the Professional Standards Authority for Health and Social Care (the PSA, the regulating body for healthcare professionals in the UK) releasing a statement in response to a tragic high-profile murder (of a woman by a man), saying, "it is unacceptable that any woman should live in fear of violence or assault." Note the use of "woman" rather than "person" here.[17]

In much of the statement, it is implicit that women live in fear *because of men* (and this was the widespread rhetoric surrounding the case); at one point, it even explicitly states that "we continue to see cases where male registrants behave unacceptably to female patients and colleagues". The statement then goes on to say that the PSA would intervene in cases where they feel "that fitness to practise panels do not address the action strongly enough". Indeed, they claim they have done so in two recent cases—one of which "erased the registrant"!

Again, we see an example of one group being pitted against another: despite the likelihood of women also potentially acting as a threat both to men and women, in the statement, men were presented as the threat and women as victims. One has to wonder why this was necessary when the only purpose it served was to portray an entire group as a threat. Alternatively, the PSA could have just highlighted that any unacceptable behaviour would be dealt with harshly—rather than targeting one specific group as the likely transgressors.

Vilification is happening to all groups that are *perceived* to be powerful. Indeed, in the last few years, a framework called the *Power Threat Meaning Framework: PTMF)*, has been developed and promoted by the BPS.[18] As with CSJ, this framework draws upon similar power-based critiques (drawing predominantly on immutable groups such as gender, race, and ethnicity). The growing popularity of this approach highlights the extent to which CSJ notions have become mainstream in psychology. While the PTMF uses the term "power" rather than oppression, the meanings and conclusions that are drawn are similar—systematically blaming powerful groups for societal (and individual) ills while valorising the groups that are claimed not to have power.[19]

Due to space constraints, we have seen only a few examples of the adoption of CSJ principles at an institutional level, but these examples are pervasive in the outputs from our mental health governing bodies such as the BPS.[20] There is also a clear trickle-through to practitioners with both individuals and private groups making similar proclamations, and even charging for delivering courses about group membership and the associated privilege and victimhood that they afford.[21,22]

Again, here we see groups offering mental health advice, clearly creating "us" and "them" divisions and making blanket judgments about them. White people are frequently named as oppressors or enemies (similarly with capitalist structures, men, "cis people", etc.), and oppressors are told that they have to do better—and that no attention will be given to their feelings. Indeed, we almost feel a desire for such groups to experience discomfort. It doesn't really feel necessary to discuss the ethical issues associated with "professionals" releasing outputs such as this and actively endorsing hatred and violence. However, in the next section, we will look at the wider implications of therapists endorsing CSJ.

Therapists encouraging hate

As discussed in other chapters, the adoption of CSJ by therapists is problematic for several reasons. However, the adoption of CSJ also has implications for the client, as it is presented as a lens through which to understand the world and its problems. If, for example, the client is part of an "oppressed" group, their problems will be attributed to this and the historical (as well as current) treatment of said group.

Primarily, this mindset is damaging to mental wellbeing, as the pathway to hatred is immediately created—when the client arrives at the therapist's office, they are told that their problems are due to their group membership, specifically the oppression of their group by another. Indeed, as we have seen in some of the above "real-world" examples, CSJ therapists capitalise on this with courses and advice centring around how to "cope with" characteristics of "oppressor" groups (such as "whiteness"). Again, individuals are viewed in terms of immutable characteristics such as skin colour with either negativity or positivity assigned to them.

If the client is a member of an oppressed group, anger and resentment towards the dominant group are encouraged and validated (again as we've seen with phrases such as "righteous anger", endorsement of depictions of violence, etc.). The client is finally told that the only solution to their problems, and the only way to get better, is to fight back—to become an activist and correct the injustices. "Harms" that the dominant group has caused, and the hardships encountered by the individual (through their group membership) are emphasised, and a commitment to change is justified and presented as the only way to address the client's problems.[23]

It is worth noting the initial difference in the treatment proposed depends on whether the client is part of an oppressed or oppressor group. If the client is in the latter group, they are encouraged to symbolically renounce their group membership in order to align themself with the oppressed group.[24] Clearly, the self-hatred (based on group membership) encouraged by therapists is not in the best interests of the client, and indeed can lead to all sorts of dissonance (while one may try to symbolically or emotionally distance oneself from an immutable characteristic, it is not physically possible to do so). This can lead to a never-ending process of denial, guilt, and attempts to atone. Certainly, one could question the ethics of therapists who attempt to encourage feelings of guilt or self-hatred in their clients.

However, once the CSJ-practising therapist has instilled this sense of guilt in their "oppressive" client, the next stages in the model follow the same pattern as for the members of an oppressed group. The client now should align themselves with the oppressed group rather than the oppressor, viewing the former group as virtuous and the latter as a threat. Finally, the client will come to legitimise any mistreatment of their old group as justified and even necessary to compensate and protect the new group from suffering further.[25]

The preceding discussion makes for difficult reading because when it comes to CSJ, all paths lead to hatred. However, there are things we can do to try to prevent this type of thinking, and this is what we will discuss in our final section.

How do we stop the legitimisation of hatred?

First of all, and as advocated elsewhere in this book, the primary way to avoid the pathway to hatred would be to treat people as individuals. It goes without saying that treating people as such avoids stereotyping, pre-judging, or assuming anything about their lives. It affords them the respect of allowing them to introduce themselves to others on their own terms.

Of course, this doesn't mean that group membership doesn't or can't contribute to our lives in important ways—undoubtedly, individuals can be profoundly affected by the groups that they are (or are not) part of. However, treating people as individuals allows them to disclose this at will, if and when it applies to them, rather than us making any (potentially faulty) assumptions about them—or, importantly, introducing issues that were not there in the beginning.

Similarly, we should be wary of any attempts on the part of others to assign people to groups based on immutable characteristics. This is especially relevant if "meaning" is attributed to any of these groups. As we have seen, members of groups based on immutable characteristics are not (and cannot be) the same. Within the category of "race", for example, there are so many different personality factors, life events, and cultural experiences that it would not be possible to assign similarity of experience, thoughts, or behaviour to them all (and the same goes for sex, sexuality, being able-bodied, etc.).

Ultimately, we want to avoid the problematic "us" and "them" language that we have seen the consequences of in this chapter. Whenever "we" are seen as an exclusive category based on immutable characteristics, there is by necessity an "other"—someone who is not us—a way of viewing the world that we want to try to avoid, if possible. Instead, we should focus on similarities and look for common ground between individuals. Rather than focusing on what divides us, and our differences, we need to look at our common humanity.[26]

This advice applies particularly strongly in the therapy room, both so that the therapeutic relationship can be developed (based on common ground and equality) and so that the goal of helping the patient (rather than pushing an agenda and encouraging hate) can be achieved. However, it is also important in our everyday lives.

As we have seen, it is all too easy to fall into the trap of viewing people in accordance with their group identity, creating an "us" and "them" mentality, and seeing the "others" as deserving of any harm that befalls them.

Conclusion

I started this chapter by referring to some of the worst atrocities in human history—something that many of us, social psychologists included, have fought and struggled to understand. The *Steps to Hate* model (SIMDCH) provides a perspective from social identity theory that helps us, to an extent, see how so many everyday people could come to at least stand by, if not actively celebrate, the hatred and even destruction of millions of people.

The *Steps to Hate* model shows us how easily we can fall into the trap of creating an "us" and "them" mentality, applying an all-or-nothing "good" vs "evil" meaning to the groups in our lives. This allows us to justify hatred and possibly even celebrate the destruction of another group (to the extent that it means that the in-group is protected from a potentially mortal enemy). Crucially, the model also shows us the extent to which CSJ perpetuates this behaviour, leading not only to divisions between groups but also attributing virtue to one and oppression to another—providing the basis for hatred.

Through my years of learning and teaching, the *Steps to Hate* model stayed with me. I could see how easily any of us could fall into the trap of legitimising hatred toward those we considered a threat or an enemy.

In recent years, as I have seen the outputs from members and official governing bodies of a discipline that is meant to be based on empathy, understanding, and compassion, I have seen chilling echoes of these processes. Indeed, those who speak of their anger, their mistrust, or their dislike of certain groups tend not to see any contradiction in this behaviour and their claims to be moral, professional, or effective psychologists.

To these people, those who supervise them, and those who follow in their footsteps, I ask you to reflect upon your motivations for wanting to become a psychologist. If your aim was genuinely to try to help others and to make the world a better place, then know that no good can ever come from teaching hatred (regardless of whether it's hatred towards oneself or hatred towards others).

Pay heed to the lessons that history and social psychology have taught us, for hatred—even when "legitimised" in the name of "what is right"—will never make the world a better place.

Endnotes

1. Stephen Reicher, S. Alexander Haslam, and Rakshi Rath, "Making a Virtue of Evil: A Five-Step Social Identity Model of the Development of Collective Hate", *Social and Personality Psychology Compass,* 2/3 (May 2008): 1313-1344, https://doi.org/10.1111/j.1751-9004.2008.00113.x.

2. Obviously the more explicit aspects of this footage are edited appropriately.

3. Reicher, "Making a Virtue of Evil".

4. As Reicher and colleagues mention (Reicher, "Making a Virtue of Evil"), the discussion around the "Banality of Evil" is more sophisticated than is implied by Hannah Arendt's famous quote. However, in the context of this current discussion, Reicher and colleagues were suggesting that rather than evil being mindless in its banality, instead it is very conscious and intentional, occurring because the individuals believe that what they are doing is right.

5. Reicher, "Making a Virtue of Evil".

6. Ibid.

7. Özlem Sensoy and Robin DiAngelo, *Is Everyone Really Equal?: An Introduction to Key Concepts in Social Justice Education* (New York: Teachers College Press, 2017).

8. Isaac Gottesman, *The Critical Turn in Education: From Marxist Critique to Poststructuralist Feminism to Critical Theories of Race (Critical Social Thought)* (New York: Routledge, 2016).

9. Henri Tajfel and John Turner, "The social identity theory of intergroup behaviour" in *Psychology of Intergroup Relations*, eds. Stephen Worchel and William G. Austin, 2nd edition (Chicago: Nelson-Hall, 1986). 7-24.

10. We regularly see this dichotomous thinking presented by proponents of CSJ, and those in "oppressed" groups are virtuised due to their group membership, in contrast to the out-group (for example, treating George Floyd as a hero despite him being a convicted fellon).

11. A recent dramatic example of this was seen in a talk given to Yale University's School of Medicine by psychiatrist Aruna Khilanani. The talk was titled "The Psychopathic Problem of the White Mind" and in it, she talked of having "fantasies of unloading a revolver into the head of any white person that got in my way, burying their body, and wiping my bloody hands, as I walked away relatively guiltless with a bounce in my step. Like I did the world a ******* favor".

12. Save Mental Health – Working to Protect Mental Health Services in the UK, "The Politicisation of British Psychology", updated April 14, 2021, https://save-mental-health.com/the-politicisation-of-british-psychology/.

[13] The division that oversees all practitioner psychologists.

[14] Coinciding with various investigations, the BPS has edited their website. The statement has now been moved to here: "Black Lives Matter; George Floyd's Life Matters: Statement by the DCP Representative Assembly," Division of Clinical Psychology, https://shop.bps.org.uk/clinical-psychology-forum-no-331-july-2020.

[15] "BPS statement on racial injustice," The BPS, https://twitter.com/bpsofficial/status/1267866089192591363.

[16] This is despite the male mental health crisis that places men at a disproportionate risk of suicide, homelessness, addiction, etc. For more information, see https://www.bps.org.uk/member-networks/male-psychology-section.

[17] "Authority statement on the murder of Sarah Everard", *Professional Standards Authority*, last modified March 16, 2021, https://www.professionalstandards.org.uk/news-and-blog/latest-news/detail/2021/03/16/authority-statement-on-the-murder-of-sarah-everard.

[18] "The Power Threat Meaning Framework," The BPS, accessed August 12, 2022, https://cms.bps.org.uk/sites/default/files/2022-07/PTM%20Framework%20%28January%202018%29_0.pdf.

[19] For example, "Western", "European", "white", "male".

[20] "Psychology has a sexual harassment problem", The Psychologist, June 2020, https://twitter.com/psychmag/status/1531279641004081152. Also, website—*No to Male Psychology*, 2022, https://notomalepsych.wordpress.com. Also, "Treatment of Men", *Save Mental Health*, 2022, https://save-mental-health.com/the-problem/treatment-of-men/.

[21] For example, see the information posted on the website for a group called *Race Reflections*, https://racereflections.co.uk, 2022. Charges are between £13 and £45 a month for membership, with the highest membership level providing an "anti-racist personal development membership". Corporate subscriptions range from £500–£3500 per calendar month and resources include pieces with titles such as "Neurosis Of Whiteness, White Envy And Racial Violence", "Whiteness, Names And Mirrors", "Ambivalence And Readiness For Whiteness: A Model", and "The Psychology Of White Fragility". Training courses include "Navigating Whiteness In Academia", "Self Care In The Face Of Racism"—the latter being a course (costing £399) designed for educators, parents/carers, and children, based on the statement that "Black and Brown children start to experience racism at a very young age". Lesson content includes topics on "whiteness" ("seeing whiteness", "defining whiteness", and "white privilege") as well as "anti-racism" in schools, which includes the section "preparing children for discrimination".

22 See the official Instagram page for a network called the *Radical Ther-apist Network*, https://www.instagram.com/radicaltherapistnetwork/?hl=en-gb, 2022.

    It includes statements such as "we are not here to comfort and protect oppressors. We will call you in and invite you to do better. We'll support you to do this in a way that holds you to account and honours the people/communities you have harmed. White dominance masked as fragility will not be tolerated". Another post states, "If your priority as a white facilitator is to make other white people feel comfortable to enable them to engage in anti-oppressive practice, then it's not anti-racist work. White people need to widen their tolerance for discomfort and understand that they have the capacity to harm."

23 Again, as noted elsewhere in the book, this form of "treatment" is potentially also very damaging to the client: telling a distressed person that they are discriminated against purely by virtue of things they can do nothing about is unlikely to help them feel empowered, in control, and able to overcome the difficulties that life throws at them. In addition, there is no consideration of helping clients develop a more realistic (and charitable) view of the world—feelings of resentment, injustice, and blame are encouraged, and actions that would help the individual improve their own mental health are ignored.

24 For example, seeing white people denouncing their race, men claiming to be feminists, non-trans people displaying pronouns, etc. Indeed, we regularly see those considered to be part of an "oppressor" group denouncing their group feeling the need to cognitively and publicly distance themselves from the oppressor group.

25 There is possibility that they may behave even more harshly towards their own group, as there is evidence that those on the periphery of a valued group (in this case, the oppressed group) will engage in increased derogation of the out-group in order to signal allegiance to the in-group (e.g. Jeffrey G. Noel, Daniel Wann, and Nyla R. Branscome, "Peripheral ingroup membership status and public negativity toward outgroups" *Journal of Personality and Social Psychology* 68, no. 1 (1995): 127-137, https://doi.org/10.1037/0022-3514.68.1.127.

26 These suggestions are, of course, not to deny—as DiAngelo claims (Robin DiAngelo, *Nice Racism* (Boston: Beacon Press, 2021), 31.). Penguin Books Ltd. (Kindle Edition) that people of colour (for example) may have different experiences in some contexts to white people, or that race is not relevant to the individual. Rather it is to take into account the fact that there are individual differences between all

humans, and that similarity of colour—or other immutable charac-teristics doesn't necessitate similarity in perception of experience. Similarly, it doesn't make any assumptions about potentially different experiences between racial groups; it simply suggests that we look for commonalities in experiences/values, etc., such as a desire to love and protect our families, similarities in hobbies/interests, etc.

Chapter 5:

The Intoxicating Ideas of Critical Social Justice—God-shaped Ideologies for God-sized Holes

by Bret Alderman

Many people have noted a quasi-religious element to Critical Social Justice (CSJ), claiming that its adherents often exhibit the same unbending, absolutist attitudes of religious fundamentalists: ideological purity tests help to form in-groups and out-groups that bear a striking resemblance to congregations of the saved and those who remain unredeemed.[1] Compulsory confessions of privilege evoke parallels with religious confessions of sin. Online and off, an inquisitional spirit seeks to identify innumerable phobias and oppressions, articulating its accusations in the vocabulary of social justice activism. Often, the imagery conjured in describing this spirit borrows metaphors from some of the more horrific chapters of our collective religious past, evoking pogroms and witch burnings, admissions of heresy, and pleas for expiation. CSJ amounts to a secular religion, they tell us, though what they describe might be more accurately deemed secular zealotry.

One can certainly argue that it is easy to make a bit too much of these analogies; ideas firmly grounded in secular academic disciplines like the social sciences and humanities are not comparable to theological dogma. It may be that the term *woke*, often associated, for better or worse, with advocates of CSJ, is itself a religious metaphor, suggesting a spiritual and moral awakening, but it is, after all, just a metaphor and just a figure of speech. Not too much should be read into it. Yet it is also easy, perhaps, to make too little of such analogies. In this chapter, I will consider how the work of Carl Jung can help us understand the religious aspects of CSJ, as well as its intoxicating allure.[2] I do so in the belief that the disciplines of psychology and psychotherapy, rather than simply being influenced and destabilized by CSJ, can help shed light on it, a bit like a skilled therapist might help a client shed light on themselves through adept intervention.

Jung delved deep into the realm of comparative religious studies and was struck by the fact that religious patterns of thought and behavior often shape secular beliefs. His age was one of religious decline: the pews of churches, temples, and mosques were increasingly vacant, and for a growing number of people, traditional religious symbols and stories simply did not mean what they had meant for their ancestors.

On the contrary, they appeared to be little more than anachronistic absurdities and superstitious beliefs worthy of ridicule. Yet, it was his conviction that in the wake of waning religious belief, "god" or "gods" had merely taken on new forms. Increasingly, what in other ages had been known as gods or spirits, angels, or demons, with all of their supernatural power, took the form of unquestioned ideologies and dogmatic beliefs that seized moderns with no less ferocity than their more religious forebearers. The enlightened, reasonable, and civilized appearance of moderns was just that: appearance. Despite the veneer of reasonableness, they were in no way immune to fanatical obsession and irrational frenzy—what might have been described as demonic possession in another age, or even possession by the holy ghost. In fact, they were in some respects more prone to such states because they could easily hide them behind a pretense of rationality.

The unquestioned ideologies and dogmatic beliefs that, at times, granted cover for these obsessions and frenzies, Jung often referred to as *isms*, with the clear intent of evoking the dueling specters of Nazism and Marxism; these were two ideologies that he witnessed grab hold of a massive swath of the world's populace and cause undeniable devastation.

On his account, the failure to truly confront the death of God, the demise of religion, had as its consequence a "fog of -isms, [and] the catastrophe" of World War II.[3] A German-speaking Swiss, he watched in horror as the German-speaking peoples descended into an anti-Semitism that he saw as a revival of medieval persecutions.[4] He took notice of the mystical imagery that the Nazis borrowed from other religious traditions, most notably the swastika, an ancient Tibetan symbol. He observed how Germans seemed to deify their Fuehrer, seeing in him a savior as he promised national *rebirth* and *redemption*, two quintessentially religious themes prevalent in mythic tales the world over.[5]

Jung saw similar patterns on both extremes of the political spectrum, observing that "even the Bolsheviks, whose radicalism leaves nothing to be desired, have embalmed Lenin and made a savior of Karl Marx".[6] For Jung, such cults of personality were just that: cults. It seemed to him that religion, although perhaps a rather malevolent form of it, was alive and well, despite all pretension to the contrary. On his account:

> The demons have not really disappeared but have merely taken on another form: they have become unconscious psychic forces ... Just when people were congratulating themselves on having abolished all spooks, it turned out that instead of haunting the attic or old ruins the spooks were flitting about in the heads of apparently normal Europeans. Tyrannical, obsessive, intoxicating ideas and delusions were abroad everywhere, and people began to believe the most absurd things, just as the possessed do.[7]

Jung's time is, of course, not our time. We live in a different era. One would hope that we are somewhat more enlightened than our forebears. One might also wonder, however, if, metaphorically speaking, our demons have really disappeared. *Are we perhaps still prone to possession by obsession ... still, at times, just as much the victims of our own tyrannical beliefs?* Jung might say that we are:

> We can never be sure that a new idea will not seize either upon ourselves or upon our neighbors. We know from modern as well as from ancient history that such ideas are often so strange, indeed so bizarre, that they fly in the face of reason. The fascination which is almost invariably connected with ideas of this sort produces a fanatical obsession, with the result that all dissenters, no matter how well-meaning or reasonable they are, get burnt alive or have their heads cut off or are disposed of in masses by the more modern machine gun. [8]

The intoxicating ideas of Critical Social Justice

The speed with which certain ideas take hold is astonishing. They seize the collective imagination with shocking rapidity. Not long ago, it was commonly believed that there were only two genders. The word *gender* was synonymous with the word *sex* and was used to avoid the multiple connotations that the latter term can evoke.

Today, this is not so much the case. The term *gender* increasingly refers to a social category and its characteristics, which are related to biological sex but not identical to it. One term refers to the biological, genetic division of a species, whereas the other refers to the myriad ways that we interpret the meaning of this division within a social and cultural context.[9] Within the English-speaking world, the idea of a simple male/female gender binary is being abandoned in favor of a growing number of terms denoting a growing multiplicity of genders that have entered popular vernacular:

non-binary, agender, bigender, genderfluid, genderqueer, pangender, cisgender, and, of course, transgender.[10] The proliferation of terms, it would seem, speaks to a psychological need: some people find the simplistic male/female gender binary to be confining, reductive, and even oppressive, and the usage of a new vocabulary to describe themselves feels like an act of liberation.

Similar observations might be made of terms like *whiteness, privilege, systemic,* and *normative.* These are words that have a long history, certainly; nevertheless, they have recently acquired uncanny power. Like talismans, they can magically shift the course of a conversation, whereas before they could not. Now, like magnets pulling to themselves the iron filings of our feelings, they have acquired a new power to evoke emotion, conjure connotations, and allude to associations present within our collective imagination. In a very short time, they have taken hold of the way that many of us talk, think, and feel, even if, and perhaps especially if, we do not agree with the meanings granted these words or follow along lockstep with the thought processes behind them; they force us to question what we are willing to say on a given issue. They provoke the need for counter-arguments precisely because disagreement has become emotionally charged.

Many people have little knowledge of the origins of such words or their newfound power. Many people who self-identify as one of these new genders may have little to no direct exposure to Gender Theory as taught in universities. They may have never heard the names of prominent theorists like Judith Butler or Judith Lorber, much less understand the intellectual underpinnings of their theoretical frameworks.[11,12] Yet echoes of these theorists' work reverberate throughout popular culture and have had a resounding effect on it. One such echo is the belief that gender is little more than a social construct. It bears little if any relation to biological sex, and biological sex, in turn, is increasingly understood to be a construct as well.

Social constructionism, while not unique to Critical Social Justice and being central to earlier forms of feminism that are now widely considered problematic to many CSJ scholars, is a school of thought that plays an outsized role in CSJ as a whole, not just in disciplines like Queer Theory and Gender Studies. It also has had a deep influence on schools of thought ranging from Critical Race and Postcolonial Theory to feminist, fat, and disability studies, as well as the intersectional approaches that occupy the spaces where all of these overlap.[13]

In the words of sociologist and renowned authority on Critical Race Theory, Robin DiAngelo, and her co-author Özlem Sensoy, in their introductory text to social justice education, CSJ scholars:

> ... argue that a key element of social injustice involves the claim that particular knowledge is objective, neutral, and universal. An approach based on Critical Theory calls into question the idea that objectivity is desirable or even *possible*. The term used to describe this way of thinking about knowledge is that knowledge is socially constructed. When we refer to knowledge as socially constructed we mean that knowledge is reflective of the values and interests of those who produce it. This concept captures the understanding that all knowledge and all means of knowing are connected to a social context.[14]

Throughout the work cited above, DiAngelo contrasts objectivity with social construction, presenting her readers with a simplistic, stark, and ultimately false dichotomy: either knowledge is objective, neutral, and universal, or it is a reflection of the values and interests of those who produce it. Either there are facts, or we are all producing fiction to suit our own needs, although we do not do so in an equitable manner; those in dominant positions within a social hierarchy impose their interests to a far greater degree in the form of self-serving ideas and ideologies, couched in a language of their own creation. Yet what they espouse says more of their relative position than anything else, and "for this reason, the concept of *positionality* has become a key tool in analyzing knowledge construction".[15]

Authorities may pretend to objectivity, but this is mere pretension, a philosophical ruse that only serves to legitimize their own entrenched and underserved authority.

For this particular understanding of social construction and objectivity, the idea that gender is a binary is merely the product of a power structure privileging its own worldview, one that splits people into two reductive categories, grants greater power and prestige to one side of the binary (males), and denies this same power and prestige to the other (females).[16]

It *cannot be* that the binary is in any way grounded in a biological or objective reality that transcends the interests of the authorities in question. It is not a fact that we are a sexually dimorphic species, like many others in the natural world, and that we reproduce by way of this dimorphism. Such a fact has no say in the matter because nothing is a matter of fact to begin with. Terms like *male* and *female*, *man* and *woman* are not so much rooted in nature or biology, but socialization. For DiAngelo, "One of the persistent myths of mainstream society is that the knowledge we study in schools is factual and neutral."[17]

The particular brand of social constructionism served up by DiAngelo is an intoxicating brew of ideas, one imbibed by an astonishing array of scholars.[18] The version of it put forth by DiAngelo, but also by prominent Queer Theorists like Butler, works like a magical elixir. Drunk to the dregs, it can have an almost hallucinatory effect. Taken in a single gulp, it can dramatically alter what one believes to be true. Under the influence of a belief in the utter absence of objectivity, no one needs to feel that they are bound by the dictates of the objective world. Reality itself can be constructed or construed in a multiplicity of ways, none of which needs to be confined by fact, natural laws, physics, or biology. These are, after all, just constructions espoused by those who hold institutional power within a stratified social structure. Empirical, demonstrable truths have little say in the matter.

If words, ideas, and ideologies are mere constructs that cannot portray anything objectively but merely serve human interests, then each one of us, or each social group, can create our own ideologies to suit our whims. Nobody needs to be subject to truths that may not be to their liking. It is an enticing idea, one that suggests that knowledge can simply be molded to the contour of one's needs. In fact, it does more than this. It states that this is what knowledge already is: attire tailor-made to fit one's own values and interests. Changing vocabulary and altering the linguistic constructs we use to describe our world becomes an emancipating, even exhilarating endeavor. If constructions are not built upon a foundation of objectivity, and if no ground supports the architecture of our ideas, then we can build castles in the sky without concern for their collapse.

Under the spell of this potent intellectual concoction—to echo Jung's words—people can believe the most absurd things, just as the possessed do because no empirical truth or appeal to objectivity can serve as an antidote to the beliefs it inspires. Or so it seems to those who have abstained from the inebriating elixir, those who remain steadfast in their sobriety, maintaining that in some form or another, even in some highly qualified, nuanced, and philosophically astute manner aware of the importance of cultural and historical differences, *some* sense of objectivity must be maintained.

From Jung's point of view, the abject denial of the possibility, or even desirability, of objective knowledge in favor of a rather absolutist understanding of what is meant by *social construction* is symptomatic of what makes certain ideas and ideologies intoxicating. For one thing, they fail to bear any relation to the outside (i.e. objective) world, so they are somewhat impervious to proof or disproof.[19] They are, as such, beyond discussion, in the same way that for some people it is beyond discussion that God created heaven and earth in seven days. To suggest that this might be a metaphor will get you nowhere.

Another characteristic that, for Jung, tends to make certain ideas tyrannical, obsessive, and intoxicating is their reductive one-sidedness. He describes this in terms of a psychology of the *nothing but*, which is "the insistent leitmotiv of all one-sidedness".[20]

Within the context of social constructionism, this might take the form of the belief that both sex and gender are *nothing but* constructs or that the entirety of science is, in fact, *nothing but* a set of stories and practices that reflect little more than the interests of a certain group, easily defined in demographic and historic terms. Depending on the particular CSJ theory, this group is deemed white supremacist, colonialist, patriarchal, fat-phobic, or ableist and, it would seem, little more. The facts, theories, hypotheses, narratives, and knowledge that any scientific or humanistic discipline produces say little about any object of study and a great deal about the social positions, interests, and biases of those who practice it. This is because the reductive mindset of ideological possession draws into intense focus one aspect of a complex situation while all other aspects blur into a hazy background. The possessed are both myopic and monocular. They have no depth of vision.

In Jung's reading, the power of tyrannical ideas renders even the best of us, at times, "liable to possession by an infatuation, a vice, or a one-sided conviction".[21] Under their sway, certain things simply *must* be so. Debate, discussion, and dialogue become a sort of inverted, diabolic trinity. Pointing out logical incongruities amounts to blasphemy. True believers bend their logic to fit their convictions and place their reasoning minds at the service of an unreasoned compulsion. They cannot consider the antithesis to their thesis because both have become too emotionally charged.

Words have become talismans, magical objects with properties that evoke overwhelming emotions. They have been invested with the same power that clings to religious symbols, and therefore they demand the same sacred solemnity. Under the spell of a one-sided conviction, it is as if one is in the presence of some supernatural force or possessed by a spirit. One must simply take a knee, raise a fist in solidarity, recite the truism, chant the mantra, or in some way genuflect before the one true principle which has now taken the place of the one true god. Entertaining possibilities to the contrary is no longer evidence of curiosity but of heresy.

Once one has drunk from the sacred chalice of social constructionism, words become a profoundly important issue. They are not merely descriptors that might serve to *reveal* reality— objective, subjective, or otherwise—but, rather, tools for *constructing* reality, or at least our knowledge of it.

Furthermore, language, as the medium through which knowledge is constructed, is also the medium through which social justice and injustice must pass. It can serve to marginalize a community or to put it front and center. It can oppress or it can liberate. Whatever the dominant discourse on an issue, by virtue of its dominance, it enacts oppression. Tossing new words about is like tossing wrenches into its machinery—a subversive, righteous endeavor that grinds the cycle of oppression to a halt.

So much depends upon words, the linguistic constructs we use to form our views. In a sense, this is all we really have: views, viewpoints, positions, and positionality. But the object we are viewing is strangely absent. If we speak of it, we are really just reflecting our own values and interests.

From social constructionism to social contagion

Social constructionism is a theory of knowledge that is well adapted to the age of social media and "a life online": views, viewpoints, and positions are what social media thrive on. Social context *is* their context. There is no other. "Hot takes" generate likes and followers, and the hotter the take, the more followers one acquires, regardless of the validity of the views one espouses. Ideas and memes go viral less due to their veracity than their ability to appeal to wants and needs. Or perhaps they go viral *because* of their lack of veracity and our thirst for illusion. Online, as elsewhere, narratives are contrived to suit people's values and interests, yet what relation these narratives might have to an objectively existing world is difficult to discern. Objectivity, if such a thing exists, quickly disappears behind an avalanche of opinion.

Indeed, "objective reality" is what is most absent online; cyberspace is *not* objective space. It presents us with pixels on a screen, text, image, and sound, but they are all reproductions and representations removed from their original context. We see the façade of a world, but the world itself is nowhere to be found. We see avatars, photoshopped images, and carefully curated videos presenting carefully curated personae. We see virtual bodies, made infinitely malleable by technology that few of us understand. But actual human bodies, actual human beings do not present themselves through the illuminated screens before us, not human beings with real-life, objectively existing bodies that breathe, sweat, urinate, defecate, make love, fall asleep, grow hungry, and need to be touched. Even being online, scrolling through posts, reading the news, checking email, watching videos, or participating in a conference call requires a degree of dissociation from our physical bodies and their needs.[22]

Both social constructionism and social media, in turn, are conducive to social contagion. While the latter provides the means to spread viral ideas and ideologies, the former lowers our immune system's defenses by assuring us, as DiAngelo has, that facts are really just myths. So, myths might just as well be facts. This is territory that Jung knew well: the disturbing amalgamation and conflation of myth and literal fact. The territory where mythic and religious forms easily hide behind a pretense of rationality was precisely what he sought to shed light on with his reference to the "isms" of ideological possession and their intoxicating influence. To DiAngelo's belief in the persistent myth of the factual, Jung would have countered with the persistent fact of the mythical.

Regardless of the particular variety of CSJ—whether we concern ourselves with Critical Race, Postcolonial, or Queer Theory; feminist, fat, or disability studies—the myth that its advocates enact is inevitably one of a heroic battle and martyrdom in relation to a pervasive, all-encompassing, often "systemic" oppression. Warriors for the "just cause" fight the good fight against the evildoers or, in lieu of them, an omnipresent power that has riddled its way into every aspect of our institutions. But a crusade by any other name is still a crusade, and its basic outline is not difficult to decipher.

A psychologically astute observer might question such myths of heroic battle and martyrdom. It is the job of psychologists, therapists, and analysts to discern when their clients' stories provide convenient cover for the very issues that bring them to therapy in the first place. CSJ can serve as camouflage, just as the perception of, or fixation on, social injustice can serve as a form of psychological avoidance. This is why the adept clinician does not blindly affirm the narrative the client presents but rather helps him or her to discern its true origin and relative merits.

When, for example, a client finds herself in the grips of depression, filling an existential emptiness with empty calories, a skillful therapist will not blindly accept her belief that what really ails her is a culture of *fattism*—a pervasive form of bigotry against the obese. Nor will the therapist give a blanket endorsement of the client's allegiance to a fat liberationist movement. Similarly, when faced with a client who believes himself to be under constant, covert attack by colleagues for his gender or ethnicity, the discerning professional seeks to find underneath the discourse of micro-aggressions the micro-aggrieved personality that it may hide.

Finding that personality beneath the discourse is never an easy task, but it grows ever more difficult in an era of dogmatic ideological conformity. The well-intentioned therapist who fails to question and explore the multiple dimensions of a client's explanations for their suffering risks, more than ever, *turning stigma into stigmata,* that is to say, turning psychological conditions into oppressed identities. Personal suffering becomes performative suffering—the visible scars of oppression at the hands of an unjust world. Then, the stigma of an emotional or psychological issue becomes easily transmuted by social justice theories into permanent, defining aspects of one's identity. And they are increasingly *valuable* aspects of an inflated social currency: it is sad to suffer from gender dysphoria—a distress resulting from a gender identity differing from one's sex at birth—but adopting the identity of transgender and learning to think in the terms provided by gender discourse can garner one instant friends and membership into a worldwide community.

Such an observation is in fundamental agreement with the portrait of Rapid-Onset Gender Dysphoria (ROGD) put forth by journalist Abigail Shrier, physician Lisa Littman, Jungian Analyst Lisa Marchiano, and others.[23,24] Adopting a transgender identity can result in the instant esteem of one's peers. Although an announcement of such an identity "is often preceded by anxiety, depression, social isolation, loss, or trauma", what follows, at least temporarily and conditionally, is a flood of in-group validation.[25] TikTok, Tumblr, YouTube, and other outlets provide instant celebrity and stages upon which to spotlight the literal scars of gender reassignment surgeries and the stigmata of transgender identity. What all of these researchers tell us is that social media is high-octane fuel for ROGD.

But, perhaps no less importantly, ROGD is fueled by what might be called RODC—Rapid-Onset Diagnostic Complicity: "Current psychotherapeutic practice involves immediate affirmation of a young person's self-diagnosis."[26] It is increasingly difficult to take anything other than a blindly affirmative approach as multiple states adopt legislation banning conversion therapy for *both* sexual orientation *and* gender identity.[27] The net effect of senselessly lumping the two concepts of sexual orientation and gender identity together in this way is to pre-empt further exploration of the latter within the therapeutic setting.

A therapist must simply affirm the client's belief: a boy who believes himself to be a girl or a girl who believes herself to be a boy must not only have their fantasy indulged but the fantasy must also be taken as true, lest the therapist is accused of attempted conversion. One must simply affirm the identity. As a consequence, relevant psychological issues cannot be explored and trans-identified individuals risk making unnecessary changes to their bodies.[28]

Such gender-affirming practices are but another variant of the aforementioned figurative raising of the fist in solidarity or genuflection before the one true god masquerading as the one true principle. The principle, in this case, is *affirmation*, which must be unquestioning and total "with the result that all dissenters, no matter how well-meaning or reasonable they are, get burnt alive" for their supposed phobia.[29]

Such is the demand of all one-sidedness, the insistent leitmotiv of the ideologically possessed.

Such is the reductive *nothing but* attitude.

In a world where fact is myth, all fantasies must be affirmed. Theories possess supernatural power, and, in turn, they possess us. When a fact is myth and that myth has become factual, it is hard to resist the allure of intoxicating ideas.

Endnotes

1   Joseph Bottum, *An Anxious Age: The Post-Protestant Ethic and the Spirit of America* (New York: Crown Publishing Group, 2014); Ross Douthat, "The Religious Roots of a New Progressive Era Welcome to the post-Protestant Reformation", *New York Times,* July 7, 2020, https://www.nytimes.com/2020/07/07/opinion/protestant-progressive-reformation.html; Laurie Johnson, *Ideological Possession and the Rise of the New Right: The Political Thought of Carl Jung* (New York: Taylor & Francis, 2019); John McWhorter, *Woke Racism: How a New Religion Has Betrayed Black America* (New York: Penguin Publishing Group, 2021).

2   Carl Jung was a colleague of Sigmund Freud and founded the school of analytic psychology.

3   Carl Jung, Gerhard Adler, *Collected Works of C.G. Jung, Volume 11: Psychology and Religion: West and East* (Princeton NJ: Princeton University Press, 2014), p. 88.

4   Jung has been frequently criticized for not having denounced Nazism more aggressively and earlier. For a fair-handed critique of Jung's response to Nazism which was, by his own admission, not beyond reproach, as well as a description of his work with the Allies in WWII as an undercover operative, see Deirdre Bair, *Jung: A Biography* (New York: Little, Brown, 2004). Jung has also been the target of accusations of anti-Semitism. For an in-depth exploration of this accusation, as well as accounts of numerous instances of assistance that he gave to Jewish analysts before and during the war years, see Aryeh Maidenbaum, *Jung and the Shadow of Anti-Semitism.* (London: Nicolas-Hays, 2002).

5   Carl Jung, *Four Archetypes: Mother, Rebirth, Spirit, Trickster* (Abingdon, UK: Routledge & Kegan Paul, 1972); Mircea Eliade, *Rites and symbols of initiation: the mysteries of birth and rebirth* (New York: Harper & Row, 1975).

6   Carl Jung, Gerhard Adler, *Collected Works of C.G. Jung, Volume 17: Development of Personality* (Princeton NJ: Princeton University Press, 1981), p. 181.

7   Carl Jung, Gerhard Adler, *Collected Works of C.G. Jung, Volume 10: Civilization in Transition* (Princeton, NJ: Princeton University Press, 2014), p. 212.

8   Jung, *Civilization in Transition*, p. 230.

9   Sherwood Thompson, *Encyclopedia of Diversity and Social Justice* (Lanham MA: Rowman & Littlefield Publishers, 2014).

10 This list was culled from an LGBTQ Glossary provided by the student affairs website for Johns Hopkins University, accessed August 8, 2021: https://studentaffairs.jhu.edu/lgbtq/education/glossary/.

[11] Judith Butler is an American philosopher and gender theorist who has been remarkably influential in Queer Theory and feminist studies. In her second, widely cited and controversial book, *Gender Trouble: Feminism and the Subversion of Identity* (New York: Routledge, 1990), Butler built upon the broadly held assumption that gender is socially constructed and further elaborated it by arguing that it is also constituted through action or "performative": less what one is and more what one does.

[12] Judith Lorber is a highly influential American theorist of the social construction of gender. Among her many writings, her book *Paradoxes of Gender* (New Haven CT: Yale University Press, 1994) has become a staple in many women's studies courses. In it, she portrays gender as a system of social stratification that structures every aspect of our lives including family, workplace, the state, sexuality, language, and culture.

[13] The concept of intersectionality refers to the ways that aspects of our social lives like our race, ethnicity, social class, gender identity, sexual orientation, and others intersect to constitute an individual's lived experience. The term *intersectionality* was introduced by Kimberlé Crenshaw in 1989, although intersectional approaches preceded this coinage. See Thompson, *Encyclopedia of Diversity,* p. 435.

[14] Özlem Sensoy and Robin DiAngelo, *Is Everyone Really Equal? An Introduction to Key Concepts in Social Justice Education* (New York: Teachers College Press, 2017), p. 29.

[15] Ibid, p. 29.

[16] A prime example of this line of thinking that regards gender as a product of power is Judith Lorber's "Shifting Paradigms and Challenging Categories", *Social Problems* 53, no. 4 (November 2006): 448–453 in which she puts forth four aspects of a paradigm shift that has taken place within feminist social sciences. The first involves a transformation of the concept of gender as an organizing principle of social order extending far beyond the family to include everything from economy to medicine. The second involves the acknowledgement of gender as a social construct. This construction is inextricably linked to the third aspect, which is the hegemony of dominant heterosexual men, what I have referred to here as "a power structure privileging its own worldview". The fourth involves methodologies that have helped bring into clearer view perspectives that have been marginalized due to class, racial ethnicity, religion, and sexuality.

[17] DiAngelo and Özlem, *Is Everyone*, p. 23.

[18] I say "particular brand" of social constructionism because there are, in fact, numerous approaches that have developed since the original publication in 1966 of Peter Berger and Thomas Luckmann's seminal work *The*

Social Construction of Reality: A Treatise in the Sociology of Knowledge (New York: Open Road Media, 2011). Some of these approaches offer far more nuance and have far greater merit than DiAngelo's. I do not here wish to deny the truth of social construction as much as suggest that it is a partial truth, one that cannot be taken as an epistemological ground. For further discussion of my views on social construction as it relates to the linguistic turn and postmodernism, see Bret Alderman, *Symptom, Symbol, and the Other of Language: A Jungian Interpretation of the Linguistic Turn* (New York: Taylor & Francis, 2016).

[19] Jung, *Civilization in Transition.*

[20] Jung, *Development*, p. 73.

[21] Jung, *Civilization in Transition*, p. 139.

[22] Lee Bailey, *The Enchantments of Technology* (Chicago: University of Illinois Press, 2005); Robert Romanyshyn, *Technology as Symptom and Dream* (New York: Taylor & Francis, 2003); George Zarkadakis. *In Our Own Image* (New York: Pegasus Books, 2016).

[23] Abigail Shrier, *Irreversible Damage: The Transgender Craze Seducing Our Daughters* (Washington DC: Regnery Publishing, 2020).

[24] Lisa L. Littman, "Rapid onset of gender dysphoria in adolescents and young adults: a descriptive study," *Journal of Adolescent Health* 60, no. 2: S95-S96, February 01, 2017, https://doi.org/10.1016/j.jadohealth.2016.10.369.

[25] Lisa Marciano, "Outbreak: On Transgender Teens and Psychic Epidemics," *Psychological Perspectives* 60, no. 3 (2017): 345-366, October 06, 2017, https://www.tandfonline.com/doi/full/10.1080/00332925.2017.1350804.

[26] Marciano, "Outbreak", pp. 345-366.

[27] There is a consensus belief, which I share, that conversion therapy for sexual orientation is exceedingly harmful. But exploring the issue of gender identity in a way that is not merely affirmative should not be understood as an attempt at conversion. Unfortunately, the conflation of the two concepts of sexual orientation and gender identity within a legal context contributes to this misunderstanding. For more information on these laws, see https://www.lgbtmap.org/equality-maps/conversion_therapy.

[28] Robert Withers, "Transgender medicalization and the attempt to evade psychological distress," *Journal of Analytical Psychology 65, no. 5 (2020)*, pp. 865–889.

[29] Jung, *Civilization in Transition*, p. 230.

Chapter 6:

Transitioning Children—The Clinician's Assumption and Client Suggestibility

by Sasha Ayad and Stella O'Malley

Prior to the early 2010s, childhood gender identity issues were vanishingly rare. In the UK, for example, the data for 2010–2011 show that 136 children per year were referred to the Tavistock Gender Identity Service, and most of those children were boys. But by 2021–2022, a complete sex ratio reversal had occurred, and the clinic saw 3,585 children that year, with females outnumbering males by more than double.[1] Meanwhile, in the United States, only one youth gender clinic existed in 2007, but today more than sixty clinics and hospitals medically treat children for gender identity concerns.[2,3]

This astronomical rise in gender distress among children simply cannot be explained by greater societal acceptance. Is the explosion of a once-rare psychological condition unprecedented? What explains this epidemiologically strange spike in a particular mental health issue? Let's begin by looking at another example of a sensational and dramatic psychological phenomenon that was both socially mediated and disproportionally impacted young women.

Before the publication of the book *Sybil*, Multiple Personality Disorder (MPD)[4] was so rare that only 100 cases had ever been reported in the medical literature. The book—later turned into a television film—told the story of a young woman's "discovery", with the help of her psychiatrist, that she embodied several distinct and separate internal "identities" which had emerged as she repressed horrific abuse from her conscious memory.[5] The media soon became transfixed by the seductive drama.

In less than ten years, thousands had been diagnosed, and by the early 90s, as many as one in every twenty people suffered from "multiples".[6] Psychiatrist Dr Allan Frances recalls the hundreds of patients he had seen claiming multiple personalities: "in every single instance, I discovered that the alternate personalities had been born under the tutelage of an enthusiastic and naive therapist, or in imitation of a friend, or after seeing a movie, or upon joining a multiples' chat group—or some combination."[7]

In the 1980s and 1990s, clinicians trained in "uncovering" the repressed memories extracted such false memories from thousands of patients. False accusations began spreading across the United States, and many innocent day-care providers were imprisoned until the truth eventually emerged. Sensational media coverage of novel miracle cures has led to similar outcomes. Between the 1940s and late 60s, for example, patients suffering from a broad range of ailments and mood disorders willingly subjected themselves to then-popular frontal lobotomies until the horrible outcomes were exposed in later years and a critical mass of disapproval finally peaked.

What does this tell us? When patients are vulnerable and clinicians are emphatic zealots, the stage is set for a medical scandal. A disturbingly similar parallel exists today. Gender clinics around the world have cropped up to serve the needs of unhappy teenagers who claim to be transgender, a population with exponentially rising numbers in the last decade. With an unsubstantiated air of certainty and urgency, these ambitious—and perhaps well-meaning—clinicians have recommended irreversible medicalised pathways for such children. And subsequently, we're seeing an inevitable rise in the number of young people who feel harmed and traumatized by the treatments.

To examine this issue, we explore the core Gender and Queer Theories that underpin the explosion of gender identities in the English-speaking world. Next, we trace the way an experimental puberty blockers study in the Netherlands has inadvertently created a template for doctors to medicalize gender distress. Finally, we review the emergence of the "trans kid" conceptualization which has reshaped our understanding of gender non-conformity and gender dysphoria. These factors coalesce in a perfect storm for a medical scandal, which is further explored in the following chapter. There, we discuss Rapid-Onset Gender Dysphoria (ROGD) and the forceful prioritization of the new "gender affirmative" therapeutic approach to dysphoria, which leads down a (concerning) one-size-fits-all pathway toward gender identity dogma and aggressive medicalization.

The Gendered Soul-Gender Identity Theory

Sex has been conceptualized in a variety of ways across time throughout the Western world. In ancient Greece, for example, the physician and philosopher Galen subscribed to a "one-sex model", believing that men and women were similar, except that women were an inferior version with "exactly the same organs but in exactly the wrong places".[8]

Thankfully, knowledge of human anatomy progressed, and by the 18th century, the "two-sex model" meant that male and female were universally understood as separate categories.[9] Charles Darwin further added to our knowledge in the 19th century with his study of the origin and the significance of the two sexes. Nonetheless, notwithstanding Darwin and colleagues,

Magnus Hirschfeld, a German physician, began to conceptualize sexuality and biological sex with greater fluidity.[10]

Hirschfeld, a brave, forward-thinking gay man and advocate for gay rights, initially supported a "three-sex model" which viewed homosexuals as the "third sex". He soon readjusted his theory, however, and proposed many types of naturally occurring sexual intermediaries within the human population such as "hermaphroditism", homosexuality, and transvestitism.[11] As Helen Joyce states in her book *Trans: When Ideology Meets Reality*, "After Darwin, any definition of 'male' and 'female' other than as developmental pathways directed towards and shaped by reproductive roles should have been dead in the water. But for Hirschfeld and his colleagues at the Institute, it was as if Darwin had never existed."[12]

Hirschfeld's theory that sex is on a spectrum, that male and female were "abstractions, invented extremes", and that homosexuals and transvestites were intermediaries, seems to be the foundation from which much of contemporary gender identity theory has evolved.[13]

The essence of femininity and masculinity have long been understood to exist independent of the sexed body. Indeed, deviations from the gender role associated with one's sex have historically been proscribed across many cultures and religions.

In the realm of psychology, a symbolic and archetypal view of masculinity and femininity was taken by Carl Jung in the mid-20th century. Jung hypothesized that each person has a necessary contra-sexual inner image—a male Animus figure in women, and a female Anima figure in men—which, when accessed appropriately, served to balance and complete the personality.[14]

The current language around gender, however, frames gender as both a literal and subjective form of personal identity. This conception might be traced back to John Money and Robert Stoller, mid-20th century clinicians whose patients had Disorders of Sexual Development (DSDs, and sometimes known as intersex people). DSDs are "congenital conditions in which the development of chromosomal, gonadal, hormonal or anatomical sex is atypical".[15] In 1955, Money, a psychologist and paediatrician, sought to describe a metaphysical, subjective sense of self when he coined the terms "gender role" and "gender expression". Nine years later, in 1964, Stoller, the American professor of psychiatry, further developed Money's concept with the term "gender identity", which he defined as "a complex system of beliefs about oneself: a sense of one's masculinity and femininity. It implies nothing about the origins of that sense (e.g., whether the person is male or female). It has, then, psychological connotations only: one's subjective state".[16] Money agreed and pronounced that "Gender identity is the private experience of gender role, and gender role is the public manifestation of gender identity".[17]

Physicians in the 1950s and 60s frequently encouraged operating on intersex children's genitals to create a more normative physical appearance. The theory of "gender identity" was used to support the claim that biological sex and gender role development are completely independent.[18] With scientific understanding then unable to detect biological sex in some intersex individuals, sometimes mistakes were made with genetically male children being raised as girls, and genetically female children as boys. It was also believed at the time that surgical intervention was primarily for aesthetics and that a child could adjust to any gender role he/she is raised in. The physical, psychological, and emotional impact of hormones such as testosterone and oestrogen were de-emphasized while hubristic theories of identity were actualized onto children's bodies, spelling disaster for many. Bruce/David Reimer is one such case.

Twin boys, Bruce and Brian Reimer, were born healthy, but at seven months old, a botched circumcision left Bruce with a damaged penis. Bruce was brought to Johns Hopkins Hospital in 1967 to see John Money, who was developing a reputation as a pioneer in the field.[19] Money, insisting that gender is malleable in the first thirty months of life, recommended that Bruce should be operated on and raised as a girl. The parents reluctantly agreed.[20] Unfortunately, however, Reimer struggled profoundly. In his pre-adolescent years, he learned the truth about being born male. He changed his name to David and, at the age of fifteen, returned to living socially as a boy. Sadly, he continued to struggle with severe depression. As an adult, Reimer underwent operations to construct a neo-penis; he married and tried to settle down. Tragically, David died by suicide in 2004, when he was thirty-eight years old.[21]

Another reckless mid-20th century physician and co-founder of gender identity theory is endocrinologist Harry Benjamin. Benjamin was introduced to a homosexual male child who claimed he "wanted to become a girl" so he could "marry, have a house and children".[22] Despite numerous protestations and warnings from psychiatrists involved in the case, Benjamin advised the mother to take the child to Europe where doctors could surgically operate on his penis. The child had a series of surgeries to create a pseudo-vagina out of skin from his thigh. Nothing is known about what became of the young patient. Seemingly incurious about the outcome of such experimental interventions on the body of a child, Benjamin pressed on to treat hundreds of patients with similar controversial recommendations. He soon became known as an authority figure in the world of sex reassignment. Hirschfeld, Benjamin, Stoller, and Money are, to this day, revered and credited as the true pioneers of transgender treatment.

The development of treatments for (adult) gender-identity concerns has always been more patient-led than other conditions, perhaps because it is buttressed by an unfalsifiable belief in a personal sense of gender identity. In 1954, at a symposium sponsored by the American Journal of Psychotherapy, Benjamin argued that humans are made up of a "mixture of male and female components and that male trans-sexualists had a constitutional femininity, perhaps due to a chromosomal sex disturbance".[23]

Later on, a wealthy transsexual patient, Reed Erickson, funded a research group that Benjamin would lead, joined by Money, with the aim of setting up an American sex-change programme. Erickson also funded a series of research symposia which ultimately, in 1979, became the Harry Benjamin International Gender Dysphoria Association (HBIGDA). This loose network of medical and mental health clinicians sought to advocate for transsexualism (as it was known at the time). In 2008, this organization was renamed the World Professional Association for Transgender Health (WPATH)[24] and is now the self-described authority on transgender care.

The publication of Benjamin's 1966 book, *The Transsexual Phenomenon*, sparked a rise in the demand for sex-change operations.[25] Transsexual patients' desire for surgeries and medical transition, rather than psychological exploration, set the tone for the development of trans health care for decades to come. Benjamin and Money didn't entirely agree on the theory; Benjamin believed that sex exists on a spectrum, while Money believed that it was our gender identity, and not our biological sex, that makes us a man or woman.

However, on one point they very much agreed: "sex-change operations", as they were known then, should be provided to those who seek them. Although these surgeries remained a fringe industry, sex change, as a concept, made its way into public consciousness, especially with the arrival of high-profile transwomen such as Christine Jorgensen, April Ashley, and Jan Morris. Now the concept of "gender identity" was well positioned to eventually supersede the importance of biological sex.

In the meantime, postmodernism was seeking to question our most basic assumptions about knowledge and Queer Theory was seeking to invert hierarchies and disrupt norms. In this perfect storm, our long-established understanding of sexual identity and gender was soon to be regarded as highly questionable and, ultimately, unfashionable.

The impact of Queer Theory on gender

Critical Theory, generally, seeks to examine and critique society and culture. Queer Theory, originating informally in the 1980s and then more formally in the early 1990s, is one branch of Critical Theory.[26] Emerging out of Queer Studies, Women's Studies, and the work of Michel Foucault, Queer Theory views common understandings of sex, sexuality, and gender as a form of power, control, and oppression and suggests we rethink everything we know about them. The central concept, "heteronormativity", points out that heterosexuality is the norm in society. The Queer Theory analysis of sexuality, however, differs from the moderate liberal position that homosexuality and bisexuality are healthy and normal variations of sexual orientation, albeit less common than heterosexuality. Rather, "heteronormativity" implies that heterosexuality is socially constructed and enforced oppressively to maintain the status quo and prevent non-normative sexuality.

The term "queer" has evolved significantly in its use, meaning, and scope over the last several decades. Today, however, it is used both as a noun and verb and is increasingly used to describe a broad spectrum of non-normative sexual orientations and gender identities. As a verb in today's context, it usually indicates a politically motivated disruption of sexuality and gender norms.[27] Judith Butler, a central figure in Queer Theory, claims that "gender reality is performative" and therefore we should consider a woman to be anyone who performs "womanhood".[28,29] Jay Stewart, CEO of Gendered Intelligence, states that "Queer theory and politics necessarily celebrate transgression in the form of visible difference from norms".[30]

With transgressing norms as its raison d'être, Queer Theory now opens the door for bearded males declaring themselves "women" and teenage girls insisting that they are gay boys.[31] Self-declaration (as a man, woman, or neither) becomes the most valid way to define terms, especially if the declaration disrupts hierarchy and defies normative categorical classification. According to the Gendered Intelligence Trans Youth Sexual Health Booklet, "A woman is still a woman, even if she enjoys getting blow jobs. A man is still a man, even if he likes getting penetrated vaginally. How you have sex need not affect your identity".[32]

Understanding the modern manifestations of Queer Theory, we can see that affirmation is the only possible response to an individual's declaration of gender. There is no stable, objective reality defining "gender", and therefore there are no valid challenges to an individual's stated gender identity. Each individual is who they say they are, and any challenge to a self-declared identity is a form of status-quo-preserving oppression. Body modification is viewed as a personal (and sometimes political) choice because it further facilitates the disruption of the so-called "arbitrary" constructs of sex and gender. This is a significant departure from gender identity theory, which suggests that body modification can be a medical necessity when someone's "gender identity" doesn't match their biological sex.

Yet, these apparently contradictory theories reach the same conclusion: every individual should be supported in their desire to call themselves a different gender and to medically transition if they so wish—no matter what age.

Furthermore, to respond in any way but agreement and compliance is considered harmful and oppressive. It's little wonder that physicians who subscribe to these theories have begun to medically transition children. They have sought to destroy the biological barriers, like puberty itself, which make "gender-confirmation" so challenging.

Experimental treatment paths

Before the 1980s, little had been written about childhood gender identity. At that time, even pioneers of transgender medicine, like John Money, understood that cross-gender identification in childhood was strongly correlated with homosexuality.[33]

Perhaps, because current research suggests that 61–98% of children with childhood gender dysphoria outgrow the condition by young adulthood, clinicians like Kenneth Zucker and Susan Bradley initially encouraged the individual to identify with their biological sex, and eventually developed a more neutral "watchful waiting" method to support the child in an unencumbered manner.[34,35]

GnRHa is a class of drugs that reduces the levels of sex hormones, testosterone, and estrogen. They have been used as a treatment to reduce the sex drive in male criminal sex offenders.[36] Informally known as puberty blockers, these drugs have also been utilized since the 1980s to treat "precocious puberty", which occurs when a child begins puberty before the age of eight in girls, and age nine in boys.

However, in the 2000s, clinicians in the Netherlands decided to study the efficacy of these drugs on children with gender dysphoria. Through an experimental pathway, the gender-dysphoric child would be started on puberty-suppressing drugs during the early stages of puberty. This would be followed by cross-sex hormones when the child is approximately sixteen years old (if there are no contraindications).[37] In a 2011 paper, these Dutch researchers suggested that the use of puberty blockers would give the young person time to contemplate whether they would like to pursue further intervention.[38]

In practice, however, almost all the adolescents in the study appeared to seek further medicalization. Of the seventy subjects, sixty-two were same-sex attracted.[39] Researchers found an overall improvement in functioning; however, there was no alleviation of gender dysphoria during the one-year follow-up. It is also unclear whether it was psychotherapy, puberty blockers, or other supports that helped improve functioning.

The clinicians in Amsterdam continued to follow this experimental treatment path, and in their second study, they followed fifty-five young adults from the original seventy participants.[40] According to a footnote in the study, despite each of the seventy participants initially stating they'd like to continue with further medicalization, several refused to participate in the follow-up and many of these fifteen participants developed complications that made them ineligible for surgery. The remaining fifty-five participants were assessed three times in total: at intake, after puberty suppression, and after cross-sex hormones (ages thirteen, sixteen, and twenty years old, respectively). Although researchers reported improvements in psychological functioning and subjective well-being in the fifty-five patients who had sex-change surgeries, there was no control group and one of the male participants died due to surgical complications. Thus, the "Dutch Protocol" was born, and these researchers inadvertently created the template for childhood medical transition.

It is notable that the physicians who pioneered the Dutch Protocol for puberty suppression have warned contemporary physicians about the experimental nature and lack of research on this kind of intervention.[41] The Dutch researchers have stated clearly that the population they studied is qualitatively different from the new cohort of adolescents seeking medical transition. Firstly, the Dutch study participants developed gender dysphoria at a very young age, while dysphoric adolescents today exhibit a sudden and dramatic arrival of gender issues around puberty. Additionally, the Dutch participants were highly functional and stable, from a psychological perspective, while today's gender-dysphoric adolescents display a high rate of clinically significant psychopathology.[42] As though hoping to return the explosive contents back into Pandora's box, the

Dutch researchers lament that "the rest of the world is blindly adopting [their] research".[43]

Thomas Steensma, lead researcher of the Dutch Protocol, expressed concern about the misapplication of their studies in clinics around the world when he said to the Dutch newspaper *Algemeen Dagblad:*

> More research is really needed, and very much needed ... We don't know whether studies we have done in the past are still applicable to today. Many more children are registering, and also a different type ... Little research has been done on the treatment with puberty inhibitors and hormones in young people. Therefore, it is also seen as experimental.[44]

Despite Steensma's disquiet, the Dutch Protocol has inadvertently become known as the foundation for all modern medical childhood transitions among gender-affirming therapists worldwide.

The emergence of "trans kids"

It is only within the last fifteen years or so that sensationalist stories in the media began to shape the public consciousness into believing that certain children were "born in the wrong body" and needed to medically transition as soon as possible.

In 2006, the poster child for childhood medical transition, Jazz Jennings, first came to prominence when she was profiled in the *Village Voice* and affirmed as a five-year-old "trans girl" (male child) with the pseudonym Nicole Anderson.[45]

At the same time, a conflict between gender identity and sexual orientation began to arise: "pre-gay" children, in their traits, mannerisms, and presentation, are remarkably similar to the newly defined "trans kids". So, it now fell on parents and clinicians to distinguish one from the other, and the risk of conflation remains unresolved to the present day.

In a 2007 paper, the psychotherapist Catherine Tuerk (who specializes in working with gender identity issues in gay boys) describes parents becoming more inclined to believe that those feminine male children were transgender girls rather than "pre-gay" boys. She points out, "This trend was initiated and supported by the intense interest in stories in the media of children beginning gender transition at early ages."[46]

It is very concerning, therefore, that the crusaders of the gender-identity movement seem uninterested in the future sexual orientation of the child. Their approach implies that gender trumps sex every time.

Diane Ehrensaft—whose fertility workshop we shall discuss in the next chapter—is a developmental psychologist and leading proponent of social and medical transition. Ehrensaft believes that all of a child's behavior is a type of communication about "gender". She makes the stunningly absurd claim that a baby girl tearing barrettes out of her hair repeatedly and a baby boy unsnapping his onesie to "make a dress" are both sending a "gender message" about being trans.[47]

Meanwhile, the endocrinologist Dr Norman Spack reports that he was "salivating" the first time he heard of the possibility of using puberty blockers on children.[48] Paediatric physician Johanna Olson-Kennedy, another true believer in the notion of the "transgender child", has become infamous for persuading a young gender-nonconforming girl that she's "really a boy on the inside" by using a metaphor about mislabelled pop tarts.[49] Olson-Kennedy has been awarded a $3.4m research grant by the National Institute of Child Health and Human Development of the NIH to study prepubescent trans and gender-nonconforming children at the Children's Hospital Los Angeles.[50]

Conclusion

Clinicians are in a position of great responsibility since we can have tremendous influence over our patients. To conclude, it would be helpful to recall the instructive example of multiple personality disorder—a similar therapy fad—given at the beginning of this chapter. One patient who was a victim of the MPD phenomenon in the mid-80s, Jeanette Bartha, who had struggled for years with depressive feelings, tells her story of seeking mental health support at this time: "I came with depression and left with multiple personalities."

Her psychiatrist, well trained in the psychological theory of MPD and repressed memories, knew the techniques to find "clues" about Jeanette's other "identities". And so it was (in pursuit of his diagnosis validation) that in one of their first sessions, he asked her repeatedly, "Who am I talking to?" She felt confused and uncertain about what he meant, but he continued to ask the question until she responded with the first name that came to her mind: *Danny*.[51] The psychiatrist soon introduced hypnotic drugs into their therapy sessions. He focused their treatment on her other "personalities" and on uncovering the (supposedly) repressed trauma. Over time, and through drug-induced suggestive questioning, Jeanette came to believe that she'd been horribly abused by her parents in a satanic cult and that she had many personalities living inside of her. Only after stopping treatment and coming off her medications did it become clear to her that nothing of the sort had ever happened.

Even as an adult, at the age of twenty-nine, when she first sought therapy, Jeanette was susceptible to the influence of authority, persuasion, and a diagnostic category with massive cultural relevance. This suggestibility is even greater in children, and therefore the responsibility of therapists and physicians treating gender-dysphoric youth is greater still. Theories to explain gender nonconformity and deviations in normative expression began with a concept of identity and subsequently converged with Queer Theory to culminate in the "transgender child". By the 2000s, trans advocacy was gaining momentum and influencing both psychological theory and treatment practices for children with gender issues. Both culturally captivating and financially lucrative, the "transgender child" has now emerged, and the concept has usurped the pre-gay child we've known of for decades. And to greet this modern-day archetype, medically experimental interventions are used with great urgency despite the warnings of those who see ominous portents all around.

Despite the lessons painfully learned throughout the history of psychiatry, once again a medical scandal has emerged.

Endnotes

1   "Gender Identity Development Services", The Tavistock and Portman NHS Foundation Trust 2022. Referrals to GIDS, financial years 2010-11 to 2020-21. https://gids.nhs.uk/number-referrals.

2   Lisa Marchiano, "Outbreak: On Transgender Teens and Psychic Epidemics", *Psychological Perspectives* 60, no. 3: 345–66, October 6, 2017, https://doi.org/10.1080/00332925.2017.1350804.

3   "Interactive Map: Clinical Care Programs for Gender-Expansive Children and Adolescents." Human Rights Campaign, accessed September 1, 2021, https://www.hrc.org/resources/interactive-map-clinical-care-programs-for-gender-nonconforming-childr.

4   Today, this is called Dissociative Identity Disorder (DID).

5   Flora Rheta Schreiber, *Sybil* (Valby, Denmark: Borgen, 1990).

6   Ian Hacking, *Rewriting the Soul: Multiple personality and the sciences of memory* (Darby, PA: Diane Publishing Co., 2003).

7   Allen J. Frances, "Multiple personality: Mental Disorder, Myth, or Metaphor?," *Psychology Today,* January 30, 2014, https://www.psychology-today.com/us/blog/saving-normal/201401/multiple-personality-mental-disorder-myth-or-.

8   Cyndy Hendershot, "Vampire and Replicant: The One-Sex Body in a Two-Sex World," *Science Fiction Studies* 22, no. 3: 373-98, November 1995, https://www.jstor.org/stable/4240458.

9   Thomas Laqueur, *Making Sex: Body and Gender From the Greeks to Freud* (Cambridge, MA: Harvard University Press, 1990), pp. 25-63.

10 Magnus Hirschfeld founded the Institute of Sexual Science in Berlin in 1919 and the World League for Sexual Reform in 1928.

11 Hirschfeld is credited with coining the terms "transvestite" and "transsexual".

12 Helen Joyce. *Trans: When Ideology Meets Reality* (London: Oneworld Publications, 2021), p. 13.

13 Ibid, p. 14.

14 Carl G. Jung and Herbert Read, "Researches into the Phenomenology of the Self," in *The Collected Works of C.G. Jung: Aion* (Princeton, NJ: Princeton University Press, 1959), 9:20.

15 Randy J. Nelson and Lance J. Kriegsfeld, *An Introduction to Behavioural Endocrinology,* rev.ed. (Sunderland, MA: Sinauer Associates, 2017).

16 Robert J. Stoller, "A Contribution to the Study of Gender Identity," *The International Journal of Psychoanalysis 45*, no. 2-3 (1964): pp. 220–226.

[17] John Money, "The concept of gender identity disorder in childhood and adolescence after 39 years," *Journal of Sex & Marital Therapy* 20, no. 3 (1994, published online 2008): 163-77, https://doi.org/10.1080/00926239408403428.

[18] Dwight B. Billings, and Thomas Urban, "The Socio-Medical Construction of Transsexualism: An interpretation and Critique," *Blending Genders* 29, no. 3 (1982, published online 2014): 129-148, https://doi.org/10.2307/800159.

[19] Sandi Mann, *Psychology: A Complete Introduction* (London: John Murray Learning, 2016).

[20] Associated Press. "David Reimer, 38, Subject of the John/Joan Case," *The New York Times*, May 12, 2004, https://www.nytimes.com/2004/05/12/us/david-reimer-38-subject-of-the-john-joan-case.html.

[21] Press, "David Reimer".

[22] Leah C. Schaefer and Connie C. Wheeler, "Harry Benjamin's first ten cases (1938-1953): A clinical historical note," *Archives of Sexual Behavior* 24, no. 1: 73-93, February 1995, https://doi.org/10.1007/BF01541990.

[23] Joyce, *Trans* p.20.

[24] World Professional Association for Transgender Health, WPATH 2022, www.path.org.

[25] Harry Benjamin, *The Transsexual Phenomenon* (New York: Ace Pub. Co., 1966).

[26] Annamarie Jagose. "Queer Theory." *New Dictionary of the History of Ideas.* Ed. Maryanne Cline Horowitz. Vol. 5. (Detroit: Charles Scribner's Sons, 2005).

[27] For example, "queering" womanhood may refer to anything from women wearing non-conforming clothing to a male person identifying as a woman while appearing rather masculine.

[28] Butler claims that the term "queer" should never be "fully owned, but always and only redeployed, twisted, queered from a prior usage and in the direction of urgent and expanding political purposes."

[29] Judith Butler, "Performative Acts and Gender Constitution: An Essay in Phenomenology and Feminist Theory." *Theatre Journal* 40, no. 4: 519–31, December 1988, https://doi.org/10.2307/3207893.

[30] Christina Richards, Walter P. Bouman, and Meg-John Barker, eds., *Genderqueer and Non-Binary Genders* (London: Palgrave MacMillian, 2017), p. 62.

[31] This idea of norm-transgression, a major theme in contemporary queer narratives, actually undermines Butler's theory of performativity, since performance *itself* requires a coherent set of behaviours and traits that

might constitute the "performance of womanhood," for example. Self-declaration becomes the highest form of epistemology, especially if the declaration disrupts hierarchy and defies normative categorical classification.

32 Gendered Intelligence, Trans Youth Sexual Health Booklet (London:Terence Higgins Trust).

33 John Money and Anthony J. Russo, "Homosexual outcome of discordant gender identity/role in childhood: Longitudinal follow-up," *Journal of Pediatric Psychology* 4 no. 1: 29–41, March 1979, https://doi.org/10.1093/jpepsy/4.1.29.

34 Thomas D. Steensma et al., "Factors associated with desistence and persistence of childhood gender dysphoria: a quantitative follow-up study," *Journal of the American Academy of Child and Adolescent Psychiatry 52, no. 6*: 582-90, April 3, 2013, https://doi.org/10.1016/j.jaac.2013.03.016.

35 Diane Ehrensaft, "Gender nonconforming youth: current perspectives," *Adolescent Health, Medicine and Therapeutics 8*: 57–67, May 25, 2017, https://doi.org/10.2147/ahmt.s110859.

36 David K. Ho et al., "Treatment with triptorelin in mentally disordered sex offenders: experience from a maximum-security hospital," *Journal of Clinical Psychopharmacology* 32, no. 5: 739-40, October 2012, http://dx.doi.org/10.1097/JCP.0b013e318266c6f5.

37 Henriette A. Delemarre-van de Waal and Peggy T. Cohen-Kettenis, "Clinical Management of Gender Identity Disorder in Adolescents: A Protocol on Psychological and Paediatric Endocrinology Aspects," *European Journal of Endocrinology* 155: 131-137, October 2006, https://doi.org/10.1530/eje.1.02231.

38 Annelou L. C. de Vries et al, "Puberty suppression in adolescents with gender identity disorder: a prospective follow-up study," *The Journal of Sexual Medicine* 8, no. 8 : 2276–2283, August 2011, https://doi.org/10.1111/j.1743-6109.2010.01943.x.

39 de Vries, "Puberty suppression".

40 Annelou L.C. de Vries et al., "Young Adult Psychological Outcome After Puberty Suppression and Gender Reassignment," *Pediatrics* 134, no. 4: 696-704, October 2014, https://doi.org/10.1542/peds.2013-2958.

41 Berendien Tetelepta, "Urgently needed more research into transgender care for young people: Where does the large flow of children come from?" *The Algemeen Dagblad*, February 27, 2021, https://www.ad.nl/nijmegen/dringend-meer-onderzoek-nodig-naar-transgenderzorg-aan-jongeren-waar-komt-de-grote-stroom-kinderen-vandaan~aec79d00/.

[42] Riittakerttu Kaltiala-Heino, Hannah Bergman, Marja Työläjärvi, and Louise Frisen, "Gender dysphoria in adolescence: current perspectives," *Adolescent Health, Medicine and Therapeutics*, 9, (2018): 31–41, https://doi.org/10.2147/ahmt.s135432.

[43] Grace Williams, "Dutch puberty-blocker pioneer: Stop 'blindly adopting our research'," 4th *Wave Now*, March 16, 2021, https://4thwavenow.com/2021/03/16/dutch-puberty-blocker-pioneer-stop-blindly-adopting-our-research/.

[44] Tetelepta, "Urgently needed research".

[45] Julia Reischel, "See Tom Be Jane," *The Village Voice*, May 30, 2006, https://www.villagevoice.com/2006/05/30/see-tom-be-jane/.

[46] Catherine Tuerk, "Considerations for Affirming Gender Nonconforming Boys and Their Families: New Approaches, New Challenges," *Child and Adolescent Psychiatric Clinics*, 20, no. 4: 767-777, October 2011, https://doi.org/10.1016/j.chc.2011.07.005.

[47] Peachyoghurt Genderfree, "How to tell if babies are transgender?", July 23, 2018, video, https://www.youtube.com/watch?v=M7KBZeRC1RI&t=10s.

[48] Anemona Hartocollis, "The New Girl in School: Transgender Surgery at 18," *The New York Times*, June 16, 2015, https://www.nytimes.com/2015/06/17/nyregion/transgender-minors-gender-reassignment-surgery.html.

[49] Dailymotion, "A trans kid is like a strawberry pop tart in the wrong package", 2019, video, https://www.dailymotion.com/video/x7kqndv.

[50] Children's Hospital Los Angeles, The Center for Transyouth Health and Development, "*Improving our understanding of children and gender*", Press release, April 8, 2019, https://www.eurekalert.org/news-releases/832679.

[51] Retro Report, "Is Multiple Personality Disorder Real? One Woman's Story," Retro Report video, 12:39, November 24, 2014, https://www.retroreport.org/video/sybil-a-brilliant-hysteric/.

Chapter 7

Transitioning Children—New Cohort, New Interventions

by Sasha Ayad and Stella O'Malley

On April 7, 2021, the developmental and clinical psychologist Dr Diane Ehrensaft led a Zoom training session for the University of California San Francisco Child and Adolescent Gender Center (UCSF CAGC) titled *Fertility Issues for Transgender and Nonbinary Youth.* Over 100 participants attended to hear Ehrensaft explain her recommendations for fertility preservation in transgender children. She acknowledged that "gender-affirming" medical interventions (puberty blockers, subsequent cross-sex hormones, and sometimes genital surgeries) render children sterile. Ehrensaft described egg harvesting and sperm preservation in children with a calm confidence that made light of the grave consequences. The justification for this radical medicalization, according to Ehrensaft, is that individuals struggling with fertility are not suicidal whereas "trans kids" are in that state. She provided zero evidence to support these wild assertions. Later, Ehrensaft made the sensational prediction that this medicalized pathway moves a child from "gender dysphoria to gender euphoria".[1]

One might presume that childhood "sex change", with its grave consequences of foreclosing on future fertility, stunting physical, and cognitive function, altering brain development, and impairing sexual function must be a well-researched and carefully executed form of treatment where no safer alternatives exist.[2,3,4,5,6]

One might also hope that such interventions have extremely high success rates to justify such a severe medical burden. And lastly, one might imagine such intervention is exceedingly rare, given that childhood gender issues must only affect the smallest minority of the population. However, based on our exploration in the previous chapter, we know none of these assumptions turn out to be true.

Referrals of children to the UK's largest gender clinic, Gender Identity Development Service (GIDS), at the Tavistock, in London, have seen a 1,607% increase in the last ten years.[7] In the Western world, countries such as Sweden, New Zealand, the United Kingdom, Canada, and Amsterdam have recorded dramatic exponential increases in youth seeking out gender-related services.[8,9,10]

Growing numbers of children struggling with their gender, along with a handful of politically—and ideologically—motivated physicians, psychologists, and transgender activists, are flooding the medical institutions, school systems, and psychological professions. It is seldom acknowledged that the more we seek out "education" on transgender issues, assessment tools, and treatment options for gender dysphoria, the more transgender identification we seem to create. This is known as iatrogenesis.

As therapists working in the field, the most common question we are asked is "How did this happen?" How can it be that medical "gender affirmation", as outlined in workshops such as Ehrensaft's, is now the norm for treating gender dysphoria in children? How can it be that counselors and therapists attending the fertility workshop showed little scepticism about the sterilization of children but left dozens of enthusiastic, gratitude-filled comments about how valuable the content will be for their expanding patient population? This chapter addresses this development by considering the following question: *what happens when a socially mediated epidemic meets Critical Social Justice Therapy?*

In order to answer this question, we first take a brief detour to examine how affirmative medical care, despite being highly controversial, came to be considered the gold standard of gender treatment for children. Next, we explore how Rapid-Onset Gender Dysphoria (ROGD) has rocketed into the social landscape, making transgender identity appealing to the most vulnerable unhappy teens. We then take a closer look at the characteristics of psychogenic illness and explore additional examples. Lastly, through discussing detransition, we expose the consequences of using a simplified social justice narrative to treat gender issues, particularly as it involves urgent and unrestricted access to irreversible medical intervention.

From conversion to affirmation

Conversion Therapy (also known as Reparative Therapy) is a highly controversial practice, broadly discredited as unethical, which aims to reduce homosexual attractions and encourage heterosexuality. Over the last several decades, these conversion practices ranged wildly. Hypnosis, castration, lobotomy, electroshock therapies, and other physical forms of torture have been employed to attempt to reduce homosexual attraction. Aversion therapies were aimed to pair disgust or pain with samesex attraction to undermine these attractions. Interventions with heterosexual pornography and prostitutes also attempted to turn gay men straight. As the gay rights movement emerged in the 1960s and 70s, efforts to de-medicalize homosexuality gained ground, and psychiatry and medicine started to abandon conversion therapies.

Perhaps the backdrop of such brutality and intolerance towards homosexuality helps explain the pendulum swing towards affirmation of whatever the client declares about herself.

The term "affirmative" offers a contrast to the damaging practices that were hitherto used when attempting to convert homosexual people to heterosexuality.[11] Today, most proposed bans on conversion therapy list gender identity along with sexual orientation, simply tacking on another identity category that a therapist mustn't challenge. Instead, the therapist must only "affirm".

On the surface, affirming sexual orientation seems similar to affirming gender identity, but they are quite different. In fact, affirming one usually requires a disavowal of the other. For example, imagine a young female client with same-sex attraction who is also claiming to be a boy. Affirming her sexual orientation as a lesbian requires some skepticism about her gender identity. And on the other hand, affirming her as a boy requires the therapist to interpret that she is not a lesbian, but a heterosexual boy. The inherent conflict between the needs of "trans kids" and "pre-gay kids" continues. One could say these conversion therapy bans are using a sledgehammer to crack a nut, as they severely restrict therapists from carrying out meaningful exploration of their clients' gender distress.

Affirmative gender care: the new standard

In 2012, World Professional Association for Transgender Health (WPATH) published its seventh version of the guidelines, *Standards of Care for the Health of Transsexual, Transgender, and Gender Nonconforming People*. Without a clear or standardized definition, most interpret the affirmative model of care as a pathway that includes:[12]

1. Social affirmation—name changes, pronoun changes, and generally treating the individual as belonging to their stated gender.
2. Psychological affirmation—mental health professionals are to view each individual as a member of their desired gender. Considering whether other pathology may be impacting the

child's declared "gender identity" is considered biased and unsupportive. The therapist follows the child's lead, even if the child wants immediate medical interventions.

3. Biomedical affirmation—hormonal and surgical interventions such as puberty blockers, cross-sex hormones, and/or surgeries that will alter the individual's appearance, sex characteristics, and/or reproductive system.

Systematic reviews of the SOC 7 guidelines have found them to be both vague and lacking in internal consistency.[13] There is no long-term, evidence-based research to support the affirmative model.[14] Additionally, what makes these guidelines so troubling is their interpretation of the physician and therapist's role. Any attempt by the provider to encourage birth-sex identification is proscribed. Instead, providers should help alleviate distress *related* to gender dysphoria and be prepared to support and encourage medical interventions for youth. In this manner, it understands gender dysphoria and transgender identity in a purely literal manner rather than a psychological or symbolic one.

This new standard of care laid out in SOC 7 can explain, at least in part, how seemingly rational professionals are keen to support childhood medical transition, despite the research that points to a 61–98% rate of childhood resistance, and the vast majority of these children growing up to be lesbian, gay, or bisexual.[15,16]

The American Psychological Association's (APA) task force on gender identity's 2015 recommendations also make it clear that the therapist's role has little to do with exploration, evaluation, or assessment; "trans-affirmative care" is the goal.[17] When working with a gay or lesbian person, therapists should "explain any discordance" through the lens of gender identity and "provide information" about transgender and gender nonconforming identities, "offer[ing] language" the patient can use to understand their experience, especially if the patient is unaware of the many different "gender identities" they can choose from. Further,

"Cisgenderism"—the recommendations claim—is a systemic bias that wrongly associates gender identity with "sex assigned at birth". It also warns that therapists familiar with gay, lesbian, and bisexual client populations may still be ill equipped to meet the needs of transgender and gender-nonconforming people.

So here, the APA tells us that decades of wisdom about gender noncomformity and gender expression in LGB people is now insufficient. Never mind that many LGB people live comfortably with cross-gender expression; instead, therapists should "educate" clients about newer contemporary identities.

The gender identity affirmative model encourages the therapist to reinterpret other symptomology through a gender-identity lens despite critics arguing that this can induce gender dysphoria more often than it resolves gender-related distress. The phrase "insistent, consistent, and persistent" is often used to clue in the parent or clinician about a child's potential for being transgender.[18] Bizarrely, the psychology or even the personality traits that might drive a certain type of child to be "insistent, consistent, and persistent" is roundly ignored by affirmative therapists.

In a 2019 EPATH Conference (the European version of WPATH), Dr Aidan Kelly posits that gender dysphoria may present as loneliness, autism, borderline personality, or depression, among others. Rather than asking if other mental distress makes children more susceptible to gender issues, the gender therapist holds the fundamental assumption that gender dysphoria is the root cause of other distress.

Proponents of the gender identity affirmative model seem to be influenced by both Gender Identity Theory and Queer Theory, defining gender identity as "the gender the child articulates as being—male, female, or something else".[19] The "something else" in this model could, at its extremity, manifest as innumerable different gender identities.

Currently, one can find hundreds of gender identities discussed in online forums. Dr Ehrensaft describes evolving categories which include "gender priuses, gender oreos, and gender smoothies".[20] Dr Ehrensaft also asserts that it doesn't matter how old a child is when first announcing a transgender identity. In fact, she labels children who first came out as gay and later transgender as "pro-totransgender". There seem to be no circumstance whatsoever in which the gender therapist can imagine that a child's self-diagnosis may be incorrect. In this worldview, gender identity swallows up all possible avenues for exploration. "Each individual will spin his or her own unique gender web, from threads of nature, nurture, and culture. Like fingerprints, no two gender webs will be exactly alike."[21] Indeed.

Rapid-onset gender dysphoria

Around 2016, Dr Lisa Littman, an OBGYN and public health researcher in the United States, noticed entire peer clusters "coming out" as transgender in her community. Littman sought to study what may be contributing to this remarkable and epidemiologically implausible development. Her peer-reviewed survey of 256, mostly politically liberal, parents indicated that an increase in social media use and other mental health diagnoses typically preceded their child's self-diagnosed gender dysphoria. This type of adolescent-onset gender questioning has been descriptively termed by Littman as Rapid-Onset Gender Dysphoria (ROGD).[22] Littman reports that 64% of these children have "one or more diagnoses of a psychiatric disorder or neurodevelopmental disability preceding the onset of gender dysphoria" and that trans identification among this population tends to follow extended periods of time spent online.[23]

Until very recently, gender dysphoria had mostly afflicted two main cohorts: pre-pubescent boys and middle-aged men. Suddenly, however, a new type of patient, the adolescent female, started presenting to gender clinics in droves. Transgender identification among adolescent girls at this scale is historically unprecedented and cannot simply be explained by greater social acceptance. Social contagion appears to be a factor; having a trans person in the friend group makes an adolescent seventy times more likely than the wider population to identify as trans.[24] In addition to the several thousand-fold increase of children referred to gender services in the UK and Ireland, in the USA the number of gender surgeries for biological females quadrupled between 2016 and 2017.[25] Sudden sharp rises among teenage boys reporting gender dysphoria have also raised concerns.[26]

Meanwhile, countries like Sweden, New Zealand,[27] Finland,[28] and Canada[29] have recorded similar dramatic exponential increases in youth seeking out gender-related services. As journalist Jon Kay wisely points out, this must be understood not as a purely novel presentation, since gender dysphoria is, in fact, a real condition, but instead, this is an issue of extrapolation whereby dysphoria is now impacting more and more people.[30]

Syndromes and mass psychogenic illness

If we are to fully understand why so many adolescents have suddenly fixated their mental distress upon their gender, we should further explore mass psychogenic illness. While we touched briefly on Multiple Personality Disorder and repressed memories in the previous chapter, we will now examine the way such phenomena develop and the reciprocal process by which novel forms of a mental health condition are created and maintained.

New syndromes evolve in a variety of ways. The philosopher Ian Hacking explains that new scientific classifications bring a new kind of person into being. He describes this as the phenomenon of "making up people".[31] We might also understand this as the creation of brand-new categories of people. When a person identifies himself with a diagnostic label, he is encouraged to take on all the features of that label.

The "looping effect" occurs when individuals also manifest their own unique version of that diagnostic label and this, in turn, changes the broader classification itself or creates new classifications.[32] In the example of gender identities, Hacking's "making up people" is arguably demonstrated with the "trans kid" descriptor; until this century, the concept of the "trans kid" simply did not exist, but it is now an accepted cohort. Likewise, the "looping effect" is perhaps evident in non-binary and other gender identities, as hitherto there had never been individuals known as "non-binary" or "agender"—these new identities are variations on the concept of "transgender people".

The neurologist, Suzanne O'Sullivan, points out that socially mediated conditions are passed on through "proximity, expectation, and embodiment".[33] Experts have identified several features of a psychogenic origin when there is a sudden outbreak of symptoms among a group of people. These include the lack of a plausible organic basis and the inability to perform an objective test for the condition, symptoms with rapid onset, the spread of symptoms through communication between individuals, a preponderance of female participants near puberty and adolescence, and the prior existence of high levels of stress and anxiety.[34]

In her book *The Sleeping Beauties,* O'Sullivan reports on an array of different manifestations of mass psychogenic illness. O'Sullivan's analysis of "Resignation Syndrome" in Sweden and the "Sleeping Sickness" in Kazakstan provides fascinating examples of psychogenic illness working through communities.

In Sweden, between 2003 and 2005, 424 cases of children fell asleep, as if in a coma, and remained catatonic for months. Some have remained in this state for years, and hundreds more cases have since been reported.[35] This appears to be a culture-bound syndrome; it is only found among refugees in Sweden and seems to be a response to the trauma of living in legal limbo as an asylum seeker.

Yet, for no apparent reason, a similarly strange syndrome afflicted the citizens of Kazakhstan in the years between 2010 and 2015. Approximately 130 residents of two small towns, Krasnogorsk and Kalachi, fell ill with a Sleeping Sickness.[36] Although many sufferers fell into a catatonic sleep, others demonstrated a "looping effect" and manifested new symptoms such as uncontrollable laughing, hallucinations, or convulsions.[37] The residents of the towns assumed a poison must have been causing the Sleeping Sickness, but no physical explanation was ever identified.

The mind has a powerful ability to mitigate chaos by seeking simple and imaginative explanations for unexplained phenomena. When considering the symptoms of others, people can become curious first, enraptured to understand the condition, then can re-interpret their own distress through the new lens of the condition. Individuals can become over-identified and begin to feel similar symptoms. Co-rumination, excessive empathy, reassurance, lengthy discussion of emotional problems, positive reinforcement, and competitive friendship cliques are found to be risk factors for social contagion. They amplify and facilitate identification with the symptoms of the culture-bound syndrome. It's worth noting that these behaviors are particularly common among teenage girls. Perhaps this explains why teenage girls are more prone to social contagion: because of their biopsychosocial stage of development and/or other societal factors.

To demonstrate how these types of contagions can be contained and mitigated, let's consider one more example. In 2011, in the town of LeRoy, some 350 miles north of Manhattan, teenagers began to develop outbursts that were similar to Tourette's syndrome—their faces spasmed, their arms jerked, and they let out involuntary grunts and shouts.[38] The teenage girls appeared on NBC News twitching and jerking on live television. This became the lead story for multiple news stations and media outlets around the world. This was only ten years after the film *Erin Brockovich,* and initially the residents of LeRoy thought—just as the residents of Krasnogorsk and Kalachi believed—that they were being poisoned, perhaps by toxins in the water or the soil. Indeed, Erin Brockovich appeared on ABC News to provide an analysis of what could be happening in LeRoy.

While the media and the broader public were fixated on tangible and physical causes of the condition, an extensive investigation found it highly unlikely that poisonous toxins were the culprit. The doctors staunchly insisted that these symptoms were psychosomatic.[39] Families were unhappy with the implication that their teenagers were in some way psychologically disturbed and withdrew in frustration. When the teenagers were removed from the malign influence of the hysterical media and the excessively zealous support, the teenagers' symptoms faded away. Ultimately, level-headed doctors were able to curb mass hysteria from getting completely out of control.

Affirmation: necessary but not sufficient

Sadly, level-headed doctors do not seem to be providing the same guidance to ROGD teenagers. Instead, the most zealous gender experts seem eager to encourage more cases of gender dysphoria.

Any competent therapist knows that we affirm our clients' emotions, we affirm their thoughts and beliefs, and we affirm and validate the depth of their distress, but we do not *confirm* their emotions, thoughts, or beliefs. To affirm the patient is to validate how they are feeling and yet ethical therapy must offer a good deal more than affirmation. Indeed, it is arguable that an affirmative approach to therapy is necessary but not sufficient.

The purpose of psychotherapy is to bring about psychological change, not to blindly celebrate the patient's perspective. Nor should we confirm that everything the individual thinks or wishes is literally true. Therapists help the patient to bring about psychological awareness, which allows the client to help themselves. Affirmation alone will not provide this opportunity.

The current affirmative model of therapeutic care suggests that therapists become akin to political advocates and facilitators of medical transition. Although therapists may need to provide support, support alone will not enable deeper understanding, change, or growth. Family and friends can provide support while therapists should strive to provide something more—effective and engaging treatment.

If we are to truly help our patients, we need to engage in a deeper therapeutic process than offering simple affirmations of what the client already believes. Instead, we need to complexify the narrative so that we can more fully understand the individual we are working with and the border difficulties associated with being an adolescent in the 21st century.

Gender dysphoria: a stand-in for general dysphoria

Why are large numbers of adolescents seeking to wipe out all traces of their previous identity? According to Suzanne O'Sullivan, "Culture-bound syndromes are often a metaphor for something that cannot be expressed more explicitly within a certain community",[40] This consideration feels particularly startling when we remember how unhappy and distressed many gender-dysphoric teenagers are today. Many of them share similar personality traits: they are intelligent, socially awkward, and quirky, and they often describe feeling a profound sense of alienation and loneliness. Many of these distressed kids seem afraid of their sexual development and have intense self-loathing about their bodies. These individuals belong to the iGen, the generation born after 1995. They became the first generation raised on cell phones and social media. Being of this digital generation, they turn to the internet to seek out answers to their emotional angst, while some theorize the devices themselves may exacerbate that angst.[41] Unfortunately, it seems they are not finding meaningful solutions to their problems, as this cohort has unprecedented rates of anxiety, depression, and other mental health issues.[42]

Detransition—the real impact of an abstract theory

As we have seen, ROGD appears to be a peer-mediated condition that is spread by social contagion among friend groups and online. When these vulnerable adolescents meet gender-affirmative clinicians, medical transition quickly ensues, arguably causing needless bodily harm to gender-dysphoric youth.

The culmination of a social contagion and an ideologically enforced abdication of therapeutic responsibility is demonstrated in the horrific experiences of detransitioners. They echo the terrible stories of other medical scandals such as the opioid crisis, the lobotomy movement, the thalidomide scandal, the Satanic ritual child abuse scandal (for which Dr Ehrensaft wrote a journal paper before she became focused on gender issues), and the Multiple Personality Disorder phenomenon outlined in the previous chapter.[43]

Detransitioners are individuals who underwent medical transition and discontinued medications, or had surgery to reverse the effects of transition, or both. Many detransitioners feel the entire transition process, and especially the affirmative therapeutic approach, was profoundly harmful to their mental and physical wellbeing.

A peer-reviewed study of 100 detransitioners offers us invaluable data which should inform future support for trans-identifying teens.[44] 60% of the respondents detransitioned because they became more comfortable identifying as their natal sex; 38% detransitioned because they came to the view that their gender dysphoria was caused by something specific such as trauma, abuse, or a mental health condition; and 55% of respondents felt that they did not receive an adequate evaluation from a doctor or mental health professional before starting their medical transition. The fact that only 24% of respondents had informed their clinicians that they had detransitioned suggests that the true figures of detransition are difficult to ascertain.[45]

In 2020, Keira Bell, a detransitioned woman and ex-GIDs patient, was named as a claimant on the Judicial Review in the UK that argued against the use of puberty blockers as an appropriate treatment for young children. Bell was a troubled adolescent when she first attended the Tavistock GIDS clinic at the age of sixteen, and describes how it was damaging that she "was welcomed and affirmed as a boy" at GIDS.[46] She was prescribed puberty blockers after three one-hour-long appointments, prescribed cross-sex hormones a year after she started puberty blockers, and a couple of years later had a double mastectomy (euphemistically termed "top surgery"). "I was allowed to run with this idea that I had, almost like a fantasy, as a teenager ... and it has affected me in the long run as an adult."

Bell has now detransitioned, regrets the entire process, and believes the gender identity affirmative model was to blame. "I should have been challenged on the proposals or the claims that I was making for myself," she said. "And I think that would have made a big difference as well. If I was just challenged on the things I was saying."[47]

Conclusion

The enthusiasm to educate clients about potential diagnoses is not a new phenomenon; however, while eccentric and esoteric psychological theories can open doors for new treatments in psychotherapy, they should only be considered through a very cautious lens.

The gender-affirmative approach to gender-dysphoric young people has been adopted widely because we have failed to scrutinize its genesis and have blindly ignored our field's contribution to this epic iatrogenesis. This literalized and medicalized approach to gender dysphoria has had profoundly damaging psychological, physical, and emotional effects on the patients it purports to serve. In other socially mediated psychological epidemics, the condition begins to fade out of the population when clients, who were harmed by the eccentric theories, tell their stories.

Perhaps now, we are at a tipping point, with more detransitioners going public about their harrowing experiences. They will need a vast amount of support to process their traumatizing slog through this "affirmative" modality of care. In the meantime, though, the integrity of psychotherapy needs to be vigorously defended.

We implore psychotherapists treating gender-dysphoric youth to return to the well-worn and empirically validated treatments which have served our clients for many decades. We need to build an honest relationship, remain interested in the client as a unique, individual person, and stay curious about underlying issues, family dynamics, personality traits, and childhood experiences. Perhaps, we could all do well to regain a symbolic understanding of what a young person means when they say, "I'm not who you think I am."

Endnotes

[1] 4thWaveNow, "TMI: Genderqueer 11-year-olds can't handle too much info about sterilizing treatments–but do get on with those treatments," 13 April, 2021, accessed September 5, 2021, https://4thwavenow.com/2021/04/13/tmi-genderqueer-11-year-olds-cant-handle-too-much-info-about-sterilizing-treatments-but-do-get-on-with-those-treatments/.

[2] Peter Hayes, "Commentary: Cognitive, emotional, and Psychosocial functioning of Girls treated with Pharmacological Puberty blockage for Idiopathic central precocious puberty," *Frontiers in Psychology* 8, (2017), article no. 44 https://doi.org/10.3389/fpsyg.2017.00044.

[3] Krishna K. Bangalore, John S. Fuqua, Alan D. Rogol, Karen O. Klein, Jadranka Popovic, Christopher P. Houk, Evangelia Charmandari, and Peter A. Lee, "Use of Gonadotropin-Releasing Hormone analogs in Children: Update by an international consortium," *Hormone Research in Paediatrics*, 91, no. 6 (2019): 357–372, https://doi.org/10.1159/000501336.

[4] Sebastian E. Schagen, Femke M. Wouters, Peggy T. Cohen-Kettenis, Louis J. Gooren, and Sabine E. Hannema, "Bone development in transgender adolescents treated wth GNRH analogues and Subsequent Gender-Affirming Hormones," *The Journal of Clinical Endocrinology & Metabolism*, 105, no. 12 (2020): e4252–e4263, https://doi.org/10.1210/clinem/dgaa604.

[5] Annemieke S. Staphorsius, Baudewijntje P.C. Kreukels, Peggy T. Cohen-Kettenis, Dick J. Veltman, Sarah M. Burke, Sebastian E.E. Schagen, Femke M. Wouters, Henriëtte A. Delemarre-van De Waal, Julie Bakker, "Puberty suppression and executive functioning: An fmri-study in adolescents with gender dysphoria," *Psychoneuroendocrinology*, 56 (2015): 190–199, https://doi.org/10.1016/j.psyneuen.2015.03.007.

[6] Tim C. van de Grift, Zosha J. van Gelder, Margriet G. Mullender, Thomas D. Steensma, Annelou L.C. de Vries, Mark-Bram Bouman, "Timing of puberty suppression and surgical options for transgender youth," *Pediatrics*, 146, no. 5 (2020) https://doi.org/10.1542/peds.2019-3653.

[7] Gender Identity Development Services, The Tavistock and Portman. Referrals to GIDS,financial years 2010-11 to 2020-21, https://gids.nhs.uk/number-referrals.

[8] John W. Delahunt, H.J. Denison, D.A. Sim, J.J. Bullock, J.D. Krebs, "Increasing rates of people identifying as transgender presenting to Endocrine Services in the Wellington region," *N Z Med J.* 131, no. 1468 (2018):33-42. PMID: 29346355.

[9] Nastasja de Graaf, Guido Giovanardi, Claudia Zitz, Claudia; Polly Carmichael, "Sex Ratio in Children and Adolescents Referred to the Gender Identity Development Service in the UK (2009–2016)," *Archives of Sexual Behavior,* (2018): 47. 10.1007/s10508-018-1204-9.

[10] Ibid.

[11] Susan Bradley and Ken Zucker, "Children With Gender Nonconformity: Drs. Bradley and Zucker reply," *Journal of the American Academy of Child & Adolescent Psychiatry* 42, no. 3 (2003): 266–268, https://doi.org/10.1097/00004583-200303000-00004.

[12] Marco A. Hidalgo, Diane Ehrensaft, Amy C. Tishelman, Leslie F. Clark, Robert Garofalo, Stephen M. Rosenthal, Norman P. Spack, Johanna Olson, "The Gender Affirmative Model: What We Know and What We Aim to Learn," *Human Development*, 56, no. 5 (2013): 285–290, https://doi.org/10.1159/000355235.

[13] Sara Dahlen, Dean Connolly, Isra Arif, Muhammad Hyder Junejo, Susan Bewley and Catherine Meads, "International clinical practice guidelines for gender minority/trans people: Systematic review and quality assessment," *BMJ Open*, 11, no. 4 (2021), https://doi.org/10.1136/bmjopen-2021-048943.

[14] Eli Coleman, Walter Bockting, Marsha Botzer, Peggy Cohen-Kettenis, Griet Cuypere, Jamie Feldman, Lin Fraser, Jamison Green, Gail Knudson, Walter Meyer, Stan Monstrey, Richard Adler, George Brown, Aaron Devor, Randall Ehrbar, Randi Ettner, Randi, Evan Eyler, Robert Garofalo, Dan Karasic, and Kenneth Zucker, "Standards of Care for the Health of Transsexual, Transgender, and Gender-Nonconforming People, Version 7," *International Journal of Transgenderism,* 13, no 4 (2012):165-232, http://dx.doi.org/10.1080/15532739.2011.700873.

[15] Thomas D. Steensma 1, Jenifer K. McGuire, Baudewijntje P. C. Kreukels, Anneke J.Beekman, Peggy T Cohen-Kettenis "Factors associated with desistence and persistence of childhood gender dysphoria: a quantitative follow-up study," *J Am Acad Child Adolesc Psychiatry*, 52, no. 6 (Jun 2013): 582-90. doi: 10.1016/j.jaac.2013.03.016.

[16] Kelley D. Drummond, Susan J. Bradley, Michele Peterson-Badali, and Kenneth J. Zucker, "A follow-up study of girls with gender identity disorder," *Developmental Psychology, 44, no. 1 (2008):* 34–45, Doi: 10.1037/0012-1649.44.1.34. Devita Singh, Susan Bradley and Ken Zucker. "A Follow-Up Study of Boys With Gender Identity Disorder," *Front. Psychiatry*, (2021), https://doi.org/10.3389/fpsyt.2021.632784.

17 "Guidelines for psychological practice with transgender and gender non-conforming people." *American Psychologist*, 70, no. 9 (2015): 832–864. https://doi.org/10.1037/a0039906.

18 Christine Aramburu Alegría, "Supporting families of transgender children/youth". *Today's Transgender Youth,* 19, no. 2 (2020): 132-143. https://doi.org/10.1080/15532739.2018.1450798.

19 Marco A. Hidalgo, Diane Ehrensaft, Amy C. Tishelman, Leslie F. Clark, Robert Garofalo, Stephen M. Rosenthal, Norman P. Spack, Johanna Olson, "The Gender Affirmative Model: What We Know and What We Aim to Learn", *Human Development* 56 (2013): 285-290. Doi: 10.1159/000355235.

20 Diane Ehrensaft, "From gender identity disorder to gender identity creativity: True gender self child therapy," *Treating Transgender Children and Adolescents,* (2014): 55-74. https://doi.org/10.1080/00918369.2012.653303.

21 Ibid.

22 Lisa Littman, "Parent reports of adolescents and young adults perceived to show signs of a rapid onset of gender dysphoria," *Yearbook of Paediatric Endocrinology*, (2019), doi:10.1530/ey.16.6.13.

23 Ibid.

24 Ibid.

25 Abigail Shrier, *Irreversible Damage: The Transgender Craze Seducing Our Daughters* (Washington DC: Regnery Publishing, 2020).

26 Angus Fox, "When Sons Become Daughters: Parents of Transitioning Boys Speak Out on Their Own Suffering," *Quillette,* (April 02, 2021), https://quillette.com/2021/04/02/when-sons-become-daughters-parents-of-transitioning-boys-speak-out-on-their-own-suffering/.

27 Delahunt, "Increasing rates of people identifying".

28 Riittakerttu Kaltiala-Heino, Maria Sumia, Marja Työläjärvi and Nina Lindberg, "Two years of gender identity service for minors: overrepresentation of natal girls with severe problems in adolescent development," *Child and Adolescent Psychiatry and Mental Health* 9 (2015): article 9. https://doi.org/10.1186/s13034-015-0042-y.

29 Madison Aitken, Thomas D. Steensma, Ray Blanchard, Doug P. VanderLaan, Hayley Wood, Amanda Fuentes, Cathy Spegg, Lori Wasserman, Megan Ames, C. Lindsay Fitzsimmons, Jonathan H. Leef, Victoria Lishak, Elyse Reim, Anna Takagi, Julia Vinik, Julia Wreford, Peggy T. Cohen-Kettenis, Annelou L.C. de Vries, Baudewijntje P. C. Kreukels, Kenneth J. Zucker, "Evidence for an altered sex ratio in clinic-referred adolescents

with gender dysphoria," *J Sex Med.* 12, no. 3 (Mar 2015):756-63. doi: 10.1111/jsm.12817.

[30] Jonathan Kay, "The search to explain our anxiety and depression: Will 'long covid' become the next gender ideology?, *Quillette,* (April 16, 2021) Accessed May 03, 2021, https://quillette.com/2021/04/15/the-search-to-explain-our-anxiety-and-depression-will-long-covid-become-the-next-gender-ideology/.

[31] Ian Hacking, "Making Up People," *London Review of Books*, (17 August 2006), Vol.28, No. 16. https://www.lrb.co.uk/the-paper/v28/n16/ian-hacking/making-up-people.

[32] Ibid.

[33] Suzanne O'Sullivan. *The Sleeping Beauty and Other Stories of Mystery Illness* (London: Pan McMillan, 2021), p. 130.

[34] Robert E. Bartholomew. *Little green men, meowing nuns and head-hunting panics: A study of mass psychogenic illness and social delusion* (Jefferson, NC: McFarland & Company, 2001).

[35] O'Sullivan, *The Sleeping Beauties*, p. 28.

[36] Ibid, p. 91.

[37] Ibid.

[38] Nicholas Jackson, "It Could Just Be Stress: The Teens of LeRoy and ConversionDisorder." The Atlantic, (5 August 2012), https://www.theatlantic.com/health/archive/2012/02/it-could-just-be-stress-the-teens-of-leroy-and-conversion-disorder/252582/.

[39] O'Sullivan, *The Sleeping Beauties*.

[40] Ibid, p. 89.

[41] Jean Twenge, *Igen why today's Super-Connected kids are growing up Less rebellious, more tolerant, Less happy-and completely unprepared For adulthood*: *(And what This means for the rest of us)* (New York: Atria Publishing, 2017).

[42] Ibid.

[43] Diane Ehrensaft, "Preschool child sex abuse: The aftermath of the Presidio case." *American Journal of Orthopsychiatry* 62, no. 2 (1992): 234-244. https://doi.org/10.1037/h0079332.

[44] Lisa Littman, "Individuals Treated for Gender Dysphoria with Medical and/or Surgical Transition Who Subsequently Detransitioned: A Survey of 100 Detransitioners." *Archives of Sexual Behavior,* Vol. 50,8 (2021): 3353-3369. doi:10.1007/s10508-021-02163-w. .

[45] Ibid.

[46] Keira Bell, "Protect Gender Dysphoric Children from the Affirmation Model", (2020), https://www.crowdjustice.com/case/challenge-innate-gender/.

[47] Alison Holt, "NHS gender clinic 'should have challenged me more' over transition", BBC News, 1 March, 2020, https://www.bbc.com/news/health-51676020.

Chapter 8:

Critical Social Justice in the Consulting Room with Gender-Dysphoric Children—How Applied Postmodernism Undermines the Search for Resilience

by Lisa Marchiano

For the last century, talk therapies have aimed to address personal suffering by helping people resolve internal conflicts, grow more resilient, and develop new skills for responding to adverse circumstances. In the face of irremediable suffering, psychotherapy helps people to grieve losses, cultivate acceptance, and make meaning of tragedy. Recent incursions of Critical Social Justice (CSJ) theories into the realm of psychotherapy threaten to undermine psychotherapy's ability to help in these ways. In their book *Cynical Theories,* James Lindsey and Helen Pluckrose identify four main themes of applied postmodernism: the blurring of boundaries, the power of language, cultural relativism, and the loss of the individual and universal in favor of group identity.[1] Although all four of these themes play a role in cutting us off from inner resources that can help us address suffering, I will be focusing on two of these: the blurring of boundaries and the loss of the individual and universal.

To explore how CSJ undermines psychotherapeutic treatment, I will be examining current modalities for addressing gender dysphoria in children and young people. I intend to trace the influence of postmodern thinking on psychotherapy practice "on the ground", to show how these ideas have shaped practice in the consulting room and how this is eroding the practice of therapy. The affirmative model of care, as elaborated by Diane Ehrensaft, among others, has become the dominant way of working in therapy with gender-dysphoric children and youth in the United States and has been endorsed by most major professional organizations.[2,3] It has been directly influenced by Queer Theory, which separates gender from sex and asserts that both are socially constructed.[4]

An affirmative approach requires that practitioners validate a child's belief that he or she is transgender with minimal exploration. Therefore, it subverts several essential principles of psychotherapy, which aim to help clients adapt to reality and make their own meaning out of their experience rather than having this imposed on them by the therapist. By looking at affirmative care, we can see how the blurring of boundaries along with the loss of the individual and the universal have eroded foundational principles of therapy in this area of practice and made it difficult for therapists to help clients cultivate resilience and acceptance.

Psychotherapy

The term "psychotherapy" comes from two Greek words meaning something like "care of the soul". Psychotherapy, therefore, is an endeavor that aims to address our deepest, most personal suffering. The focus of inquiry and intervention is on the level of the individual in front of us in the consulting room.

Because it focuses on the personal, psychotherapy has been accused of being a means of shifting the blame for society's ills onto the backs of individuals and ignoring the wider systemic issues that may be at play.[5] This critique has merit. I witnessed this as a social work intern on an inpatient psychiatric unit in a New York City hospital. I was with several senior male psychiatrists, a male psychiatric resident, and a female Ph.D. psychology intern. All of us were white.

We were interviewing a woman who had immigrated from the Dominican Republic and was living in a public housing complex in the Bronx notorious for drug-related crimes. This woman had been hospitalized due to paranoid delusions and hallucinations. As we sat with her that day, she was calm but hesitant and deferential. The psychiatrists were trying to persuade her to continue taking her antipsychotic medication, but she wanted to speak to us of her fears—that her young adult son would be murdered by the drug gangs that ruled the complex or that she would be hit by a stray bullet. The others on the team sidestepped these fears and continued to insist that the medication would take care of these problems, but I wasn't so sure. Although, as the most junior person on the team, I didn't dare to say anything, I thought to myself that her concerns seemed at least somewhat reality-based. By framing her fears as delusional and paranoid, we located the cause of the problem in her, covering up or denying the very real outer forces that were impacting her and her family.

It should go without saying that social forces affect our lives on a personal level in profound ways, and even our most private suffering is nested within a social context. The biopsychosocial model has been integrated into mainstream therapies for many years. It incorporates an understanding of the social factors that may be influencing or causing a client's distress while leaving room for exploration of intrapsychic or physical contributors. It can therefore serve as a corrective to an approach that sees all pathology as the result of personal factors.[6]

Yet, psychotherapy is essentially an intervention at the level of the individual.[7] It has proven to be effective at helping clients reduce or manage distress in their personal lives, but it has not traditionally concerned itself with systems-level change.

CSJ theories have altered this focus away from the individual to center on identity group affiliation as the locus of inquiry. The change in focus, in and of itself, renders psychotherapy less effective, as few interventions can be applied at this level of analysis. Rather than helping a client change what can be changed in the inner or outer environment, an emphasis on group identity conflict and oppression is likely to leave a client feeling outraged but also disempowered.[8]

The blurring of boundaries

Postmodern thought is characterized by a suspicion of previously commonly accepted categories and boundaries.[9] We see this most strikingly perhaps in Queer Theory, which "regards the very existence of categories of sex, gender, and sexuality to be oppressive".[10] Queer Theory downplays the importance of biological sex, implying that sex itself is socially constructed. Key Queer Theorist, Judith Butler, suggests that biological sex is not in and of itself a foundational reality.

> If the immutable character of sex is contested, perhaps this construct called 'sex' is as culturally constructed as gender; indeed, perhaps it was always already gender, with the consequence that the distinction between sex and gender turns out to be no distinction at all.[11]

Sometime in the 2000s, these arcane beliefs were imported into the consulting room via practitioners.[12] In their influential 2008 book for parents, Stephanie Brill and Rachel Pepper explain that "gender is not actually inherently connected to one's bodily anatomy. Biological sex and gender are very different".[13]

Brill and Pepper go on to discuss culturally proscribed gender norms and acknowledge that these are mostly culturally constructed. However, they then assert that one's sense of gender is an innate, unchangeable aspect of core identity. With this assertion, they displace anatomy as that which determines sex, replacing it with gender identity. "People do not choose to feel like a boy or a girl, or like both, or neither. They simply are who they are. From this perspective, transgender people and all people whose gender identity does not align with their anatomical sex are simply born this way."[14]

Here we see the confusion wrought in the wake of jettisoning biological sex. Queer Theory teaches that categories themselves are oppressive, but in fact, categories are conceptual tools that allow us to navigate complex situations with more ease. Grouping people into the naturally occurring categories of male and female is an innate ability that is arguably essential for negotiating the world, especially when it comes time to reproduce or evaluate safety. Brill and Pepper have effectively supplanted biological sex with gender identity. We can see the downstream effects that this has had on clinical work with gender-variant children by exploring the writings of other practitioners.

In her work with gender-dysphoric children and youth, Diane Ehrensaft practises according to the affirmative model of care. In a paper published in 2017, Ehrensaft describes the basic principle of this approach: "When it comes to knowing a child's gender, it is not for us to tell, but for the children to say."[15]

She goes on to purport that once a clinician has fully assessed a child's "gender status", that child should be supported in making a social or even medical transition regardless of the child's age.[16] "Such decision-making is governed by stages, rather than ages, both for social transitions and later for medical interventions. Once the child's gender comes into clear focus, which is posited as happening with a child of any age, no need is seen to hold off until adolescence to affirm that gender."[17]

In a paper published in 2014, Ehrensaft describes working with a ten-year-old girl with gender dysphoria. At the urging of Ehrensaft, the child's mother presented her daughter with the possibility of puberty blockers. The introduction of this option, at first, made the child distressed but eventually led the child to make a declarative statement about herself. Ehrensaft describes this moment as it occurred in treatment: "Jacqueline, who rarely made direct eye contact except when beating me at a board game, slowly looked up and said, 'I'm pretty sure I'm a boy.'"[18] The child did indeed go on to take puberty blockers, according to Ehrensaft's report.

But Jacqueline was not, in fact, a boy, regardless of how she felt. The basis for believing that this child needed to embark on a project to artificially delay puberty comes directly from postmodern-inspired theories that say that it is gender identity and not biology that should be determinative. And yet, gender identity is not even a clearly defined concept, much less an empirically supported one. Puberty blockers given to children for gender dysphoria disrupt normal development and lead to decreased bone density and certain infertility when followed by cross-sex hormones.[19]

Meanwhile, the evidence in their favor has been subject to several recent systematic reviews, including a 2020 one conducted by the UK National Institute for Health and Care Excellence or NICE. The NICE review found that puberty blockers result in little or no change in such metrics as gender dysphoria, mental health, body image, or psychosocial functioning. The reviewers noted that the studies evaluated in the review had results of "very low" certainty.[20]

A necessary part of life is mourning—that which cannot be changed—so that we can adapt to reality. Disguising or misrepresenting biological facts to a child or teen distorts her relationship with her embodied reality and may make it more difficult for her to make healthy choices. Poor choices in turn may have real consequences for her long-term physical and psychological health.

The importance of the individual

Informed by applied postmodernism, the affirmative model of care for gender-dysphoric children and youth rests on a foundational assumption that each person has a gender identity that may be mismatched with one's biological sex. Though gender identity is a poorly defined concept that rests on a purely subjective feeling, according to the affirmative model, we are meant to offer children "support for them to evolve into their authentic gender selves, no matter what the age".[21] In this context, a child with gender dysphoria is understood not as an individual, but as a "trans child"—a member of an oppressed group.

Affirmation is a "one size fits all" treatment approach. Dysphoria is seen as having only one possible cause and one possible solution, and that is a transition (either social or social and medical, depending on the age of the child). Rather than exploring all aspects of a child's inner and outer life that may contribute to the feelings of distress, treatment focuses on validating the child's belief that her body and gender identity do not match and that, therefore, *her body is wrong*.

In the therapy that follows, gender eclipses other issues. Any other symptoms that may be present are understood to be a result of "cultural reactions" (e.g., transphobia, homophobia, sexism) rather than from within the child.[22] The patient ceases to be seen as a wholly unique and complex person whose life is embedded in a particular context. Her feelings and experiences are interpreted exclusively through the lens of group identity.

Without the ability to explore the nuances and particularities of her experience, the client is offered only one way to understand what she is going through. With a single story about the nature of her suffering, a single solution is offered. Seeing our life solely through a group identity lens offers us a borrowed narrative that traps us in a narrow story of disempowerment because we are not free to make our own meaning of our experience. It is also inimical to mental health because a sense of ourselves as an individual is vital to the kind of "meaning-making" that is required to bear suffering.

Encouraging a young patient to see herself only through the lens of group membership makes it difficult for her to ponder her uniqueness and individuality. It also robs her of what may be the only true agency we have—that of deciding for ourselves how to make meaning of suffering that cannot be assuaged or removed. According to Viktor Frankl, "The last of one's freedoms [is] to choose one's attitude to any given set of circumstances, to choose one's own way".[23,24]

In the end, we live our life as an individual, and we interact with the world as an individual. We love as an individual, and we grow old and die as an individual. The Swiss psychiatrist, Carl Jung, famously noted this.[25] "In the last analysis, the essential thing is the life of the individual. This alone makes history, here alone do the great transformations first take place, and the whole future, the whole history of the world, ultimately spring as a gigantic summation from these hidden sources in individuals."[26]

It is, above all, the individual we tend to in therapy, not an identity group or a social movement, and it is at the level of our individual lives that we are able to (and must) make meaning. Jung recognized this. "The real carrier of life is the individual. He alone feels happiness, he alone has virtue and responsibility and any ethics whatsoever. The masses and the state have nothing of the kind ... Anyone, therefore, who thinks in terms of men minus the individual, in huge numbers, atomizes himself and becomes a thief and a robber to himself."[27]

When we frame all problems strictly in terms of group identity and oppression, we take away from patients their ability to adapt to their individual reality and to make their own meaning.

The importance of the universal

According to the affirmative model of care, the distress a young person feels about his or her body is understood as evidence that she is transgender—a new category of human experience divorced from historical context. (Although there have always been gender-nonconforming people, it wasn't possible to consider the possibility of medical transition until the recent development of hormones and surgeries.)

Affirmative care for youth exceptionalizes gender dysphoria, taking an entirely normal and universal experience of feeling uncomfortable with one's body in adolescence and construing it as a special experience that requires a radical treatment approach. It, therefore, removes dysphoria—a Greek word that simply means "suffering"—from its very human context.

When a young client comes to us with gender dysphoria, it would be important to explore the unique aspects of her experience, but it would also be key to contextualize her experience by letting her know that others have suffered as she has. This will be especially important in the case of same-sex attracted young people who may not realize that gender dysphoria is a common struggle that often occurs in the process of the consolidation of a same-sex orientation. Because Queer Theory rejects the concept of a common human nature, the possibility of experiencing the comforting universality of our painful experiences is denied us. Instead of offering the profound and ordinary solace that we are not alone, we are offered a grandiose promise of specialness. This may feel good in the immediate term, but longer term it leaves us isolated and stranded from the rest of humanity.

In recent years, there has been a dramatic rise in the number of young people seeking hormones and surgeries for gender dysphoria—and most of these are adolescent females.[28] This shouldn't be surprising. Adolescence is a time when one begins to question one's place in the world.

In our culture, the trials of adolescence are frequently belittled or pathologized—the angsty teen is a trite trope. But the challenges faced on the lonely and often frightening road to adulthood are anything but trivial. It isn't a coincidence that many of the world's great novels deal with coming of age and treat themes of estrangement and existential loneliness.

At some point in life, everyone struggles with issues of meaning, belonging, safety, and self-acceptance. These are not insignificant matters—they go to the very core of what it means to be human.

There are no pat or easy answers to these questions, and we ought to be suspicious of any ideology that offers one. Understanding that our suffering is part of the universal human experience can give us a sense of connection with those who have come before us. It can make us feel less alone, and it is also essential to the meaning-making process. Jungian analyst Marion Woodman has written that "Without an understanding of myth, without an understanding of the relationship between destruction and creation, death and rebirth, the individual suffers the mysteries of life as meaningless mayhem alone".[29] With a connection to the universal aspects of the human experience, our suffering is part of the mysteries of life. This makes our suffering bearable. Without such a connection, we are hapless victims.

There is a Buddhist tale about a woman named Kisa Gotami, who lost her only son, a young child. She refused to accept his death and carried his lifeless body through the streets, begging someone to give her medicine to bring him back to life. At last, she went to the Buddha and asked him to bring her son back. He told her that before he could do that, she needed to bring him a handful of mustard seeds from a home that had not been touched by loss and sorrow. She looked far and wide for such a home, but, of course, she found none. This helped her to realize the universality of death and suffering.

We understand intuitively that when we feel connected with others who have suffered as we have, it is a balm to our anguished souls. No life is free from suffering. When we meet suffering with an open heart, then it transforms us.

Grieving is the painful process by which we disinvest our energy from a beloved person, object, belief, or plan so that we can invest this energy elsewhere. Grief requires an acceptance of the situation as it is, no matter how much we may dislike it. Psychotherapy can facilitate mourning so that patients can accept that which cannot be changed and move forward into life. Therapeutic approaches that cut us off from a universal perspective make it harder for us to do this important work.

When we face a challenging circumstance that cannot be remedied, we will need to find acceptance. In these cases, making meaning of the suffering will be an important aspect of bearing the pain. "In some ways," wrote Victor Frankl, "suffering ceases to be suffering at the moment it finds a meaning."[30]

The great philosophical, mythological, and religious traditions of the world all address meaning-making in the face of loss and suffering as a central aspect of their teachings. They offer us a wider, larger-than-self context in which to understand our suffering.

In contrast, CSJ theories provide a single narrow story—that our suffering is the result of oppression. This understanding militates against acceptance and short circuits our ability to access a larger-than-self perspective that would help us place our suffering in its universal context. Making meaning from suffering is a spiritual act, a demanding process of coming to terms with our fate. There is no shortcut for this. No one can hand us a ready-made meaning that has integrity. It has to be hard-won.

Conclusion

Traditionally, psychotherapy has aimed to help clients change things in their inner or outer environment that may be painful or not in the service of adaptation. Where a change is not possible, therapy aims to help patients mourn, accept, and, when ready, to move forward. Doing so fosters resilience, as we are then helping clients to handle the hardships they will inevitably face rather than encouraging them to feel wronged when difficulties arise.

As applied postmodernism has influenced psychotherapeutic practices, it has undermined therapy's ability to help people mourn and reach acceptance. Furthermore, when we teach young people that the main cause of their suffering has to do with them being a member of an oppressed group, we cut them off from possible sources of meaning and comfort. We encourage a mentality of victimhood which keeps them trapped in outrage and powerlessness.

The psychotherapeutic process is at its best when it fosters resilience and responsibility. Offering children and adolescents a chance to come to terms with reality while they make meaning of their experiences as individuals connected to a universal human story does just that.

Endnotes

1. Helen Pluckrose and James A. Lindsay, *Cynical Theories: How Activist Scholarship Made Everything about Race, Gender, and Identity-and Why This Harms Everybody* (Durham, NC: Pitchstone Publishing, 2020), p. 38.

2. Diane Ehrensaft, "Gender Nonconforming Youth: Current Perspectives," *Adolescent Health, Medicine and Therapeutics* 8, (2017): 57–67, https://doi.org/10.2147/ahmt.s110859.

3. For example, in 2018, the American Academy of Pediatrics published a policy statement promoting affirmative care. See Jason Rafferty, "Ensuring Comprehensive Care and Support for Transgender and Gender-Diverse Children and Adolescents." *Pediatrics* 142, no. 4 (2018), https://doi.org/10.1542/peds.2018-2162.

4. For a full discussion of Queer Theory and its impact on our understanding of gender, see Kathleen Stock, *Material Girls: Why Reality Matters for Feminism* (London: Fleet, 2021).

5. This was a point made by the anti-psychiatry movement of the 1960s. See for example Thomas S. Szasz, "The Sane Slave." *American Journal of Psychotherapy* 25, no. 2 (1971, published online April 2018): 228–39, https://doi.org/10.1176/appi.psychotherapy.1971.25.2.228. For a contemporary exploration of this idea, see Lucy Johnstone and Mary Boyle, *The Power Threat Meaning Framework: Towards the Identification of Patterns in Emotional Distress, Unusual Experiences and Troubled or Troubling Behaviour, as an Alternative to Functional Psychiatric Diagnosis* (Leicester: British Psychological Society, 2020).

6. The biopsychosocial model was introduced in psychiatry in 1977 by psychiatrist George Engel. It continues to be influential in mental health treatment in many settings. See G.N. Papadimitriou, "The 'Biopsychosocial MODEL': 40 Years of Application in Psychiatry." *Psychiatriki* 28, no. 2 (2017): 107–10, https://doi.org/10.22365/jpsych.2017.282.107.

7. There are approaches in therapy that focus on the group level, such as family systems therapy.

8. Sally Satel, "Keep Social-Justice Indoctrination out of the Therapist's Office," *Quillette*, May 10, 2021. https://quillette.com/2021/05/07/keep-social-justice-indoctrination-out-of-the-therapists-office/.

9. Pluckrose and Lindsay, *Cynical Theories*.

10. Ibid, p. 89.

11. Judith Butler, *Gender Trouble: Feminism and the Subversion of Identity* 2nd ed. (Routledge, 1999), pp. 10-11.

12 See for example Diane Ehrensaft, "Raising Girlyboys: A Parent's Perspective," *Studies in Gender and Sexuality* 8, no. 3: 269–302, https://doi.org/10.1080/15240650701226581.

13 Stephanie A. Brill and Rachel Pepper, *The Transgender Child a Handbook for Families and Professionals* (Hoboken, NJ: Clies Press, 2008), p. 7.

14 Brill and Pepper, *The Transgender Child*, p. 14.

15 Ehrensaft, "Gender Nonconforming Youth", p. 63.

16 Social transition may involve changes to name, pronouns, clothing, and hairstyles. Medical transition may involve the use of puberty blockers, cross-sex hormones, and surgery. Medical interventions are not usually offered to pre-pubertal children.

17 Ehrensaft, "Gender Nonconforming Youth", p. 63.

18 Diane Ehrensaft, "Listening and Learning from Gender-Nonconforming Children", *The Psychoanalytic Study of the Child* 68, no. 1 (2014, published online Nov 2016): 51, DOI: 10.1080/00797308.2015.11785504.

19 Michael Biggs, "Revisiting the effect of GnRH analogue treatment on bone mineral density in young adolescents with gender dysphoria", *Journal of Pediatric Endocrinology and Metabolism* (2021), https://doi.org/10.1515/jpem-2021-0180.

20 The evidence review is no longer available on the main NHS site. A copy can be accessed here on the website of the Society for Evidence-based Gender Medicine, https://segm.org/sites/default/files/20210323_Evidence%2Breview_GnRH%2Banalogues_For%2Bupload_Final_download.pdf.

21 Ehrensaft, "Gender Nonconforming Youth", p. 62.

22 Marco A. Hidalgo, Diane Ehrensaft, Amy C. Tishelman, Leslie F. Clark, Robert Garofalo, Stephen M. Rosenthal, Norman P. Spack, and Johanna Olson, "The Gender Affirmative Model: What We Know and What We Aim to Learn," *Human Development* 56, no. 5 (2013): 285, https://doi.org/10.1159/000355235.

23 Victor E. Frankl (1905–1997) was an Austrian psychiatrist, philosopher, and Holocaust survivor. He founded logotherapy, a school of psychotherapy that posited that a search for meaning was a central motivating force in people's lives.

24 Victor E. Frankl, *Man's Search for Meaning: an Introduction to Logotherapy* (Beacon Press, 1992), p. 75.

25 C. G. Jung (1875–1961) was a Swiss psychiatrist. He developed the school of psychoanalysis known as analytical psychology.

[26] Carl Gustav Jung, *The Symbolic Life: Miscellaneous Writings Vol. 18* (Princeton, NJ: Princeton University Press, 1980), para. 1400.

[27] Carl Gustav Jung, *Collected Works of C.G. Jung, Volume 14* (Princeton, NJ: Princeton University Press, 2014), para 194.

[28] Kenneth J. Zucker, "Adolescents with Gender Dysphoria: Reflections on Some Contemporary Clinical and Research Issues," *Archives of Sexual Behavior* 48, no. 7 (2019): 1983–92, https://doi.org/10.1007/s10508-019-01518-8.

[29] Marion Woodman, *The Pregnant Virgin: a Process of Psychological Transformation* (Inner city Books, 1985), p. 24.

[30] Frankl, *Man's Search for Meaning*, p. 116.

Chapter 9:

Critical Social Justice Indoctrination in Sexuality Education for Therapists

by Tim Courtois

This book contains many examples of how the theory and practice of Critical Social Justice (CSJ) are reshaping the therapy
professions to the detriment of the clients those professions are
supposed to serve. This chapter provides a glimpse into how this
ideological takeover is being enacted in the realm of sexuality
education for therapists. It serves as a case study of how an academic course teaching views rooted in CSJ is being used to train
professionals who are in turn instructed to spread this gospel to
children, parents, and vulnerable clients.

I was unlucky enough to have a front-row seat to one such
academic course: an internationally known year-long training program at the University of Michigan—conducted in affiliation with
AASECT (the American Association of Sexuality Educators, Counselors, and Therapists)—for medical health professionals, educators, and therapists specializing in sexuality: the Sexual Health
Certificate Program (SHCP).

As a case study, this chapter is by its very nature anecdotal.
As such, it cannot serve as conclusive evidence of how counselor training, rooted in CSJ, will *always* go. But it can provide an
in-depth look at how it went in one significant case. Readers may

judge for themselves whether the patterns described here resemble the way CSJ is being enacted in culture more broadly.

It is important to recognize, at the outset, that proponents of CSJ—as with any ideology—often don't explicitly align themselves with a particular label. The SHCP did not bill itself as a Critical Social Justice program. However, ideas and practices can be rooted in CSJ even when those who implement them don't talk about—or perhaps even know about—the label "Critical Social Justice". Indeed, such ideas can be all the more insidious when labels are not used because the ideology can fly under the radar: "We're not teaching CSJ; we're just providing a good education for therapists."

This begs the question: *What is good education?* Here, I submit, are three self-evident principles of "good" education that, in my experience, were consistently violated in the SHCP program:

- First, education should develop in students a liberal **conscience** that can freely think and choose for itself; it should introduce students to a well of knowledge and wisdom about a given topic and invite them to think critically about that topic.
- Second, education should develop **curiosity**, helping students to look at topics from a diversity of lenses and viewpoints.
- Third, education should practice **caution**; it should acknowledge the limits of present knowledge, patiently consider new ideas, and allow consensus to emerge over time.

From my perspective, the SHCP, in its devotion to the CSJ worldview, sought *not* to develop a liberal conscience but to indoctrinate by compelling thought and action. Instead of fostering curiosity, it encouraged students to view the world through the reductive lens of *power*. (In this regard, a superficial commitment to diversity—a proclaimed value for the experience of minorities—was negated, as all stories were subsumed under the "oppressor–oppressed" metanarrative that arises from a belief in *power* as the ultimate reality.) Finally, it appeared to abandon all caution, displaying a tendency to canonize faddish ideas as established fact—so long as they could be framed as "anti-oppression" ideas.

This is not to say that CSJ-informed education can *only* proceed along these lines or that it can bring nothing valuable to the table. But I believe that the SHCP wielded tenets of CSJ orthodoxy so clumsily and myopically as to render the attempt at education destructive rather than helpful.

When I signed up for the SHCP, I hoped for an experience that would deepen my understanding of sexuality, better equipping me to care for the clients who come to me with issues related to sexual health. I applied and was accepted for the 2019–2020 cohort. When I showed up, I was thrilled to find that my class included participants from around the world—including Iceland, Egypt, Lebanon, and China.

Having completed the program, I can attest that, notwithstanding whatever mission AASECT once had as the most prestigious certifying body for sex therapists in the USA, it now appears to operate largely as a de facto activist group seeking to reshape standards of healthcare and education according to a CSJ worldview.

Further, AASECT has released a series of position papers littered with CSJ buzzwords declaring, for example, that sexuality education must incorporate "the perspectives of anti-oppression, equity, inclusivity, and polyculturalism", and that "educators must be ever-growing in their knowledge of anti-oppressive, anti-racist … intersectional … approaches".[1] One such paper proclaims that "Social justice plays an essential and foundational role in the organization's mission. … [AASECT] disavow[s] any therapeutic and educational effort that, even if unwittingly, violates or impinges on AASECT's vision of human rights and social justice".[2]

The purpose of this chapter is not to criticize AASECT for opposing oppression and racism but to show the harmful manner in which these values are being implemented. My opinion— informed by my own experience of their training—is that the imposition of this new orthodoxy of beliefs has superseded a focus on academic inquiry and responsible clinical practice. As a result, the above-mentioned principles of a good education have been abandoned,

Instead of the development of a liberal conscience: compelling thought and action

My doubts about the SHCP started to creep in on the first day. Our first classroom module was titled "Sexual Attitude Reassessment". I amused myself with the thought that this sounded like an unsettling euphemism for a brainwashing session. Sadly, this was not far from the truth.

It quickly became clear that the program did not have the goal of developing participants' capacity for critical thinking. The topic of sexuality often served merely as a pretext for harangues about the need to remake society according to AASECT's ideological blueprint.

In a keynote lecture that began the program, the speaker declared that the world we inhabit is socially constructed.[3] The speaker told us with striking candor, "I'm not here 'neutral' ... I'm here to try to recruit you to a particular kind of point of view of how kink should be viewed." He later addressed the accusation that "liberals" support any sexual behavior, as long as it is consensual. "Ya got me!" he said.

The point here is not to critique this professor's stated moral values but to note that it is not the role of a good education to declare to students what their moral values should be. This program began not with an invitation to academic inquiry but with declarations that moral values are socially constructed, alongside absolutist proclamations of "correct" moral beliefs about sexuality. Our attitude "reassessment" was well underway.

As I learned, "Sexual Attitude Reassessment" (SAR) is an established term in the field used to describe a class that serves to educate sexual health professionals about the wide range of sexual experiences that they may encounter among clients.[4] This is a valid goal, and essential for a prospective sex therapist. Unfortunately, the SAR in the SHCP descended into an exercise in overstimulation and indoctrination—two days of pornographic videos and interviews interspersed with lectures about intersectionality and oppression.[5,6]

Among the videos we watched were a series of videos of people masturbating (one of which involved a strange interaction with a cat); a woman with "objectiphilia" who had a sexual attraction to her church's pipe organ; a presentation on polyamory designed to convince viewers that the polyamorous lifestyle is healthy, wholesome, and problem-free; and various sadomasochistic acts.

Sadomasochism—or BDSM more broadly—appeared to be a particular fixation throughout the year-long program. In the SAR, we were shown videos of a woman meticulously applying genital clamps to the scrotum of a willing man and a dominatrix teaching a class how to properly beat people while demonstrating on an eager participant. We also watched an interview with a sex-dungeon "dom" (the male equivalent of a dominatrix) who described one of his experiences: his client had instructed him—as the dom recounted it—"I want you to bind me and then beat me until I scream. And no matter how much I scream or beg you to stop, I want you to keep beating me." The dom did as he was told, continuing the beatings through the customer's begging and pleading until the client went limp and silent, seeming to dissociate. At this point, the dom unbound the man, who then began to weep uncontrollably in the dom's arms.

BDSM is a real and active sexual subculture; I don't object to its inclusion in the course materials or wish to bring any blanket judgments against those who practise it. What surprised me was the degree of fixation on this subculture, along with an insistence that all BDSM behaviors must be uncritically viewed as wholesome and beautiful. Good therapy asks questions about deeper meanings and is unafraid to look beneath the surface. But when it comes to "sexual minorities", the program treated such questioning as a perpetuation of systems of oppression and could allow only for celebration.

In my opinion, the SHCP actively sought to convert therapy offices and classrooms into venues for moral re-education. For example, when one professor was discussing a couple that had come to therapy for help with the husband's compulsive pornography use, the professor suggested that the wife's prudish anti-porn attitude was the real problem that needed treatment. When I asked the professor whether he might have an alternative suggestion for clients whose values preclude them from using pornography, he reiterated his belief that a refusal to use pornography is unhealthy in itself!

The study of sexuality should allow for a nuanced conversation about issues such as compulsive sexual behavior, pornography, and sexual morality. A one-sided discussion of such complicated issues is a poor excuse for professional training. And the suggestion that therapists should take it upon themselves to "correct" the moral beliefs of clients with whom they disagree violates the codes of ethics of the counseling profession.[7] I would argue that this is dogma masquerading as therapy.

Another tenet of the SHCP—compliance with which was enforced by the threat of contempt and mockery—is that sexuality education shall not be deemed truly inclusive unless it incorporates, from the youngest possible age, explanations of every kind of sexual activity. AASECT's official position on the topic states,

"AASECT affirms that limiting access to comprehensive sexuality education equates to violence against individuals across the lifespan." Any alternative is declared to be "shame-based and harmful to sexual minorities".[8]

When I directly asked one professor in the program whether very young children were really psychologically ready for exposure to some kinds of sexual content, he argued that "age appropriateness" was a conservative myth. It would seem that for the AASECT faithful, no age is too young to encourage a child to wonder whether they identify as non-binary, polyamorous, kinky, or pansexual.

Here's how the enforcement of this belief played out: a professor had the class vote (anonymously) about the age at which they think a variety of topics in sexuality education should be taught. For each topic, the bulk of the class voted "elementary school". Whenever votes for a later stage of education were revealed, exclamations of shock, horror, and derisive laughter rippled throughout the room. The professor gave a nod to impartiality, saying, "We need to be careful not to commit microaggressions against people who might have different opinions."

But the professor's expression of tolerance was short-lived. Later that morning, he declared, "In this work, we have a long way to go. And we are going to be opposed by people who are going to attack us and bring accusations against us. So, it's important that we be aware of the arguments and strategies they are going to use." Then, to inform the class about the kinds of arguments "we" would face, he showed the class an episode of *Last Week Tonight* with comedian John Oliver. Mocking laughter filled the room as Oliver set up and then knocked down a series of caricatures of conservative views on sex education. The ensuing class "discussion" was focused on venting anger and contempt for such conservative views—this time, unchecked by the professor.

Instead of helping clinicians to be informed and independent thinkers, the SHCP appeared to me to be training clinicians to respond to clients who express "wrong-think" by re-educating them or laughing them out the door. It was unsettling to see AAS-ECT representatives use their classroom pulpit to advance a narrow set of simplistic "right" answers to complex and controversial questions.

Instead of curiosity and a value for multiple viewpoints: power as a reductive lens for all of life

Good education should foster curiosity by looking at topics through a variety of lenses. In contrast with the SHCP's self-proclaimed "underpinnings"—with the goal to overturn "all the binary/either, or ways of thinking"—the pattern I noticed when dealing with complex topics was to acknowledge only two possible viewpoints and then to extol one side of the debate and mock the other.[9] The SHCP demonstrated a commitment to viewing all of life through the reductive lens of *power* as the ultimate truth underlying all reality. Thus, a cynical metanarrative emerged in which there are only two kinds of people in the world: oppressors (who have power) and the oppressed (who do not). As a result, a superficial commitment to diversity was negated as all stories were subsumed under this metanarrative.[10]

In line with the aims of CSJ, the program was focused on "centering" the experience of sexual minorities. In principle, making room to attend to viewpoints that are sometimes ignored is a good thing. But this becomes problematic when the value of a person's perspective is determined primarily by their membership in an "oppressed" class. *Instead of valuing people for their own sake, individuals are reduced to tools for the advancement of an ideology.*

Indeed, the same can be said for the study of sexuality itself. As stated in class materials, "It is crucial that all efforts are viewed through a social justice lens that contributes to and advances sexuality education as an anti-oppressive force."[11]

In my opinion, for AASECT, sexuality education is no longer even about sexuality per se; it is an excuse to spread social justice ideology. One professor in the program—a founder of an influential organization spreading this ideology called the Transgender Training Institute—boldly proclaimed, "Anti-oppression frameworks are the future of sex education."[12] Thus, we often spent more time in class talking about power, oppression, and privilege than we did about sexuality.[13]

In the SHCP, even science itself was treated as subservient to the cause of "social justice". I noted that professors' declarations were not typically rooted in science or rational discourse, but in a myopic focus on enacting "social justice" via kneejerk opposition to anything that could be framed as "oppression".

For example, one professor acknowledged that proponents of social justice have deliberately distorted scientific data about sexual orientation in order to advance LGBTQIA+ rights. According to this professor, it has been common to exaggerate the extent to which sexual orientation is known to be inborn, but now that LGBTQIA+ rights have made progress, there is more willingness to admit that many experience sexual orientation as fluid. Notably, this professor did not condemn the practice of falsifying scientific claims.[14]

Even pedophilia was treated as something that could be overlooked in the service of social justice. While pedophilic behavior was typically condemned in the program, one professor declared, "We make a distinction with gay males who have sexual experiences with older gay men, because they don't have as many available opportunities to experiment with people who are their own age." Thus, the lens of oppression was even used to justify pedophilia, so long as the victim and perpetrator are both members of an oppressed class!

In short, education that insists on viewing all of life through one lens precludes curiosity. If *power* is the lens through which the world must always be viewed, then only one cause of all problems can be imagined; we are led to believe that the reason sex is such a difficult area of life for so many people is not—as one might think—because sexuality is complicated and humans are morally fallible, but solely because of *systems of oppression* that marginalize minorities and instill sexual shame. In a reversal of Alexander Solzhenitsyn's famous claim, the SHCP approach to sexuality appears to suggest that the line separating good and evil passes not through every human heart, but between those identity groups who have power and those who do not.[15]

Instead of cautiously acknowledging the limits of present knowledge: canonizing faddish ideas

Good education should acknowledge the limits of present knowledge, remaining cautious when solid conclusions have not yet emerged. The CSJ movement is not marked by such humble caution.

In conjunction with the tendency to evaluate claims based on their perceived utility to social justice rather than veracity, CSJ often canonizes faddish ideas as established facts while dismissing critiques, unknowns, and risks. This inclination was shown in the program's previously described blanket celebration of trendy sexual practices such as polyamory and BDSM, but manifested most strongly in the SHCP concerning "gender identity".

There is more to be said about the debate surrounding gender identity than can be fully addressed here. What can be said is that there have been rapid shifts in recent years, not only in the vocabulary and definitions surrounding sexuality and gender, but also in the ways gender identity and gender dysphoria have been manifesting in culture—particularly among young people.[16] The causes and consequences of these shifts should be patiently studied, and conclusions should not be hastily drawn.

However, AASECT has cemented itself within a trendy perspective arising from its CSJ lens: those who proclaim a non-cisgender identity are an "oppressed" class; therefore, any such proclaimed identity must be unequivocally affirmed without curiosity or caution. AASECT has formally denounced the position that "sex means a person's status as male or female based on immutable biological traits" as "legally untenable, scientifically inaccurate, and morally reprehensible".[17]

Of course, gender dysphoria is a real phenomenon. Some people go through their entire lives with a longing to bring outward appearance in line with their inner felt sense of identity. But it's also true that some people come to identify as trans later in life, or desist from a previously declared trans identity. In fact, studies indicate that *most* trans-identified minors end up reverting to a self-identified gender that aligns with their birth sex.[18]

Yet, in the SHCP, I heard one professor confidently declare that at birth, we are all handed a "gender envelope" containing our gender identity, and this identity can't be affected by outside forces such as trauma or culture. This ignores emerging data suggesting that this sort of thing happens often, especially in the case of teenage girls.[19] This quasi-religious conception of gender was used to support the conclusion that trans-identifying children should be given easy access to puberty-blocking drugs and cross-sex hormones. Both treatments were breezily declared to be safe, with little risk of adverse consequences—despite studies that indicate otherwise.[20]

For cases in which parents hesitate to allow their children to undergo such treatments, we were taught to leverage the threat that their children might commit suicide: "Do you want a *live* trans-child or a *dead* cisgender-child?" is the question participants in the program were trained to use to manipulate parents into allowing currently trans-identified children to transition medically.

This brought to light a striking contradiction in the doctrine of the SHCP: while we were told the desire of children is always authoritative concerning their proclaimed gender identity, the program was staunch in its declaration that minors are not able to consent to sexual contact with adults. Thus, the SHCP taught that if a child wants to have an adult pedophile stimulate his genitals, his desire should be disregarded. But if a child wants to have an adult surgically remove those genitals, his desire must be honored. To do otherwise is "oppressive".

Such contradictions became less surprising to me throughout the program, as I observed that the SHCP showed little commitment to rational consistency. Definitions were subject to change from moment to moment. When convenient, gender identity and sexual orientation could be held to be either immutable from birth or flexible throughout life. It would be assumed sometimes that trans people are those who persistently identify as such and who must be allowed to transition medically; at other moments, transgenderism could be redefined as "encompass[ing] any individual who crosses over or challenges their society's traditional gender roles and/or expressions". Under this definition, even "feminine men" and "masculine women" were declared to fall under the "transgender umbrella".[21]

The SHCP's slipshod wielding of truth claims—causing many of the teachings to be more "trendy" than "true"—was best demonstrated by the use of a *Calvin & Hobbes* comic in class to illustrate the "current underpinnings" that guided the program. In the comic, Calvin is asked to answer a factual question on a history exam. In response, Calvin declares that he doesn't believe in linear time, and that "Existence in the temporal sense is illusory". He then looks at the reader with a smile and says, "When in doubt, deny all terms and definitions."[22]

I would submit that such willingness to play games with truth may make Critical Social Justice popular, but it cannot provide a good foundation for therapy.

In short: bad education

When I set out to study sexuality at an internationally respected training program, I hoped the experience would enrich my work as a therapist and grow me as a person. Instead, I found myself immersed in an atmosphere that paradoxically merged relativism with dogmatic indoctrination.

Further, I was treated from the outset as if my enrollment in the program had implicitly bound me to an activist team; I was told precisely what to think and what actions I should take—not simply to be a good therapist, but to achieve the societal changes that "we" all know are necessary to enact the cause of social justice. In my experience, moments of quality therapeutic training were few and far between.

I concluded that the focus was on turning participants into evangelists for CSJ orthodoxy who will root out unorthodox beliefs in schools and therapy offices wherever they go.

In short, while the SHCP provided, in my eyes, a very bad education, it also gave me firsthand experience of just what Critical Social Justice threatens to do to the therapy professions: reducing them to a tool for the spread of a faddish and foolish ideology.

Endnotes

1   "Position on Sexuality Education", American Association of Sexuality Educators, Counselors and Therapists (AASECT), last modified 2022, https://www.aasect.org/position-sexuality-education.

2   "Position on Sexual Expression Including Orientation and Identity," AASECT, last modified 2022,https://www.aasect.org/position-sexual-expression-including-orientation-and-identity.

3   Russell J. Stambaugh, "Why Fetishism Matters", delivered April 12, 2019 at University of Michigan School of Social Work, Ann Arbor, MI, video, 1:31:42, https://ssw.umich.edu/offices/continuing-education/certificate-courses/sexual-health/plenaries.

4   For a good example, see "What is a SAR? (Sexual Attitude Reassessment)," Sexual Health Alliance, last modified 2022, https://sexualhealthalliance.com/nymphomedia-blog/what-is-a-sar-sexual-attitude-reassessment.

5   Valerie Wood and Stacy Peterson, "SAR 2019 Video Resources" (Unpublished course handouts for SAR - Sexual Attitude Reassessment, University of Michigan, Ann Arbor, MI, delivered on April 13, 2019).

6   Valerie Wood and Stacy Peterson, "Intersectionality (1)" (Unpublished course handouts for SAR - Sexual Attitude Reassessment, University of Michigan, Ann Arbor, MI, delivered on April 13, 2019).

7   American Counseling Association, 2014 ACA Code of Ethics (Alexandria, VA, 2014), A.4.b, https://www.counseling.org/resources/aca-code-of-ethics.pdf.

8   AASECT, "Position on Sexuality Education".

9   Prem Pahwa and Phillis Mims-Gillum, "Current Underpinnings" (unpublished course handouts for Core Sexual Health Education 1, University of Michigan, Ann Arbor, MI, delivered on May 18, 2019).

10 Valerie Wood and Stacy Peterson, "Intersectionality (2)" (unpublished course handouts for SAR - Sexual Attitude Reassessment, University of Michigan, Ann Arbor, MI, delivered on April 13, 2019).

11 Eli Green, "Understanding Sexuality Education Through a Social Justice Lens" (unpublished course handouts for Advanced Training in Sexuality Education 2, University of Michigan, Ann Arbor, MI, delivered on November 23, 2019).

12 The Transgender Training Institute (TTI), last modified 2022, https://www.transgendertraininginstitute.com.

13 For a more detailed description, see Tim Courtois, "I Signed Up to Study Sexual Health. What I Got Was Gender Ideology, Fetishism, and Porn," Quillette, October 31, 2020, https://quillette.com/2020/10/31/i-signed-

up-to-study-sexual-health-what-i-got-was-gender-ideology-fetishism-and-porn/.

[14] Prem Pahwa, "Core Sexual Health Education 1", (online class lecture at the University of Michigan, Ann Arbor, MI, delivered on May 18, 2019). A video of this lecture was made available to all class members after the talk. (I retain a personal copy of this recording.)

[15] "Gradually it was disclosed to me that the line separating good and evil passes not through states, nor between classes, nor between political parties either—but right through every human heart—and through all human hearts." Alexander I. Solzhenitsyn, The Gulag Archipelago, Volume 2 (New York: HarperCollins, 2007), p. 615.

[16] Abigail Shrier, *Irreversible Damage: The Transgender Craze Seducing Our Daughters,* Washington, D.C.: Regnery Publishing, 2020.

[17] "Position Statement on the Dignity and Rights of Transgender, Gender Nonbinary, and Gender Nonconforming Individuals," AASECT, last modified 2022, https://www.aasect.org/position-statement-dignity-and-rights-transgender-gender-nonbinary-and-gender-nonconforming.

[18] Devita Singh et al., "A Follow-Up Study of Boys With Gender Identity Disorder," Frontiers in Psychiatry (March 2021), https://doi.org/10.3389/fpsyt.2021.632784. Wylie C. Hembree et al., "Endocrine Treatment of Gender-Dysphoric/Gender-Incongruent Persons: An Endocrine Society Clinical Practice Guideline," The Journal of Clinical Endocrinology & Metabolism, 102, no. 11 (November 2017), https://doi.org/10.1210/jc.2017-01658.

[19] Lisa Littman, "Parent reports of adolescents and young adults perceived to show signs of a rapid onset of gender dysphoria," PLOS One. (August 2018), https://doi.org/10.1371/journal.pone.0202330.

[20] For research into puberty blockers, see the following: Lieke Josephina Jeanne Johanna Vrouenraets et al, "Early Medical Treatment of Children and Adolescents With Gender Dysphoria: An Empirical Ethical Study," Journal of Adolescent Health, 57, no. 4 (October 2015): 367-373, https://doi.org/10.1016/j.jadohealth.2015.04.004 ; Paul W. Hruz et al., "Growing Pains: Problems with Puberty Suppression in Treating Gender Dysphoria," The New Atlantis, no. 52, Spring 2017, 3-36, https://www.thenewatlantis.com/publications/growing-pains : Guido Giovanardi, "Buying time or arresting development? The dilemma of administering hormone blockers in trans children and adolescents," Porto Biomedical Journal, 2, no. 5 (September 2017): pp. 153-156, https://doi.org/10.1016/j.pbj.2017.06.001. For research into cross-sex hormones,

see the following: Talal Alzahrani, et al., "Cardiovascular Disease Risk Factors and Myocardial Infarction in the Transgender Population," Circulation: Cardiovascular Quality and Outcomes, 12, no. 4 (April 2019), https://doi.org/10.1161/CIRCOUTCOMES.119.005597; Darios Getahun, et al., "Cross-sex Hormones and Acute Cardiovascular Events in Transgender Persons, A Cohort Study," Annals of Internal Medicine, 169, no. 4 (August 2018): 205-213, https://doi.org/10.7326/M17-2785.

[21] Doug Braun-Harvey, "Beyond the Binary" (unpublished course handouts for Core Sexual Health Education 2, University of Michigan, Ann Arbor, MI, delivered on June 22, 2019).

[22] Prem Pahwa and Phillis Mims-Gillum, "Current Underpinnings" (unpublished course handouts for Core Sexual Health Education 1, University of Michigan, Ann Arbor, MI, delivered on May 18, 2019).

Chapter 10:

What is the Impact of Critical Social Justice on Therapy for Men?

by John Barry

Introduction

In recent years, theories and guidelines have emerged in several countries suggesting that men's mental health problems are a result of flaws inherent in traditional masculinity. Examples of such deficits are being stoical or competitive rather than talking about one's feelings. Masculinity is said to be bad not only for men but for those around them, causing homophobia and violence against women. Although Critical Social Justice (CSJ) is not usually referred to explicitly in such guidelines, the influence is recognisable, for example, in encouraging the view that masculinity is wholly a result of socialisation rather than being influenced in any way by biological factors or the result of evolution.

Accordingly, this chapter outlines some of the ways that CSJ has influenced the field of psychology in recent decades. Implications for the safety and efficacy of models of therapy informed by CSJ are discussed, and the benefits of a more male-friendly approach are explored. One example of taking a male-friendly approach is the view that traditional masculinity is not the root cause of men's mental health problems, and, in fact, might contain valuable resources that can enhance mental health. This viewpoint allows therapists to understand men in a way that is more likely to foster better rapport between therapist and client, facilitating a more successful therapy. The headline news is often filled with men who suffer from unresolved mental health issues and who can sometimes "act out" in dangerous ways, so improving men's mental health benefits not only men but everyone in society.

Critical Social Justice terminology in psychology

The family tree of CSJ branches off in odd ways, leaving a trail of idiosyncratic terminology and schools of thought. In psychology, "postmodernism", "cultural studies", and the "Frankfurt School" of Critical Theory (from which Theodor Adorno and Erich Fromm are still well known today in social psychology) have all left their mark, as evidenced by terms such as "the critical perspective" and "critical realism".[1,2,3] More frequently though, the influence is seen in themes common in CSJ, such as "power", "patriarchy", and "hegemonic" masculinity.

Critical Social Justice, gender, masculinity, and patriarchy

The CSJ-inspired notion that gender, and therefore masculinity, is socially constructed is one of the four main tenets of intersectional feminism and gender studies.

> Nowhere in gender studies can one find men or masculinities being studied through any lens but feminism. This is not particularly surprising because it is completely consistent with [CSJ] Theory ... in Social Justice scholarship, we continually read that patriarchy, white supremacy, imperialism, cisnormativity, heteronormativity, ableism and fatphobia are literally structuring society and infecting everything. They exist in a state of imminence – present

always and everywhere, just beneath a nicer-seeming surface that can't quite contain them.[4]

Thus, masculinity and patriarchy are just two elements of a *smorgasbord* of ways to induce "radical doubt" in people's minds about the world around them. In CSJ, gender is considered a restrictive social construct, and people are encouraged to question, criticise, and liberate themselves from traditional gender roles and create their own concepts of gender to disrupt the binary of masculine and feminine and of male and female.

Being "liberated" from oppressive norms sounds like a fantastic idea, but the world is full of examples of how the meaning of words can be distorted in order to manipulate perceptions.[5]

The CSJ view of gender is that masculinity and femininity are wholly socially constructed, completely uninfluenced by evolutionary forces or biology. Even biological sex itself—male and female as defined by reproductive function—has been argued to be a social construct. If gender is a result of socialisation, then any gender inequalities are, in the CSJ view, the product of unequal social forces, power imbalances, and oppression, leaving no room for biological factors or lifestyle preferences as explanatory factors. Thus, all inequalities in outcomes related to gender (e.g., fewer women than men working in science jobs) are seen as evidence of social inequality.

Critical Social Justice in psychology

There are lots of examples of how CSJ influences the field of psychology, often in subtle ways. For example, authors in the US claim that "feminists have made it possible for women to not only invade the (traditionally male and pathologizing) field [of psychology] but to radically take it over".[6] Any remaining male psychology students should be trained "as viruses" to see gender from the "critical" perspective, who will go on to infect spaces "where their privilege and dominance is assumed".[7] The influence of this approach might be one of the reasons the enrolment of men into undergraduate psychology programmes has plummeted over the past few decades.

One of the more infamous ways in which CSJ has infected psychology is the guidelines on therapy for boys and men issued by the American Psychological Association (APA) in 2018.[8] Although to many people the dim view of men expressed in the guidelines came as a shock—based on patriarchy theory and a negative view of masculinity—the signs of CSJ were already in the APA literature.

For example, a study published in 2012 surveyed 475 psychologists on tips for best practice in working with men and boys.[9] This was potentially a very useful study, but the researchers were, arguably, somewhat selective about what type of information they included among the information collected from participants. For example, the researchers omitted feedback from psychologists about the relevance of trauma histories of abusive males, even though trauma (e.g., childhood, combat) is known to be a cause of anger and violence in some men. Instead, issues such as gender socialisation became the preferred focus and main findings of the researchers, which is not surprising because "all researchers were pro-feminist white males who bring a critical perspective on traditional gender roles".

This same study could have been a good opportunity to find out important information on the traumatic roots of abusive behaviour by men, for the benefit of both men and women, but the opportunity was wasted. The findings were cited several times in the APA guidelines, though without reference to the influence of the critical perspective, with its socio-political rather than scientific focus.[10]

Masculinity and patriarchy in therapy

Although much criticised, the guidelines of Division 51 (Men and Masculinities) of the APA for psychological practice with boys and men include some material of merit, e.g., Guideline 9 on male-friendly therapy.[11] However, Guidelines 1 and 3 are uniformly tainted with Critical Social Justice.

Guideline 1 states that "masculinities are constructed based on social, cultural and contextual norms". It is true, of course, that manifestations of masculinity are influenced by social and cultural forces, but that is only part of the truth. When it comes to therapy, this is not just a matter of scientific credibility or an endless nature vs nurture debate, because treating masculinity as a learned behaviour implies that it can be unlearned relatively easily.

Further, the APA guidelines go on to suggest that the problematic socialisation of men can be attributed to patriarchy. Guideline 3 states that on average, "males experience a greater degree of social and economic power than girls and women in a patriarchal society". This statement presumes that the modern US can be described as a patriarchy (see the section below) and minimises the fact that men in the modern US often have the least social and economic power. For instance, men comprise the vast majority of rough-sleeping homeless people and workers employed for the dirtiest and most dangerous jobs.[12] The retort that "patriarchy hurts men too" rings hollow and highlights the flaw of "infallibility" of patriarchy theory in that it contorts itself to claim that men as a group are simultaneously both dominant and oppressed.[13]

Others, influenced by CSJ, sometimes refer to patriarchy as a specific problem and use this as a focus for interventions, though more often the reference to patriarchy is more implicit. For example, assumptions about power imbalances in relationships such as a woman not being listened to by their male partner can be seen as a manifestation of patriarchy rather than manifestations of other issues that could explain the problem.[14]

In other cases, patriarchy theory takes centre stage. For example, the Duluth model of domestic violence is based on patriarchy theory and attributes the problem to men's attempts at power and control over women.[15] Although in widespread use in several countries for decades, interventions based on Duluth have proven much less effective than more conventional therapies such as relationship enhancement; these therapies focus on the coaching and modelling of interpersonal skills without reference to patriarchy.[16] This situation means there is a widespread lack of adequate provision of therapy for male offenders and a near-total lack of therapy available for female offenders.

Is the critical view of men above criticism?

The validity of the critical view of men and masculinity depends to a large degree on the validity of its central ideas: that masculinity is learned and in no way innate, and that patriarchy influences men towards negative behaviours and poor mental health.

But what if both of these hypotheses are false? In other words, what if there is evidence that masculinity is not simply the result of social influence, but also shaped by biological and evolutionary forces? There is also the issue that masculine traits are, in many contexts, highly valuable, e.g., risk-taking in emergency services. And what if the idea of the existence and influence of patriarchy is misleading to the point of being, itself, somewhat delusional?

Is masculinity just a social construct?

In a just world where all evidence is assessed and theories developed based on such evidence, the CSJ view of gender would be dismissed as a radically one-sided exaggeration of reality. That is because there is a huge amount of evidence that biological variables such as testosterone and evolutionary adaptations influence the expression of gender in men and women. For example, exposure to higher levels of testosterone prenatally is linked to better three-dimensional mental rotation, which is a type of visuospatial ability that is useful in team sports, hunting, and engineering, all of which men choose to engage in more than women do.[17] One aspect of traditional masculinity is being a fighter, which is in keeping with the twenty-six biological sex differences supporting the idea that men are more adapted than women to combat, e.g., in general, men are taller, have heavier bodies, stronger bones, faster reactions, etc.[18]

Furthermore, if masculinity and femininity are the product of the environment, then we would expect a great deal of variation in gender internationally. However, there is a great deal of evidence that gender-typical sex differences, such as being competitive, taking risks, and crying less, occur internationally, a fact that severely undermines the idea that sex differences are merely the product of social construction.[19] So, how does CSJ deal with this evidence? It ignores it, cherry-picks minor exceptions (e.g., a remote village where gender roles are claimed to buck the international trend), or rejects the evidence for other non-scientific reasons.

We should not expect evidence that disproves CSJ ideas to be assessed rationally, because "the critical perspective does not aim to be objective and scientific, let alone aim for common sense, but aims to 'emancipate' people from scientific and common-sense views of the world by introducing 'radical doubt' into studies of gender".[20]

In other words, CSJ is about socio-political ideology rather than science. This being the case, it is surprising how effective this strategy has been in persuading otherwise rational people to support ideas inspired by CSJ. For example, gender "equality" programmes are based on the idea that patriarchy is the reason there are more men in science, technology, engineering, and mathematics (STEM) careers, and the way to make things more equal is to favour women disproportionately when it comes to STEM professions.[21] The influence of CSJ in science is all the more remarkable given how these ideas are transparently unscientific.

Is patriarchy a malign influence in the modern West?

Some readers might be wondering what exactly is meant by patriarchy, and this is an important question that is not asked often enough. Although the term is bandied around the media and social sciences, its panoramically wide use as an explanation begs the question of what specifically it means. The Oxford English Dictionary defines it as "the rule of the father" and is properly applied to communities of related families with a male leader known as a "patriarch".

However, a more political version of this concept was introduced into academia in 1970 by radical feminist sociologist Kate Millet as a way of theorising the oppression of women in the modern world.[22] This reconceptualization of patriarchy reveals the influence of Marxism, with men cast in the role of the bourgeoisie and women cast as the downtrodden workers, and traditional gender roles (e.g., being a housewife) and "hegemonic masculinity" as the method of using power (e.g., economic power of the breadwinner) to achieve the oppression of women.

While CSJ forms of feminism are largely critical of older radical "feminisms" due to their tendency to reject trans activism (known as trans-exclusionary radical feminists, or TERFs) and sex work as a freely chosen profession (known as sex worker exclusionary radical feminists, or SWERFs), this concept of patriarchal domination remains.

Although patriarchies still exist in some less modernised parts of the world today, much less attention is given to the fact that men are currently disadvantaged compared to women in many parts of the world, especially those countries with medium to high levels of development.[23] Ironically, calls to "smash the patriarchy" are loudest in countries where there is the least evidence of patriarchy. Instead of liberation from oppression, smashing the patriarchy in modern Western countries translates into smashing the traditional family unit and undermining the role of the father, such as through harsh treatment in the family courts.[24] The terrible irony is that a good father in the home benefits everyone, including women and girls, through having a stabilising influence that extends from the family to the wider society, e.g., in terms of crime reduction.[25]

Therefore, it appears that patriarchy theory has little relevance to modern Western culture, apart from being a toxic method of "gaslighting" men and eroding the fabric of Western culture through the undermining of the traditional family unit (see also [26]).

In the same way that the social construction of masculinity is only part of the truth, and dangerously one-sided, so too is the idea that women are oppressed by gender roles. Both men and women can be conceptualised as oppressed in various ways by their gender roles; in reality, their gender roles are shaped by evolution as well as culture, so we should recognise Mother Nature as the oppressor rather than "The Patriarchy". We should also remember that sexual selection shaped masculinity and femininity, meaning that masculine traits are those that have been most chosen by women throughout evolutionary history, and vice versa.

One of the promotors of CSJ views of masculinity observed that the biological/evolutionary view of masculinity makes "the dark side of masculinity as an unfortunate, but relatively inevitable, outcome of male heritage".[27]

Conversely, if masculinity is just a learned behaviour, people might naturally be less tolerant of men's bad behaviour. In promoting a social constructionist view of masculinity and the spectre of patriarchy, CSJ has replaced biological reality with a patriarchal conspiracy theory. The result has been an unforgiving view of masculinity and, by association, men and boys.

What is the impact of Critical Social Justice views on therapy for men?

Despite the importance of the question—what is the impact of Social Critical Justice views on therapy for men?—it has received surprisingly little research attention. In probably the first study of its kind, an online survey of 107 therapists found that although only a minority (overall) supported CSJ ideas (that masculinity is a social construct and that patriarchy holds back women today), there were strong correlations between believing these CSJ ideas and believing that they are good for men in therapy.[28]

In this same research, of a subsample of sixty therapists who described how they conducted their therapy for men, those who didn't subscribe to CSJ ideas were significantly more likely to practise male-friendly therapy than either gender-neutral therapy or therapy based on anti-patriarchy ideas.

What is male-friendly therapy?

Male-friendly therapy is an approach that recognises there are some differences in how men and women deal with their mental health issues. Further, it tries to accommodate these differences in therapy.[29] For example, there is evidence that men tend to prefer a more solution-focused approach to deal with their problems. If this approach is used, a male-friendly therapist will try to ensure the client knows this option is available and that they don't need to have an emotion-focused intervention if they don't feel comfortable with it (although the latter approach can be very useful and should remain an option). [30]

One thing that tends to get forgotten in CSJ-related discussions of gender is that there is evidence that masculinity is beneficial to physical and psychological health in various ways.[31] For example, values associated with masculinity, such as self-reliance, taking action, working as a group, being a fighter, and taking control, can facilitate coping strategies in men suffering from depression. This means that trying to eliminate "traditional" masculinity through therapy makes no sense, not only because it goes against innate tendencies but because it is completely unnecessary. So, if men have an innate tendency towards being competitive, then treating competitiveness as a flawed aspect of traditional masculinity is not only incorrect but also alienating for a client who has experienced—from childhood onwards—competitiveness as a fundamental and positive part of their life, e.g., in sports or in his career. People who come to therapy are almost by definition in a vulnerable state, and as therapists, we are ethically bound to ensure their safety and protection from harm in what we do. But imposing a CSJ approach seems to contradict this valued ethos.

In many ways, the main component of male-friendly therapy is the attitude of the therapist. The therapist should not treat their male client as a stereotypical male, or as a vehicle for dysfunctional masculine traits, but as a unique person, and one who may share characteristics with other men, in part through a common evolutionary heritage, that are relevant to their mental health. The male-friendly approach is thus client-centred. It also borrows from humanistic and positive psychology in recognising that male-typical characteristics can be harnessed to the benefit of the client's mental health.

For example, the male-typical tendency to deal with problems stoically can be useful for situations such as short-term emergencies but can backfire if relied upon too heavily. It often goes unremarked that stoicism is a cornerstone of Rational Emotive Behaviour Therapy, and male clients who might otherwise be disinclined to attend a therapy where they would need to dwell upon their feelings might be more inclined to seek help if they see it as more clearly focused on helping them to get their feelings under control. However, because the most important aspect of male-friendly therapy is the genuinely male-friendly attitude of the therapist, this means that a range of therapeutic approaches can be adapted to men, as discussed in Liddon and Barry's *Perspectives in Male Psychology,* which has been cited throughout this chapter.

Further, because men are less likely than women to seek therapy yet more likely to die by suicide and more likely to drop out of therapy, it makes sense for practitioners to make a male-friendly approach available to clients.[32]

Also, of course, some women may prefer this approach too, and some men may prefer a more emotion-focused therapy; this is all well and good and only shows that we do not live in a one-size-fits-all world.

However, we have seen, when taking a CSJ approach to therapy, a dim view of masculinity and the supposed influence of patriarchy leads therapists to utilise approaches that might not appeal to many men, might undermine rapport between the client and therapist, and ultimately, this will be relatively unhelpful.

Conclusion

At present, in academia, there is a blurring of politics and science in the social sciences.

CSJ activist projects based on "lived experience" are currently being treated as if they are on a par with scientific research, while evidence from scientific research is ignored or vilified as a tool of oppression.

Although gender studies have been found to lack scientific credibility compared to many parts of academia, it retains a disproportionately—and inexplicably—strong influence over many areas of discourse and decision-making in media, politics, the law, and more recently the world of therapy.[33]

I hope this chapter helps to demonstrate why there is an urgent need to reassess how much we are prepared to allow Critical Social Justice to influence our lives, especially as such an important aspect of our lives is mental health.

Endnotes

[1] See Chapter 6 for an engaging presentation of the history of Critical Theory in Andrew Breitbart, *Righteous Indignation: Excuse Me While I Save the World* (New York: Grand Central Publishing, 2011).

[2] J. R. Mahalik, G. E. Good, D. Tager, R. F. Levant, and C. Mackowiak, "Developing a taxonomy of helpful and harmful practices for clinical work with boys and men", *Journal of Counseling Psychology* 59, no. 4 (2012): 591–603. https://doi.org/10.1037/a0030130.

[3] L. Johnstone and M. Boyle, *The Power Threat Meaning Framework: Towards the identification of patterns in emotional distress, unusual experiences and troubled or troubling behaviour, as an alternative to functional psychiatric diagnosis,* (Leicester, UK: British Psychological Society, 2018).

[4] Helen Pluckrose and James Lindsay, *Cynical Theories* (Durham, NC: Pitchstone, 2020): 183, 184, 215.

[5] J. Whyte, *Bad Thoughts: A guide to clear thinking.* (London: Penguin, 2010).

[6] B. Fahs and M. Karger, "Women's Studies as Virus: Institutional Feminism and the Projection of Danger," *Multidisciplinary Journal of Gender Studies* 5, no.1 (2016): 945, 947, http://dx.doi.org/10.4471/generos.2016.1683.

[7] American Psychological Association, Boys and Men Guidelines Group. (2018). *APA guidelines for psychological practice with boys and men, last modified August 2018,* http://www.apa.org/about/policy/psychological-practice-boys-men-guidelines.pdf.

[8] American Psychological Association, Boys and Men Guidelines Group.

[9] L. Liddon and J. A. Barry, *Perspectives in Male Psychology: An introduction* (Chichester, UK: Wiley, 2021).

[10] American Psychological Association, Boys and Men Guidelines Group.

[11] Ibid.

[12] *Bureau of Labor Statistics (2020). National Census of Fatal Occupational Injuries.* US Department of Labour. Accessed 10 August 2021, https://www.bls.gov/news.release/pdf/cfoi.pdf.

[13] K. R. Popper, *The Logic of Scientific Discovery* (Lanham, US: University Press, 1959).

[14] C. Knudson-Martin, C., "When Therapy Challenges Patriarchy: Undoing Gendered Power in Heterosexual Couple Relationships", in *Socio-Emotional Relationship Therapy,* eds C. Knudson-Martin, M. A. Wells and S. K. Samman (New York: Springer International Publishing, 2015), pp. 15-26.

15   D. Powney and N. Graham-Kevan, "Male Victims of Intimate Partner Violence: A Challenge to the Gendered Paradigm" in *The Palgrave Handbook of Male Psychology and Mental Health*, eds J. A. Barry, R. Kingerlee, M. Seager, and L. Sullivan (London: Palgrave Macmillan, 2019), pp. 123-143.

16   J. C. Babcock, C. E. Green, and C. Robie, "Does batterers' treatment work? A meta-analytic review of domestic violence treatment," *Clinical Psychology Review* 23, no.8 (2004): 1023–1053. doi: 10.1016/j.cpr.2002.07.001.

17   J. A Barry & R. Owens, "From fetuses to boys to men: the impact of testosterone on male lifespan development", in *The Palgrave Handbook of Male Psychology and Mental Health*, eds J. A. Barry, R. Kingerlee, M. Seager, and L. Sullivan (London: Palgrave Macmillan, 2019), pp. 3-24.

18   A. Sell, L. S. E. Hone and N. Pound, "The importance of physical strength to human males", *Human Nature* 23, no.1 (2012): pp. 30–44.

19   L. Liddon and J. A. Barry, *Perspectives in Male Psychology: An introduction* (Chichester, UK: Wiley, 2021).

20   N. Blyler, "Taking a political turn: the critical perspective and research in professional communication", *Technical Communication Quarterly* 7, no.1 (1998): pp. 33–52. https://doi.org/10.1080/10572259809364616.

21   Liddon and Barry, *Perspectives in Male Psychology*.

22   Kate Millet's work is presented in summary here by her sister, Mallory Millet, "Marxist feminism's ruined lives," *Frontpagemag.com*, accessed 10 August 2021, https://archives.frontpagemag.com/fpm/marxist-feminisms-ruined-lives-mallory-millett/.

23   G. Stoet and D. C. Geary, "A simplified approach to measuring national gender inequality," *PLOS ONE* 14, no. 1 (2019), https://doi.org/10.1371/journal.pone.0205349.

24   J. A. Barry and L. Liddon, "Child contact problems and family court issues are related to chronic mental health problems for men following family breakdown", *Psychreg Journal of Psychology* 4, no.3 (2020): 57-66, https://doi.org/10.5281/zenodo.4302120.

25   Liddon and Barry, *Perspectives in Male Psychology*.

26   H. Pluckrose, "How to tell if you're living in a patriarchy," *Areo*, July 2017, https://areomagazine.com/2017/07/10/how-to-tell-if-youre-living-in-a-patriarchy-a-historical-perspective/.

27   G. R. Brooks, "Masculinity and Men's Mental Health," *Journal of American College Health* 49, no. 6 (2001): 285–297, 292. https://doi.org/10.1080/07448480109596315.

28 J. A. Barry, L. Liddon, R. Walker and M. Seager, "How therapists work with men is related to their views on masculinity, patriarchy, and politics", *Psychreg Journal of Psychology* 5, no.1 (2021): 50-64, https://doi.org/10.5281/zenodo.4889456.

29 Liddon and Barry, *Perspectives in Male Psychology*.

30 L. Liddon, R. Kingerlee, M. Seager and J. A. Barry, "What Are the Factors That Make a Male-Friendly Therapy?" in *The Palgrave Handbook of Male Psychology and Mental Health*, eds J. A. Barry, R. Kingerlee, M. Seager, and L. Sullivan (London: Palgrave Macmillan, 2019), 671–694.

31 Liddon and Barry, *Perspectives in Male Psychology*.

32 Ibid.

33 G. Madison and T. Söderlund, "Comparisons of content and scientific quality indicators across peer-reviewed journal articles with more or less gender perspective: gender studies can do better", *Scientometrics* 115, (2018):1161–1183, https://doi.org/10.1007/s11192-018-2729-3.

Chapter 11

The Negative Impact of Critical Social Justice on Suicidal Behaviour in Men

by Dennis Relojo-Howell

Introduction

Gender differences in both suicidal behaviour and suicidal ideation have been extensively studied. Research has consistently
shown that while women have suicidal thoughts more often, men
die of suicide more frequently.[1] Depression and stress are significant factors in suicidal behaviour, and decades of suicide research
have demonstrated that men are more vulnerable to depression
caused by stressful events.[2]

In spite of these indisputable facts, the narrative coming from
Critical Social Justice (CSJ) theory demonises the group most vulnerable to dying of suicide. Attacks on so-called "toxic masculinity", along with the promotion of "natural and non-harmful masculine traits" as a solution, are not helpful. In fact, CSJ discourses
negatively impact men's mental health and may contribute to suicidal behaviour.

As someone who manages a mental health platform, much of
my own work is informed by my first-hand observation of mental
health difficulties and the regrettable state of current mainstream

attitudes regarding mental health issues. My observation, none-theless, is supported by empirical findings. A 2020 study found that young people demonstrated good knowledge and a positive attitude toward mental health disorders. Yet, some continue to hold negative perceptions regarding approaching someone with a mental health issue, harbouring doubt and fear.[3] Therefore, it is of crucial importance that men, especially, are encouraged to seek help sooner.

However, as many societal attitudes have changed and now promote greater openness for men, this is only a small part of the solution to the problem of male suicide. The growing influence of CSJ has impeded the progress made in other areas due to its stig-matising of (particularly, white) men. This consequently damages men's self-esteem, making them feel guilty for their natural and non-harmful masculine traits and leading to their isolation from wider society.[4]

Over the past five decades, successive studies into resilience have emphasised the vital role of social support and a sense of belonging in providing a buffer against suicidal behaviour.[5] Rather than the isolation and devaluation of masculinity that is central to many men's experience of CSJ ideology, resilience interventions are far more effective in preventing the onset or exacerbation of suicidal behaviour among men. In this chapter, I will expand on this, as this argument needs to be made more now than ever, as I fear the current situation is here to stay for the foreseeable future.

Worrying statistics

The incidence of suicide continues to increase around the world against a backdrop of declining mortality, representing a significant public health concern. In 2018, there were 6,507 suicides regis-tered in the UK, which equates to 11.2 deaths per 100,000; this figure is significantly higher than that of the previous year but rep-resents the first increase since 2013.[6] Further, in February 2021, it was reported that a third of young men in Scotland contemplated taking their lives as the nationwide lockdowns took their toll on people's mental health.[7]

As previously noted, even though suicidal ideation (thoughts and plans about suicide) is more common among women, men are still considerably more likely to engage in suicidal behaviour (completed or attempted suicide), and more often, they die of suicide. This is known within the context of suicide research as the *gender paradox*. The *2019 Suicide Statistics Report* by the Samaritans revealed that men aged 45–49 still have the highest rates of suicide in the UK.[8]

A similar trend can also be observed globally: a 2015 report from Our World in Data showed that suicide is more prevalent in men than women in all countries.[9] In developed countries, suicide mortality has been estimated as 2–3 times higher in young males than females; 75% of suicides are by men under fifty and the suicide rate is highest among middle-aged white men, who accounted for almost 70% of all suicides in 2017.[10,11] Yet, despite this evidence, there is a noticeable lack of discussion focusing on the male perspective.

Researchers in the field of male psychology have accumulated evidence that shows that men experience significant enacted stigma that negatively affects their overall mental health.[12] For one, men seem to have a harder time managing their mental health themselves and worry about how others will see them if they talk openly about it. Men are also more likely to use potentially harmful coping methods such as drugs or alcohol and are less likely to discuss their mental health issues with family or friends.

One possible explanation for this growing trend relates to a disconnect between the roles performed by men in previous centuries and what is expected of them now. Through the ages, broad themes around what it means to be male or female have persisted. Changes happened, but usually in a gradual way and not too dramatically; this is not what is happening in today's world. Change is everywhere; it is accelerating—and it is happening on an ever-increasing scale.

Traditional masculinity

Throughout history, there has been an ingrained connection between strength and masculinity, with physical pursuits seen as highly valuable forms of training for the military.[13] Similarly, in contemporary society, contact sports and other activities which push physical stamina to the limit are extremely popular with participants and spectators. Sports institutions, media outlets, and other related businesses benefit from enormous audiences who primarily consist of competitive-minded men. Some things just don't change.

Just as in prehistoric times, where men were hunter-gatherers who bore the weight of providing for and protecting their family, many present-day men still continue to base much of their self-worth on their success as breadwinners; a failure to provide is considered as a more general and profound failure as a man. Social psychologists Jennifer Bosson and Joseph Vandello posited that men are significantly more anxious about upholding gender norms than women.[14] Men feel the need to be the strong ones in the family, and therefore refrain from displays of weakness and refuse to admit any suffering—physical or mental. To do so would be tantamount to admitting they are no longer a man; such is the level of pride inherent in masculinity. Nonetheless, the reason men are more driven to provide and protect is that these are the traits "sexually selected" for them by society throughout history, and remain popular today.

Almost every culture has a specific view of manhood: deeming only certain, select behaviours acceptable, demanding that men maintain their lifestyle within a limited range of traits. In many cases, that aspiration toward masculinity means the need to perform feats of social and physical strength. The modern hazing rituals found in US universities are an example of this.

There seems to be a strong evolutionary basis for this tendency that probably explains why men have, throughout history, been expected not to disclose any problems in relation to their mental health. It is also why they are generally more competitive. But there is no one, or nothing, that this mentality can be blamed on in particular. It is simply how evolution has transpired. Men have historically been brought up not to discuss their mental health; they are generally more competitive among themselves than women, and so displays of vulnerability are more likely to lead to a loss of status for men.

Prevailing concepts of masculinity

The concept of masculinity is by no means a static entity. It metamorphoses across history and cultures; it is also intimately intertwined with social class. The most pervasive expression of masculinity right now is the one characterised by the Australian sociologist Raewyn Connell as *hegemonic masculinity*: the cultural ideal within societies, characterised predominantly by a belief in men's superiority over women.[15]

Stereotypical masculine traits are seen as the ideal, and sometimes even necessary traits of being a man. This notion of masculinity enjoys support from those who do not fulfil these criteria but who support hegemony in return for the rewards of being compliant. This has been termed *complicit masculinity*; those who are neither dominant nor complicit belong under the umbrella of subordinated masculinities, including those who are not white, young men, and homosexual men.

The subordination and lack of belonging are expressed in a variety of ways. Alfred Adler, the founder of the concept of individual psychology, claimed that when men experience a sense of inadequacy or perceived lack of virility, they often enact a "masculinity protest" as a means of compensation.[16] Adler's work on the inferiority complex was at the forefront of the literature on masculinity in the field of psychodynamic psychology.

Many of the reasons for which modern men and boys are reprimanded can fall into the category of masculinity protest. For example, a boy who does not fit into the group of alpha males in his class at school may, at first, attempt to benefit from their social success by becoming complicit in the hegemony. After some time, he may feel he is not benefiting as much as he should and so becomes resentful.

Initially, he might not know how to act in a way that demonstrates his agency but eventually compensates for his lack of belonging through amphetamine use. At first, the novelty is enough to distract him from his troubles, but as his day-to-day life continues to show no signs of improvement, the draw of an instant if temporary solution to all his problems becomes too much to resist. This could be a deviation in the boy's life, or it could be the beginning of a path leading to suicide. A drug habit can often make forming genuine relationships significantly more difficult. Lack of belonging or connection is possibly the biggest risk factor for depression; if one is living a chaotic life in the shadow of depression, an existing substance abuse problem is very likely to become worse. As evidenced by decades of research, this kind of spiral is all too common among men.[17]

Women, of course, encounter similar situations, but the particularities of masculinity mean that men and boys are far more likely to fall into this kind of trap. Although this model is simplistic, it does include some premises which are supported by more rigorous psychology. Research has shown that sex-related differences in the brain can influence the responses to drugs of abuse, progressive changes in the brain after exposure to drugs of abuse, and whether addiction results from drug-taking experiences.[18]

A modern masculinity?

It is only relatively recently that men have started to "come out" with their mental health stories in a genuinely vulnerable way. There has been a marked change in the level of institutional and societal support for men who choose to discuss their feelings. Prominent male public figures have contributed to this new atmosphere of support; if they can open up, so can men in general (consider Prince Harry, for instance).[19]

This changing mindset is crucial as, speaking generally, women are much more likely to talk about what is bothering them, while it is more common for a group of men to actively avoid acknowledging emotions and instead talk about shared interests. In such scenarios, it is difficult not to want to avoid being seen as the weak, emotional one of the group.

While there are still shortcomings within mental health services, societies have undeniably achieved significant progress in encouraging men to talk about their feelings. This progress is a double-edged sword, however, as it seems to suggest that the barrier to men getting the help they need is simply their unwillingness to ask for help or their inability to engage properly when help is offered to them. Consequently, the quality of the support or the aggregate of wider social attitudes are not considered problematic to the same extent.

To clarify, men do not need to be treated with kid gloves when it comes to encouraging them to talk, but it needs to be done in a way in which they will feel comfortable and do not feel "un-masculine". As mentioned previously, most women are open to discussing their emotions more readily, whereas due to evolved traits (then, consolidated by culturally ingrained habits), many men either cannot or will not share. Evolution and sexual selection account for many typical masculine traits. However, the way these traits manifest (and whether or not positive manifestations are maximised and the negative ones mitigated) comes down to culture and society.

The constellation of causes of suicidal behaviour is not fully understood. However, it is clearly the result of complex interactions between many different factors. A large body of research has demonstrated that there are specific factors that can help attenuate vulnerability to suicidal behaviour.[20] An awareness of these factors enables mental health professionals to provide targeted psychological treatment for those at risk. Unfortunately, well-established psychological theories operate in ways that directly contradict the tenets of CSJ theory.

Masculinity, suicide, and Critical Social Justice

CSJ has a rather unique way of viewing suicidal behaviour: it highlights the complex interactions between individual and group experiences of suicidality and various social pathologies including inequality, intergenerational poverty, racism, sexism, and homophobia.[21] Proponents of CSJ also obsessively accentuate how rising rates and disproportionate concentrations of suicide within specific populations can be linked to wider social, political, and economic inequalities.[22]

While social justice *per se* can offer a nuanced view of mental health, groups that suffer disadvantage and discrimination are expected to suffer high rates of mental ill health. It might seem well-intentioned, but CSJ can exacerbate mental health issues, including suicidal behaviour, in multiple ways.

First, CSJ offers an established narrative that its proponents use to push back against dominant white, male, Western discourses which they aim to dismantle. This can alienate men, especially those who are already disenfranchised or vulnerable for other reasons. One such example is young men from working-class communities who are over-represented among victims of "The Troubles" in Northern Ireland with suicides, crimes, school suspensions, expulsions, and academic underachievement.[23]

Second, the idea of resilience—especially within the context of mental health—has been absent from CSJ discourses. Men who struggle to stand firm during adverse life events may be further impeded from developing an action-oriented approach to personal change when they are regularly being told how they are on the side of the oppressor and need to shut up and "check their privilege".

Third, and most importantly, things are made worse by standpoint epistemology: the idea that the more privilege one has, the less of the world one can see and understand.[24] White men are told that they are racist and uphold white supremacy; those who are not white are told that they are oppressed and that the only solution is to tear down the very structures that in many ways have improved their own lives, and the lives of everyone else. This gets in the way of a more nuanced, individual, and evidenced-based approach to addressing mental health issues experienced particularly by men.

Disappointingly, even professional bodies can distort the way we view this, often for the worse. In 2019, the American Psychological Association pathologised maleness when they released their "first-ever guidelines for practice with men and boys", where they claimed that "Traditional masculinity—marked by stoicism, competitiveness, dominance, and aggression—is, on the whole, harmful".[25]

Arguably, the widespread adoption of CSJ beliefs does not bode well for men's well-being overall and, particularly, may lead to an increase in the incidence of suicide in this population.[26]

Things are changing

We must work particularly hard during this period of great social upheaval not to cede power to a set of beliefs that is actively harmful to men's mental health on a large scale. It could be that a notional roadmap for the way society treats mental health and other social issues for the next twenty years is being drawn up as we speak. Nevertheless, we must do everything possible to ensure that the mental health field develops in a way that maximises positive outcomes and minimises the number of men dying by suicide. I would argue that there are three clear steps that those involved in men's mental health should be talking about right now:

- **Counter the stigma.** As a society, we often fail to address the many traumas faced by boys and men, and we commonly punish behaviours without addressing the underlying causes. The person displaying these behaviours often does not feel comfortable asking for help and so, often, very little is done to make a fundamental change in their life. We need to eliminate the stigma around mental illness and remind men that expressing emotions and seeking therapy are approaches not just beneficial for the individual but can have positive consequences on their relationships and are necessary for the betterment of our society.

- **Promote resilience.** For men with mental health challenges, both the practice and the personal quality of resilience can manage distress in the face of adversity. Consequently, it can protect against negative outcomes such as suicidal behaviour by spending time focusing on the individual's power to change their own circumstances, on self-respect, and personal responsibility in life in general.

- **Research and communicate effective ways forward for men.** Findings from longitudinal studies reveal that higher personal growth initiative is associated with reduced psychological distress as well as improved mental health outcomes.[27] It is vital, therefore, that as a society we understand the various ways lack of purpose and lack of belonging can contribute to men's suicidal behaviour. This can serve as the key to the effective promotion and maintenance of positive mental health.

Conclusion: being there for men

There is significant evidence that exposure to CSJ ideologies may well be a risk factor for suicidal behaviour. To promote optimal mental well-being, we need strong relationships with others and must seek our own journeys that generate a sense of belonging and purpose. CSJ does not help with this but may actually engender social isolation as well as feelings of hopelessness and disassociation.

I would suggest that more of us need to listen to mental health professionals and those in allied fields who work "on the ground" with both men who are suffering and also those who once were suffering but have managed to rebuild their lives.

People who have first-hand experience in helping suicidal and/or dysfunctional men often don't feel the need to engage with CSJ—as it doesn't provide many answers. Understanding what has led someone to decide to end their own life necessitates a focus on the individual, yet currently, that is very much outside the territory of CSJ.

Each of our stories cannot be broken down to fit neatly into a set of boxes labelled as "race", "gender", "sexuality", and so on. But, if you listen long enough to men who express suicidal ideation, then common themes begin to emerge. These are the narratives that we need to be listening to in order to address the real challenges faced by a demographic group that is in particular trouble at the moment. *External* narratives such as CSJ are not designed to talk about an individual's *internal* struggles.

Endnotes

[1] Amy Chandler, "Masculinities and suicide: unsettling 'talk'as a response to suicide in men." *Critical Public Health* 32, no. 4 (2022): 499–508. https://doi.org/10.1080/09581596.2021.1908959.

[2] Laura Orsolini, Roberto Latini, Maurizio Pompili, Gianluca Serafini, Umberto Volpe, Federica Vellante, Michele Fornaro et al. "Understanding the complex of suicide in depression: from research to clinics." Psychiatry Investigation 17, no. 3 (2020): 207–221. https://doi.org/10.30773/pi.2019.0171.

[3] Irma Puspitasari, Ingka Tisya Garnisa, Rano Sinuraya, and Witriani Witriani, "Perceptions, Knowledge, and Attitude toward Mental Health Disorders and Their Treatment among Students in an Indonesian University", *Psychology Research and Behavior Management* 13 (October 27, 2020): pp. 845–54. https://doi.org/10.2147/prbm.s274337. (Bear in mind that every culture has a different way of looking at mental health issues.)

[4] Peter J. Helm., Lyla G. Rothschild, Jeff Greenberg, and Alyssa Croft. "Explaining sex differences in existential isolation research." *Personality and Individual Differences* 134 (2018): pp. 283–288. https://doi.org/10.1016/j.paid.2018.06.032.

[5] Irina Roncaglia, "Challenges vs Opportunities: A Different Perspective of Resilience", *Psychreg Journal of Psychology,* 3, no. 3 (2019): 46–49. https://doi.org/grh2.

[6] Office for National Statistics, "Suicides in the UK: 2018 Registrations", Office for National Statistics, 2018, https://www.ons.gov.uk/peoplepopulationandcommunity/birthsdeathsandmarriages/deaths/bulletins/suicidesintheunitedkingdom/2018registrations.

[7] Mark McLaughlin, "Alarm Over Rise in Suicidal Thoughts in Young Men," *The Times,* February 15, 2021, https://www.thetimes.co.uk/article/alarm-over-rise-in-suicidal-thoughts-in-young-men-t9fp2nnlf.

[8] "Suicide Statistics Report. Latest Statistics for the UK and Republic of Ireland," Samaritans, December 2019, https://media.samaritans.org/documents/SamaritansSuicideStatsReport_2019_Full_report.pdf.

[9] Ritchie, Hannah, Max Roser, and Esteban Ortiz-Ospina. "Suicide." Our World in Data, June 15, 2015. https://ourworldindata.org/suicide.

[10] Andrea Miranda-Mendizabal, Pere Castellví, Oleguer Parés-Badell, Itxaso Alayo, José Almenara, Iciar Alonso, Maria Jesús Blasco, et al., "Gender Differences in Suicidal Behavior in Adolescents and Young Adults: Systematic Review and Meta-Analysis of Longitudinal Studies", *International Journal of Public Health* 64, no. 2 (2019): 265–83. https://doi.org/10.1007/s00038-018-1196-1.

[11] Christine Yu Moutier, "Innovative and timely approaches to suicide prevention in medical education". *Academic Psychiatry 45*, no. 3 (2021): 252–256. https://doi.org/10.1007/s40596-021-01459-2.

[12] Louise Liddon, Roger Kingerlee, and John A. Barry, "Gender Differences in Preferences for Psychological Treatment, Coping Strategies, and Triggers to Help-Seeking"' *British Journal of Clinical Psychology* 57, no. 1 (2017): 42–58. https://doi.org/10.1111/bjc.12147.

[13] Kimberly Atherton, "The Concept of Masculinity and Male Suicide in North East England," Psychreg Journal of Psychology 3, no. 2 (2019): 37–5, https://doi.org/gb6m.

[14] Jennifer K. Bosson and Joseph A. Vandello, "Precarious Manhood and Its Links to Action and Aggression", *Current Directions in Psychological Science* 20, no. 2 (2011): pp. 82–86. https://doi.org/10.1177/0963721411402669.

[15] David Karen, and Robert Washington, "An Iron Man: The Body and Some Contradictions of Hegemonic Masculinity". In *Sociological Perspectives on Sport*, eds David Karen and Robert Washington (New York: Routledge, 2015). Pp. 141–149.

[16] Adler was an Austrian medical doctor, psychotherapist, and founder of a school of individual psychology. The overarching goal of Adlerian psychotherapy is to help the patient overcome feelings of inferiority. See Mark D, Kelland, "Adler's Individual Psychology", https://www.oercommons.org/authoring/22859-personality-theory/5/view.

[17] Sarah E. Zemore, Camillia Lui, and Nina Mulia, "The Downward Spiral: Socioeconomic Causes and Consequences of Alcohol Dependence among Men in Late Young Adulthood, and Relations to Racial/Ethnic Disparities." *Alcoholism: Clinical and Experimental Research* 44, no. 3 (2020): pp. 669–78. https://doi.org/10.1111/acer.14292.

[18] Jill B. Becker, Michele L. McClellan, and Beth Glover Reed. "Sex Differences, Gender and Addiction". *Journal of Neuroscience Research* 95, no. 1–2 (2016): 136–47. https://doi.org/10.1002/jnr.23963.

[19] Cecilia Rodriguez, "Prince Harry Opens up about His 20-Year Mental Struggle," April 18, 2017, https://www.forbes.com/sites/ceciliarodriguez/2017/04/18/prince-harry-opens-up-about-his-20-years-of-mental-struggle/?sh=6250c2f878ab.

[20] Paula Siegmann, Tobias Teismann, Nathalie Fritsch, Thomas Forkmann, Heide Glaesmer, Xiao Chi Zhang, Julia Brailovskaia, and Jürgen Margraf, "Resilience to Suicide Ideation: A Cross-Cultural Test of the Buffering Hypothesis". *Clinical Psychology & Psychotherapy* 25, no. 1 (2017): e1–e9. https://doi.org/10.1002/cpp.2118.

[21] Mark E. Button and Ian Marsh, *Suicide and Social Justice* (New York: Routledge, 2020), Preface.

[22] Anna Bussu Anna, Claudio Detotto, and Valerio Sterzi, "Social Conformity and Suicide". *The Journal of Socio-Economics* 42 (2013): 67–78. https://doi.org/10.1016/j.socec.2012.11.013.

[23] Ken Harland and Sam McCready, "Rough Justice: Considerations on the Role of Violence, Masculinity, and the Alienation of Young Men in Communities and Peacebuilding Processes in Northern Ireland". *Youth Justice* 14, no. 3 (2014): 269–83. https://doi.org/10.1177/1473225414549696.

[24] Elizabeth Anderson, "Feminist Epistemology and Philosophy of Science", Stanford Encyclopedia of Philosophy, February 13, 2020, https://plato.stanford.edu/entries/feminism-epistemology.

[25] "APA Issues First-Ever Guidelines for Practice with Men and Boys", American Psychological Association. Accessed October 13, 2021. https://www.apa.org/education-career/ce/1360513.

[26] Dennis Relojo-Howell, "Being a Snowflake Is Bad for Your Mental Health," The Critic, August 8, 2021, https://thecritic.co.uk/being-a-snowflake-is-bad-for-your-mental-health.

[27] Koen Luyckx and Christine Robitschek, "Personal Growth Initiative and Identity Formation in Adolescence through Young Adulthood: Mediating Processes on the Pathway to Well-Being," *Journal of Adolescence* 37, no. 7 (2014): 973–81. https://doi.org/10.1016/j.adolescence.2014.07.009.

Chapter 12:

Critical Race Theory in the Therapist's Chair—Introduction and Overview

by Carole Sherwood and Dina McMillan

Why would anyone object to a theory that promotes the rights of minorities? The following two chapters aim to address this question by exploring the ideas and beliefs that underpin Critical Race Theory (CRT).[1] This theory has come under attack, particularly in the US, from those concerned about its detrimental effect on mental healthcare and on children who are being taught CRT in schools.[2,3,4]

CRT is one of the main branches of Critical Social Justice ideology, which originates from Marxist thought and postmodernist theory. CRT is concerned with issues of race and racial discrimination. Its principles were developed by a group of legal scholars in the late 1980s.[5] Their underlying premise was that race is a socially constructed category originally established to oppress and exploit people of colour, especially black people. CRT has a set of tenets it applies to our current social, political, and legal structures.[6] They include the following ideas:

- racism is normal and permanent
- interest convergence[7]

- whiteness is property[8]
- counter-storytelling[9]
- critiques of liberalism.[10]

In essence, CRT's view is that racism will always be present in society, white people are responsible for maintaining it, and liberal ideas such as colour-blindness are either inadequate or seen, by some proponents, as a "mask to hide racism".[11]

In recent years, and particularly since the death of George Floyd, which led to widespread Black Lives Matter protests, there has been a notable and rapid incursion of CRT into the field of therapy.[12] The American Psychological Association states that it is "working to dismantle institutional racism" while the British Psychological Society, and the UK Council for Psychotherapy, are integrating the "anti-racist" ideas of Ibram X. Kendi into their organisations and training programs.[13]

Although this movement started out with the best of intentions, psychiatrist Dr Sally Satel raises concerns that an "overtly ideological approach is becoming increasingly prominent among a cadre of counseling professionals", citing, amongst others, the Graduate Counseling Program at the University of Vermont, where "the coordinator has issued a proposal to 'structurally align' the program with the Black Lives Matter movement, and begin 'the work of undoing systemic white supremacy'".[14]

We, the authors, share this growing sense of unease. Division and confusion are replacing common humanity and empathy and we fear that, in the longer term, psychological distress will be exacerbated rather than diminished by these initiatives, however well meaning their aims.

When considering how to present the complexity of CRT and its arguments in our chapters, we decided to adopt the novel approach of putting it "in the therapist's chair" to help readers understand CRT's worldview.[15] We gave it a "voice", enabling CRT to express its views through encounters with two psychologists—one white, and one black, with differing backgrounds, expertise, and life experiences. Our accounts of what unfolds are designed to reveal the ways of thinking encouraged by CRT and the implications of these for individuals, friendships, relationships, and the wider society. Our aim is to help the reader understand why serious concerns are being raised about introducing CRT, a major branch of Critical Social Justice ideology, into the field of therapy.

In Part One, CRT meets a white clinical psychologist who considers the potential effects of CRT's worldview on the mental health of both its proponents and those it criticises.

In Part Two, a black social psychologist considers CRT's beliefs about society and how these might manifest in a workplace environment.

Endnotes

[1] "The critical race theory (CRT) movement is a collection of activists and scholars engaged in studying and transforming the relationship among race, racism, and power"; "Unlike traditional civil rights discourse, which stresses incrementalism and step-by-step progress, critical race theory questions the very foundations of the liberal order, including equality theory, legal reasoning, Enlightenment rationalism, and neutral principles of constitutional law". Richard Delgado and Jean Stefancic, *Critical Race Theory: An Introduction,* 3rd ed. (New York: New York University Press, 2017), 2, Kindle.

[2] Jonathan Butcher and Mike Gonzalez, "Critical Race Theory, the New Intolerance, and Its Grip on America", The Heritage Foundation, 7 December, 2020, https://www.heritage.org/civil-rights/report/critical-race-theory-the-new-intolerance-and-its-grip-america.

[3] Sally Satel, "When Therapists Become Activists", *Persuasion,* August 13, 2021, https://www.persuasion.community/p/when-therapists-become-activists.

[4] Evan Gerstmann, "Should The States Bank Critical Race Theory in Schools?", Forbes, July 6, 2021, https://www.forbes.com/sites/evangerstmann/2021/07/06/should-the-states-ban-critical-theory-in-schools/?sh=3787427111a0.

[5] The first annual workshop on Critical Race Theory was held in 1989 and attended by Derrick Bell, Alan Freeman, Kimberlé Crenshaw, Richard Delgado, Cheryl Harris, Charles R. Lawrence III, Mari Matsuda, and Patricia J. Williams. Chris Demaske, "Critical Race Theory", *The First Amendment Encyclopedia*, 2009, https://www.mtsu.edu/first-amendment/article/1254/critical-race-theory.

[6] Jean Stefancic and Richard Delgado, *Critical Race Theory: The Cutting Edge* (Philadelphia: Temple University Press, 2013), Kindle.

[7] White people only act in ways that benefit them, even when they claim these efforts are to assist black people and correct past injustices (ibid).

[8] Due to the extensive history of white advantage, whiteness itself is treated as "property" within many institutions. It is a tangible asset, likened to the benefits of owning property versus being forced to rent (ibid).

[9] White people must listen to and accept black narratives because they share the impact of their longstanding exploitation (ibid).

[10] The tenets dismiss progressive claims of "colour-blindness", meritocracy, equality under the law as it is applied to black people and insist that white

people enjoy considerable social and cultural advantages not afforded to those of other races, especially black people. This includes their race being treated by organisations and institutions as a significant, permanent financial asset. Nicholas Daniel Hartlep, "Critical Race Theory: An Examination of its Past, Present, and Future Implications" (Information analysis, University of Wisconsin at Milwaukee, 2009), 1-19. https://files.eric.ed.gov/fulltext/ED506735.pdf.

[11] Ibram X. Kendi, *How to Be an Anti-Racist,* (New York, One World Publishing, 2019), 10, Kindle.

[12] Larry Buchanan, Quoctrung Bui, and Jugal K. Patel, "Black Lives Matter May Be the Largest Movement in U.S. History," *The New York Times*, July 3, 2020, https://www.nytimes.com/interactive/2020/07/03/us/george-floyd-protests-crowd-size.html

[13] Ibid.

[14] Sally Satel, "Keep Social-Justice Indoctrination Out of the Therapist's Office," *Quilette*, May 7 2021: https://quillette.com/2021/05/07/keep-social-justice-indoctrination-out-of-the-therapists-office/.

[15] The term "CRT" is used throughout these chapters as a generic "shorthand" to encompass all Critical Theories of Race. Recent criticisms of CRT have been met with protests that critics do not understand the term "CRT" or that it refers simply to a legal studies theory. However, the influence of Critical Theories of Race has extended well beyond legal studies to many other arenas, including education, healthcare, the church, entertainment, the corporate sector, government institutions and, of course, mental healthcare and the therapeutic professions.

Chapter 13:

Critical Race Theory in the Therapist's Chair—Part 1

by Carole Sherwood

Introduction

I am a clinical psychologist. Clinical psychologists are mental health professionals who work with individuals, families, groups, and communities. They use talking therapies to help people experiencing psychological distress due to a range of mental or physical health problems such as depression, anxiety, trauma, and chronic pain. During my professional career, I worked in an inner-city hospital where I helped people with HIV, some of them victims of torture or sexual assault, and others who had lost family members due to war or genocide. Many of those referred to me were refugees or asylum-seekers. All of them were fellow human beings deserving of respect and sensitivity.

When I listened to the painful stories they told me of brutality and degradation, I would often feel a strong sense of injustice. First and foremost, though, I considered it my job to do what I had been trained to do: to listen and bear witness to people's stories, helping them find ways of coping with overwhelming feelings of pain and despair while giving them some hope for the future.

In the account that follows, Critical Race Theory (CRT), one of the main branches of Critical Social Justice ideology, is given a voice, as explained in the introduction.

CRT meets a white clinical psychologist

It was clear from the outset that CRT did not want to see me—a white psychologist—discussing its beliefs. It considered all white people to be inherently racist and constantly looked for signs of racism in everything I said, monitoring me closely and asking itself, "How did racism manifest?"[1] In response, I cautiously monitored myself, worried that I might inadvertently cause offense and be accused of a microaggression.[2,3]

What CRT saw when it looked at me was "white privilege"—a "manipulating, suffocating blanket of power" that was both "'brutal and oppressive".[4,5] I was complicit in "whiteness": a system that conferred benefits to white people that were not available to non-white minorities.[6]

CRT did not hold back when telling me exactly what it thought of me, but I was rarely allowed to speak. When I tried to raise concerns about the consequences of continuously seeking evidence of racism, even in situations where it was not clear it had actually taken place, it dismissed those concerns.

When I suggested that "confirmation bias" might explain why CRT only looked for evidence that supported its worldview, this was denied.[7] When slights were perceived, CRT reacted angrily and accused me of racism. If I became defensive, I was accused of "white fragility".[8] Any denial was viewed as further evidence of racism.[9] There was no room for innocent mistakes and no forgiveness. Even expressions of guilt were viewed with scorn.[10]

CRT was trapped in a vicious cycle of hypervigilance, anger, and recrimination.[11] When I put these observations to CRT, I was told that this was why there was no point in talking to white people.[12]

I wondered about the consequences of the behaviour CRT advocated on the friendships and relationships of those who adopted its ideology. What effect would viewing life through a CRT lens have on someone's mental health?[13] Would they not feel angry and threatened most of the time? Wouldn't accusations of racism provoke feelings of guilt, shame, anger, or hopelessness in others? CRT was teaching minorities that they were helpless victims, encouraging a sense of grievance and victimhood.[14] If they followed CRT's guidance, always relying on anger to dictate their actions, constantly accusing white people of racism and encouraging other minorities to do the same, was there not a risk that such divisive behaviour would lead to racial tensions?[15]

Ways of thinking

With these concerns in mind, I looked at the ways of thinking that CRT advocates. In my clinical experience, always trusting your feelings or jumping to conclusions that you know what others are thinking, without any supporting evidence, are seen as examples of cognitive distortions.[16] Further, these ways of thinking are associated with depression and anxiety.[17] In their book *The Coddling of the American Mind*, Lukianoff and Haidt argue that when people think in the way CRT proposes, it's like a form of reverse Cognitive Behaviour Therapy (CBT) that can harm mental health.[18] The following exercise reveals how cognitive distortions work:[19]

> Imagine, while out walking, you see a friend coming towards you. You wave, but she doesn't wave back. She passes by, ignoring you completely. What would go through your mind? Maybe you'd wonder, "What have I done to offend her?" and feel worried and upset. Or perhaps you'd think, "How dare she ignore me?" and feel angry. What would you do?
>
> You might shrug and walk on, believing she hadn't seen you. Or perhaps you'd dwell on what happened

until you felt miserable or resentful. Maybe you'd call your friend to find out what was wrong. Suppose you discovered that, just before you saw her, she had been diagnosed with a serious illness. How would you feel then? Would it change your view of what had happened?

This exercise demonstrates how the same event can be interpreted in many different ways. You may even interpret the same event differently, depending on the context and your mood. It also shows how you cannot always trust your feelings to tell you what is actually happening, particularly in ambiguous situations. CBT proposes that it's not the event itself that's important but how you respond to it.[20]

Additionally, you are encouraged to consider a range of alternative perspectives before deciding how best to interpret and respond to a situation, rather than engaging in cognitive distortions such as *jumping to conclusions*, *mind-reading*, or *emotional reasoning*, as these can have unintended consequences for you personally, for your friendships and relationships.[21]

Let's get back to CRT, which had concluded that the actions of the white woman who walked by were racist. In its worldview, the *impact* of her actions mattered more than whether or not she *intended* to cause offense.[22] I asked CRT how this friend might feel if she knew she was being accused of racism. "White women's tears," was the reply.[23] Any suggestion that there may be other ways of looking at this scenario was rejected.

CRT insisted that "lived experience" was the "only truth that matters" and denied any notions of "objective reality".[24,25] It pointed out that my science was used "to colonise other lands and peoples" and that "it is a form of violence".[26,27] I was accused of behaving in a "traumatising, harmful, and oppressive" way.

Emotional reasoning, jumping to conclusions, and mind-reading

To understand what's happening here, let's look at the cognitive distortions in the thinking advocated by CRT. We'll start with *emotional reasoning* as this is central to the claim that "lived experience is the only truth".[28]

Have you ever watched a thriller on TV and noticed your heart beating faster? Although you're just watching actors on a film set, there's a primitive part of your brain—the amygdala—that works on a "better safe than sorry" basis and is designed to keep you safe.[29] What you're watching on TV is not actually going to cause you harm, but your brain *acts* as if it is. The amygdala sends out "false alarms", rather like an oversensitive car alarm that sounds when the wind blows. *Emotional reasoning* can lead us to *mis*interpret situations as threatening when they are not.

CRT refused to accept there was any alternative perspective to the "walking by" scenario. Yet, microaggressions are in the eye of the beholder and it can be difficult to establish whether or not they have occurred.[30] While one person might view an ambiguous remark or situation as hostile, another might not.[31] These individual differences in interpretation may be due to an individual's personality or temperament, with those who tend to experience negative emotions being more likely to interpret ambiguous situations negatively.[32,33] If someone feels particularly aggrieved and places undue emphasis on microaggressions, this may perpetuate a sense of victimhood.[34]

CRT was also *jumping to conclusions* and *mind-reading* about the white woman in the "walking by" scenario.[35] Hostile intentions were attributed to her without any supporting evidence that she was being racist. In CRT's view, "A positive white identity is an impossible goal. White identity is inherently racist; white people do not exist outside the system of white supremacy."[36] However good their intentions are, white people are condemned to remain forever racist. This is a bleak, uncompromising, and pessimistic belief to hold about your fellow human beings, particularly when, as in this scenario, you have no evidence to support it.

Magnifying, minimising, and catastrophising

CRT encourages minorities to *magnify* the most negative aspects of their encounters with white people and to *minimise* the importance of other aspects.[37] In the "walking by" scenario, it focused on the fact that a white friend had apparently ignored them while dismissing the friend's understandable preoccupation with their recent diagnosis. CRT's claim that the words I used to question their interpretation of this event were "traumatising" and "harmful" are examples of *catastrophising*.[38, 39]

In recent years, the idea that words can cause harm has spread across university campuses and is sometimes used as a justification for violent protests.[40] I noted that CRT was quick to accuse others of harm but expressed no concern at all about the harm it was causing others.

All-or-nothing thinking, overgeneralisation, blaming, and shaming

Since the Civil Rights movement of the 1960s, racism has come to be seen as a "highly stigmatised behaviour".[41] Even DiAngelo acknowledges that "to suggest I am racist is to deliver a deep moral blow—a kind of character assassination".[42]

Yet, if someone behaves defensively in response to being called a racist, they are automatically accused of "white fragility".[43] This is a circular argument from which white people can never escape judgement, whatever their response. They are told they're wrong if they feel guilty and wrong if they engage in "self-flagellation" to try and atone.[44,45]

If they refuse to change their existing worldview, they are accused of "willful ignorance".[46] Yet, if they try to help, they are called "white saviours". White people can do nothing but appease their accusers and try to "educate themselves" with no hope of redemption.[47] This is an example of *blaming and shaming,* and it can lead people to self-censor and remain silent in order to avoid accusations of racism.[48]

CRT has also changed the definition of "racism" from an individual act of prejudice and discrimination which most people understand to one that suggests racism is a "complex interconnected system" brought about by the "forces of socialization" in which "whites hold social and institutional power over people of color".[49,50]

Telling people that they are racist—on the basis of immutable characteristics, using incomprehensible definitions that they may not know or understand—then claiming they are "fragile" and in denial when they try to defend themselves, or accusing them of "gaslighting" when they don't agree with you, is a punitive way of treating people, whatever their colour.[51] Punishment is not an effective way of changing behaviour because "people will learn to avoid their punishment rather than the behaviour you are wanting to reinforce".[52]

White people might, understandably, start avoiding contact with minorities who hold these worldviews. Inevitably, though, this would place them in a double-bind because their actions would be construed as racist. These ways of thinking lead to a divisive "us-and-them" mentality.

Underpinning that divisive mentality is the categorisation of people as "black" victims or "white" oppressors. This is an example of *all-or-nothing* thinking that ignores the subtleties of life, with its complexities and shades of grey.[53] Each of us, as unique individuals, experience the world in our own particular way, based on early experiences; personal, family, and societal beliefs; culture; religion; and other influences.

Yet, for CRT, people are not individuals but members of identity groups.[54] It assumes that millions of people hold exactly the same opinions and prejudices based on the colour of their skin and believes that ethnicity or skin colour determines what people think. This is an example of *overgeneralization*.[55]

On the other hand, CRT also divides minorities into ever-increasing numbers of sub-categories, according to their degree of marginalisation.[56] Sub-dividing people into categories in this way has led to some minorities—who have lighter skin—being considered to have more privilege than those with darker skin, therefore potentially leading to conflict between minority groups.[57]

Victimhood, shoulds and oughts, name-calling, and labelling

Those minorities who do not fit neatly into black-or-white categories, such as Asian or Jewish people, or people of mixed heritage, pose a problem for CRT's worldview.[58] Minorities who have been successful in their lives and careers may not view themselves as "oppressed". In the conclusion to his book *Biracial Britain*, Remi Adekoya argues that people "want to be treated as the unique individuals they are, not as nameless members of this or that race or ethnic group. We all want to be viewed as individuals, not as 'black people', 'white people', or 'mixed-race people'. We need to approach others as we would like to be approached: as complex human beings full of so many contradictions any label deployed to define us is inevitably a gross simplification".[59]

Adekoya cites the case of Ralph, the son of a white English father and Nigerian mother, who comments, "One of the popular perceptions about mixed-race people that I don't like is the idea we are these vulnerable, traumatised individuals in a perpetual identity crisis. Some of us are. But I also know a lot of mixed-race people who are very confident human beings just wanting to live their lives and not be defined by race. They don't want to dance to the tune of identity politics and victimhood."[60]

There is also a risk that repeatedly telling people they are victims may lead them to develop a sense of "learned helplessness" and a belief that they have no control over their lives, leaving them vulnerable to depression.[61,62]

Yet, CRT would accuse anyone from a minority group who expressed such contrary views of having "internalised oppression" or of "acting white".[63,64] Minorities *should* never deviate from the CRT worldview. If they argue that their "lived experience" does not equate with CRT's, they are told they do not have the right kind of "lived experience". White people who try to stand up for minorities expressing alternative viewpoints are told, "Stay in your lane and be quiet," but when they do that they are then told that "silence is violence". The *tyranny of "shoulds"* gives people no option but to do what they are told or risk being pilloried, stigmatised, or silenced.[65]

If minorities dare to disagree with CRT's tenets, its advocates often resort to *name-calling* and *labelling.*[66] They are accused of being "race traitors", "coconuts", "Uncle Toms", or worse.[67] This punitive and accusatory behaviour can lead to demoralisation and a sense of hopelessness or anger and resentment in those subjected to it.

CRT's response

What, then, did CRT make of these observations? It replied that I was simply defending "whiteness". I asked why, then, had it agreed to talk to me. "Because you help minorities cope with problems in society when it's a society that needs to change. Changing minds is not activism. An activist produces power and policy change, not mental change."[68]

Sadly, our conversation was over and I had achieved nothing. CRT's main concern was not about improving mental health but encouraging activism. It wanted my job. It wanted control of the organisation that employed me, and it wanted to take over the institutions that train therapists like me. There was no hope for anyone who had grave misgivings about CRT's worldview and its potential for causing serious harm. Its aims were political and it would take no prisoners. I concluded the conversation with a heavy heart.

Conclusion

So, were CRT's aims to be fully realised, what would be the conse-quences of it gaining dominance in the field of therapy?[69]

We have seen that it teaches people to think in ways that are harmful to mental health. Always trusting your feelings to tell you what is "true" and refusing to consider other perspectives can lead to misunderstandings, problems in relationships, feelings of shame, guilt, resentment, anxiety, depression, and hopeless-ness. Blaming and judging others, rather than taking responsibil-ity for your actions and developing resilience, produces a culture of victimhood and division, bullying, and abusive behaviours. The inflexible views, lack of compassion, intolerance, or unforgive-ness inherent in CRT are, in my view, likely to lead to, rather than reduce, division and racism in society.

What kind of therapist would want to create such unhappi-ness and provoke greater societal divisions? How can any thera-pist claiming to be antiracist ignore the mistrust, animosity, and inflaming of racial tensions that the politicised ideology underpin-ning this term creates?

By asking these questions, I do not deny the painful expe-riences of those who endure racism, whether overt or subtle. Racism still exists and continues to cause harm; more needs to be done to address prejudice and discrimination. However, the problem is that Critical Race Theory causes harm too. It should come with a health warning. If you, reader, are seeking help from a therapist, I caution you to beware of the therapist trained in this ideology. It is unethical and potentially harmful.[70]

Therapists are expected to "do no harm", to be compassion-ate, empathic, and respectful of their clients, and to treat them as unique individuals. They do not set out to impose a set of political views and values on their clients.

Therapists have a lot of power in the therapeutic relationship, and this can easily be abused when clients are at their most vul-nerable. When a therapist has already made their mind up about who and what you are on the basis of your skin colour, they are more likely to cause you harm than to help you. If you are unlucky enough to find yourself in therapy with such a practitioner, there is a risk that they could seriously damage your mental health.

Endnotes

1   Robin DiAngelo, *White Fragility: Why It's So Hard for White People to Talk about Racism* (London, Allen Lane, 2019), 106, Kindle.

2   Derald Wing Sue, Christina M. Capodilupo, Gina C. Torino, Jennifer M. Bucceri, Aisha M.B. Holder, Kevin L. Nadal and Marta Esquilin, "Racial microaggressions in everyday life: implications for clinical practice," *The American Psychologist* 62, no.4 (May-June 2007): 271-286, https://doi.org/10.1037/0003-066X.62.4.271.

3   Anna Smith, "What to know about microaggressions", *Medical News Today*, June 11, 2020, https://www.medicalnewstoday.com/articles/microaggressions.

4   DiAngelo, *White Fragility,* p.23.

5   Reni Eddo-Lodge, *Why I'm No Longer Talking to White People About Race* (London, Bloomsbury Publishing, 2018), 69, Kindle.

6   Özlem Sensoy and Robin DiAngelo, *Is Everyone Really Equal?: An Introduction to Key Concepts in Social Justice Education*, 2nd ed. (New York: Teachers College Press, 2017), pp. 142-143.

7   Confirmation bias is the tendency of people to favour information that confirms their existing beliefs or hypotheses, Iqra Noor, June 10, 2020, https://www.simplypsychology.org/confirmation-bias.html.

8   DiAngelo, *White Fragility,* p. v.

9   Ibram X. Kendi, "The Heartbeat of Racism is Denial", *The New York Times*, January 13, 2018, www.nytimes.com/2018/01/13/opinion/sunday/heartbeat-of-racism-denial.html.

10 Eddo-Lodge, *Why I'm No Longer Talking to White People,* 8, p. 146.

11 Hypervigilance is a state of increased alertness and extreme sensitivity to your surroundings. It can make you feel like you're alert to any hidden dangers, whether from other people or the environment. Often, though, these dangers are not real: https://www.healthline.com/health/hypervigilance.

12 Eddo-Lodge, *Why I'm No Longer Talking to White People,* p. 5.

13 Kimi Katiti, "This is How I Escaped The Cult of Wokeness", Youtube, May 28, 2021, https://www.youtube.com/watch?v=S5Ak5uEcDUQ.

14 Bradley Campbell and Jason Manning, *"Microaggression and Moral Cultures,"* *Comparative Sociology* 13, no.6 (January 2014): 692-726, https://doi.org/10.1163/15691330-12341332.

15 Jonathan Haidt and Lee Jussim, "Hard Truths About Race on Campus", *The Wall Street Journal*, May 6, 2016, https://www.wsj.com/articles/hard-truths-about-race-on-campus-1462544543.

16 A.T Beck, "Thinking and depression: I. Idiosyncratic content and cognitive distortions," *Archives of General Psychiatry*, 9, no.4 (1963): 324-333, https://doi.org/10.1001/archpsyc.1963.01720160014002.

17 Greg Lukianoff and Jonathan Haidt, *The Coddling of the American Mind: How Good Intentions and Bad Ideas Are Setting Up a Generation for Failure* (New York: Penguin Books, 2019), 7, Kindle.

18 Ibid.

19 In my clinical work, I refer to them as "thinking styles", explaining that everyone has at least some of these biases but that raising awareness of them and finding alternative perspectives can help overcome them.

20 Helen Kennerley, Joan Kirk and David Westbrook, *An Introduction to Cognitive Behaviour Therapy: Skills & Applications* (London:Sage Publications, 2017), pp. 193-195.

21 Ibid.

22 Lukianoff and Haidt, *The Coddling of the American Mind*, p. 40.

23 DiAngelo, *White Fragility, pp.* 129-138.

24 James Lindsay, "Lived Experience", New Discourses, Revision date: April 17, 2020. https://newdiscourses.com/tftw-lived-experience/.

25 Sensoy and DiAngelo, *Is Everyone Really Equal?*, pp. 15-17, p. 187.

26 Race Reflections, Rethinking Inequality, Injustice and Oppression, "Culturally Biased Therapy? (Part 1) Epistemic Violence and CBT", January 11 2017, https://racereflections.co.uk/articles/.

27 Gayatri Chakravorty Spivak, "Can the Subaltern speak?" in *Marxism and the Interpretation of Culture,* eds. Cary Nelson and Lawrence Grossberg (London: Macmillan, 1988), pp. 271-313.

28 *Emotional Reasoning:* "Assuming that feelings reflect fact", Kennerley, Kirk and Westbrook, *An Introduction to Cognitive Behaviour Therapy*, p.195.

29 Amygdala: an almond-shaped structure in the temporal lobe that is a component of the limbic system. The amygdala plays an important role in memory, emotion, perception of threat, and fear learning, 2020, https://dictionary.apa.org/amygdala.

30 Sue, Capodilupo, Torino, Bucceri, Holder, Nadal and Esquilin, "Racial Microaggressions in Everyday Life", 279, quoted in Scott O. Lilienfeld, "Microaggressions: Strong Claims, Inadequate Evidence", *Perspectives on Psychological Science* 12, no.1 (January 2017): 143. https://doi.org/10.1177/1745691616659391.

31 Lilienfeld, "Microaggressions", pp. 144-145.

32 Brenda Major, Shannon K. McCoy, Cheryl R. Kaiser, and Wendy J. Quinton, (2003). "Prejudice and self-esteem: A transactional model," *European Review of Social Psychology*, 14, no.1 (2003): 77–104, https://doi.org/10.1080/10463280340000027, quoted in Lilienfeld, "Microaggressions", p.147.

33 Lilienfeld, "Microaggressions", pp. 152-155.

34 Kenneth R. Thomas, "Macrononsense in Multiculturalism", *American Psychologist*, 63, no.4 (2008): 274-275, https://doi.org/10.1037/0003-066X.63.4.274 quoted in Lilienfeld, "Microaggressions", p.140.

35 *Jumping to conclusions and mind-reading* – "Making interpretations in the absence of facts to support them", Kennerley, Kirk and Westbrook, *An Introduction to Cognitive Behaviour Therapy*, p. 195.

36 DiAngelo, *White Fragility*, p. 59.

37 *Magnification and minimisation* – "Exaggerating the importance of negative events and underestimating the importance of positive events", Kennerley, Kirk and Westbrook, *An Introduction to Cognitive Behaviour Therapy*, p. 194.

38 Nick Haslam refers to the expansion of concepts such as "trauma" as "'concept creep" and argues that this risks "pathologizing everyday experience and encourages a sense of virtuous but impotent victimhood". Nick Haslam, "Concept Creep: Psychology's Expanding Concepts of Harm and Pathology," *Psychological Inquiry* 27, no.1 (January 2016): 2.

39 *Catastrophising* – "Predicting the very worst, sometimes from a benign starting point. This may happen very rapidly so that it seems that the client has immediately leapt to the most awful conclusion", Kennerley, Kirk and Westbrook, *An Introduction to Cognitive Behaviour Therapy*, p. 194.

40 Lawrence, N. (2017, February 7) Black bloc did what campus should have. *The Daily Californian*. Retrieved from https://www.dailycal.org/2017/02/07/black-bloc-campus/, quoted in Lukianoff and Haidt, *The Coddling of the American Mind*, pp. 81-98.

41 Campbell and Manning, *"Microaggression and Moral Cultures"*, 692-726, https://doi.org/10.1163/15691330-12341332.

42 DiAngelo, *White Fragility*, p. 72.

43 Ibid, p. 14.

44 Eddo-Lodge, *Why I'm No Longer Talking to White* People, pp. 146-147.

45 Ibid, p. 8.

[46] Houston A. Baker Jr., "Handling 'Crisis': Great Books, Rap Music, and the end of Western Homogeneity (reflections on the humanities in America,) *Callaloo*, 13, no.2 (Spring 1990): 173-194, https://doi.org/10.2307/2931668, quoted in: Sensoy and DiAngelo, *Is Everyone Really Equal?*, p. 6.

[47] DiAngelo, *White Fragility*, p. 143.

[48] Dr Becky Spelman, "The Weaponisation of Shame, Blame and Guilt", December 2018, https://theprivatetherapyclinic.co.uk/shame-blame-and-guilt/.

[49] *Prejudice, adverse or hostile attitude toward a group or its individual members, generally without just grounds or before sufficient evidence.* Brittanica, https://www.britannica.com/topic/racism.

[50] DiAngelo, *White Fragility*, p. v, 3, 4.

[51] *Gaslighting,* an elaborate and insidious technique of deception and psychological manipulation, usually practiced by a single deceiver, or *"gaslighter,"* on a single victim over an extended period. Brian Duignan, Brittanica, https://www.britannica.com/topic/gaslighting.

[52] Paul Gilbert and Robert L. Leahy, "Introduction and overview, Basic issues in the therapeutic relationship," in *The Therapeutic Relationship in the Cognitive Behavioral* Psychotherapies, eds., Paul Gilbert and Robert L. Leahy (New York: Routledge, 2007), 6, Kindle.

[53] *All-or-nothing thinking,* also known as *dichotomous* or *black-and-white thinking*, "Viewing things in all or nothing terms without appreciating the spectrum of possibilities between the two extremes", Kennerley, Kirk and Westbrook, *An Introduction to Cognitive Behaviour Therapy*, p. 194.

[54] Sensoy and DiAngelo, *Is Everyone Really Equal?*, pp. 43-47.

[55] *Overgeneralisation,* "Seeing a single negative event as an indication that everything is negative", Kennerley, Kirk and Westbrook, *An Introduction to Cognitive Behaviour Therapy*, p. 194.

[56] Helen Pluckrose and James Lindsay, *Cynical Theories: How Activist Scholarship Made Everything about Race, Gender, and Identity – and Why This Harms Everybody* (Durham, North Carolina: Pitchstone Publishing, 2020), pp. 125-131.

[57] Kristel Tracey, "We Need to Talk about Light-skinned Privilege," *Media Diversified*, February 7, 2019, mediadiversified.org/2018/04/26/we-need-to-talk-about-light-skinned-privilege/, quoted in Pluckrose and Lindsay, *Cynical Theories*, p. 129.

[58] Pluckrose and Lindsay, *Cynical Theories*, p. 129.

59 Remi Adekoya, *Biracial Britain: A Different Way Of Looking At Race*, (London: Constable, 2021), 304, Kindle.

60 Ibid, p. 103.

61 Martin E.P. Seligman and C. Peterson, Learned Helplessness, International Encyclopedia of the Social & Behavioural Sciences, 2001, pp. 8583-8586, https://doi.org/10.1016/B0-08-043076-7/00378-8.

62 Reading one short passage of CRT was sufficient to reduce African-American respondents' sense of control over their lives. Eric Kaufman, "The Social Construction of Racism in The United States", Report April 2021, 20-23, https://media4.manhattan-institute.org/sites/default/files/social-construction-racism-united-states-EK.pdf.

63 Sensoy and DiAngelo, *Is Everyone Really Equal?*, p. 72.

64 Devon W. Carbado and Mitu Gulati, *Acting White? Rethinking Race in "Post-Racial" America* (Oxford UK: Oxford University Press, 2013), p. 43.

65 Rob Pascale and Lou Primavera, "The Tyranny of Musts and Shoulds: learning to fight against our irrational beliefs", Psychology Today, April 17, 2017, https://www.psychologytoday.com/gb/blog/so-happy-together/201704/the-tyranny-musts-and-shoulds.

66 "Cognitive Distortions: Labeling," Cognitive Behavioral Therapy Los Angeles, May 8, 2015, https://cogbtherapy.com/cbt-blog/cognitive-distortions-labeling.

67 Serina Sandhu, "Race report: commissioners have faced death threats and 'racial slurs like Uncle Tom' says Kemi Badenoch," inews UK, April 20, 2021, https://inews.co.uk/news/uk/race-report-commissioners-death-threats-racial-slurs-kemi-badenoch-964801.

68 Ibram X. Kendi, *How to be an Anti-racist,* (London: Penguin Random House, 2019), 209, Kindle.

69 The Contradictions of Critical Theory and Counseling, Tristan Fitz, *New Discourses*, July 2020: https://newdiscourses.com/2020/07/contradictions-critical-theory-counseling.

70 Why Critical Social Justice Activism Could Increase Suicide Risk, Steve Dreesman, *Areo*, August 2020: https://areomagazine.com/2020/08/10/why-critical-social-justice-activism-could-increase-suicide-risk/.

Chapter 14:

Critical Race Theory in the Therapist's Chair—Part Two

by Dina McMillan

Introduction

I am a social psychologist. My approach is therefore different from that of a clinical psychologist. Social psychologists are not therapists, per se. Instead, we assess the impact of personal, social, and environmental factors on individual beliefs and behaviors. We consider how people learn and how they're persuaded and influenced. However, my specialism is researching the dynamics that operate in abusive relationships, and this has allowed me to offer a consultancy service. Essentially, I help people who believe they are experiencing unfair power imbalances, manipulation, or maltreatment in their intimate or workplace relationships.

Viewed through both my professional knowledge and specialist experience, in this chapter, I will explore the effects of Critical Race Theory's (CRT) worldview on both individuals and wider society. I consider a few of the problems that might realistically arise with CRT in the workplace, demonstrating how its tenets, assumptions, and advocated behaviors can lead to conflict and division. This is especially the case when it is used as a template for its advocates' own interactions and they try to impose their beliefs onto others.

Critical Race Theory has become more than a broad theory developed in the 1980s by legal scholars. It has increasingly been introduced into the structure of both private sector and government agencies. In recent years, its ideological premise has become embedded within our legislative, educational, and health systems. This includes mental health services.

CRT proposes the concept of race is not a scientific concept. Rather, they maintain it is a socially constructed category designed by whites to exploit and exclude people of color, in particular black people. Advocates of CRT view racism against blacks as foundational, not an aberration, and insist it continues to inform our legal, judicial, and social systems.[1]

CRT has several fundamental principles, called tenets, that underlie its doctrine. It maintains that those whose intention is not overtly racist can nonetheless act in a manner that promotes white supremacy. Therefore "color-blindness" is a myth, as are other liberal ideas supported by whites to address racial injustice.[2] CRT asserts racism is such a fundamental aspect of our society that it is a permanent fixture, interpreted by many to indict all whites as racist, whether conscious of it or not.

CRT's tenets insist that whites only act in a way to benefit black people if they also gain, something they label "interest convergence". They assert that being white is such a significant advantage in social outcomes it is comparable to the benefits of having a legal deed to a home, called "whiteness as property". CRT advises whites who are interested in rectifying these injustices should adopt a passive stance. They must allow black voices and other people of color to share storytelling, and actively listen as they relate their lived experiences without being interrupted or judged.

Previously, we anthropomorphized Critical Race Theory into a fictional client, named CRT, to illustrate this more clearly. We saw that CRT's responses to a white psychologist were hostile and dismissive. Would meeting a psychologist who is also black make a meaningful difference? Or would CRT's acceptance of me be contingent on my sharing its worldview?

Critical Race Theory meets a black social psychologist

When CRT entered the room, it did not automatically object to me, in sharp contrast to the way it had responded to my white colleague. As a black woman who wears her hair naturally, not straightened, I expected to garner at least superficial approval.

CRT had difficulty getting comfortable. Its back was poker straight and its muscles tight in a classic pose of defensiveness. The tenets underlying its worldview left it permanently scanning the environment for indicators of racial bias and systemic injustice. I knew this would include me; everything from my dress and style of speech to the diploma on the wall indicating where I had received my formal training. I had a moment of concern that it would view my standard professional dress as indicating I was an "assimilationist", and therefore someone who had adopted the beliefs and standards of "white supremacists" rather than supporting black empowerment.[3]

Critical Race Theory tenets at work

CRT wished to discuss problems at its workplace. It complained that the top executives, all white men, refused to acknowledge their privilege and continued to deny their race afforded them unearned opportunities. They dismissed the merit of "whiteness as property", a central CRT tenet exposing a wide range of substantial, measurable systemic benefits linked with being white.[4] They would not alter their promotion policies to place more black people in positions of authority, an equity solution that CRT endorsed as a fair method to correct past injustices.[5]

CRT claimed the executives' "reasons" were excuses. There was insufficient interest convergence to motivate them to act. When it said this, I recalled "interest convergence" is the willingness of whites to take action that benefits black people, but only when whites also gain. The executives had rejected all suggestions that CRT demanded of them. Attempts to change their minds had led to profound discord at the company.

CRT had been sent to therapy to gain some active tools to help it interact more congenially with others. It appeared, after chatting for a while, that CRT's real purpose in seeking this meeting with me was to gain insight into getting more concessions from its employers regarding anti-racism policies. It was certain it had been racially stereotyped by its employers as just another "angry black person".[6] We both understood this as a limiting trope used by whites for centuries to dismiss the genuinely oppressive experiences of black people, pathologizing normal emotional reactions to being treated unfairly or even cruelly.

Yet, CRT was unwilling to consider whether there could be issues on both sides. While its employers may have been too quick to stereotype CRT as angry, CRT may also have been behaving in ways that made interactions too arduous for employers, colleagues, and customers. CRT's attitude was described by its employers as "persistently confrontational". They insisted it was "unacceptable" for customers and colleagues to be accused of racism or made to feel self-conscious whenever a request by CRT was not immediately granted. CRT expected me to find this accusation from its employers a typical example of racial bias. I did not concur. How could I? The assessment of CRT's effect on others was probably accurate. Being accosted with constant hostility is wearing.

Expecting racial discrimination

CRT also proclaimed its outrage that the white psychologist that had been seen previously had believed it was misinterpreting the racial hatred it encountered. She had not honored CRT's "lived experience" as the most valid criterion for assessing the situation.[7] She had appeared unenthusiastic about the counter-storytelling that's key, in its view, to getting whites to recognize the cost of their longstanding exploitation of black people.

On hearing this, I knew that my colleague, as a clinical therapist, would have been more than willing to listen to CRT's interpretation of events. However, healthy interactions require considering the perspectives of others. CRT was completely opposed to considering the impact of its behavior on anyone in its workplace if they were white.

When I probed further, CRT admitted that it kept its guard up all the time around white people in the expectation of racial discrimination. It was always on the lookout for conscious bias. It was also scanning for unconscious bias, often found in microaggressions, the more subtle words and gestures that indicate prejudiced perceptions, contempt, or even hatred against members of historically marginalized groups.[8] CRT stated that certainty of rejection was the reason it avoided interactions with whites, other than when compelled to do so for work or when performing tasks such as shopping or travelling.[9]

CRT did not believe white people when they attempted to convince black people they were not racist, viewing these attempts as performative and empty gestures. I wondered whether CRT had ever had a positive relationship with a white teacher, boss, or friend. I feared CRT would perceive the actions of any whites who had assisted it or attempted to be friends as having selfish and racist motives.[10]

In addition to insisting that racism permanently underlies the foundation of our society, CRT declared the damage of racism is only generated by the behavior of whites (as the empowered group) towards blacks (as the disempowered group) and never the other way around.

CRT contended that racial inequality hadn't improved since the middle of the 20th century when Malcolm X spoke before he was assassinated. CRT still believed in the currency of all of Malcolm X's assertions, especially when he stated outright that he did not trust white liberals.[11] CRT also decried gestures like whites putting "Black Lives Matter" on their social media profiles or adding a black square on Instagram during the widespread protests in 2020.[12] It asserted these were done under duress and did not represent any fundamental change in the way white people view black people. Resolutely, CRT insisted any critique of white liberalism was still valid.

I doubted CRT would perceive any attempt to address racial inequality as sincere. Popular authors including Ibram X. Kendi, Michael Eric Dyson, and other Critical Social Justice advocates insist that racism is as strong as it has ever been, or even worse.[13] A cursory examination of basic principles would likely show CRT dismissing most, if not all, anti-racism efforts as placating gestures or racism in disguise.[14]

I noted again how consistently CRT's focus was only targeting wrongs by whites towards black people. It acknowledged nothing about its own destructive patterns or behavior. It certainly did not consider that any of its principles or tenets could be incomplete, obsolete, or incorrect. Did personal responsibility, accountability, or self-correction have a chance? What about the black community's efforts to address harmful issues like high crime, single parenthood, and poverty? Would the temptation to ascribe all ills directly to racism be too strong? Did CRT consider we could ever move past historical wrongs? Or was its fundamental identity centered only in reference to its grievances? I became concerned: could anything be forgiven? Could any action by whites be accepted as a genuine attempt to heal?

And importantly, had CRT ever considered the impact of teaching black people they are perennial victims who will always be underestimated, disrespected, and despised?

I wondered whether CRT would interpret these questions as a sign I was experiencing "internalized white supremacy". Would it think I only perceived the world with consideration of the benefits for white people?[15] Would my views be summarily dismissed in the same way as my white colleague's had been?

CRT asked me if I had ever experienced racism. I admitted I had, and still do. Racism is included in some of my earliest memories. This admission calmed the situation somewhat.

How to help?

I took the conversation back to the core topic. CRT had been repeatedly unsuccessful when attempting to convince its employers to fundamentally shift their policies. Perhaps there was something in its approach that was limiting the appeal. Did they feel attacked rather than advised? Did they believe CRT was being unfair in its attempt to redress historical wrongs? "White fragility" was the answer, again. CRT defined any resistance as due to the discomfort whites experience when asked to reconsider the unfair advantages provided to them by systemic racism.

I wondered silently if any approach would be successful when all questions were met with anger and accusations. CRT did not seem to consider the impact of incessant antagonism and derogatory interpretations on whites, or even on blacks who were not yet convinced. I dared to ask, "Is it wise to ascribe any and all points of contention or alternative viewpoints as racism?" "Absolutely!" was the immediate response, with a look of disappointment indicating that I did not understand this fundamental premise.

As seen in the last chapter, adherence to dogmatic philosophies leave adherents prone to cognitive distortions. Lukianoff and Haidt have proposed that a hypervigilant and persistently negative mindset can have a deleterious effect on mental health.[16]

However, I doubted the ability of Cognitive Behavior Therapy (CBT) to assist proponents of Critical Race Theory (CRT). CBT works with clients to teach them how to consider various alternative perspectives before drawing conclusions or choosing a particular course of action.[17] Utilizing only the fixed lens of racism would severely restrict the options of CRT when interacting with others.

CRT also placed considerable emphasis on "lived experience" as the only basis for interpreting situations. This stance echoes the underlying principles of postmodernism, with its emphasis on truth being subjective and knowledge linked to power.[18] According to CRT, whites can never live the experience of blacks, and therefore it is selfish for whites to dismiss whatever interpretation of events is offered by black people.[19] CRT declared there had been more than enough stories about the lives of whites and that it was time for whites to quietly listen to counter-storytelling and the new, possibly painful, version of events being offered by blacks.[20]

Cognitive distortions

Everything had to be presented according to the perspective through which CRT viewed the world or risked being immediately dismissed. This rigidity led to an overwhelming level of "cognitive distortions".[21] Part of this biased thinking—CRT assuming it automatically knew what others were thinking—gave me a small advantage in this context. Unless I explicitly disputed a notion, CRT would presume my experiences were similar and that I supported its principles and approach.

Therefore, I felt it may be helpful to assess the cognitive distortions experienced by CRT from a slightly different angle. I wanted to acknowledge that racial bias and discrimination still exist. I also wanted to explore how CRT may be demanding such strict adherence to a specific paradigm of tenets, thereby constraining its adherents from dealing with other underlying issues.[22] It was necessary to focus on a few aspects of CRT's current thinking that were making attempts difficult for it to address its workplace problems.

First, the "egocentric" viewpoint.[23] CRT focused only on its own evaluation of the world and its presumed impact on black people. It demonstrated no consideration of the effect its actions had on the feelings, needs, or requirements of others and seemed not to understand why it should try. There was no indication of empathy for others, including those black people who did not share their perspectives or concur with its suggested social remedies.

CRT's hypervigilant awareness was perpetuated by expectations of harm due to racism. It made decisions according to chronic feelings of self-righteous anger and anticipation of being wronged due to racial bigotry. CRT demanded this should be rectified in a way that was beneficial only to itself, and perhaps to those black people who shared its beliefs.

For example, CRT told me of an incident at its workplace where a young white female staff member complimented a black colleague on their hair. CRT was outraged, seeing this as a microaggression, and made a complaint about her to management.[24] CRT insisted that the white employee be disciplined and enrolled in an anti-racism program to teach her the error of her ways. No consideration was given to the young woman's feelings, the negative impact this might have on her in the workplace, or to the black colleague who may have disagreed with CRT's actions.

Second, CRT refused to consider alternative viewpoints. This is not unusual when someone is a member of a group that demands rigid adherence to a set of dogmatic beliefs and identifies specific targets to blame for all wrongs. For devotees of CRT, the only explanation for faulty processes and failed outcomes for black people, as individuals or as a people, is racial oppression due to white supremacy. There is no consideration given to the possibility of flawed in-group social norms, unsound personal decisions, or more general factors that may be at fault.[25]

Third, CRT expected an automatic free pass whenever it made a mistake or did not achieve the requisite outcomes for someone in its position at the organization where it worked. Its mindset defined any dissent, resistance, or demands for accountability as white supremacy or, if the person criticizing CRT was also black, internalized racism. When CRT or a black colleague behaved badly at work, severely underperformed, insulted a customer, or caused damage to the company's reputation, managers would immediately be accused of racism if they dared to call them to account. There was no consideration by CRT that the accusation could be valid and the problem needed to be redressed. This is in stark contrast to the punitive way CRT advocated managers deal with white colleagues if any of the same behaviors were noted.

There was an exception. Whenever a black colleague disagreed with CRT's worldview, they would be treated as though they were white and their opinions dismissed as an example of internalized white supremacy. Sometimes, the black colleague would suffer even harsher punitive measures than a white person, being viewed as traitorous.

Cognitive biases

Besides the cognitive distortions discussed above, there were other biases evident in CRT's behavior and approach to life.[26] In this section, I will be focusing on three in particular: disqualifying the positive, personalization, and control fallacies.

For CRT, the only constructive approaches or actions were those aligned with its worldview.[27] Black people should only do positive things for other black people if these did not serve white supremacy in some manner or support existing power structures. CRT disqualified anything supportive or generous from whites towards blacks as demonstrations of either interest convergence or placating gestures due to a perception of black problems as part of the "white man's burden".[28] White people would only act with fairness or kindness to keep black people from responding violently or because their interests were also served by the action.

CRT left no possibility for genuine kindness, fairness, friendship, love, consideration, or any other positive emotion or interaction between the races.

When CRT spoke of disruptive interactions at work, it personalized every negative occurrence as something done because of racial differences. CRT refused to consider that it may have simply been due to its own unacceptable behavior. It was all about CRT as a black person dealing with white supremacy. Everything unpleasant that occurred, every challenging event, was viewed as a personal affront and underpinned by racism. CRT claimed there was a campaign to get it to quit and prevent it from being able to sue the company for discrimination.

Despite CRT's ability to quote the tenets of Critical Race Theory verbatim, it did not feel any control over its life and was firmly convinced that all whites hate all blacks. To CRT, the rigid system structurally underlying our entire society was predicated on whites accepting black people only as sources of entertainment, sports figures, and useful workers propping up white infrastructure. When asked about healing from the trauma of past experiences and possibly changing its interpretation of the motivations of others, CRT refused. It insisted it is crucial to be conscious of what is really occurring, which meant strict adherence to the "Approved Narrative" and its prescribed worldview.[29] For CRT, its limited perspective and the accompanying chronic rage were companions not yet ready to be left behind.

CRT maintained total obedience to the principles of its philosophy and upheld its constrained view of the world. Included in this is a call for tenacious activism to aggressively seek to remedy this imbalanced power dynamic.[30] These perspectives, combined with a lack of emotional, cognitive, or compassionate empathy for others, created a significant challenge for anyone trying to assist or even interact.[31] It was evident that CRT had little or no flexibility. Unless each person in their life shared their worldview in every respect, CRT would either try to convert them or reject them. It demanded "ideological purity".[32]

This standpoint resulted in a person prone to making judgmental, irate, and rejecting comments toward anyone who dared ask questions or disobey the Approved Narrative. This could be as simple as refusing demands for incessant activism in all contexts. A special point of contention seemed to be white people who insisted they did not maintain, in CRT's words, "the internalized sense of superiority that all whites possess".[33]

According to CRT, racism is so inherent in the structure of our culture that there is no redress.[34] Racism is permanent. Black people must accept they are perpetual unwelcome victims. There is no mention of how this is a lose/lose proposition, that this mindset is totally disempowering for black people.[35]

I asked CRT if it was useful to label all whites as ceaseless predators. CRT insisted it was useful because it was true. It said, "It doesn't matter if it all ends in tears." CRT insisted black people need to know where they stand and build from there. It didn't offer suggestions for how to build anything that could thrive on a foundation of hatred, suspicion, and rejection.

How Critical Race Theory exacerbates vulnerability and disempowerment

Those who experience persistent feelings of indignation, which they view as righteous, tend to shield themselves from personal responsibility for their actions. They hold a pre-identified scapegoat responsible for all of their pain, traumas, and hurts; that scapegoat is ultimately accountable for their misdeeds. This source is always outside of the self. It is both a shelter and a prison, protecting the ego while also limiting the probability of genuine healing or progress.

In addition to maintaining this external locus of control, they experience a fragile sense of self that is easily threatened. It is triggered by anything but unquestioning, explicit submission to their promoted doctrine. Threat perception is heightened by attempts to hold them responsible for their actions. Their usual response to any threat is extreme aggression.

Groups that demand rigid conformity while offering a strong sense of group identity are usually more appealing to those who are emotionally vulnerable. The continued prevalence of racial bias and the lasting impact on families of severe racist policies in the recent past leave a large segment of the black population susceptible. There is a considerable body of work now that defines the experience of racism as traumatic, whether it is the result of major discriminatory acts, hate crimes, or even the compilation of small incidents and "microaggressions" over time.[36,37]

This approach makes an unapologetic, *"in your face"* ideology like CRT appealing to those who have been damaged by racism's persistent presence in our society. They are seeking answers and tangible examples of resolution.

If exposed to CRT, they would notice the many recent examples of influential people advocating for its principles and people in authority conceding to its demands, both white and black. These demonstrations of power can be heady for anyone who has experienced marginalization or discrimination. Joining in means sharing that power.

The question is whether a rigid, hostile, externally focused ideology like CRT is a viable solution. I have never witnessed a successful redress tactic that relies solely on one side being held accountable while the wronged party is permitted to act and react in any fashion without reproach. The probability this would lead to frequent abuse is unacceptably high, and common sense.

And the role of black people as permanent victims? Encouraged to blame racism for everything, with no strategy for eventual social acceptance and no personal accountability? What about cultural norms within the black community directly linked to poor outcomes?[38] Where is the solution for human flaws and excesses that impact all races? CRT would—and does—gloss over these as though they are of little consequence.

It's easy for anyone working in the healing professions, especially the field of psychology, to recognize CRT as a time bomb with a short fuse. Sociologists and political scientists should also be alarmed, as this approach could only result in more severe and permanent social schisms wherever CRT is taught and promoted.

Conclusion

In this chapter, CRT is personified as "the client". Describing it this way highlights some of the challenges with Critical Race Theory. It is angry, bitter, and aggressive, yet also vulnerable and hurt due to genuine experience of rejection and trauma. This ideology appeals to those who have waited for society to recognize their pain and continuing struggle.

However, there is no tangible solution associated with this ideology. It makes strong accusations of wrongdoing without a workable strategy of redress for the group it is designed to protect. Simply demanding promotion, favor, and forgiveness in exchange for historical wrongs is a recipe for disaster. Labeling all others as hostile enemies, and treating them as such, would feasibly become a self-fulfilling prophecy.

CRT is hoisted on its own petard of incongruency. White people are told their words are violent if they express themselves, and at the same time berated for complicity with black oppression if they do not speak up.[39] Whites are accused of fragility for being hurt by these accusations and criticized for attempting to be "white saviors" if they make any efforts to heal the racial rift.[40]

I am aware of the continuing stain of racism in our society, both personally and professionally. I am also aware of the danger of promoting ideological views within a therapeutic setting. Nevertheless, adopting and utilizing the vulnerability of a client to promote an extreme political or ideological viewpoint betrays a duty of care.

The same can be said for therapists who validate an identity or ideology simply because it is adopted by the client. It's impossible to assist someone by endorsing beliefs that are factually inaccurate and/or causing them harm, whether these views do so directly in some manner, or because they narrow the client's focus to include only solutions that fit within that limited paradigm.

Therapists are endowed with an enormous responsibility and trust to assist clients in their healing process. Reducing their options only to those that fit within a narrow ideological scope alters the dynamic and turns the role of the therapist into a fellow activist, a conceptual ally, or even an indulgent parent, rather than that of a knowledgeable professional.

CRT is a useful example. It can be incredibly challenging to navigate in a therapeutic setting. In many ways, its principles make it worse than zero-sum thinking. At least with zero-sum thinking, there is a clear winner and a definite loser. But with CRT, both sides are losers; they are permanent adversaries with no end in sight.

With this prospect in mind, I imagine CRT leaving my consulting room, still resentful, still vengeful, yet immune to any therapeutic intervention. The core pain at the center of its issues will be exacerbated and misdiagnosed regarding both immediate cause and potential remedy.

I predict, with a heavy heart, that it will continue to pollute and divide the workplace—tainting all interactions with its cynical and aggrieved worldview while utterly blind to the destruction left in its wake.

Endnotes

1. Stephen Sawchuk, "What is Critical Race Theory, and Why is it Under Attack?" *Education Week*, 18 May 2021.

2. Janel George, "A Lesson on Critical Race Theory," *American Bar Association*, (11 January 2021).

3. Ibram X. Kendi, *How to Be an Anti-Racist*, (New York, One World Publishing, 2019), Chap.2, Kindle.

4. Jared Ball, "Critical Race Theory and Whiteness as Property", *Black Agenda Report*, (February 16, 2011), https://www.blackagendareport.com/content/critical-race-theory-and-whiteness-property.

5. James Lindsay, "Equity", New Discourses, (Revision July 13, 2020), https://newdiscourses.com/tftw-equity/.

6. Yvonne McClean, "'Jezebel' is just one of three common stereotypes against all black women and girls", *Baptist News Global*, (February 12, 2021), https://baptistnews.com/article/jezebel-is-one-of-three-common-racial-slurs-against-all-black-women-and-girls/#.YXA1pHko-3U.

7. Brian D. Smedley, "The lived experience of race and its health consequences", *American Journal of Public Health*, 102, no.5 (2012): 933-5, https://doi.org/10.2105/AJPH.2011.300643.

8. Andrew Limbong, "Microaggressions are a big deal: how to talk them out and when to walk away," *NPR*, (9 June 2020). What Is A Microaggression? And What To Do If You Experience One. : Life Kit : NPR.

9. Katherine Kirkinis, Alex L. Pieterse, Christina Martin, Alex Agiliga, and Amanda Brownell, "Racism, racial discrimination, and trauma: a systematic review of the social science literature", *Ethnicity & Health*, (2018), 26, no.3: 392-412, https://doi.org/10.1080/13557858.2018.1514453.

10. Richard Delgado and Jean Stefancic, *Critical Race Theory: An Introduction*, 3rd ed. (New York: NYU Press, 2017), 8, Kindle.

11. Malcolm X, "The white liberal is the worst enemy to America, and the worst enemy to the black man". Undated speech. Malcolm X was born 19 May,1925, and was assassinated on 21st February,1965. Malcolm X White Liberals Quotes (3 quotes) (goodreads.com).

12. Paul Monckton, "This is Why Millions of People are Posting Black Squares on Instagram," *Forbes*, (2 June 2020). This Is Why Millions Of People Are Posting Black Squares On Instagram (forbes.com).

13. Ibram X. Kendi, *Stamped from the Beginning: The Definitive History of Racist Ideas in America* (New York: Bold Type Books, 2017); Michael Eric Dyson, *Tears We Cannot Stop: A Sermon to White America* (New York: St. Martin's Griffin, 2021).

[14] Reni Eddo-Lodge, *Why I'm No Longer Talking to White People About Race* (London: Bloomsbury Publishing, 2018).

[15] Roberta K. Timothy, "Five Ways to Address Internalized White Supremacy and Its Impact on Health", *The Conversation*, (March 4, 2021); E.J.R. David, Tiera M. Schroeder and Jessicanne Fernandez, "Internalized Racism: A Systemic Review of the Psychological Literature on Racism's Most Insidious Consequence," *Journal of Social Issues*, 75, no.4 (September 2019): 1-57-1086, https://doi.org/10.1111/josi.12350.

[16] Greg Lukianoff and Jonathan Haidt, *The Coddling of the American Mind: How Good Intentions and Bad Ideas Are Setting Up a Generation for Failure* (New York: Penguin Books, 2019), 7-9, Kindle.

[17] Leslie Sokol and Marci Fox, *The Clinician's Guide to Cognitive Behavioral Therapy* (Eau Claire, WI: PESI Publishing and Media, 2019).

[18] Christopher Butler, *Postmodernism: A Very Short Introduction* (Oxford, UK: Oxford University Press, 2002).

[19] Robin DiAngelo, *White Fragility: Why It's So Hard for White People to Talk about Racism* (Boston, MA: Beacon Press, 2018).

[20] Aja Y. Martinez, *Counterstory: The Rhetoric and Writing of Critical Race Theory* (Champaign, IL: National Council of Teachers of English, 2020).

[21] Courtney E. Ackerman, "Cognitive Distortions: When Your Brain Lies to You", (October 31, 2020), https://positivepsychology.com/cognitive-distortions/.

[22] Kala Burrell-Craft, "Are (We) Going Deep Enough: A Narrative Literature Review Addressing Critical Race Theory, Racial Space Theory, and Black Identity Development," *Taboo: The Journal of Culture and Education*, vol. 19, Issue 4, Article 2, October 2020; R. Nicole Johnson-Ahorlu, "Efficient Social Justice: How Critical Race Theory Research Can Inform Social Movement Strategy Development," *Urban Review: Issues and Ideas in Public Education*, v49 n5 p729-745 Dec 2017.

[23] Jodi Clarke, "What It Means to be Egocentric," (Updated April 6, 2021), https://www.verywellmind.com/what-does-it-mean-to-be-egocentric-4164279.

[24] "Microagressions" according to Critical Race Theory are non-verbal or indirect displays of racial bias by whites. (Oxford Dictionary, 2022).

[25] Elin Johnson, "Racial Inequality, at College and in the Workplace," *Inside Higher Education*, (October 18, 2019), accessed https://www.insidehighered.com/news/2019/10/18/racial-inequality-college-and-workplace.

[26] Ackerman, "Cognitive Distortions".

27 Delgado and Stefancic, *Critical Race Theory: An Introduction.*

28 "White Man's Burden" is a philosophy underlying a poem with this title by Rudyard Kipling (1899). It exhorts white men to conquer and promote Western culture to other races as part of a higher moral duty. *Collins Dictionary* (2021).

29 James Baldwin. "To be a Negro in this country, and to be relatively conscious, is to be in a rage almost all the time", (Radio interview, 1961), https://www.penguin.co.uk/articles/2021/august/best-james-baldwin-quotes-still-true-relevant-today.html.

30 Shiv R. Desai and Andrea Abeita, "Institutional Microaggressions at a Hispanic Serving Institution: A Dine (Navajo) Woman Utilizing Tribal Critical Race Theory Through Student Activism", *Equity and Excellence in Education*, (August 18, 2017), pp. 275-289.

31 The three kinds of empathy include cognitive empathy, knowing and understanding how another person feels without experiencing it yourself; emotional empathy, when you feel alongside the other person; and compassionate empathy, a combination type of empathy where there is understanding of what the other person is experiencing, feeling it with them, and being moved to help. Enid R. Spitz, "The Three Kinds of Empathy: Emotional, Cognitive, Compassionate", accessed October 20, 2021, https://blog.heartmanity.com/the-three-kinds-of-empathy-emotional-cognitive-compassionate.

32 Katrin Redfern and Richard Whatmore, "History tells us that ideological 'purity spirals' rarely end well", *The Conversation*, accessed July 1, 2020, https://theconversation.com/history-tells-us-that-ideological-purity-spirals-rarely-end-well-140888.

33 DiAngelo, *White Fragility.*

34 Diane J. Goodman, *Promoting Diversity and Social Justice: Educating People from Privileged Groups.* (New York: Routledge, 2011).

35 Daniel Subotnik, "What's Wrong with Critical Race Theory: Reopening the Case for Middle Class Values," *Cornell Journal of Law and Public Policy*, Vol. 7, Issue 3, (Spring 1998).

36 M.T Williams, I.W. Metzger, C. Leins and C. DeLapp, "Assessing racial trauma within a DSM–5 framework: The UConn Racial/Ethnic Stress & Trauma Survey," *Practice Innovations,* 3, no.4 (2018): pgs. 242–260. http://dx.doi.org/10.1037/pri0000076.

37 "Microaggressions" are defined as "verbal, behavioral, and environmental indignities that communicate hostile, derogatory, or negative racial slights and insults to the target person or group. For Black people, they

are ubiquitous across daily work and life". This is the uncited general definition that comes up when you undertake an internet search on the term. There is no mention of studies finding these gestures subjective and highly unreliable as a basis for asserting hostility or racism. Importantly, there is also no mention of mutuality—of microaggressions by black people towards whites due to the expectation of rejection. George Leef, "Microaggressions Put Under the Scholarly Microscope", *The James G. Martin Center for Academic Renewal*, (April 21, 2017), https://www.jamesgmartin.center/2017/04/microaggressions-put-scholarly-microscope/.

[38] John McWhorter, "Racist Police Violence Reconsidered," *Quillette*, (June 11, 2020), https://quillette.com/2020/06/11/racist-police-violence-reconsidered.

[39] Kendi, *Stamped from the Beginning.*

[40] DiAngelo, *White Fragility.*

Chapter 15:
Cognitive-Behavioral Therapy and Critical Social Justice Are Incompatible

by Philip Pellegrino

Critical Social Justice (CSJ) is an umbrella term for a set of theories that are informed by postmodern philosophy and have a political goal of changing society. One of these theories in particular, Critical Race Theory (CRT), has come to the foreground in terms of the provision of mental health services. Therefore, sometimes, through the course of this chapter, we will be using CRT as a proxy for all of the theories under the umbrella of CSJ.

CSJ suggests that current models of psychological treatments are invalid when applied to minorities and other oppressed groups. According to CSJ, they are invalid because they believe them to be socially constructed by the dominant cultural group (cis hetero white males) and are likely to perpetuate racism, sexism, homophobia, Islamophobia, and transphobia.

Cognitive-Behavioral Therapy (CBT) is the prevailing model of psychological treatment for a range of psychological disorders. This chapter, therefore, will highlight the key differences between CBT, a science-based approach, and CSJ, a political-based approach to the application of psychotherapy. We will demonstrate how the core principles of effective CBT treatments can alleviate emotional and behavioral problems, while an approach based upon CSJ will contribute to poor psychological health and has the potential to perpetuate harmful approaches to living.

Overall, the chapter will highlight how CSJ is dangerous to the behavioral health profession and, importantly, the lives of our clients.

Core principles of a CBT approach

Cognitive Therapy (CT) was developed by the late Aaron Beck in the 1960s; he recognized the role of thinking and belief in psychological problems.[1] What separated cognitive therapy from other dominant forms of therapy at the time was the ability to do randomized control trials and other research to show the efficacy of the treatment modality. Although originally applied to depression, CT began to show effectiveness for a wide range of psychological conditions. CT practitioners began to combine CT with behavioral therapy approaches, primarily exposure therapy for anxiety disorders. Over time, the two treatments evolved into what is now known as Cognitive Behavioral Therapy (CBT).

CBT encompasses a wide umbrella of treatment approaches for a variety of conditions. Most of these treatments share a common set of principles, each of which is relevant to understanding human suffering and behavior as well as informing interventions for change. These principles are present and relevant for the development and maintenance of most psychological conditions and play a role in their treatment.

We will review four of these core principles and then compare and contrast them with how Critical Social Justice would formulate and treat psychological conditions. These four core areas include experiential avoidance/emotional exposure, attentional bias, functional contextualism, and emotional schemas. We will review each core principle in more detail and compare and contrast this with a CSJ approach to psychotherapy.

Experiential avoidance/emotional exposure

Experiential avoidance refers to thoughts, actions, strategies, and other moves that involve the active avoidance of unwanted experiences.[2] Unwanted experiences can include difficult emotions, distressing thoughts, memories, or painful physical sensations. Examples of experiential avoidance include distraction, suppression of thoughts and feelings, drug and alcohol use, overthinking, opting out of the experience, and self-harm.

We all engage in experiential avoidance from time to time, and it can be adaptive (i.e., days off, vacation). However, experiential avoidance begins to become a problem when it is the typical mode of operating and a chronic pattern of coping with distress. When people consistently avoid uncomfortable experiences, it limits their lives and their opportunities for joy and satisfaction. Also, people who experientially "avoid" do not learn how to cope with emotions, which is a key factor in successful living.

Experiential avoidance operates under the behavioral principles of negative reinforcement. Negative reinforcement is when a behavior leads to the removal of or decreased intensity of an aversive experience. When a behavior leads to the decrease or absence of something aversive, that behavior tends to be repeated. Social Anxiety Disorder, Panic Disorder, Obsessive-Compulsive Disorder (OCD), Depression, Post-Traumatic Stress Disorder (PTSD), Generalized Anxiety Disorder (GAD), Illness Anxiety Disorder, substance use disorders, and all phobias are maintained by experiential avoidance/negative reinforcement mechanisms.[3]

Experiential avoidance limits life opportunities and the capacity to flourish as a human being. Experiential avoidance also does not allow a person to learn something new about themselves, others, or the world. In other words, experiential avoidance keeps people stuck in old patterns of living, which may not always be helpful in adapting to an ever-changing world. Typically, the goal of avoidance methods is to completely eliminate or get rid of unwanted experiences. In some ways, zero tolerance for unwanted thoughts and emotions.

Critical Social Justice and experiential avoidance

CSJ does not ask questions about if and how much racism (and sexism) exists. Instead, it claims that it exists in everything and at all times, and we need to identify it in every situation to dismantle it in all its forms.

From this perspective, the client is viewed either as an inevitable victim of societal oppression or an inevitable perpetuator of this oppression, both of which need to be addressed psychologically. This stance essentially proposes that we need to eliminate all forms of potential or perceived systemic oppression from our culture and our institutions (admirable yet misguided). The stance of the CSJ-driven therapist is to help their clients to dismantle their own privilege as a member of the "dominant" group or, if they are a member of a marginalized group, to accept that they have been influenced by systemic oppression (sometimes referred to as internalized oppression). The existence of systemic oppression is just assumed by the CSJ-driven therapist without question.

Of course, we want to take steps to limit the effects of racism, sexism, and homophobia and call them out when necessary. However, the heart of CSJ is a constant focus on elimination or "dismantling" anything that any individual who subscribes to the CSJ worldview deems as oppressive.

Fundamentally, the message is not to learn how to cope or respond to the world but that we will all be free once we have called out and eliminated systemic oppression. The messaging is that the client is a victim and is so fragile and helpless unless we dismantle and eliminate the problem.[4] Recent examples include the cancellation of speakers on college campuses, emphasis on trigger warnings, hypervigilance about pronouns, and tearing down historical statues. One of the main problems with experiential avoidance as a coping style is the focus on the elimination of thoughts and emotions. A CSJ approach to therapy and the world further exacerbates the focus on elimination vs. (the more positive and sustainable approach of) learning how to cope, change, and navigate life's problems.

Let's take the example of the application of Critical Race Theory in particular. Imagine an African American female client who is afraid of asking her white male boss for a raise. She stated that she is afraid of "causing waves" at work, making her boss angry, and doesn't want to bring unnecessary attention to herself. You learn from her history that she was punished often for speaking up as a child and was mostly given attention when she was misbehaving.

From a CBT perspective, the therapist would work with the client to assert herself and experiment with her hypotheses about what would happen. Through this process, she may learn something new about herself, her boss, and the world. From a CSJ perspective, she would not be encouraged to test out these beliefs, but her fears would be seen through the lens of racism, that there is something about working for a white male that is causing her problems and that her fear is a result of the system that keeps black women down. Note here the movement from the individual as the point of intervention to the level of the system.

Also, the therapist only has one formulation of the system. Her avoidance is not the problem from a CSJ perspective. The problem is that she is oppressed by her boss and society. If this is the case, what recourse does this woman have in this scenario? Is she learning how to take control of her own life? What opportunities is she missing out on to grow as a person? Now, racism may play a role here; however, it is not to be assumed from a CBT perspective. This formulation would be based on collecting data and information that would support the role of racism in this context.

Attentional biases

"Attentional bias" refers to an individual's inclination to focus on particular information in the environment to the detriment of other information.[5] Attentional bias is a quick way for human beings to make sense of their world, find patterns, and make connections with minimal energy or effort. Attentional bias is an adaptive trait that gives us a good snapshot of what is happening in our environment and allows us to make quick decisions.

Generally speaking, these biases can be very effective for survival and making decisions, particularly for pre-civilization humans. For example, attentional bias allows us to focus on certain information that seems important and to filter out irrelevant information, such as how when studying for a test you want to be biased towards information that is likely to be on the test. This allows us to sift through all the noise and be better prepared for the test. Additionally, these biases allow us to make quicker decisions while using little energy.

The downside to this biased approach is that we are prone to miss valuable information that can lead to false positives. These biases are very helpful when it comes to test-taking; however, when applied to a complex and nuanced world, they can lead to poor decisions and unhelpful approaches.

Attentional bias has been found to play a role in developing and maintaining a range of psychological conditions. In Social Anxiety Disorder, there is a bias toward potential rejection or embarrassment.[6] In depression, there is a bias toward a hopeless future, negative self-criticism, and low energy. CBT looks to help individuals identify information in their environment that is inconsistent with their attentional biases. In the above example, a CBT therapist would help this client by bringing attention to times she asserted herself and was not punished or other information about her boss that would make him unlikely to respond negatively to her request. This is done through various skills to bring attention to new data or alternative information.

Attentional bias and Critical Social Justice

Fundamentally, CSJ is one large attentional bias that views people as either oppressors or the oppressed based on their immutable characteristics. The bias is stated as follows: oppression and power differentials are a factor in any and every interaction between people of different groups, and this oppression can explain any and all differences between groups. Therefore, anytime a person from a marginalized group is questioned or denied a job, the explanation is because of some form of oppression or bigotry. No other possible explanation is considered from the CSJ perspective. The reader is invited to think about how this begins to shape how one interacts with the world—even the most benign of interactions can be interpreted as being a problem because if we look hard enough, we can find sexism or homophobia to be the cause of all problems if we want to.

Clinically, individuals who struggle with depression and anxiety tend to hold one explanatory belief about the events in their life. A common belief among those with depression is "These things keep happening to me because I am a bad person". There is no room for any other explanation.

When individuals are this rigid in their beliefs and are unable to understand the complexity of their interactions with others, they are going to develop significant interpersonal problems. This can present itself as depression or other difficulties.

Therefore, I strongly believe that approaching therapy by advocating for an already preconceived assumption about the nature of interactions with others will continue to create problems for the client and they will continue to be perplexed by the responses from others. Creating meaningful relationships not based on one's racial and gender identity will be limited. Concerningly, from a CSJ perspective, the only strategy is to blame those around them for their own problems and take up the victim mentality. How does this person then solve the problem? One option is to attack, tear down, or dismantle the perpetrators. Again, not a very effective solution to building and maintaining relationships, something at the core of each person's wants and desires.

Context matters

Functional contextualism is the idea that behavior and actions are only beneficial, harmful, or neutral depending on the context in which they occur.[7] For example, being more inhibited at work or school may have significant benefits but is not so rewarding on a date or in a social scenario. Functional contextualism also explains the development of behaviors through the context in which behavior is acquired. For most people, this is the family/home environment where they grew up. Culture is also a context in which some behaviors are rewarded and other behaviors are punished. The norms and values of one's family, neighborhood, and ethnic background all impact how one begins to view the world and the particular behaviors that are rewarded or punished.

From the CBT viewpoint though, behaviors that become problematic later in life once served a significant adaptive purpose in early environments and are no longer adaptive in the current context. Functional contextualism also suggests that a behavior developed in one context can be misapplied in another. For instance, what happens if you try to hit a golf ball like a baseball? Therefore, psychological conditions can be thought of as strategies for coping or responding to the world that were adaptive in previous contexts but are ineffective in the present environment. Avoiding germs is adaptive to not getting sick; however, the overuse of control strategies to avoid germs in all contexts is debilitating (see elimination strategies and experiential avoidance above).

Critical Social Justice and context

Context never changes in CSJ. The only context is that we live in a society built upon oppression and therefore oppression informs each and every interaction. From the perspective of Critical Race Theory, society, particularly the United States, was built upon racism, and racism is baked into the foundations of every institution. Further, depression, anxiety, and other problems are all the result of oppressive power structures. There is never nuance in CSJ. The only thing that matters is the role of race, gender, and sexuality in interactions and discourse. The norms and values we currently hold are based on white supremacy and this is making us ill. The only way to change mental health is to change the entire structure of our environment, unlike CBT, which is about changing coping strategies to fit contextual demands. Each client is seen as a victim of this environment and is therefore coached to advocate for dismantling that environment. Therapy would appear to be more focused on political action than on helping an individual grow and make changes that enhance their own lives.

Let's take the example of a female who enrolls in college. During her first semester, she experienced negative looks from other students and overheard a group of male students making sexist and rude comments toward women. Overall, she is having trouble adapting to the current environment at her school. The CBT therapist who takes a functional contextual approach encourages the client to meet new people, address the negative emotions she is experiencing about the remarks, and generally guides her to find activities, people, and behaviors that will work out for her so she can thrive. She would learn how to cope with the difficult people at her school while also persisting in her life endeavors.

However, the CSJ-driven therapist would paint the entire school and the "patriarchy" as the problem, given the actions of a few people. This student would be encouraged to make complaints to the school about their blatant sexism and to request special demands from the administration. She would not learn how to navigate this challenging transitional stage in her life but learn that others are to blame for her situation and her feelings. Again, leaving it up to other people to make her life better, further reducing her self-agency. So, instead of learning new skills for the context, this client learns the same (damaging) strategy that is to be applied in all contexts.

Beliefs about emotion

Beliefs about emotions have a significant impact on how people respond to the range of their own emotional experiences. What a person believes about the cause of an emotion, how long it will last, the emotion's meaning about the person, and the individual's judgment of their emotions will have an impact on how they cope with emotions and interact with others and the world.

Dr Robert Leahy has developed an innovative CBT approach to treating emotionally based disorders based on the role of beliefs about emotions called Emotional Schema Therapy.[8] Based upon this theory, if an individual believes that they are "weak or bad" for being sad, this will have an impact on their normal experience of sadness. This person may be sad about a common scenario, such as a breakup. If this person believes they are weak for feeling this way, then this will increase the intensity of sadness, leading to other emotional experiences, and likely delay the emotional processing of the loss (furthering experiential avoidance).

A person with a belief that sadness and emotional experiences are normal would not have the same response. They would not see their emotions as problems and therefore would respond more effectively, grieve the loss, and move on with their life. In other words, people who learn to validate and experience validation for their own emotional experiences will tend to respond more effectively to those emotions rather than individuals who do not see their experiences as valid.[9]

Critical Social Justice and beliefs about emotion

A core tenet of CSJ is that emotional harm is comparable to physical harm; when you cause someone to feel a negative emotion, you are causing harm to that individual. Any level of discomfort is considered harmful and, in some cases, the equivalent of violence.[10]

This approach promotes the idea that experiencing discomfort is itself harmful and devasting; therefore, the subsequent response is to attack or "cancel" the perpetrator that "caused" the negative emotions. These messages can be seen in common CSJ ideas such as "trigger warnings", "micro-aggressions", and "safe spaces."[11] Individuals who misgender someone are often seen as having hostile intentions towards trans people.

Within the CSJ movement, there is often a focus on being "marginalized" that, at times, has no real concrete explanation of how the person is being marginalized. Often, CSJ advocates are referring to "feeling" states. The person—because of some aspect of their "identity"—feels excluded, hurt, disrespected, rejected, or attacked in some way. When individuals of the oppressed feel these in the presence of less oppressed identities, the oppression and marginalization of the oppressor are identified as the problem.

To clarify, let's imagine the case of a gay Hispanic male who has had a history of challenging interpersonal relationships. He reports that he has difficulties with his emotions in relationships, feeling that his partners will leave him and then reacting emotionally in ways that end the relationship. From an emotional schema perspective, the therapist would help this individual identify his beliefs about his emotions and his general approach to emotional coping as they arise. He would learn more helpful beliefs and run experiments on what actually happens with his emotions during these moments so he can learn to respond in more helpful ways.

These skills would then be practised and rehearsed so that he can practice them in real-world contexts.

However, a CSJ-driven therapist would teach this individual that their emotions are the harm caused to him by a white heteronormative culture. The pain he experiences in his relationship and his outbursts are the direct result of his coming to accept himself in this culture. The culture as a whole is to blame, not the person's coping style or his learning history. We can see here how a CSJ approach would teach him that he is a victim; this would exacerbate his anger and frustration in relationships. One would be hard-pressed to imagine how this approach would help this young man have more meaningful and fulfilling relationships, which is why he is coming into therapy in the first place. In fact, instead of developing new skills and new behaviors, this client's condition is worsened and exacerbated by the CSJ approach.

The ultimate price of a Critical Social Justice approach to psychotherapy

We have outlined how a CSJ-driven approach to psychotherapy would exacerbate and worsen problems for individuals seeking psychotherapy. A CSJ-driven approach teaches clients to see their emotional experiences as harmful and blame their emotional experiences on oppression. Clients would learn to be constantly focused on racism, sexism, homophobia, and oppression as the cause of their problems. Further, they would learn that their own emotions are only valid in the context of oppressor and oppressed, not that they can be tolerated and are valid for being a human being.

Essentially, taking a CSJ approach to psychotherapy does not allow people to grow, learn new skills, and learn new things about themselves and others. They would stay in a constant state of anger, avoidance, blame, and hypervigilance, all of which have been found to decrease functioning and overall psychological health.

Cognitive-behavioral therapy targets the above areas while CSJ-driven therapy seeks to exploit and magnify them. CBT helps people to approach emotional discomfort, to take on challenges, and increase awareness of how our own personal biases impact our interactions with others and the world. The CSJ approach teaches clients to take political action, while CBT advocates for personal growth and individual life enhancement. These two approaches are not compatible. One seeks to address problems at the level of the individual whereas the other blames an oppressive society. The contrast between the two strategies is obvious and glaring. There is no doubt where training programs should be placing their energy.

Endnotes

1   Aaron T Beck, *Cognitive Therapy and the Emotional Disorders.* (New York: Penguin Publishing, 1979).

2   Stephen C Hayes, Kelly G. Wilson, Elizabeth V. Gifford, Victoria M. Follette, Kirk Stroshal, "Experiential avoidance and behavioral disorders: A functional dimensional approach to diagnosis and treatment," *Journal of Consulting and Clinical Psychology* 64, no.6 (1996):1152-1168. https://doi.org/10.1037/0022-006X.64.6.1152.

3   Multiple studies have shown the impact of experiential avoidance in contributing to overall psychiatric distress for a number of psychological conditions. However, measuring EA for disorder-specific symptoms has proven challenging; EA plays a significant role in psychopathology across a number of psychological disorders. Neharika Chawla & Brian Ostafin, "Experiential avoidance as a functional dimensional approach to psychopathology: An empirical review," *Journal of Clinical Psychology,* 63, no.9, (2007): 871-890. https://doi.org/10.1002/jclp.20400.

4   Trigger warnings facilitate experiential avoidance and send the message that certain topics are "too difficult" for students to handle and therefore should be avoided. This is contrary to effective CBT, which is about approaching and coping with challenging life scenarios. Trigger warnings is a concept promoted mostly in academia, where students are informed that emotionally evocative material will be discussed in a class before the presentation of the material. See Pamela Paresky, "Harvard Study: Trigger Warnings might coddle the mind". *Psychology Today* (2018) accessed on 22 August 2022, https://www.psychologytoday.com/us/blog/happiness-and-the-pursuit-leadership/201808/harvard-study-trigger-warnings-might-coddle-the.

5   Attentional bias is the process of attending to, focusing on, and generalizing potential threat information from the environment. These biases are automatic and can be outside the individual's awareness, not allowing them to notice any competing information. It is believed by most CBT theorists to play a significant role in the etiology and maintenance and specific anxiety conditions. Aaron T. Beck & David A. Clark, "An information processing model of anxiety: Automatic and strategic processes", *Behaviour Research and Therapy* 35 (1997):49-58. https://doi.org/10.1016/s0005-7967(96)00069-1.

6   Attentional bias has significant implications in maintaining and contributing to anxiety conditions and has been found to be consistent with type and function of anxiety disorders. In other words, individuals with social

anxiety have bias towards threat of embarrassment and rejection and individuals with contamination OCD tend to focus on germs and contamination. Bram Van Bockstaele, Bruno Verschuere, Helen Tibboel, Jan De Houwer, Geert Crombez and Ernst H W Koster, "A review of current evidence for the causal impact of attentional bias on fear and anxiety", *Psychological Bulletin* 40, no. 3 (2014): 682-721. https://doi.org/10.1037/a0034834.

[7] Functional contextualism has long been a major piece of Acceptance and Commitment Therapy (ACT). ACT moves away from a mechanistic model of mental health to understanding that behaviors are adaptive or non-adaptive based on context. Behaviors are not seen as universally negative or positive but as functioning and working for an individual in a given context. Russ Harris, *ACT made simple: An Easy to Read Primer on Acceptance and Commitment Therapy.* (New York: New Harbinger Publications, 2009).

[8] The cognitive model's basic theoretical underpinning consists of the role of thinking and beliefs on emotions and behavior. Leahy extends this further to beliefs and thinking about emotions specifically and how that can impact beliefs about the self. Robert Leahy, *Emotional Schema Therapy.* (New York: Guilford Press, 2015). For example, when one sees their emotions as "out of control" and "all over the place", they are likely to begin to see themselves as out of control or crazy. These negative labels and judgements of oneself have a direct impact on the development of psychological conditions.

[9] Validation and compassion have long been known to help individuals who struggle with the shame they have for their behaviors or beliefs. Through validation, the individual then becomes more accepting of themselves, which is a key component of any form of psychotherapy. CSJ would advocate for this, but only based upon an individual's racial or gender identity, not their own unique life experiences. CSJ also fails to advocate for any effective form of making changes in that individual's life. Validation is important; however, the main purpose of any psychotherapeutic endeavor is to make effective changes in an individual's life.

[10] Social Justice advocates have openly stated that speech can be violence and treat any type of threatening speech as "problematic". Barret Feldman, "When is Speech Violence." *New York Times*, July 14, 2017. https://www.nytimes.com/2017/07/14/opinion/sunday/when-is-speech-violence.html?_r=0.

[11] Safe spaces have been significantly discussed at the university level and highlighted by Greg Lukianoff and Jonathan Haidt in their best-selling book *The Coddling of the American Mind*. Multiple universities have safe spaces advocated on their websites. The idea of safe spaces comes from the concept that certain topics, emotions, or people are too distressing and people, particularly those of marginalized groups, need to be protected from these in safe spaces. Typically, the events they need protecting from are seen as hate speech. Essentially, anything that disagrees with the Critical Social Justice ideology is viewed as hate speech and marginalized people need to be protected from hate speech. Greg Lukianoff and Jonathan Haidt, *The Coddling of the American Mind: How Good Intentions and Bad Ideas are Setting up a Generation for Failure* (New York: Penguin Books, 2018).

Chapter 16:

How Critical Social Justice is Incompatible with the Therapeutic Relationship—The Ground of Therapy

by Val Thomas

Introduction

From the very first time that you, Reader, encounter me as your therapist and right up until the final moments of the last therapy session, I will have one primary underlying focus: the therapeutic relationship. I will start by establishing a working alliance with you, and from then on I will be developing and maintaining our relationship, monitoring it, and alert to any opportunity for drawing on its therapeutic potential.

When I attend clinical supervision, I will be reflecting on how you and I are interacting. In this regard, I am no different from any other counsellor or psychotherapist. You might wonder why there is such a focus on the relationship; surely the issues you bring to therapy are much more significant? The answer is that research has established unequivocally that without a good enough relationship between therapist and client, there is little prospect of any positive outcome.[1] This is true no matter what therapeutic approach is espoused. The fundamental importance of the therapeutic relationship is universally accepted.

In this chapter, we will be exploring the contradictions that lie at the heart of the claims for the Critical Social Justice (CSJ)-driven practice as a therapeutic approach. We will analyse its obsession with power, its collective worldview, and the political agenda that are not coherent with the established ground of therapeutic practice, namely the relationship between therapist and client.

In fact, we will take one step further and assert that therapy is not the goal of CSJ-driven practice. If you have engaged the services of a practitioner who espouses a CSJ worldview, then unbeknownst to you, you are being recruited for a different kind of project altogether.

How the therapeutic relationship became established as the ground of therapy

One of the defining characteristics of the therapy field over the last few decades has been its pluralism. Many different therapeutic approaches and methods have evolved in response to the complexity of the human condition. One of the notable achievements of the disciplines of counselling and psychotherapy is the way in which they have been able to value and maintain such a rich heritage. All the different modalities within the field contribute to its creativity and dynamism.

Running in tandem with this proliferation of new approaches and methods has been a countervailing tendency, one that seeks to identify commonalities across the different schools of therapy. This has resulted in a trajectory beginning in the 1970s towards integration and theoretical convergence.[2] In the early days of the counselling and psychotherapy disciplines, the founders believed, understandably enough, that the efficacy of their approach rested solely on the correct application of their particular theoretical model to therapeutic practice.[3] However, cumulative

empirical research over the course of many decades corrected
this misapprehension.

During the first half of the 20th century, claims for the efficacy
of therapy, in particular psychoanalysis, rested mainly on anecdotal evidence and the fervent advocacy of practitioners. This all
changed in 1952 when Eysenck delivered a devastating critique
of psychotherapy: he pointed out that the long-term outcome for
untreated depressed patients was the same as that for comparable patients who were treated with psychoanalysis.[4] The obvious
inference that psychoanalytic psychotherapy was ineffective gal-
vanised the field into a programme of intensive research. By the
mid-to-late 1970s, these research programmes focusing on the
outcomes of therapy were able to establish that talking therapies
in general were effective.[5]

But there was another unexpected by-product of this research
enterprise that was to have a profound impact on shaping our
understanding of how therapy works. Some of the research studies included comparisons of cohorts receiving different treatments, and the findings indicated that there were no significant
differences in effectiveness between different models of therapy.[6]
A new research focus came into being which attempted to identify the main ingredients in effective therapy across the different
approaches.

By the end of the century, it was established beyond doubt
that the most significant common factor implicated in positive
therapeutic outcomes is the quality of the therapeutic relationship—confirming the findings of Carl Rogers' seminal research
decades earlier.[7,8]

Ultimately, no matter what therapeutic approach is provided,
if the relationship between therapist and client is not established
or is perceived by the client as problematic, then it is unlikely that
the therapy will be successful. Consequently, at the beginning of
the new millennium, the vast majority of therapists were united

in their belief in the importance of the therapeutic relationship. Standing on this shared ground, each therapeutic modality would then deliver therapy differently depending on its particular theorising of the therapeutic potential of the relationship.

CSJ advocates would most likely claim that their approach is no different from any other type of therapy: the therapeutic relationship is the foundation of its practice. But is that true? This investigation starts by comparing the philosophical position and worldview of CSJ-driven practice with established schools of therapies concerning the therapeutic relationship.

How different schools view the therapeutic relationship

The different approaches in counselling and therapy have been historically grouped into larger categories sometimes known as "forces" (as described in the first chapter). Each of these groupings has a particular philosophical position which in turn leads to a characteristic way of making therapeutic use of the relationship between therapist and client. They include both the earlier 20th-century modern schools which locate the client's problems solely within the individual, as well as later schools, which view the client's difficulties as arising not just within themselves but also being shaped by a wider environment.

One way of illuminating this is to consider how different philosophical positions result in particular ways of making sense of the world; this method of interpretation is referred to as hermeneutics in the continental philosophical tradition.[9] The type of lens that is used by a therapy modality to interpret the world is of fundamental importance as it will shape all aspects of its theory and practice, including how it approaches the therapeutic relationship. This works at the level of the individual. Think about how you make sense of your social world. If you employ the hermeneutic of charity, then you will be inclined to perceive the actions and responses of others as expressions of good faith by default and you will be reluctant to assume ill intent unless given a strong reason to do so. A relevant example of a logical entailment of this hermeneutic would be that you would not be predisposed toward the detection of microaggressions by default.

Applying this hermeneutic framework to the therapy field can help shed light on an otherwise complex pluralistic territory. Taking a very broad brush, we can now look at three of the main groupings of therapeutic approaches (the "forces") and show how their different hermeneutics inform their theory and practice in relation to the encounter between therapist and client (with the caveat that this complex and nuanced matter is presented in a very simplified fashion).[10,11]

Psychodynamic therapies employ the hermeneutic of suspicion.[12] Taking this interpretative position, nothing is what it seems to be on the surface. Apparently, everyday human interactions disguise hidden motivations and/or repeat relationship patterns created in childhood. Consequently, the therapist holds a questioning position in relation to how the client interacts with them. The therapeutic relationship is the place where unconscious/hidden processes can be brought into the light of consciousness and thereby transformed.

Behaviourist (now Cognitive Behavioural Therapies) therapies employ the hermeneutic of evidence; making sense of the world is based on empirical evidence. Therapies are viewed as testable, scientifically proven methods designed to improve emotional/mental/behavioural problems.[13] Early on, the relationship between therapist and client was not viewed as significant to therapeutic efficacy. However, the incontrovertible evidence base for the importance of the therapeutic relationship has led to an emphasis on developing a strong therapeutic alliance between therapist and client.[14]

Humanistic/existential therapies employ the hermeneutic of authenticity.[15] The philosophical commitments of this "force" rest on phenomenology and existentialism.[16,17] Making meaning of the world is based on getting as close as possible to a direct experience of reality and discriminating between what is false (bad faith) and what is authentically true. The therapist works with the client to help align them with their authentic selves. The therapeutic relationship is used as a means whereby the client can experience an authentic relationship and truthful self-expression. There is a strong belief in the healing potential of a real human relationship.

So, what is the interpretative stance of a therapist who espouses CSJ? This ideology views power as the ground of human societal experience. Furthermore, each person's experience of power is determined by their membership in groups deemed to be either oppressed or the oppressor. Consequently, a CSJ-driven therapist employs a hermeneutic of oppression.[18]

Viewed through this lens, all encounters between people will be understood as expressions of power relations. If this is then mapped onto therapeutic practice, the relationship between therapist and client would be interrogated concerning perceived differences in societal power.

The collective worldview of CSJ

However, there are additional characteristics of CSJ that will also come into play in the encounter between therapist and client. These factors, when combined with its hermeneutic of oppression, make CSJ incompatible with the notion of the therapeutic relationship.

First, and foremost, this ideology has a collective worldview. The other three "forces" discussed here view the client as a unique individual. For CSJ, people are not individuals as such but rather representatives of particular identity groups located within a matrix of power. Therefore, when two people engage with one another, it is understood primarily as encounters between constellations of intersected identities. I do not encounter you, Reader, as a unique person in your own right but rather I, as a heterosexual white woman, encounter you as whatever mix of identities you might possess. There is very little room here for a meeting between two individuals as a unique interpersonal relationship.[19]

Furthermore, both therapist and client will be primarily understood as members of either an oppressed or an oppressor identity group. All human interactions, and there can be no exceptions, are characterised by the power dynamics operating across differently positioned identity groups. The clinical setting is no different. It is the client's identity (or set of intersecting identities) that will be foregrounded. The CSJ-driven therapist will be interrogating the encounter with the client from the perspective of power relations. In other words, the relationship between therapist and client will be problematised from this ideological perspective.[20] The clinical work will then be informed by this analysis.

A simple example of this would be the encounter between a white therapist (and therefore a "privileged" group member) and a client who is a person of colour (therefore, automatically, a member of an oppressed identity group). Critical Theories of Race would oblige the therapist to take a particular stance towards the client, one whereby the therapist demonstrates their commitment to allyship and working towards mitigating historical racial injustices.[21] These commitments override the requirement to develop an interpersonal relationship in service of a therapeutic goal. Another example would be a street homeless white man as a patient of a white female psychotherapist consultant. CSJ automatically assigns oppressor status to males and oppressed status to females.[22] Its power relations impose an unhelpful upside-down reading of this encounter, and this jeopardises the development of trust and empathy.

This combination of the hermeneutic of oppression with a collective worldview results in encounters that can only be transactional. The relationship between therapist and client cannot be a vehicle for therapeutic processes in any way conceived of by traditional established therapies. *No such interpersonal relationship is possible because CSJ, by its very nature, is not relational.*

And finally, and possibly most important of all, there is another feature that sets the CSJ view of the relationship apart from other approaches: *CSJ has an unspoken primary agenda that has nothing to do with therapy.*

The political goal of Critical Theory

The Critical Theory component of CSJ stamps its application to therapy with a political objective—the dismantling of oppressive systems of societal power—and a utopian vision of an ensuing perfect society. Wherever CSJ arrives, it brings with it this political goal. This agenda trumps everything else. Whatever the primary focus of the arena might be, behind the scenes all efforts will be made by activists to refocus on political ends. These objectives primarily comprise the instilling of a worldview in people's minds (aka critical consciousness) and thereby recruiting them for the battle against oppressive societal structures.[23] Each arena retains its original name or label, but the contents will be changed to align with Critical Theory.

The disciplines of counselling and psychotherapy are no different from any of the other arenas where CSJ has arrived. The process whereby CSJ takes control is happening along predictable lines (as outlined in the first chapter). Critical Theory is pragmatic and will make use of whatever is already established within the field and co-opt it for self-serving ends. This is true of both the theory and practice related to the therapeutic relationship.

So, in terms of the practice, the alliance between the therapist and client is used for the purposes of moral re-education—clients are encouraged to view their problems through the lens of societal oppression. The relationship offered by the therapist is then a transactional one of advocacy and allyship in the fight against injustice. In terms of theory, CSJ is not interested in working through any contradictions between itself and the theoretical ground. It will instead seek to superficially adapt itself to already existing knowledge and clinical theory.

That the therapeutic alliance is just a means to a political end is implicit in *The APA Guidelines to Multicultural Practice* issued in 2017.[24] Informed by intersectionality, these guidelines recommend that the psychologist actively fosters conversations with clients about their different identities.[25] It is suggested that any resistance to self-disclosure on the client's part is something that needs to be overcome. A range of strategies is offered in order to bring the client around, "such as clinician authenticity, tone, spontaneity, therapist self-reflection, practice, patience with stumbling, supervision, and consultation".[26] Note that no possibility is allowed for any legitimate objection to engaging in mutual disclosures of identities. Manipulative techniques are going to be employed to get the client to comply with the therapist's agenda.

In summary, CSJ does not stand on the same ground as conventional established counselling and psychotherapy approaches. Instead, its political ideology automatically lends itself to a cynical manipulation of the relationship between therapist and client for non-therapeutic ends.

How can the therapy field respond?

Despite the argument that CSJ is a cynical practice that exploits already established theory and knowledge, it should not be taken to mean that the issues it raises should be dismissed. There is a collective dimension to the therapeutic encounter which requires our attention.

There are multiple ways in which collective group identity can come to the fore in the clinical space. At a basic and material level, it may determine our choice of therapist. For example, a disabled client may have their choice limited by lack of wheelchair access, or a female client may decide that only a female therapist could fully empathise with her experience of misogyny.

Sometimes, a client's issues may be explicitly related to their identity; for example, a black client wants to deal with earlier race-related trauma and believes that a black therapist would have more insight and understanding. Conversely, a client's identity-related issues might lead them to select a therapist with a different identity; a female client wanting to work through the trauma of a sexual assault might choose a male therapist in the belief that this would give her more opportunities to confront her experience.

However, there is a more subtle and complex manifestation of the collective that is implicit rather than explicit. It is ever-present in potential as the collective is an irreducible dimension of human existence.[27] A client may have brought issues to therapy ostensibly unrelated to their identity or social context, and yet, at some point, their group identity may become a salient issue and start to affect the relationship. An example of this could be a gay male client and a straight male therapist working on generalised anxiety disorder. A rupture in the relationship could occur through the therapist's failure to grasp the level of anxiety arising for the client in situations where his sexuality may be inadvertently disclosed.

It could be argued that the therapy professions have not paid sufficient rigorous attention to this collective dimension; this neglect may have been a factor in the seemingly uncritical acceptance of a new collective political worldview in the therapy field.

In CSJ, the subtle reality of the ever-present collective dimension has been reduced to the simplistic idea of systems of power shaping all human interactions. As this ideology establishes itself as the orthodoxy, it can sideline the personal and universal dimensions of human relating which generated the original wealth of knowledge about the therapeutic relationship.

Integrating the collective dimension into the therapeutic relationship

In terms of the therapeutic relationship, we are faced with a previously undervalued collective aspect that is now being presented as the most important and fundamental dimension. It is imperative that attempts are made within the disciplines of counselling and psychotherapy to correct this regressive move. We need to value all dimensions of relating in a balanced way.

The first step is to pay more critical attention to the intercultural aspects of interpersonal relating so that we can integrate these more deeply into the therapeutic endeavour. *How can the collective and the individual dimensions of the self be brought together in a coherent yet fluid and balanced way?*

Some ground on this already exists. In the last couple of decades of the 20th century, the trajectory towards integration— mentioned earlier on—was focusing people's minds on finding ways to bring together radically different perspectives and approaches. Clinical theorists had started to wrestle with the conundrum created by different views of the therapeutic relationship. How could integrative therapists resolve the contradiction between offering an authentic relationship to the client (humanistic) with the diametrically opposed psychodynamic approach of interpreting what was happening between client and therapist as symbolic?

One elegant solution was provided by Petruska Clarkson, who developed the *5 Relationship Framework*.[28] Her framework allows a way of thinking about the dynamic flow of different types of relationships that come into play at particular points in the encounter between therapist and client. This complex relational process is driven by a combination of factors including both the conscious decisions made by the therapist and also the underlying unconscious dynamics that begin to become apparent between the client and therapist.

So, let's apply this framework to our encounter. When you, Reader, begin therapy with me, I will start by establishing a therapeutic alliance through a collaborative process that includes set-ting agreed goals. Then, I will work to foster a "real" trusting rela-tionship grounded in authentic, non-judgemental, and empathic responses to you. At some point, I might begin to detect that something unconscious is interfering in this real relationship: you appear to be withdrawing. In discussions with my clinical supervi-sor, I conclude that you are reacting to me as if I were your origi-nal critical parent. Informed by this analysis, I might then start to deliberately provide you with a reparative relationship whereby I offer opportunities for you to feel fully validated. This is a subtle dynamic process, and the needs of the relationship will neverend-ingly cycle through different relationship types.

Clarkson's model has established itself as a classic approach due to the way that it successfully captures the complex multidi-mensional nature of interpersonal relating. A reality that every-one is familiar with from their own experiences of the ever-shift-ing nature of intimate relationships.

As this framework was developed during the last decades of the 20th century, it drew on therapy traditions that focused on the individual. However, there is no reason why this model cannot be developed and expanded beyond the original five relationship types to include the collective and cultural dimensions.

Further, I propose that a sixth type could be included and pro-visionally termed the *intercultural relationship*. This relationship type would come to the fore when the client and/or therapist experience the other person in terms of their group identity. An example might be when a client from a minority group begins to feel that their white therapist is failing to grasp how different their experience of society is. Unacknowledged and unrecognised, this has the potential to undermine the therapeutic relationship and consequently negatively affect the outcome of the therapy.

Integrating the intercultural relationship into such a framework would support the relational encounter between therapist and cli-ent. It would offer a means of holding different perspectives on the relationship. For example, it would allow a therapist to hold a colour-blind view but at the same time recognise its limitations—there are times when identity overrides the universality of human experience.

In order to move forward productively, we cannot side with privileging either the collective or the individual dimensions.

Conclusion

It has taken decades of research, clinical observations, and theory development to establish the therapeutic relationship as the solid ground of all established and traditional counselling and psychotherapy practices. And yet, in a very short period, approaches informed by a new worldview have begun to appropriate this ground for non-therapeutic ends. At best, CSJ-driven practice is purely transactional; at its worst, it is a cynical manipulation of the relational encounter for political ends.

It is time for the therapy professions to reclaim the territory; this can be done by attending to both the individual and collective dimensions of relating in a balanced way. If we incorporate a contemporary focus on the collective into the already existing ground of the therapeutic relationship, it will safeguard the integrity of counselling and psychotherapy.

We need to continue to expand our understanding of the encounter between therapist and client and not allow it to be diminished and exploited. The therapeutic relationship is dynamic, and complex, and, in the final analysis, can never be reduced to a formula.

We have some insight into the processes at work, but it is still mysterious and ungraspable. All we can do is commit to developing this ground—the base of all of our work. Each client who enters the clinical space trusts the therapist to offer an authentic and respectful relationship that serves their true needs. Therefore, we need to honour the relational experience that happens between therapist and client and treat its healing potential with the reverence it deserves.

Endnotes

1 See the meta-analysis that concluded the power of the therapeutic relationship was reflected across more than 1000 research studies. D. E. Orlinsky, K, Grawe, K., & B. K. Parks, "Process and outcome in psychotherapy—Noch einmal", in *Handbook of psychotherapy and behaviour change* (4th edn), eds. A. Bergin & J. S. Garfield (New York: Wiley, 1994), pp. 270-378.

2 John C. Norcross & Lisa M. Grencavage, "Eclecticism and integration in counselling and psychotherapy: Major themes and obstacle", *British Journal of Guidance & Counselling*, 17 no 3 (1989), pp. 227-247.

3 For example, psychoanalysts would focus on helping the client see how unconscious patterns of relating (established in childhood) are playing out in present encounters, whereas behavioural therapists would be helping the client to identify negative behavioural habits that need to be consciously changed (and later in CBT to identify and change automatic cognitions that drive maladaptive behaviour).

4 Hans Eysenck, "The Effects of Psychotherapy: An Evaluation", *Journal of Consulting Psychology*, 16, (1952), pp. 319-324.

5 The earliest meta-analysis of therapy outcome research that established the effectiveness of therapy was carried out by M. L. Smith, & G. V. Glass, "Meta-analysis of psychotherapy outcome studies", *American Psychologist*, 32 no 9, (1977), pp. 752- 760.

6 An example of a significant early study was carried out by R. B. Sloane, F. R. Staples, A. H. Cristol, & N. J. Yorkston, "Short-term analytically oriented psychotherapy versus behavior therapy", *Am J Psychiatry,* 132 no.4 (April 1975), pp. 373-7.

7 Researchers have determined that after non-therapeutic variables such as external life changes and events, it is the therapeutic relationship that is the most significant in relation to positive outcomes. See the particularly influential report by T. R. Asay, & M. J. Lambert, "The empirical case of the common factors in psychotherapy: quantitative findings", in *The heart and soul of change: what works in therapy,* eds. M. A. Hubble, B. L. Duncan, & S. D. Miller (Washington DC: American Psychological Association, 1999), pp. 23-55.

8 Carl Rogers has a classic paper based on his ground-breaking research, "The Necessary and Sufficient Conditions for Therapeutic Personality Change", *Journal of Consulting Psychology*, 21, (1957): 95–103.

9 The term "hermeneutics" originally referred to the means whereby biblical texts were interpreted. During the 20th century, hermeneutics was

taken up and developed within the continental philosophical tradition as an interpretative method for making sense of the world. It was understood that a particular philosophical position would result in a particular stance towards the world. Consequently, different philosophical schools would generate different types of hermeneutics—the characteristic way in which the method of interpretation would be applied. Lawrence Kennedy Schmidt, *Understanding Hermeneutics,* (London & New York: Routledge, 2006).

[10] For the sake of brevity, I have restricted this discussion to the three original "forces" established by the latter part of the 20th century. However, this framework could be applied to the fourth force in therapy. There are several contenders for this, but one in particular is systemic/contextual. See C. Fleuridas & D. Krafcik, "Beyond Four Forces: The Evolution of Psychotherapy", *SAGE Open.* 2019, 7. https://doi.org/10.1177/2158244018824492. Systemic/contextual therapies would be characterised by the hermeneutic of context. Taking this interpretative position, the individual is understood in terms of their relationship to the wider setting. In terms of the therapeutic relationship, it is both the means of illuminating how the client is operating within a wider system (e.g., systemic family psychotherapy) and/or the trusted arena where the client can explore the impact of social context (e.g., feminist psychotherapy).

[11] For the sake of simplicity, these three forces are represented here by the classic schools rather than the more sophisticated and evolved contemporary versions—such as psychoanalytically informed relational approaches, third-wave CBT, and process-oriented psychotherapy.

[12] First identified as such by Paul Ricoeur, *Freud and Philosophy: An Essay on Interpretation* (New Haven, CT: Yale University Press, 1970).

[13] Hence, the question that is often posed to the client in classic CBT procedures and protocols: "Where is your evidence for that?" See Kristina Fenn and Majella Byrne, "The key principles of cognitive behavioural therapy", *InnovAiT.* 6, no. 9 (Sept. 2019):579-585. https://doi.org/10.1177/1755738012471029.

[14] See Paul Gilbert and Robert L. Leahy, "Introduction and overview, Basic issues in the therapeutic relationship", in *The Therapeutic Relationship in the Cognitive Behavioral* Psychotherapies, eds., Paul Gilbert and Robert L. Leahy (New York: Routledge, 2007), pp. 3-23.

[15] There are other contenders mooted for the humanistic therapies such as the hermeneutic of love—see Brent Dean Robbins (2015) "The Heart of Humanistic Psychology: Human Dignity Disclosed Through a Hermeneutic of Love", *Journal of Humanistic Psychology,* 56 no 3 (Fall, 2016):

223-237. However, since this force also encompasses existential perspectives, the hermeneutic of authenticity is arguably a better match.

[16] Phenomenology is the philosophical study of subjective experience, in particular how it is structured and the nature of consciousness. Significant philosophers in this field would be Edmund Husserl (1859–1938), Martin Heidegger (1889–1976), and Maurice Merleau-Ponty (1908–1961). See Dermot Moran, *Introduction to Phenomenology,* (London and New York: Routledge, 1999).

[17] Existentialism refers to a loosely associated group of 19th–20th century philosophers who inquired into the nature of human existence. Significant philosophers would include Soren Kierkegaard (1813–1855), Friedrich Nietzsche (1844–1900), and Jean-Paul Sartre (1905–1980). See Kevin Aho, *Existentialism: An Introduction,* 2nd ed. (Cambridge: Polity Press, 2020).

[18] CSJ does not have a neutral reading of power; therefore, to characterise its hermeneutics as power would be too broad. This ideology frames any situation from the perspective of membership of an oppressed or oppressor group; therefore the hermeneutic of oppression would be a more accurate characterisation. See further exploration of the epistemic side of oppression in José Medina, *The Epistemology of Resistance: Gender and Racial Oppression, Epistemic Injustice, and the Social Imagination* (New York: Oxford University Press, 2013). https://oxford.universitypresss-cholarship.com/view/10.1093/acprof:oso/9780199929023.001.0001/acprof-9780199929023.

[19] CSJ theorists take a strategic view on individuality, as demonstrated in the following statement by Robin DiAngelo, *Nice Racism* (London: Penguin Books Ltd. Kindle Edition) 35. "Granting Black people individuality interrupts a racist dynamic within a culture that has denied their individuality. Conversely, suspending individuality for white people is a necessary interruption to our denial of collective advantage."

[20] Problematising is a focus for CSJ—all efforts are made to identify the ways in which present conditions do not meet an ideal.

[21] A clear introduction to CRT can be found in Richard Delgado and Jean Stefancic, *Critical Race Theory: An Introduction,* 3rd ed. (New York: New York University Press, 2017), Kindle.

[22] A criticism of intersectional feminism for not recognising why poor white men might object to being told they are privileged is delivered by L Gordon, " 'Intersectionality', Socialist feminism and contemporary activism: Musings by a second-wave socialist feminist", *Gender and History,* 28 no.2, (July 2016): 340-357. https://doi.org/10.1111/1468-0424.12211.

23   Critical consciousness is defined as the ability to recognize and analyse
     systems of inequality and the commitment to take action to dismantle
     these oppressive systems. See James Lindsay's use of the virus analogy
     to illustrate the way in which CSJ operates in the same way, in all arenas,
     "The Virus of Critical Social Justice", *New Discourses, podcast with James
     Lindsay, Episode 40,* (June 12, 2021), YouTube video, https://www.you-
     tube.com/watch?v=Kilz4-SxLlw

24   American Psychological Association, *Multicultural Guidelines: An Ecolog-
     ical Approach to Context, Identity, and Intersectionality* (2017).

25   Patricia Hill Collins and Sirma Bilge, *Intersectionality: Key Concepts,* 2nd
     edn, (Cambridge, UK: Polity, 2020), 2, describe intersectionality's core
     insight as "in a given society at a given time, power relations of race,
     class, and gender, for example, are not discrete and mutually exclusive
     entities, but rather build on each other and work together; and that,
     while often invisible, these intersecting power relations affect all aspects
     of the social world".

26   APA, *Multicultural Guidelines,* 2017, p. 23.

27   See the contemporary philosopher Ken Wilber's elegant AQAL frame-
     work, which lays out the four main irreducible dimensions (or "quad-
     rants") of the individual's existence as individual/interior (the subjective
     contents of the mind), individual/exterior (the body), collective/interior
     (intersubjectivity and culture), and collective/exterior (the structures of
     society). An accessible overview can be found in Ken Wilber (2007). *The
     integral vision: A very short introduction to the revolutionary integral
     approach to life, God, the universe, and everything.* (Boulder, Colorado:
     Shambhala Publications, 2007).

28   Clarkson posited five different types of relating that could be operating
     between client and therapist. These different ways of relating would
     change in a dynamic and fluid way; one moment one type would be in
     the foreground, and then another would take its place. The five types of
     relationships map to a certain extent onto the different therapy schools.
     1: The working alliance, which involves an adult-to-adult relationship
     working towards a common goal. 2: The transference-countertransfer-
     ence relationship, where unconscious relationship patterns are played
     out. 3: The reparative relationship, whereby the therapist provides
     developmentally needed conditions. 4: The real relationship, which is
     an authentic person-to-person encounter. 5: The transpersonal relation-
     ship, which refers to the mysterious intangible connection experienced
     between people. See Petruska Clarkson, *The Therapeutic Relationship.*
     2nd edn. (London: Whurr, 2003).

Chapter 17:

Therapeutic Presence and the Inadequacy of Critical Social Justice

by Birgit Ewald

Introduction

Although counselling and psychotherapy have traditionally been viewed as secular practices in the West, there are other approaches in this pluralistic field that also include a transpersonal or spiritual dimension.[1] A transpersonal approach to therapy views a client as a whole person who is in an intimate relationship with a diverse, interconnected, and evolving world. This perspective also pays attention to experiences that go beyond the boundaries of the individual self as normally defined; the perspective also includes spiritual, mystical, and other related, exceptional human experiences.[2]

Transpersonal approaches to therapy are notoriously challenging to articulate as they postulate an ineffable mystery at the heart of the healing process. The embrace of this mystery makes these approaches very different from generic empirically-based psychological practices such as Cognitive Behavioural Therapy (CBT) with which many people will be familiar.[3]

However, a therapist informed by a transpersonal/spiritual perspective will share key assumptions with practitioners from other schools regarding therapeutic practice, one of these being the fundamental importance of the therapeutic relationship.[4]

In this chapter, I will be using the concept of the therapeutic relationship to reflect on key differences between a therapeutic approach informed by a transpersonal perspective and a Critical Social Justice (CSJ)-driven approach to therapy. In particular, I will be focusing on the notion of the therapist's *presence,* an important concept developed within the humanistic therapeutic traditions especially (I will be using italics throughout the following chapter to indicate this specialised meaning of the term "presence"). *Presence* can be understood as the therapist's embodied multi-dimensional awareness in their engagement with the client.[5] In other words, the therapist's attention is open to the client on multiple levels, including information and communication emanating from beyond the confines of the separate individual. A growing body of research points to the important role that the therapist's *presence* plays in facilitating the healing and growth of the client.[6]

I will be providing some clinical vignettes in order to illustrate how therapeutic *presence*—including its intangible transpersonal dimension—can operate in clinical practice. I will then contrast this approach, which emphasises connectedness and the potential for shared human experience, with a CSJ-driven approach, which focuses on separation and difference.

The importance of the therapeutic relationship

People come to therapy because they are scarred, hurt, and traumatised by other people and/or events in their life. The experience of a consistent and trusting relationship with a therapist who listens to them facilitates healing and growth. Such a relationship enables a client to open up. Through telling their story, patterns and emotions manifesting in external relationships and life situations can be transferred into the therapy encounter to be explored and worked through.

The centrality of the client–therapist relationship has been emphasised since the inception of Freud's psychoanalysis in the early 20th century. Today, there is a broad research base to support this, and not surprisingly the existential therapist Irvin Yalom famously stated, "It is the relationship that heals, the relationship that heals, the relationship that heals."[7,8]

However, while we know *that* the relationship is central to successful therapy, we still know much less about *what* exactly it is in a relationship that is healing; for example, what are the common therapist or client factors that contribute to a successful therapeutic relationship?[9]

"Successful" therapeutic relating

In the 1950s, Carl Rogers, the founder of Person-Centred Therapy, pioneered the discovery of key factors that facilitate therapeutic change and growth.[10] He proposed six "necessary and sufficient conditions of therapeutic personality change"—three of these became known as the core conditions, namely congruence, unconditional positive regard, and empathy.[11,12]

Congruence means that a therapist presents themself as who they are in their own experience and awareness. Unconditional positive regard denotes the acceptance of *all* of the client's experience, and empathy refers to the therapist's ability to understand a client's world as if it were their own. Such understanding also includes the ability to communicate insights that are out of the client's awareness.[13]

Recent research gives a wider, more nuanced picture regarding factors for therapeutic change. While congruence, unconditional positive regard, and empathy may not be necessary and sufficient to engender change in *all* clients, they remain key for *many* clients in providing a safe and effective therapeutic relationship.[14]

In the latter years of his life, Rogers spoke of an additional "condition" that he had begun to view as even more important and central, something that goes beyond a therapist's attitude towards a client:

> I am inclined to think that in my writing perhaps I have
> stressed too much the three basic conditions … Perhaps
> it is something around the edges of those conditions that
> is really the most important element of therapy – when
> my self is very clearly, obviously present.[15]

The humanistic therapeutic traditions especially have developed a term for this "something around the edges", calling it *presence*. It is proposed that *presence* is a key component of a therapeutically beneficial relationship.[16] In the following section, I want to explain what *presence* is, how it is facilitated, and how it impacts the therapeutic relationship.

Presence in the therapeutic relationship

Presence, as it manifests in the therapeutic encounter, is complex, multifaceted, and somewhat ineffable. It involves the therapist's and client's self, the relationship they engage in, and a spiritual or transpersonal dimension.[17] A therapist plays an important role as a facilitating *presence* in a session. It is an engagement that encompasses their whole way of being.

> Presence is the "state of having one's whole self in
> the encounter with a client by being completely in the
> moment on a multiplicity of levels – physically, emotion-
> ally, cognitively, and spiritually".[18]

Being present also involves three key "stances". Firstly, a therapist needs to become open and receptive. It means shelving one's own values, thoughts, worldviews, and preconceptions as much as possible.[19] Therapists who are fully present have an awareness of how they are in relation to themselves on a physical, cognitive, emotional, and intuitive level and how these sensations, thoughts, and perceptions might shift and change during a session. This includes being fully grounded in oneself, as well as the ability to become receptive to a client and their internal and external world.[20]

Therefore, secondly, a present therapist attunes to their client on multiple levels; they listen to the verbal, emotional, and symbolic content, to what is being talked about, and notice body language. Attuning to clients also includes a therapist's ability to communicate verbally and non-verbally with a client so they feel safe, heard, and understood.[21]

Being present in a therapeutic relationship is, therefore, almost paradoxical. For example, a present therapist needs the capacity to suspend their knowledge and expertise and meet a client without applying diagnostic categories, expecting clients to be or behave in a certain way, or having intentions about the direction of the therapeutic process in that particular session. At the same time, a therapist also draws on their knowledge and expertise to inform therapeutically helpful responses and allow focus and direction to emerge.[22]

Thirdly, a present therapist is also receptive to a greater spiritual or transpersonal reality. Research shows that therapists experienced moments within therapy when they felt an expansion or opening of space. They felt connected to a larger reality or energy that extended beyond the connection they had with the client. This sense of expansion also coincided with experiences of heightened awareness of self and client and/or increased intuition.[23]

It appears that Rogers spoke of this dimension when he observed:

> As I recently said, I find that when I am the closest to my inner, intuitive self – when perhaps I am somehow in touch with the unknown in me – when perhaps I am in a slightly altered state of consciousness in the relationship, then whatever I do seems to be full of healing. Then simply my presence is releasing and helpful. At those moments, it seems that my inner spirit has reached out and touched the inner spirit of the other. Our relationship transcends itself and has become part of something larger. Profound growth and healing and energy are present.[24]

Such experiences indicate an altered, or transpersonal, state of consciousness—a state that can generate profound insight into the client's experience and subsequently inform interventions that are potentially transformative and healing.[25] The therapist and client may, or may not, talk about such experiences in the session, depending on a client's belief system and what is most beneficial for them. However, if a reference to the transpersonal is made, different names for these experiences may be employed, for example, Higher Self, God, Goddess, Spirit, Inner Wisdom, (Universal) Energy, etc.[26]

In summary, a therapist is present to their client at the level of body, mind, emotions, and spirit, and at the same time, the therapist is also present to the dynamics within the therapeutic relationship. This relationship has three dimensions comprising the therapist's self, the connection between therapist and client, and attunement to a larger transcendent reality. These dimensions are inseparably and dynamically interwoven, and *presence* can manifest at different levels—so that there can be lighter or deeper *presence* engagement between therapist and client.[27]

It appears that *presence* is at its deepest when all levels and dimensions are held and realised simultaneously. It is from this place that deep healing can arise. As Geller and Greenberg comment:

> The session is guided by this dance of awareness and attunement with self and other, pausing between what is known and what is not known, and listening deeply from that still place that exists between self and other. This develops into a sense of relational copresence that promotes emergence of the novel and facilitative healing.[28]

As a therapist, I can facilitate the conditions for such a deep relationship grounded in *presence*, but it is not something that can be generated at will.[29,30]

The following vignette, from my work with a client who we shall name Sylvia, illustrates what such "relational therapeutic *presence*" might look like in a therapy session:[31]

Sylvia, a woman in her mid-thirties, and I worked together in therapy for close on three years. There was a period when she was working through a complex relationship with her mother. As she described a particular situation, I noticed a vivid and repeated hand movement that was accompanying Sylvia's story. Drawing on the Gestalt therapeutic technique of exaggeration, I brought her awareness to this hand movement and invited her to repeat and exaggerate it, while simultaneously describing her internal process to me as much as she was able to.[32]

Sylvia began to exaggerate her gesture and described how she felt. I found myself physically attuning to her by mirroring her body posture and hand movement, while also speaking her words back to her. My speaking and mirroring in turn encouraged a deepening intensity and further exaggeration of her hand movement. As she entered more deeply into feelings of deep distress stored in her body's memory, these feelings began to find release in tears.

During this process, I felt that we were engaging in an ever-deepening "dance", where the boundaries between us were becoming transparent and dissolved; I "knew" how she felt, and I could also mirror this awareness back to her.[33]

Sylvia subsequently described that she, too, had felt this deep connection and dance between us. "I didn't know what was going to happen and once I was in it, I just went with it," she told me, "... and I certainly didn't expect that this would happen" (referring to her emotional reaction and the insight she was gaining through this exercise).

In general, clients—like therapists—have also experienced the process of deep, *presence*-based relating as significant and healing.[34] Clients have described key characteristics of this type of relating as being deeply held and cared for by their therapist; feeling vulnerable, but safe, being "seen" and understood, not just in this moment, but in their totality as a whole person.

Some clients also spoke of experiencing a transpersonal dimension, a sense of merging of personal boundaries and of oneness with their therapist, while they were still also aware of their own, separate self. In such an encounter, the client and therapist are deeply immersed in the present moment experience of relating to one another. Through this relationship, clients felt whole and were able to get in touch with themselves as a "real" person. They also experienced their therapist as being real.[35]

It seems that this kind of relating comes close to an "I–Thou" relationship, as described by the philosopher Martin Buber.[36]

I–Thou and I–It

For Buber, "all real living is meeting" and healing happens in meeting the other in their uniqueness.[37,38] A human person lives in two relationships—an I–Thou and an I–It relationship—that both manifest in distinctive ways.[39]

An I–It relationship is what we are most used to in life. It is a stance of seeing another person, thing, or situation through the lenses of our own psychological makeup, values, social realities, and cultural conditioning. The "other" becomes an *object* of our perception, an "It" that is different and separate from us. Such "objectifying" is necessary for living, helping us to define ourselves and "the other". It enables us to gain knowledge and a sense of control over the world we live in.[40] I–It, however, cannot address the true core of each participant.[41]

An I–Thou relationship, in contrast, denotes a meeting between two persons, as it occurs in the present moment. At this moment, the other person is met *as* they *are*, beyond one's own perceptions and pre-conceptions. I–Thou is characterised by openness and directness, even an attitude of wonder, and flows dynamically between co-subjects.[42,43]

This type of relationship opens a "space in-between", where dialogue can happen. True dialogue does not happen in *talking about* the other. It happens in *engaging with* another from the core of oneself. In I–Thou relating, the "I" comes into being in its encounter with the "Thou", as does the "Thou" in its encounter with the "I". I–Thou touches on the mystery between people— glimpses of the eternal, divine "Thou" can be experienced in the encounter.[44]

A healing therapeutic relationship will necessarily move back and forth between therapist and client relating to each other in both an I–Thou and I–It relationship. It appears that in the session with Sylvia that I described earlier, we engaged in an I–Thou rela- tionship and experienced an I–Thou "peak" moment.[45]

Reflecting on the interaction itself, and the therapeutic gain for Sylvia afterward, brought us back to I–It relating—the *talking about* rather than a direct experiencing. However, if the client and therapist are open, once "seen" as a Thou, a client can always become a Thou again.[46]

The following case example by existential therapists Emmy van Deurzen and Claire Arnold-Baker, summarises how an open and trusting therapeutic relationship can support therapist and client through challenging cultural and social differences and experiences, toward personal growth and healing.[47] Please note that although van Deurzen and Arnold-Baker do not refer to the concepts of I–Thou relationship or *presence,* in this case study, it seems to me that this piece of therapeutic work illustrates the dynamics of an I–Thou therapeutic relationship at play.

Rahim, a gay Persian man in his early forties had experi- enced persecution in his home country, Iran, due to his sexuality. Having been in a secret relationship with his partner, Firouz, for ten years, the pair were arrested in a hotel raid while spending time together. Rahim was released due to his father's connections within the courts and by shifting the blame onto Firouz, who was later executed.

Van Deurzen describes that Rahim and herself formed a trusting and affectionate therapeutic relationship. Eventually, therapy reached a point where significant cultural differences began to surface and were played out. Rahim began to express his hostility and doubts about her ability as a Western, female, atheist therapist to understand him, an Iranian, Muslim, gay man. He also appeared to feel superior to her. Van Deurzen describes her conflicting responses; on one hand, welcoming Rahim's newfound ability to express his feelings openly and confidently, but on the other hand, feeling deeply challenged herself:

> ... Rahim had definitely gotten under my therapeutic skin ... Far from me regretting this, it made me feel more real in my relationship with Rahim and more truly connected to him. I think it makes a huge difference when I allow a person to affect me and change me.[48]

Reflecting on this, I realized how much I had to learn. Van Deurzen and Arnold-Baker acknowledge the impact the therapeutic relationship had on both the client's and the therapist's growth:

> For me, this case highlighted the way in which we are not detached in the therapeutic relationship; we are interconnected beings and therefore we learn something about ourselves from our clients' struggles.[49]
>
> We came together in that way, both learning something new, as is always the case when therapy touches the depth of our shared human existence. There is something extremely satisfying about such human communion as is possible in therapeutic work.[50]

I would argue that van Deurzen was manifesting a healing *presence* in this therapeutic relationship. And it was this *presence* that enabled her to hold the paradox of empathising with and affirming the client's current reality and experience, acknowledging differences and challenging him, and holding the potential for what the client (and therapist) might become.

Simultaneously, the therapist allowed herself to be challenged while remaining true to her own key values. Buber uses the term "inclusion" or "imagining the real" for this dynamic aspect of I–Thou relating:

> It is "imagining" what you are perceiving, thinking, feeling, and willing ... I can be empathetic or intuitive in our relationship, but unless I swing boldly and wholeheartedly in your direction, I will not make you fully present to myself ... Inclusion is 'imagining the real', which means to experience the other side of the relationship while not losing your own ground in the process.[51]

Firmly grounded in their own self, the therapist facilitates a deepening of relationship in which the client can become more present to themselves; the client's increased *presence* in turn impacts the therapist's unconscious patterns, assumptions, and resulting behaviours.[52]

I strongly purport that in a "true" meeting of persons, both therapist and client will be changed. *Presence*-based relating encourages the client's expression and healing and also touches the therapist.

In defence of therapeutic presence

So far, I have explored the dynamics, processes, and benefits of a *presence*-based therapeutic encounter. Therefore, in my view, this approach is diametrically opposed to therapy that is driven by Critical Social Justice, the key differences being how the person of the therapist and client are viewed and how relational dynamics are understood.

CSJ-driven therapy understands therapist and client, first and foremost, as people that have been shaped and affected by the complex, socially constructed, intersecting group identities that each party brings to the encounter, such as race, gender, age, class, and religious affiliation. CSJ theory asserts that inherent, negative power dynamics in these intersecting identities *necessarily* create positions of privilege and marginalisation, oppression, and dehumanisation.[53] Relationships in general, and the therapy relationship would be no exception, are primarily viewed through a lens of oppressive power dynamics at play.

Consequently, both the client and therapist are not primarily seen as human persons in relation to each other and the socio-cultural world around them.[54] Instead, they are viewed as defined by their intersecting group identities and, importantly, the differences and inequalities these identities create.[55] Dynamics of oppression are at the heart of the CSJ-driven therapy relationship.

This is the opposite of a therapeutic encounter grounded in *presence*. It renders *presence*-based relating impossible. A *presence*-based relationship with core characteristics like openness and receptivity where the therapist strives for an attitude of un-knowing cannot manifest where both client and therapist are pre-determined in their identities and their relationship is essentially seen as oppressive from the outset.[56]

Recalling the case study of Rahim, I wonder whether Rahim would have been able to reconcile his sexuality with his faith and find peace eventually, had his therapist operated from a CSJ-driven approach and emphasised their differences rather than their common humanity.[57]

Further, I hypothesise that such an emphasis would have led to the termination of therapy, as the encounter would have increasingly become marked by separation and disconnection. If the relationship itself had been consistently problematised and scrutinised under a predetermined lens of oppressive dynamics, it would have been deprived of its creative, present-moment potential, where differences can be worked through and transcended by newfound insights. *When a relationship is reduced to operating within fixed parameters, there is no space to receive the other openly—the relationship loses its dynamic healing potential.*[58]

The relationship in CSJ-driven therapy essentially seems akin to I–It relating. I–It objectifies the other, which, although a necessary form of relatedness, cannot become and be the ground of a deeply therapeutic, healing encounter.[59]

By staying grounded in meeting the client with an attitude of not-knowing, and being open to struggling with differences, the ineffable mystery of therapeutic relating, of an I–Thou relationship, could emerge. This therapeutic "stance" led to transformation and a new life perspective for Rahim, and the therapist was not left unchanged. This is inclusion, as described by Buber—it is inclusive therapy in the truest sense.

The meaning of I–It only unfolds in the service of I–Thou relating and not the other way round.[60] At its best, therefore, a CSJ-driven approach to therapy is putting the cart before the horse. At its worst, such an approach undermines more than a century of insight, experience, wisdom, and research into the healing nature of the therapeutic relationship.

Endnotes

1   For example, Roberto Assagioli, *Psychosynthesis: A Manual of Principles and Techniques* (Wellingborough, UK: The Aquarian Press, 1990).

    Ken Wilber, *Integral Spirituality* (Boston MA: Shambhala, 2006). The terms "spiritual" and "transpersonal" are often used interchangeably. For further detail see John Rowan, *The Transpersonal: Spirituality in Psychotherapy and Counselling.* 2nd Ed. (London: Routledge, 2005).

2   Glenn Hartelius, Geffen Rothe, and Paul J. Roy, "A Brand From the Burning: Defining Transpersonal Psychology", in *The Wiley Blackwell Handbook of Transpersonal Psychology,* ed. Harris L. Friedman H. L. and Glenn Hartelius (Chichester UK: Wiley Blackwell, 2015), p.14.

3   Judith S. Beck, *Cognitive Therapy: Basics and Beyond* (New York: Guilford Press, 2021).

4   I am writing from an ontological position that integrates socially constructed and transcendent paradigms of self and reality, postulating that "people are both/and: both a social self and a transcendent self … inhabitants of both physical reality and of a transcendent dimension." P. Gregg Blanton, "Adding Silence to Stories: Narrative Therapy and Contemplation", *Contemplative Family Therapy* 29 (2007): p. 218, https://doi.org/10.1007/s10591-007-9047-x.

5   See a more detailed definition and explanation further down under 'Presence in the therapeutic relationship'; cf. endnote 18.

6   For example: Jamal Granick, *Transpersonal Aspects of Therapist's Presence: What do Clients Experience?* Institute of Transpersonal Psychology. ProQuest Dissertations Publishing, 2011. 3495276. https://www.proquest.com/docview/923617889/B955E2D86C974AB0PQ/1.

    The following also all reference the importance of presence in the therapeutic relationship:

    Shari M. Geller and Leslie S. Greenberg, *Therapeutic Presence. A Mindful Approach to Effective Therapy* (Washington: American Psychological Association, 2012).

    Shari M. Geller. *A Practical Guide to Cultivating Therapeutic Presence* (Washington: Psychbooks Collection. American Psychological Association, 2017).

    Shari M. Geller and Stephen W. Porges, "Therapeutic Presence: Neurophysiological Mechanisms Mediating Feeling Safe in Therapeutic Relationships", *Journal of Psychotherapy Integration*, 24, no. 3 (2014): 178-192, https://doi.org/10.1037/a0037511.

Not all research includes a transpersonal dimension, for example: Ken A. Colosimo and Alberta E. Pos, "A Rational Model of Expressed Therapeutic Presence", *Journal of Psychotherapy Integration*, 25, no.2 (2015): 100-114, https://doi.org/10.1037/a0038879.

I am indebted to Geller's and Greenberg's work, especially in articulating my own experiences and understanding of *presence*. I acknowledge that they may hold different views to the ones expressed in this chapter.

[7] See Val Thomas' chapter in this book, "How Critical Social Justice is Incompatible with the Therapeutic Relationship: The Ground of Therapy".

[8] Irvine Yalom, *Love's Executioner and other Tales of Psychotherapy* (London: Penguin Books, 2013), p. 101.

[9] Geller and Greenberg, "Presence", p. 3.

[10] Howard Kirschenbaum and April Jourdan, "The Current Status of Carl Rogers and the Person-centred Approach," *Psychotherapy: Theory, Research, Practice, Training* 42, no.1 (2005): p. 44, https://doi.org/10.1037/0033-3204.42.1.37.

[11] Carl Rogers, "The Necessary and Sufficient Conditions of Therapeutic Personality Change," *Journal of Consulting and Clinical Psychology* 60, no.6 (1992): pp. 827 – 832.

[12] Tudor, K. (2011), "Rogers' therapeutic conditions. A relational conceptualization". *Person-centred & Experiential Psychotherapies,* 10(3), pp. 165-180. https://doi.org/10.1080/14779757.2011.599513.

[13] Rogers, "Conditions", pp. 827-832.

[14] Mick Cooper, "Carl Rogers's 'core conditions'. Are they necessary and sufficient?", April 2, 2019, https://mick-cooper.squarespace.com/new-blog/2019/4/2/carl-rogerss-core-conditions-are-they-necessary-and-sufficient#.

[15] Michele Baldwin, "Interview with Carl Rogers on the Use of Self in Therapy", in *The Use of Self in Therapy*, ed. Michele Baldwin (New York: Haworth Press, 1987), p. 45.

[16] For example, James F. Bugental, *The Art of the Psychotherapist. How to Develop the Skills that Take Psychotherapy Beyond Science* (New York: Norton Inc, 1992).

[17] Geller and Greenberg, "Presence".

[18] Ibid, p. 7.

[19] This process is also known as "bracketing", emptying oneself, or un-knowing: Ernesto Spinelli, *Practicing Existential Therapy: The Relational World* (London: Sage 2015).

20 Geller and Greenberg, "Presence".

21 Colosimo and Pos, "Rational Model".

22 Cf. Geller and Greenberg, "Presence", 55f.

23 Geller and Greenberg, "Presence".

24 Baldwin, "Interview", p. 50.

25 Bradford speaks of "unconditional presence" manifesting. G. Kenneth Bradford, "From Neutrality to the Play of Unconditional Presence," in John J. Prendergast and G. Kenneth Bradford, *Listening from the Heart of Silence* (St. Paul, MN: Paragon House, 2007), pp. 55-75.

26 Cf. Rowan, "The Transpersonal", p. 4.

27 Geller and Greenberg have developed a model of five deepening levels of presence. See Geller and Greenberg, "Presence", p. 139.

28 Ibid, p. 257.

29 Mearns and Cooper introduce the related concept of "relational depth", which refers to *both* a particular moment of deep encounter *and* a relationship with deep connection.

    See Dave Mearns and Mick Cooper, *Working at Relational Depth in Counselling and Psychotherapy*, 2nd ed, (London: Sage, 2018).

    For Geller, relational therapeutic presence goes beyond relational depth, as it encompasses a transpersonal dimension. I concur with her that presence is the foundation of relational depth. Shari Geller, "Therapeutic Presence a Foundation for Relational Depth," in *Relational Depth: New perspectives and Developments*, ed. Rosanne Knox et al (Basingstoke UK: Palgrave Macmillan, 2013), p.181. However, Rowan identifies a transpersonal dimension in relational depth. John Rowan, "The Transpersonal and Relational Depth", in Knox, *Relational Depth*, p.211.

30 Rowan, "The Transpersonal and Relational Depth", p. 214, questions this position.

31 Geller and Greenberg, "Presence".

32 Dave Mann, *Gestalt therapy: 100 key points & techniques* (Abingdon, UK: Routledge, 2021), 265ff.

33 This phenomenon is also called "linking", Rowan, *The Transpersonal*, pp. 162-166.

34 Rosanne Knox, "Relational Depth from the Client's Perspective," in Knox, *Relational Depth*, 21-35. However, Knox herself does not explicitly link "relational depth" with "presence".

35 Ibid.

[36] Martin Buber (1878–1965) was deeply critical of Western individualism and the idea of an independent, objective, and self-sustaining individual. For him, relationship and dialogue are at the heart of all being. Existential and Gestalt approaches to therapy have been strongly influenced by his thinking.

[37] Buber, 1958, 11 in Maurice Friedman, "Buber and Dialogical Therapy. Healing through Meeting", *The Humanist Psychologist* 36, (2008): p. 300, https://doi.org/10.1080/08873260802350014.

[38] Friedman, "Buber", 300: Awareness of a person "means to perceive the dynamic centre that stamps on all utterances, actions, and attitudes the recognizable sign of uniqueness … It is possible only when he or she becomes present for me as a partner in dialogue".

[39] Buber distinguishes between an "individual" and a "person". Being a person is "an expression of what it is to be human – a being who inhabits an inseparable relation with the world and is an expression of that relation". Ernesto Spinelli, *Practising Existential Therapy: The Relational World* (London: Sage 2015), p. 20.

[40] Spinelli, "Existential Therapy", p. 20.

[41] Gary Ventimiglia, "Martin Buber, God, and Psychoanalysis, "*Psychoanalytic Inquiry* 28, no.5 (2008): p. 615.

[42] Friedman, "Buber", p. 306.

[43] Spinelli, "Existential Therapy", p. 19.

[44] Ventimiglia, "Martin Buber", pp. 612-621.

[45] Mann, "Gestalt Therapy", 222ff identifies a general therapist I-Thou attitude and an evanescent I-Thou peak moment: "The I-Thou attitude makes the I-Thou moment possible".

[46] John G. Scott et al, "Healing relationships and the existential philosophy of Martin Buber". *Philosophy, Ethics, and Humanities in Medicine* 4, no. 11 (2009) https://doi.org/10.1186/1747-5341-4-11.

[47] Existential therapy is philosophy-based and concerned with questions and crises of human experience, emphasising client responsibility, choice, and freedom: Linda Finlay, *Relational Integrative Psychotherapy* (Chichester UK: Wiley, 2016).

Emmy van Deurzen and Claire Arnold-Baker, C. "Existential-Phenomenological Therapy Illustration: Rahim's Dilemma", in *The Wiley World Handbook of Existential Therapy*, ed. Emmy van Deurzen et al (Chichester UK: Wiley, 2019), pp. 181–197.

[48] Ibid, p.194.

49 Ibid, p. 197.

50 Ibid.

51 Friedman, "Buber", p. 304. In therapy, inclusion cannot be entirely mutual, as it is the therapist's role is to help the client and not vice versa. Friedman, "Buber", 305f.

52 Geller and Greenberg, "Presence", p. 55.

53 Özlem Sensoy and Robin Di Angelo, *Is Everyone really Equal?: An Introduction to Key Concepts in Social Justice Education,* 2nd Ed (New York: Teachers College Press, 2017).

54 Cf. Endnote 36.

55 The psychoanalytic school is developing ways of integrating intersectionality into therapeutic practice, for example Dwight Turner, *Intersections of Privilege and Otherness in Counselling and Psychotherapy: Mockingbird* (London: Routledge, 2021);

Max Belkin and Cleonie White, *Intersectionality and Relational psychoanalysis: New Perspectives on race, gender, and Sexuality* (London: Routledge, 2020).

For more extensive literature and discussion concerning CSJ integration into psychotherapy and counselling, see other chapters in this book.

56 Spinelli, "Existential Therapy", 147f.

57 Van Deurzen and Arnold-Baker, "Rahim". My view and hypothesis expressed here do not claim to represent van Deurzen's and Arnold-Baker's position.

58 Lago and Christodoulidi give a succinct summary of potential diversity-related obstacles to relational depth. However, they contend that deep meeting is possible, listing relational stances and attributes that echo presence-based relating.

Colin Lago and Fevronia Christodoulidi, "Client-Therapist Diversity: Aspiring towards Relational Depth", in *Relational Depth: New perspectives and Developments*, ed. Rosanne Knox et al (Basingstoke: Palgrave Macmillan, 2013), pp. 114-124.

59 Scott, "Healing Relationships".

60 Ibid.

Chapter 18:

Systemic Family Therapy and Critical Social Justice: Happy Marriage or Grounds for Divorce?

by Piers Newman

Introduction

Systemic family therapy is a psychotherapeutic approach that differs from almost all other psychotherapies. While other psychotherapies consider the internal or intrapsychic world of the individual client, family therapy focuses on the real-time interactions between family members in a therapy room. Family therapy's origins are unusual, and it draws on a wide variety of influences to inform its theoretical base. Aspects of postmodernism started to appear in the late 1980s, but it is in the last ten years that influences from Critical Social Justice (CSJ) have entered the field.

Given CSJ's suspicion of the individual, it would appear that a therapy that does not prioritise the individual would be a good fit. This chapter will take a brief look at the origins and key ideas that have developed, over time, in family therapy and will use a vignette of a family to further clarify how these ideas work in practice. I will then offer my opinions to demonstrate that CSJ approaches negate core principles of family therapy and undermine a key psychological tenet of the family unit.

Origins and key ideas

During the 1950s and 60s, various individual psychotherapies aimed at severe clinical problems, such as schizophrenia, had failed to yield results. At this time, prior to the emergence of antipsychotic medication, research was funded into the role family communication had in maintaining these difficulties, leading to professional interest in family interaction. Individual therapies generally focus on an individual's biographical and historic circumstances, whereas the family approach considered the family's current circumstances, especially relationship difficulties and disputes.[1]

There was also a great deal of interest in General Systems Theory and its applicability to human relationships.[2] The early years of family therapy conceived of the family as a type of system, a collection of interacting parts that were greater than its sum. The parts of any system affect the state of each other using an exchange of information known as feedback. Within human systems, such as families or groups, feedback was initially seen as behavioural and communicative and able to affect the members within them.[3]

These initial descriptions of family systems were rather mechanistic, deriving from engineering, mathematical and reductive biological theories. However, insights arose from this, such as psychological difficulties being maintained by relationships or the persistence of such difficulties being a family's unsuccessful attempt to resolve them.

Family therapy works by having the members of a family in the room together to talk about what difficulties they feel they are experiencing. Interestingly, different members of the family may perceive these difficulties in different ways. For example, parents of an anxious child may have differing accounts of when the anxious behaviours started and what they believe caused them. A variety of factors could hypothetically contribute, such as anxiety as a response to disputes with a peer group, concern with a parent who is sick or who has been made redundant, or parents who are in a highly conflictual relationship. Therefore, the problem ceases to be located in the child but is seen as a response to other circumstances in the wider family system.

In family therapy, a conversation starts between the therapist and family members, with opinions often being expressed by family members to one another about the reasons for their difficulties. While a great deal has been written about family therapy practices, the fundamental principle behind family therapy is the therapist asking questions. This sounds incredibly simplistic, but a great deal has been written in family therapy literature about how questions elicit information.[4] Ultimately, the family members' responses to the therapist's questions serve as feedback to one another.

When communication is going well in the family, this feedback can be heard as encouragement, support, care, concern, and love. When families are faced with difficult circumstances, this feedback may be heard as criticism or animosity.

In everyday life, families may have little time and space to reflect together on their circumstances, and a comment I sometimes hear is one family member saying to another, "I didn't realise you thought that." An essential role of the therapist in this environment, therefore, is to encourage helpful communication as well as to think with the family about difficult emotions that may need to be addressed.

Training in family therapy became more formalised in the 1970s, with the approach being focussed primarily on behavioural issues and communication processes, using directive tasks to elicit change. The family was seen as a simple system with the therapist metaphorically "pulling levers and turning dials" to adjust the family.[5]

However, one of the most profound influences on family therapy took hold in the late 1970s and early 1980s. The Milan Team comprised four child psychiatrists and psychoanalysts based, unsurprisingly, in Milan, Italy.[6] They emphasised developing multiple ideas of why families struggled to function, accentuating the reciprocal nature of relationships and the importance of the therapist not appearing to take sides with one member of the family over another. While not explicitly postmodernist, the idea of multiple perspectives appeared to have some overlap with postmodern concepts, such as scepticism towards objectivity in relation to families. To demonstrate this, consider a dispute in your family. Finding the "objective" truth about the causes of the dispute may well exacerbate the dispute rather than resolving it, as different family members may have differing views about its causes.

Around this time, the role of the therapist shifted from an instigator of change (one who "pulls the levers") to a collaborator with the family to achieve change. Family therapists became warier about imposing their own beliefs and views of how a family should function.[7] They also wanted to demystify therapy by making it more transparent and for therapists to adopt a less-knowing, more curious position towards the family. Feminist family therapists critiqued the earlier models, pointing out that family therapy could end up reinforcing the role of women as homemakers and providers of childcare.[8]

The interest in postmodernism grew and developed in two related ways: how power was conceptualised within the family and the role of language. With the former, some feminists regarded the family as the seat of patriarchal power with women being subjugated within it.

In the case of the latter, language and, in particular, narrative—the stories that families tell themselves—became a focus of therapy and were seen as another way pre-existing power structures within society were maintained.

Michael White, an Australian family therapist, was instrumental in bringing these ideas into family therapy.[9] White surmised that within every family there were dominant narratives that the more powerful family members held and subordinated narratives, which were the less-heard exceptions to the dominant ones.

The tendency to focus on language and narrative resulted in two potential ways of working with it within family therapy. The first approach sees therapy as a conversational partnership, whereas the second is framed as socio-political activism; this latter one is strongly associated with White's narrative family therapy.[10] Supposedly, narrative family therapists counter oppression within the family and wider society by revealing alternative constructions to potentially rigid categories as a means to liberate families from them. They consider problems in families through a political lens to examine wider cultural or societal problems, such as racism and sexism, as well as more subtle ones, such as what constitutes a "healthy" relationship.[11]

In this chapter, I will use the terms "narrative therapist" and "activist therapist" interchangeably, although I would add that not all narrative family therapists would necessarily consider themselves activists.

Activist therapeutic concepts have become more established in recent years in the UK. The Association for Family Therapy and Systemic Practice (AFT for short) is the principal professional organisation for family therapists in the UK.[12] AFT produces two publications: the *Journal of Family Therapy* and *Context*, the former being an academic journal and the latter having a magazine format. *Context* regularly publishes articles that reiterate core principles of Critical Social Justice.

Issue 129, in 2013, was on the subject of masculinity, framing it from a feminist perspective as problematic, with men occupying the dominant position of power and women as a subordinated class.[13] Issue 155, in 2018, on Queer Practice and Systemic Practice, repeated the contention that biological sex is socially constructed.[14] Further, Issue 164, in 2019, was subtitled "The professional and the political". One article even suggested the need to look again at Marxist philosophy as a way to broaden the social mind of the discipline of family therapy.[15] This would not be a problem if other philosophies or conceptualisations about the family and society were presented. However, they were not because, in my opinion, those who produce knowledge in the field of British Family Therapy are strong proponents of Critical Social Justice.

Ideas into practice: the Richards family

In order to illustrate how these different family therapy approaches would work in practice, I will use a case study. In this instance, I am using a case from my own clinical practice and showing how three different versions of family therapy would be applied in their particular circumstances. The first is an early behavioural and communication model; the second uses a less interventionist, more conversational approach; and the final one is an activist approach. Names and some details have been changed to maintain client confidentiality.

> The Richards family was referred to the psychotherapy service where I was working at the time. The mother, Cynthia, was described by her referrer, a general practitioner, as depressed. She was from a black-British background and lived primarily on benefits. She had been using cannabis on a daily basis. Three of her sons, Courtney, aged fifteen, Ben, aged thirteen, and Aaron, aged ten, lived with her. There were also concerns about the boys. They were described as having conduct difficulties and problems with attending school. Social care agencies had been or were currently involved with the family. Slightly over a year before the family's referral to mental health services, an older brother, Delroy, aged eighteen, had been fatally stabbed in an altercation with a gang of boys. It was postulated, in the referral, that

Delroy might have been involved with gangs. There was another older brother, Errol, aged twenty-four, who lived with his partner and young children nearby. Cynthia had separated from the boys' father, Winston, a number of years previously. Winston was intermittently involved with his sons' lives.

An early family therapy approach from the 1970s would have focussed primarily on behavioural issues and communication processes. The boys' behaviour can be seen as serving to distract from their grief, and Cynthia's grief, at the loss of Delroy. Cynthia's difficulty in asserting her role as a parent in the family would also be addressed. The role of the family therapist would be to provide interventions and adjustments to how the family functions. This would be by setting directive tasks, such as a system of rewards for appropriate behaviour and consequences, including their behaviour in school.

Also, the family would be asked to deliberately do different things together, such as spending time together or finding a way to acknowledge the loss of Delroy. This therapeutic approach is directive.

As a therapist, I am sympathetic to the conversational partnership approach described earlier, and therefore I am using my own experience of clinical work with this family as an example of the second type of approach.

My initial session was one with Cynthia, and all her sons were present. She said that they needed to talk about what had happened, particularly Delroy's death. Over the next few months, as I listened to their stories, I had the feeling that they had been in a kind of stasis. Cynthia recognised she was medicating herself by using cannabis, and we discussed her giving it up. Her faith became more important to her, although her presence at church was met with occasional prejudice, as her boys were perceived as "bad".

Courtney, her fifteen-year-old, asked to come and see me alone. I agreed, and we spoke about the difficulties of his life, both the loss of Delroy, but also the pressures and fear he felt as a young, stigmatised black man. He also spoke about having to have a "front". Several times in our meeting, he was close to tears and would become silent. Sadly, some months later, Courtney was involved in a serious altercation and was detained in a young offenders' institution.

Courtney's brothers spoke about their experience of discrimination. There were concerns that Ben, the thirteen-year-old, was on the periphery of gang activity, so he was moved to a specialist education unit and soon began to succeed academically.

Aaron, the youngest at ten, was told that he would amount to nothing by a teacher. I was shocked that much of the discrimination the family experienced was not on the basis of race. Instead, they were being judged through a moralising lens by members of their own community as well as professionals.

Several other statutory agencies such as social care and charities were involved with the family. Often, the family was given contradictory and uncoordinated advice. The Richards were treated as a "problem" family, constantly told by professionals, both black and white, what they had to do. During one session where they told me of another incident of being on the receiving end of poor treatment from professionals, I noticed that I felt an almost overwhelming inability to be helpful. I then asked them, "What can I, as a middle-aged, middle-class white man do to help you?" Cynthia chuckled at me and said, "You listen to us; nobody else does."

This comment was a turning point for me. I felt the family regarded me as a useful professional, and this emboldened me to challenge the boys' attitude toward their mother. Aaron and Ben regained their respect for their mother as they saw her cease smoking cannabis and begin to assert herself with professionals who she felt were treating them unjustly. The family began to watch television and films with each other and also began to spend more time together. Courtney communicated with the family from the young offenders' institute, telling his brothers to study hard at school. I was unable to involve Winston in any of our sessions, and Errol was only able to attend a few sessions.

Unfortunately, I had to stop working with the family, as I was redeployed in a restructuring of the service I was working in. Our last session together was a moving experience for us all. I told them that I felt anger at the injustices they had experienced. The family gave me a thank-you card. In it, Ben had written that they were going to miss me and drew an eye weeping a tear.

I wonder what it would have been like if I had taken an approach directed by Critical Social Justice ideology with the Richards family. If I worked with them from this perspective (of oppression), then their experience of racism and stereotyping, toxic masculinity, and the role of a single parent might have been brought to the foreground of the conversation. I could then have discussed resisting the pernicious dominant discourses and begin to construct alternatives. I could have taken an approach just focussing on the wider context of discrimination. This would have allowed a detailed conversation about the difficulties black families and, in particular, young black men face in British society today.

Perhaps I could have recruited other people from a similar cultural background to the family to comment on and provide meaning from a cultural perspective as a way of providing some form of cultural expertise to the therapeutic system. I could have assembled other pupils from Ben and Aaron's school to talk about the misrepresentation they experience. I could have explicitly critiqued my own need to focus on the emotions of the family rather than the Richards family's experience of racism, violent masculinity, and the role of a single parent.[16] Additionally, I could have repeatedly acknowledged my "whiteness" and its contribution to systemic racism.

Do you think that would have been a helpful approach? I don't. I believe that some of the ideas described above would have been inappropriate for a family therapist to employ with families. In the following section, I will outline why in further detail.

The problems with importing Critical Social Justice tenets into family therapy

Using CSJ principles has several implications for family therapy. As was previously described, family therapy has changed over time. The therapist was originally seen as the primary agent responsible for the change. Nowadays, the therapist is a facilitator helping the family to address mutually defined goals. This has had the helpful effect of depathologising many presentations by seeing them as relational, as given in the anxious child previously described.

However, the introduction of CSJ concepts reintroduces the concept of pathology, albeit one framed in narrow definitions of power and oppression. The activist therapist risks viewing a family's difficulties as a manifestation of the oppressive nature of society, associating dominant discourses with pathology and subordinated discourses as healthy. This may well convey to a family that, faced with the idea of living in an oppressive society, lack the agency to change anything. In the case of the Richards family, this also risks bypassing their very real grief at the loss of Delroy.

This inversion of pathologising may also have another effect. Family therapy practice turns into something that blindly affirms subordinated members and castigates dominant members. Even if we assume that these societal dynamics exist, it does not necessarily follow that they are replicated in all families. Applying a binary view of subjugated and dominant narratives is a poor application of theory to therapy, as not all presenting difficulties manifest in this way.[17] Sometimes, narratives in families are subjugated because they might be unhelpful to the family. At times, members of families keep information from one another in order to protect their loved ones rather than to have power over them.

Another key concept in family therapy is curiosity.[18] Interactions within family systems can be complex, with family members not always understanding the stances other members might take. Curiosity on the part of the therapist creates multiple descriptions for a family that pragmatically facilitate understanding of one another rather than depending on a monolithic, linear explanation from a powerful, all-knowing therapist.

The activist approach, however, is anti-curious, or to an extent certain about the difficulties families face. Descriptions of difficulties are located within the theoretical presumption of oppression. In doing this, the therapist paradoxically becomes that which was initially critiqued by the profession, namely the powerful figure who is directive, basing their interventions on a limited number of unproven theories and assumptions about the nature of power and language derived from postmodernism.

Furthermore, locating a family's difficulties within language, narrative or discourse fails to acknowledge a core reason why many enter therapy. People who have had traumatic experiences do not have a language or even words for these and often have strong feelings of guilt and shame. Some people that I have met describe themselves as contaminated or cursed. In these cases, this linguistic turn of therapy reveals a profound inadequacy to help traumatised people address these difficulties as traumatic responses are pre-verbal.

Fundamentally, difficult feelings and emotions arising from previous experiences must be addressed in order for people to develop a sense of agency, both as individuals and as a group. However, an agential self is viewed with suspicion in postmodern quarters. An agential self is a modernist concept, yet for some, the development of agency is an important step to transcending the experience of abuse or neglect.[19]

Ultimately, psychotherapy based on the constructs of language is a strange and somewhat unrecognisable thing, as the following quote suggests: "... the psychotherapeutic task is to recognise the deeply embedded implicit metaphors lodged in the language in terms of which we currently unthinkingly think, and replace them with others."[20]

Some Feminist and Queer Theorists have challenged the concept of family, describing it as maintaining patriarchal and heteronormative discourses within society. However, there is more to the role of parents in a family than carriers of discourse. Increasingly, neurological research is showing the important role that parents play in their child's development. Interaction and stimulation are critical to brain development in children.[21] There is something that parents provide which is the development of personhood.

In any good enough parent–child relationship, the child exists as a construct in the parent's mind. The child experiences this construct of themselves in the way the parent relates and develops a sense of themselves relationally. What appears to be important for children are parents who are consistent, reliable, and able to provide some structure to daily living. I wish to state that I am not arguing for some politically conservative notion of what a family is, with a father and a mother and 2.4 children. This sort of arrangement does not guarantee children to grow into adults able to relate well to people and resolve the difficulties the world throws at them. Rather, I am arguing for fundamental principles of evidence-based parenting to be considered concerning children's development, and I believe that a deconstructive or de-colonising approach to parenting—an approach prioritising particular Feminist and Queer Theories—is not feasible.

I am concerned that an over-reliance on CSJ concepts will have implications for the future of family therapy, and not in a good way. As a tutor in family therapy, I have become increasingly troubled that teaching is moving away from a theoretically diverse base and a pragmatic attaining of skills. Indeed, a great deal of ideological terminology, such as oppression and liberation, has been adopted, with the aim of teaching a purely socio-political activist approach to family therapy to students.

As with any purely ideological teaching, a minority will be enthusiastic about these ideas. However, the majority will be ambivalent or oppositional, either participating with the aim of jumping through hoops in order to gain a qualification or dropping out of the course entirely. This contrasts with the idea of creating transparent, collaborative therapists. A training syllabus based on CSJ principles will focus on a variety of social categories focussing on domination and oppression, conflating membership of an identity group and personal experience.

Training family therapists involves them looking at their own experiences of family, requiring vulnerability in revealing their own stories of family, and being sensitive when listening to the stories of other trainees.

Activist family therapists, however, prioritise the narratives of those with subordinated identities and characterise dominant identities as oppressive. This reduces students to a collection of markers of identity. Concomitant with that is the risk of inculcation of guilt and the necessity of confessions of inadequacy to the group.[22]

Family therapy has always been an outlier in the psychotherapeutic field as its approach is very different from many other therapies and it has been open to ideas from unusual sources. However, activist family therapy appears increasingly antithetical to the heteronormative notion of family.

While there is a truth that some societal beliefs around family have had a negative effect on some heterosexual women, gay men, and lesbians, it is important to note that familial structures are fundamental to child development. CSJ ideas imply that men are a category of suspicion, with their role in the family and society both ignored and negated. In some cases, I would contend this is misandry.

Conclusion

Activist family therapy espouses its connection to postmodernism. However, the activist's goal of imposing their views on a family is not a postmodern project. It is as modernist as early family therapy, psychiatry, or psychology, redolent with the power of the therapist to stigmatise and pathologise—in this case, based on categories of identity.

The history of mental health care, unfortunately, contains many incidents of "care" based on highly dubious beliefs and prejudices. Psychotherapies informed by CSJ will inevitably repeat these earlier mistakes, as they are yet another example of well-meaning professionals, wanting to do "good".

Endnotes

1   I have briefly summarised the excellent and far more detailed overview of the history of family therapy that can be found in Rudi Dallos and Ros Draper, *An Introduction to Family Therapy: Systemic Theory and Practice* (Maidenhead: Open University Press, 2015).

2   Rudi Dallos and Ros Draper. *An Introduction to Family Therapy : Systemic Theory and Practice.* (Maidenhead: Open University Press, 2015), Ch. 1.

3   Systemic family therapy needs some explanation, given the current overuse and misuse of the word "systemic". A simple system is a central heating system: I can walk into my home, feel cold, and turn up the thermostat. The thermostat signals to the boiler to turn on, and the boiler pumps warm water through the radiators in the house. On reaching the appropriate temperature, the thermostat feeds back to the boiler to turn off. The people who I share my house with are another system. They may strongly disagree with my setting of the thermostat, and feedback to me is that it is too warm or too cool. Thus, systems of varying complexity interact.

4   Karl Tomm is a Canadian psychiatrist and family therapist who has written several papers on questions that therapists can ask. He divides them into four categories: lineal, circular, strategic, and reflexive. The first two categories help the therapist understand the family's difficulties better; the latter two are ways the therapist might influence a family.

Lineal questions are purely investigative: who did what when? Circular questions focus on how family members' behaviours, communications, and emotions act on each other: "When your parents argue, what does your brother do?" Strategic questions can be leading or challenging and have a corrective element to them: "How can you and your wife stop these arguments?" Reflexive questions are facilitative attempts to get family members to consider alternatives: "If these arguments ceased, how would your day-to-day lives be different?" See, for example, Karl Tomm, "Interventive Interviewing: Part III. Intending to Ask Lineal, Circular, Strategic, or Reflexive Questions?" *Family Process* 27, no. 1 (March 1988): 1–15. https://doi.org/10.1111/j.1545-5300.1988.00001.x.

5   One early model of family therapy, structural family therapy, paid attention to the roles of subsystems within a family, such as whether the parents worked together effectively and whether children were brought into disputes or became confidantes of parents. Another model, strategic family therapy, focussed on pragmatic solutions that involved consciously changing patterns of communication and behaviour. An example

of an intervention would be to request an argumentative family to argue at a specific time of day for a fixed amount of time. This is intended to disrupt the unboundaried pattern of argumentation the family is in.

6   Mara Palazzoli Selvini et al., "Hypothesizing - Circularity - Neutrality: Three Guidelines for the Conductor of the Session", *Family Process* 19, no. 1 (March 1980): 3–12. https://doi.org/10.1111/j.1545-5300.1980.00003.x.

7   Lynn Hoffman, *Exchanging Voices: A Collaborative Approach to Family Therapy.* (London: Karnac Books, 1993), Ch. 3.

8   For example, see Rachel T. Hare-Mustin, "A Feminist Approach to Family Therapy". Family Process 17, no 2 (1978): 181–94. https://doi.org/10.1111/j.1545-5300.1978.00181.x.

9   White, in collaboration with David Epston, sees language as the primary means of constructing meaning and as an active relational process rather than passive representation. White and Epston view therapists as "inevitably engaged in a political activity" and believes that they have a responsibility to challenge "techniques that subjugate persons to a dominant ideology". Michael White and David Epston, *Narrative Means to Therapeutic Ends* (New York; London: W.W. Norton & Company, 1990): p. 29.

10   Gerald Monk and Diane R. Gehart, "Sociopolitical Activist or Conversational Partner? Distinguishing the Position of the Therapist in Narrative and Collaborative Therapies". *Family Process* 42, no. 1 (March 2003): 19–30. https://doi.org/10.1111/j.1545-5300.2003.00019.x.

11   Mark Hayward, a British family therapist, wrote, "At a stretch, for example, you could have identified yourself as a Strategic, Structural, or post Milan therapist, and maintained a left or right-wing political position, been for or against equality in society, valued neutrality or non-neutrality, centred or de-centred yourself as a therapist, been knowing or not-knowing, adopted modernist or postmodernist, structuralist or post-structuralist frames. Narrative practices are available for anyone to use in whichever (ethical or unethical) ways they like, but to identify yourself as a narrative therapist is to imply your alignment with fairly specific values, practices, politics, ethics and theories." Mark Hayward, "Critiques of Narrative Therapy: A Personal Response," *Australian and New Zealand Journal of Family Therapy* 24, no. 4 (December 2003): 183–89. https://doi.org/10.1002/j.1467-8438.2003.tb00558.x.

12   AFT Association for Family Therapy and Systemic Practice, accessed October 2022, https://www.aft.org.uk/

13   Ged Smith, "Working with men in systemic therapy: challenging masculinities". *Context* 129 (October 2013): pp. 29-35.

14 Amanda Middleton and H Howitt, "Trans sexualities in the therapy room". *Context* 155 (February 2018): pp. 44-48.

15 Jim Wilson, "The politics of practice and the state we are in". *Context* 164 (August 2019): pp. 3-6.

16 I chose the examples in this paragraph based on the experience of a family therapist attending a conference demonstrating narrative family therapy.

   Salvador Minuchin was a hugely influential family therapist who was critical of narrative approaches and outlined a series of objections he had to how narrative therapists had avoided the family in their work. Salvador Minuchin, "Where is the Family in Narrative Family Therapy?" *Journal of Marital and Family Therapy* 24, no. 4 (October 1998): 397–403. https://doi.org/10.1111/j.1752-0606.1998.tb01094.x.

   Other family therapists express more concern with the narrative approach. On the one hand, the narrative use of a person's story implies an individualism, yet narrative therapists wish to reduce the self to linguistic interaction. Additionally, the story told is not the individual's story but the story told to the therapist. Finally, much can be communicated in therapy without language. Silence and non-verbal communication can paradoxically be expressive. Paolo Bertrando, *The Dialogical Therapist: Dialogue in Systemic Practice* (London: Karnac, 2007).

17 Bertrando, *The Dialogical Therapist,* pp. 39-40.

18 Gianfranco Cecchin, "Hypothesizing, Circularity, and Neutrality Revisited: An Invitation to Curiosity", *Family Process* 26, no. 4 (December 1987): 405–13. https://doi.org/10.1111/j.1545-5300.1987.00405.x.

19 Carmel Flaskas, an Australian family therapist, has written extensively on the effect of postmodernist thought in family therapy. She identifies the limits of language in conveying traumatic experiences and the inadequacy of a postmodern, fluid self for the client in therapy. Carmel Flaskas, *Family Therapy beyond Postmodernism: Practice Challenges Theory* (Hove, UK: Routledge, 2002).

20 John Shotter, "Consultant re-authoring: the 'making' and 'finding' of narrative constructions", *Human Systems* 2, no. 2 (1991): pp. 105-119.

21 Bateman and Fonagy give an account of the importance of the parenting role in child development in their book: Anthony Bateman and Peter Fonagy, *Psychotherapy for Borderline Personality Disorder : Mentalization-Based Treatment* (Oxford ; New York: Oxford University Press, 2004).

22 Robert Lifton describes these processes taken to extremes in his book. Robert Jay Lifton, *Thought Reform and the Psychology of Totalism: A Study of "Brainwashing" in China* (Mansfield Centre, CT: Martino Publishing, 2014).

Chapter 19:

Critical Social Justice—Today's Pseudoscience in American Professional Psychology

by Nina C. Silander and Robert D. Mather

Thirty years ago, the sitting American Psychological Association (APA) president called on psychologists to "explicitly blend our data and values in order to make strong arguments for the kinds of [radical] change we think is necessary".[1]

While *politicization* is not new to professional psychology, over the last twenty years, and especially during the last five to ten, concerns about *political bias* due to a lack of ideological diversity have increased.[2] And many have argued that this bias threatens the credibility of the profession, so much so that one recent study showed that even the general public could detect widespread political bias across an array of social psychological research articles![3]

Unfortunately, ideological bias in social psychological research has a downstream effect. Essentially, it shapes the many ways in which this research is applied. Perhaps the most concerning effect is how ideological bias influences mental health services. We will show how this ideological bias, and with it, Critical Social Justice (CSJ), manifests at the organizational level in American professional psychology.[4] We will then explain what this means for the consumer of psychological services, including one of the most valuable and well-supported therapeutic approaches.

The prevalent bias in American professional psychology

Psychologists studying political ideology in the United States (US) typically use the "conservative vs. liberal" binary that coincides with the primarily two-party system of Republicans and Democrats. Regrettably, this binary excludes other ideological categories (e.g., libertarians) and overlooks other important ideological/political nuances (e.g., classical liberals vs. progressives). Nonetheless, we will use the terms "conservative" and "liberal" in this chapter to remain consistent with research conducted in the American cultural context.

With that said, the liberal-to-conservative ratio in the American public is relatively balanced.[5] However, this is not the case in the field of psychology. In 2015, Duarte and colleagues, for instance, reported a ratio of 10.5 liberal psychology professors to every 1 conservative psychology professor.[6] Other measured ratios are even more pronounced (e.g., 76 to 1, in the 2012 presidential voting patterns).[7]

Particularly strong undercurrents of CSJ, typically embraced by "liberal" (or, more typically, "leftists" and progressives), have become thematic and promoted across specialty disciplines and professional contexts. Terms such as "marginalization", "systemic oppression", "privilege", "equity", and "decolonization" pervade many of them.

The Heterodox Academy's Psychology division is one of the louder voices expressing concern about ideological bias and calls for greater intellectual diversity. On its previous social media page, they explain that:

> Too often research, training, and practice in psychology are captured by particular ideological orthodoxies and are not welcoming of diverse ideas, particularly

with respect to sociopolitical perspectives. This insularity in the field decreases the accuracy, comprehensiveness, and practical application of psychological research, impedes psychologists' ability to effectively serve diverse populations, and reduces the credibility of psychology with policymakers and the public.[8]

The ideological bias is shaping many psychologists' roles in research, advocacy efforts, higher education and admissions, training/supervision, program development, consultation, and mental health services. Activities across these roles tend to predictably match the dominant ideology—now CSJ—broadly embraced by the profession.

Examples of politicized psychology in the US

All the primary American mental health organizations share a mission. The American Psychological Association (APA), American Counseling Association, and National Association of Social Work have all committed themselves to a version of "social justice" that corresponds with CSJ. Additionally, the APA promotes critical constructivist and liberation theories in psychology.[9,10]

Commitment to scientific integrity appears to have fallen by the wayside in favor of a political theory. The author of one recent academic article titled *Intersectionality Research in Psychological Science: Resisting the Tendency to Disconnect, Dilute, and Depoliticize* urges readers to avoid ideological objectivity and instead read everything through an intersectional lens.[11] The following sections reveal the influence of CSJ in several topic domains.

Biology and sex

The APA's bias regarding the treatment of men and women's issues is most clear in the *Guidelines for Psychological Practice with Girls and Women* compared to the equivalent ones for boys and men.[12] In the former, girls/women suffer for reasons such as structural oppression, sexism, and power differentials. In the latter, boys/men experience mental health crises because of "toxic masculinity" or the particularly perplexing term, 'masculinity ideology'. Widespread public and academic criticism of the guidelines for practice with boys and men was met with dismissal.[13]

Within these guidelines, psychologists are encouraged to educate on and challenge male privilege, reflect on their own critical consciousness, only assign diagnoses to girls/women when absolutely necessary and only in an unbiased manner, and ensure girls/women have access to "folk, indigenous, and complementary or alternative forms of healing".[14]

Unsurprisingly, there was no mention of the biological bases of behavior within these guidelines' commentaries. Further, on the APA's website, under the topic heading of "women and men"—ironically hosted by the *Women's* Program Office (italics added for emphasis)—the organization concludes:

> Women and men aren't as different as you might think: A review of dozens of studies found that men and women are basically alike when it comes to personality, thinking ability and leadership. The differences that do exist may reflect social expectations, not biology. Despite this evidence, the media continue to spread the idea that the sexes are fundamentally different — with real-life consequences.[15]

But this statement does not contradict media messaging. Rather, it contradicts a lengthy and comprehensive history of rigorous research on biological sex differences across cultures, ages, and species—*even* one of APA's advertised books on the evolutionary biology of sex differences![16]

It is unclear to what extent the absence of biology on sex differences has on clinical practice, yet psychologists who uphold a biological view of sex can face considerable consequences. For

example, one scholar was removed from the listserv belonging to
the Society for Behavioral Neuroscience and Comparative Psychology (Division 6 of the APA) for casually suggesting the sex binary
exists.[17] This certainly begs the question—what would happen to
those who might try to report biologically based sex differences
in their research?

Ethnicity/Race

Consistent with the APA's commitment to social justice activism,
the organization attributes group disparities to systemic injus-
tice/racism. As such, it views part of its mission to seek legislative
change and to ally with political and contentious organizations
(e.g., BLM).[18] The use of Critical Race Theory (CRT) and "decolo-
nialization" can be identified in the:

1. adoption of terms such as systemic oppression and inequity
2. symbolic racism, microaggressions, and related constructs
3. research on implicit bias and the Implicit Association Test
   (IAT)[19]
4. white privilege, fragility, and guilt
5. even potentially the racial identity development models.
   These models explain the racial attitude changes supposedly experienced over time by members of different racial
   groups (e.g., white, black) when exposed to racially different people. The models instruct on the appropriate final
   attitude stage one should achieve, which is also different
   based on the racial group. Efforts to "de-colonize" psychology (i.e., "deconstruct" Western *white* psychological science) is also an increasingly popular topic for professional
   webinars and trainings, as well as seminars on addressing
   specifically *white* racism in psychotherapy.[20]

The APA's *Race and Ethnicity Guidelines in Psychology* advise psychologists to simultaneously avoid racial and ethnocultural bias,

assess their own "positionality", and prioritize ethnic and racial minorities in their professional work.

In the *Multicultural Guidelines: An Ecological Approach to Context, Identity, and Intersectionality*, the APA explicitly promotes Robin DiAngelo's book, *White Fragility*, one of the most central works of CRT.[21] A blog site frequently used by psychology graduate trainees published an article encouraging readers to "stop hesitating" and begin speaking to their black clients about race, which assumes that race is a central concern to everyone in this demographic. The author also promoted the heavily discredited Implicit Association Test (IAT), popularly used to identify people's racism.[22]

The National Register of Health Service Psychology promoted an article about how to "Africanize" the discipline of scientific psychology by identifying "alternative ways of knowing" apart from the scientific method.[23]

Further, the very progressive Society for the Psychological Study of Social Issues hosted a webinar on "The White Supremacist State through the Racial Triangulation of Black, Asian, and White Communities". The webinar description explained that "invisible structures and manifestations of the White Supremacist state in America" is the root cause of "deep divisions among BIPOC communities".[24]

Authoritarianism

One frequent manifestation of ideological bias in social and political psychology is the "explaining" of the out-group (i.e., those belonging to a different group), which, in left-leaning psychology, means explaining how conservatives (or Republicans) deviate from the ("liberal") norm. CSJ entails presenting the political opposition as oppressive. Thus, conservatives, or non-progressives, are easily labeled "Nazis" or "Fascists". This pattern is reflected in research on "authoritarianism", which has historically been viewed as something that characterizes conservatives—not liberals (i.e., *right*-wing authoritarianism"). Conservatives were described as possessing bigotry, valuing conformity and the status quo, and creating echo chambers of misinformation, unlike enlightened "liberals".[25]

However, flaws in decades of research have been exposed. Notable bias in the most commonly used measure of authoritarianism was found in the way that it framed questions to focus on right-of-center values. When the questions were modified to include issues salient to "liberals" using parallel phrasing, then authoritarianism, dogmatism, and prejudice were all found to be equally present among "liberals".[26] This was ultimately named the "ideological conflict hypothesis" (ICH).[27] Yet another study identified a non-partisan authoritarian personality profile, as well as authoritarian traits unique to both right-wing and left-wing political groups.[28]

Objective truth? Causes and consequences of psychology's political bias

Evidence-based treatments

Professional psychology in the US is in the curious situation of having a contradictory relationship to objective truth. On the one hand, clinical psychology, for instance, places immense value on "evidence-based treatments", or therapeutic treatments found effective through scientifically rigorous randomized clinical trials (or RCTs)—the gold standard for clinical practice. One such treatment is Cognitive-Behavioral Theory (CBT). It presumes an objective reality exists and can be collaboratively identified through Socratic dialogue and therapeutic and experimental efforts (e.g., via reality testing).[29]

Through this process, a client gains a more realistic understanding of the causes of personal distress, resulting in emotional relief. On the other hand, proponents of CSJ have criticized CBT on the grounds that it is not generalizable across multicultural groups, partly because it implies the existence of an objective reality or truth—an allegedly Western value. In fact, the author of one article went so far as to critique efforts to establish evidence-based interventions, such as CBT, as demonstrating Western fear of globalization and anti-immigration sentiments.[30]

Instead, critics recommend "alternative ways of knowing", notions of "lived experience", and popular constructs such as microaggressions presume that reality is subjective—or in the "eye of the beholder". They also accuse CBT of victim-blaming by promoting improved wellbeing via individual effort and change (e.g., through "behavioral activation" or increasing activity levels, "cognitive restructuring" or re-framing one's initial negative thoughts into more realistic and helpful ones). This re-framing tool is contradicted by the concept of microaggressions (e.g., "this person is racist for asking me where I am from" despite other plausible explanations). The actual intention of an ambiguous comment does not matter relative to how the comment is received.[31]

In other words, constructs and approaches such as these promote reliance on subjective perception, often fraught with bias and distortions, rather than broader or more realistic perspective-taking, a valuable therapeutic goal.

Postmodernism and language

Postmodern influence, especially through the use of language, as described by Tarescavage, is present in the APA's Multicultural Guidelines and likely among many other guidelines proposals as well. He identified it by terms such as "intersectionality", "privilege", and "oppression" across multiple practice recommendations for clinicians.[32]

Yet, there is little to no empirical support for these terms, suggesting that they are promoted based on ideology rather than scientific rigor and support. What does the absence of empirical support mean? There is no way to "falsify" such theories. A falsifiable theory can be tested and found to be valid (true) or not. A frequently used example would be how *questioning* the notion of "white privilege", regardless of the legitimacy of concerns, is simply *evidence* of "white fragility". There is simply no way out of the white privilege discussion—or to fully exempt oneself from the accusation of racism if one is seen as "white"—a true Kafka trap!

The postmodern constructivist influence is also easily identified in more recent language changes that seem manipulative and leveraged toward political purposes. Haslam calls this shift in language "concept creep". It reflects a broadening of definitions and the inclusion of new and more benign terms.[33] Now, "trauma" and "violence" can, for instance, allegedly result from simply sharing non-progressive ideas in public spaces.[34] While some salient words are trivialized (e.g., trauma), other benign words are exaggerated (e.g., microaggressions, micro assaults), both of which ultimately exacerbates the perception of an offense.

Akresh noted a similar pattern regarding the changing definition of racism (as power + privilege, *not* merely racial superiority/animosity). This allows for condemnation of people who possess mainstream conservative, libertarian, or classically liberal values (e.g., opposition to affirmative action, support of color-blindness, and meritocracy).[35] These values can be attributed to the notion of "symbolic racism" when evidence of explicit racism and discrimination is absent.

Science vs. activism

Moreover, the profession's tenuous relationship with objective truth has resulted in encouraging competing scientist and activist roles both individually and at organizational levels. This has not been limited to psychology. Various STEM-affiliated societies and even the National Institutes of Health (NIH) have spoken out on political and activist topics.[36] The APA is actively involved in advocacy efforts and makes frequent press releases on partisan policy topics.[37] Emails from the organization during 2020 and 2021 have included notices about the promotion of psychological research to mitigate the spread of COVID-19 "misinformation", advocating for the contentious Equality Act, support for firearm reforms, and $500 million worth in congressional funding requests for healthcare *equity* research.[38]

In a recent advocacy update email, the APA notified its members that the organization is praising the presidential administration for its involvement in international climate policy engagement.[39] In another, the APA's Advocacy Office partnered with the Society for Pediatric Psychology's Anti-Racism Task Force to further the use of Critical Social Justice-based Diversity, Equity, and Inclusion (DEI) efforts at federal, state, local, and institutional levels, including in the APA Division's structure and practice.[40]

Despite an array of topics promoted, the unifying theme of those that are sociocultural or political in nature is that they consistently coincided with progressive or left-wing agenda items and reflect a CSJ undercurrent. This is not to say that "misinformation" has not been a legitimate concern regarding COVID-19, but rather promoted content about the coronavirus predictably featured only left-of-center concerns when others also existed (e.g., infringement of personal rights and religious protections, mental health consequences secondary to very restrictive governmental policies, socioeconomic impact on livelihoods, the effect of school closures on nutritional and physical health needs, educational attainment, social/emotional development, child abuse, and neglect rates, etc.). These patterns inevitably undermine the other reasonable and occasional calls for mutual understanding and depolarization that the APA has made.[41]

What are the ramifications for psychotherapy (services)?

We are only just beginning to grasp the impact that political bias has on clinical services such as psychotherapy. Without setting a new course, time will continue to reveal ideology triumphing over scientific integrity to the detriment of quality services. We will share our primary concerns here.

First, with over 74 million votes cast for Donald Trump in the 2020 presidential election, a substantial number of Americans have shown that they do not possess the leftist or progressive ideals that have pervaded psychology. As such, American professional psychology's reputation suffers, and many potential mental health clients are evaluating their therapists based on their perceived politics. Many conservative clients are often concerned that their therapists might mistreat them based on their political values and therefore seek conservative therapists or opt out of needed treatment altogether.[42] To meet this need, some mental health professionals are launching new websites to market conservative-friendly mental health services—potentially furthering polarization professionally.[43]

Second, when professional psychology lacks ideological diversity and is driven by ideology instead of scientific integrity, good clinical services will be compromised. Interventions guided by ideology could result in a ripple effect of problems. For example, the APA's formalizing of "toxic masculinity" and attributing societal problems to men/masculinity was perceived to potentially worsen men's regard for mental health services.[44]

Furthermore, prioritizing ideology could promote negative psychological coping, for instance, through promoting external (vs. internal) locus of control (i.e., encouraging externalization of responsibility) as we have seen coincide with the victimhood mentality. It could also entail affirmation of unhelpful but politically correct and popular axioms (e.g., loving oneself to the negation of self-improvement and health, prioritizing self-expression and advancement over important familial/social responsibilities).

Third, therapists consciously or unconsciously beholden to CSJ are at risk of conceptualizing their patients' problems consistent with its framework. These ideological influences may cause therapists to feel justified in using certain stereotypes. Diminished humility, sensitivity, and authentic understanding of one's ideological counterparts can cause poorer clinical judgment in therapy. For example, a lens that employs an "oppressed vs. oppressor" narrative can easily cause a therapist to classify clients according to this binary. Since an "oppressor" status is so easily associated with non-progressive ideological values, a large lay population could be viewed as racist, sexist, bigoted, or otherwise characterized by internalized prejudice of some form. For those clients who would be assigned the "oppressed" class, therapists would view them as lacking self-efficacy or self-agency and being dependent upon the "privileged" for socioeconomic elevation.

In this vein of reasoning, the clients most easily attributable to the "oppressor" class are also the most likely to find themselves at risk of a rupture in the therapeutic relationship. If at least one-third of psychologists are very or moderately willing to discriminate against conservative colleagues, how willing would (leftist) mental health professionals, broadly speaking, be to protect their clients from their own ideological values and beliefs?[45]

Recent and pertinent research by Redding uncovered that 23% of therapists identified politics as the most likely factor that could bias their attitude towards their clients, 40% suspected they may impose their values on their clients, and, unsurprisingly, an ideological mismatch between therapists and client presented a risk to the therapeutic relationship.[46]

Unfortunately, many psychologists likely do not realize the extent to which political ideology informs their viewpoints and attitudes, particularly towards those across the political aisle and including in the provision of their professional services, nor the extent to which professional organizations like the APA promote the inculcation of political ideologies.

Conclusion

CSJ, and with it, an inconsistent regard for objective truth, is undermining the important and otherwise scientifically based professional discipline of psychology. Issues of race/ethnicity, sex/gender, and treatment of political outgroups are just several topics that reveal strong and damaging ideologies, and professional activities within research and applied psychology are profoundly affected.

At this point, many questions remain regarding the prospects for good psychotherapeutic services amid this rampant ideological bias. Will research psychologists ultimately recommit to rigorous scientific inquiry? To what extent do psychologists treat their clients according to CSJ tenets? Can prospective clients be well served by mental health professionals seeking to further a political agenda in the therapeutic milieu? Will greater partisanship, through conservative subculture movements in psychology and counseling, encourage these professionals to cater to their own "political communities"? To what extent will prejudice continue to foment toward their ideological foes?

Psychology and counseling organizations must consider what ideological and political bias will mean for the future of these professions and whether the bias will contribute to greater political polarization paralleling the broader culture.

We encourage these organizations to reassess political activism efforts and agendas relative to the ethics codes that promote universal principles, many of which are primarily aimed to protect the general public. We hope that efforts to expose the problem of political and ideological bias will encourage professional psychology and counseling organizations, like the APA, to embrace methods that will reduce bias, preserve and uphold scientific integrity, and embrace the pursuit of objective truth and the regard for shared humanity amongst consumers of mental health services.

Endnotes

1   Dennis R. Fox, "Social science's limited role in resolving psycholegal social problems," *Journal of Offender Rehabilitation, 17*, no. 2 (October 1991): 159-166. https://doi.org/10.1300/J076v17n01_12.

2   Jose L. Duarte, Jarrett T. Crawford, Charlotta Stern, Jonathan Haidt, Lee Jussim, and Philip E. Tetlock, "Political Diversity Will Improve Social Psychological Science." *Behavioral and Brain Sciences, 38* (2015): E130. https://doi.org/10.1017/S0140525X14000430; Yoel Inbar & Joris Lammers, "Political Diversity in Social and Personality Psychology." *Perspectives on Psychological Science, 7*, no. 5 (September 2021): 496-503. https://doi.org/10.1177/1745691612448792; Matthew Woessner, Lee Jussim, & Jarrett Crawford, "Academe is overrun by liberals. Here's why that should disturb you." *Heterodox: The Blog,* May 2016, https://heterodoxacademy.org/blog/academe-is-overrun-by-liberals-heres-why-that-should-disturb-you/ ; Philip E. Tetlock, "Political Psychology or Politicized Psychology: Is the Road to Scientific Hell Paved with Good Moral Intentions?" *Political Psychology, 15*, no. 3 (1994): 509-529. https://doi.org/10.2307/3791569.

3   Orly Eitan, Viganola Domenico, Yoel Inbar, Anna Dreber, Magnus Johannesson, Thomas Pfeiffer, Stegan Thau, and Eric L. Ulhmann. "Is Research in Social Psychology Politically Biased? Systematic Empirical Tests and a Forecasting Survey to Address the Controversy", *Journal of Experimental Social Psychology, 79* (November 2018): 188-199. https://doi.org/10.1016/j.jesp.2018.06.004.

4   Intersectionality is defined as "a provisional concept linking contemporary politics to postmodern theory" - Crenshaw, 1991, "Mapping the Margins...." Footnote 9, 1224.

5   Gallup Poll, "Party Affiliation," accessed September 12, 2021: https://news.gallup.com/poll/15370/party-affiliation.aspx.

6   Duarte et al., "Political Diversity".

7   David M. Buss and William Von Hippel, "Psychological barriers to evolutionary psychology: Ideological bias and coalition adaptations", *Archives of Scientific Psychology, 6*, no. 1 (2018): 148–158. http://doi.org/10.1037/arc0000049.

8   Heterodox Psychology Facebook page, accessed October 12, 2021: https://www.facebook.com/groups/hxpsychology/about.

9   Heidi M. Levitt, *Essentials of Critical-Constructivist Grounded Theory Research* (American Psychological Association, 2021). https://www.apa.org/pubs/books/essentials-critical-constructivist-grounded-theory-research-sample-chapter.pdf.

[10] Lillian Comas-Díaz & Edil Torres Rivera. *Liberation Psychology: Theory, Method, Practice, and Social Justice* (American Psychological Association, 2020). https://doi.org/10.1037/0000198-000.

[11] Nicole T. Buchanan & Lauren O. Wiklund, "Intersectionality research in psychological science: Resisting the tendency to disconnect, dilute, and depoliticize." *Research on Child and Adolescent Psychopathology, 49* (2021): 25-31. https://doi.org/10.1007/s10802-020-00748-y.

[12] American Psychological Association, Boys and Men Guidelines Group, "APA guidelines for psychological practice with boys and men." *American Psychological Association.* (August 2018) https://www.apa.org/about/policy/boys-men-practice-guidelines.pdf; American Psychological Association, Girls and Women Guidelines Group. "APA guidelines for psychological practice with girls and women." *American Psychological Association.* (December 2018) https://www.apa.org/about/policy/psychological-practice-girls-women.pdf.

[13] "APA guidelines on boys and men launch important—and fiery—national conversation." *Monitor on Psychology, 50*, no. 2 (February 2019): https://www.apa.org/monitor/2019/02/male-guidelines.

One of the APA (2018) Guidelines' authors presented a number of helpful ways for psychologists to engage men in therapy and even expressed the importance of tolerating political differences with clients. Nonetheless, when asked about critical responses to the Guidelines, he commented that the critics "have nothing better to do". Frederic E. Rabinowitz. "Engaging men in therapy" video webinar hosted by National Register of Health Service Psychology, 2019, https://ce.nationalregister.org/videos/engaging-men-in-psychotherapy-archived/.

[14] American Psychological Association (APA), Girls and Women Guidelines Group, "APA guidelines for psychological practice with girls and women", p. 17.

[15] "Women & men", American Psychological Association. https://www.apa.org/topics/women-girls.

[16] David P. Schmitt, Audrey E. Long, Allante McPhearson, Kirby O'Brien, Brooke Remmert, and Seema H. Shah, "Personality and gender differences in global perspective." *International Journal of Psychology, 52*, no. S1 (2017): 45-56. http://doi.org/10.1002/ijop.12265; Elizabeth V. Lonsdorf, "Sex differences in nonhuman primate behavioral development." *Journal of Neuroscience Research, 95* (2017). 213-221. http://doi.org/10.1002/jnr.23862; W. H. Overman, J. Bachevalier, E. Schuhmann, and P. Ryan, "Cognitive gender differences in very young children parallel

biologically based cognitive gender differences in monkeys." *Behavioral Neuroscience, 110*, no. 4 (1996): 673-684. http://doi.org/10.1037//0735-7044.110.4.673.

[17] Tyler Hummel, "Scholar booted from APA discussion group after suggesting there are only two sexes", *The College Fix*, May 14, 2021, https://www.thecollegefix.com/scholar-booted-from-apa-discussion-group-after-suggesting-there-are-only-two-sexes/.

[18] Zara Adams, "The association is working to dismantle institutional racism over the long term, including within APA and psychology", *Monitor on Psychology, 51*, no. 6 (September 1, 2020): https://www.apa.org/monitor/2020/09/systemic-change; Candice Hargons, Della Mosley, Jameca Falconer, Reuben Faloughi, Anneliese Singh, Danelle Stevens-Watkins, and Kevin Cokley, "Black lives matter: A call to action for counseling psychology leaders", *The Counseling Psychologist, 45*, no. 6 (2017): http://doi.org/10.1177/0011000017733048.

[19] John Nwosu, "Implicit racial bias in counselors-in-training", *Think D.I.F.-Equity in Counseling*, (2018): https://doi.org/10.13140/RG.2.2.26335.69282; Amy K. Maslowski, "Infusing multiculturalism, identity, and social justice in asynchronous courses," *Society for the Teaching of Psychology, 49*, no. 1 (2022): https://doi.org/10.1177/009862832096477.

[20] David Drustrup, "Addressing white racism as a part of psychotherapy process" video webinar hosted by National Register of Health Service Psychology, 2020 https://ce.nationalregister.org/videos/addressing-white-racism-as-part-of-the-psychotherapy-process-archived/; "The decolonizing psychology virtual conference, by Teachers College, Columbia University" *Division of School Psychology.* (March 12, 2021), https://apadivision16.org/2021/03/the-decolonizing-psychology-virtual-conference-by-teachers-college-columbia-university/; Glenn Adams, Ignacio Dobles, Luis H. Gómez, Tuğçe Kurtiş, & Ludwin E. Molina. "Decolonizing psychological science: Introduction to the special thematic section." *Journal of Social and Political Psychology, 3*, no. 1. (2015): https://doi.org/10.5964/jspp.v3i1.564.

[21] "APA's race and ethnicity guidelines", American Psychology Association, https://www.apa.org/about/policy/summary-guidelines-race-ethnicity; Task Force on Re-Envisioning the Multicultural Guidelines for the 21st Century. "Multicultural guidelines: An ecological approach to context, identity, and intersectionality." American Psychological Association (2017): http://www.apa.org/about/policy/multicultural-guidelines.pdf; Zara Adams. "APA calls for true systemic change in the U.S. culture." *Monitor on Psychology, 51*, no. 6 (September 1, 2020): https://www.apa.org/monitor/2020/09/systemic-change.

[22] Elizabeth McCorvey, "Stop hesitating and start talking to your black clients about race", *Time2Track Blog*, June 10, 2020, https://blog.time-2track.com/stop-hesitating-and-start-talking-to-your-black-clients-about-race/.

[23] Puleng Segalo and Julia Simango, "Psychology carries a dark past: How the discipline can be Africanized", *The Conversation*, February 17, 2021, https://theconversation.com/psychology-carries-a-dark-past-how-the-discipline-can-be-africanised-155165.

[24] Society for the Psychological Study of Social Issues (SPSSI). YouTube channel - https://www.youtube.com/spssi.

[25] See: John T. Jost, Jack Glaser, Arie W. Kruglanski, and Frank J. Sulloway. "Political conservativism as motivated social cognition", *Psychology Bulletin, 129*, no. 3 (May 2003): 339-375, http://doi.org/10.1037/0033-2909.129.3.339; John T. Jost, Sander van der Linden, Costas Panagopoulos, & Curtis D. Harding. "Ideological asymmetries in conformity, desire for shared reality, and the spread of misinformation", *Current Opinion in Psychology, 23* (2018): 77-83, https://doi.org/10.1016/j.copsyc.2018.01.003.

[26] Lucian G. Conway, Shannon C. Houck, Laura J. Gornick, and Meredith A. Repke, "Finding the Loch Ness monster: Left-wing authoritarianism in the United States", *Political Psychology, 39*, no. 5 (2018): 1049-1067, https://doi.org/10.1111/pops.12470.

[27] Mark J. Brandt, Christine Reyna, John R. Chambers, Jarrett. R. Crawford, and Geoffrey Wetherell, "The ideological-conflict-hypothesis: Intolerance among both liberals and conservatives", *Current Directions in Psychological Science, 23* (2014). 27-34. https://doi.org/10.1177/0963721413510932.

[28] Thomas H. Costello, Shauna M. Bowes, Sean T. Stevens, Irwin D. Waldran, Arber Tasimi, and Scott O. Lilienfeld, "Clarifying the structure and nature of left-wing authoritarianism", *Journal of Personality and Social Psychology.* https://doi.org/10.1037/pspp0000341.

[29] Steve Dreesman, "The contradictions of critical theory and counseling" *Critical Therapy Antidote,* June 7, 2020, https://criticaltherapyantidote.org/2020/08/14/the-contradictions-of-critical-theory-and-counseling/. Joshua Miles, "What is reality testing and why is it important?" *Counseling Directory*, October 27, 2015, https://www.counselling-directory.org.uk/memberarticles/what-is-reality-testing-why-is-it-important; Sarah R Davies, Deborah M Caldwell, Jose A Lopez-Lopez, Sarah Dawson, Nicola Wiles, David Kessler, Nicky J Welton, and Rachel Churchill, "The process

and delivery of cognitive behavioural therapy (CBT) for depression in adults: a network meta-analysis" *Cochrane System Database Review,* (2018). https://doi.org/10.1002/14651858.CD013140.

30 Lauren Rogers-Sirin, "Psychotherapy from the margins: How the pressure to adopt evidence-based-treatments conflicts with social justice-oriented practice", *Journal for Social Action in Counseling and Psychology, 9,* no. 1 (Summer 2017): 55-78, https://openjournals.bsu.edu/jsacp/article/view/73/55.

31 Scott O. Lilienfeld, "Microaggressions: Strong claims, inadequate evidence", *Perspectives on Psychological Science, 12,* no. 1 (2017): 138-169, https://doi.org/10.1177/1745691616659391.

32 Anthony M. Tarescavage, "Science Wars II: The insidious influence of postmodern ideology on clinical psychology (commentary on "Implications of ideological bias in social psychology on clinical practice")", *Clinical Psychology: Science and Practice, 27,* no. 2 (June 2020): e12319, https://doi.org/10.1111/cpsp.12319.

33 Nick Haslam, "Concept creep: Psychology's expanding concepts of harm and pathology", *Psychological Inquiry, 27,* no. 1 (2016). 1–17. https://doi.org/10.1080/1047840X.2016.1082418.

34 While the DSM-IV to DSM-5 changes for Post-Traumatic Stress Disorder involved restricting the trauma exposure criteria to "actual or threatened death, serious injury, or sexual violence", many psychologists believe that mere exposure to microaggressions or racist slights is sufficient.

35 Ilana Restone Akresh, "The dangers of defining deviancy up", *Quillette,* January 24, 2019, https://quillette.com/2019/01/24/the-dangers-of-defining-deviancy-up/.

36 See: Lawrence M. Krauss, "Science goes rogue," *Quillette,* March 14, 2021, https://quillette.com/2021/03/14/science-goes-rogue/?fbclid=IwAR2_3Bk4QXWOyqUPC-IUVqY9vo27RHb6JQnxdGh0Y0vpP2F6iMx-4r0eFVIE; The NIH Director, "NIH stands against structural racism in biomedical research," National Institutes of Health, March 1, 2021, https://www.nih.gov/about-nih/who-we-are/nih-director/statements/nih-stands-against-structural-racism-biomedical-research.

37 Nina C. Silander and Anthony M. Tarescavage, "Ideological bias in American Psychological Association communications: Another threat to the credibility of professional psychology", in *Political Bias in Psychology: Nature, Scope, and Solutions,* eds. Craig L. Frisby, Richard E. Redding, William T. O'Donohue, & Scott O. Lilienfeld (in press: Springer).

[38] "Advocating for the Equality Act in the Senate", American Psychological Association, April 1, 2021, https://www.apaservices.org/advocacy/news/equality-act-senate;

"APA calls for reforms to nation's gun laws", American Psychological Association, April 1, 2021, https://www.apaservices.org/advocacy/news/reforms-gun-laws; "Supporting investments in health systems and health equity research at the Agency for Healthcare Research and Quality", American Psychological Association, March 10, 2021, https://www.apaservices.org/advocacy/news/health-systems-equity-research.

[39] "Applauding global engagement in letters to Biden administration", American Psychological Association, May 25, 2021, https://www.apaservices.org/advocacy/news/global-engagement-biden-administration.

[40] "Pediatric psychologists' anti-racism task force trained on federal, state advocacy strategies, and tactic", American Psychological Association, May 26, 2021, https://www.apaservices.org/advocacy/news/pediatric-psychologists-anti-racism.

[41] Kirk Waldroff, "Healing the political divide", *Monitor on Psychology, 52*, no. 1 (January 1, 2021), https://www.apa.org/monitor/2021/01/healing-political-divide; Interview with Cory Clark, "Psychological research provides insight into US political divisions", American Psychological Association, February 1, 2021, https://www.apa.org/research/action/us-political-divisions.

[42] Robert M. Mather, "Conservative psychologist wanted", Psychology Today, July 16, 2020, https://www.psychologytoday.com/us/blog/the-conservative-social-psychologist/202007/conservative-psychologist-wanted.

[43] In the US, there is a growing partisan therapist movement (i.e., "conservative therapists"). There are "conservative mental health therapist" groups on social media sites like Facebook and MeWe, and Dr. Stephanie Knarr, a conservative clinical psychologist, blogger, and radio show host. Her website houses a clearinghouse for conservative therapists who cater to those seeking explicitly conservative therapists. Similarly, Robert Mather, co-author of this chapter, maintains a blog, "The Conservative Social Psychologist", at Psychology Today.

[44] Quillette, "Twelve scholars respond to the APA's guidance for treating men and boys", February 4, 2019, https://quillette.com/2019/02/04/psychologists-respond-to-the-apas-guidance-for-treating-men-and-boys/.

[45] Inbar and Lammers, "Political diversity".

46 Richard E. Redding (2020), "Sociopolitical values: The neglected factor in culturally-competent psychotherapy", in *Prejudice, Stigma, Privilege, and Oppression,* eds. Lorraine T. Benuto, Melanie P. Duckworth, Akihito Masuda, & William O'Donohue (Springer, 2020), pp. 427-445.

Chapter 20:

The Miseducation of Psychotherapists

by Christine Sefein

Introduction

In 2021, after many months of sleepless nights, I reluctantly came to the conclusion that I had to resign from my post as a professor of counseling and psychotherapy.

A decade after graduating, I returned full of enthusiasm to commence teaching at the West Coast university in the US where I had originally trained. I knew the program well and felt aligned with its mission—to train psychotherapists to treat every client with kindness, empathy, and dignity without judgment.

However, over the course of my teaching career, Critical Social Justice (CSJ) theories gained currency and radically changed both the curriculum and delivery of the teaching program. It became clear to me that the worldview which informed such theories was incompatible with producing sensitive, empathic therapists able to create and maintain authentic therapeutic relationships— viewed as the most significant factor in successful therapy.[1] Furthermore, I could no longer allow myself to be part of an unethical enterprise.

My aim in this chapter is to reflect on the impact of CSJ, in particular, Critical Race Theory (CRT), on counseling and psychotherapy training programs using my own experiences as illustrations. The anecdotal flavor of this chapter is inevitable due to the scarcity of other insider accounts—unfortunately, the professional consequences of speaking out against the prevailing orthodoxy have inhibited any public discussion.[2] However, wherever possible, I will be making some general observations about the wider training field which can be supported by the literature.

The chapter will open with some relevant background both about myself and also what traditional therapy training looked like. It will then go on to identify the main ways in which CSJ gained access to the training program at my university and, by extension, to training elsewhere. I will then draw on my own experiences as an educator to demonstrate how this political ideology played out in the classroom.

My background

I am a first-generation American, born of parents who immigrated to the United States from Egypt in 1978. In Egypt, my parents were financially fairly well-off. My father worked as an executive in an engineering firm while my mother worked part-time as an engineer. They could afford extras like nannies and housekeepers to take care of household chores. Despite the comforts and luxuries they enjoyed, the political landscape was becoming increasingly hostile and unpredictable. There were fewer work opportunities, as the economy took a downturn, and there was increasing tension between Christians and a small group of radical Muslims resulting in higher rates of crime and a lack of sufficient law enforcement protection.

So, eventually, my parents legally entered the US in 1978, seeking political and religious asylum. America represented a beacon of hope. It was a country that would allow them to freely practice their religion and provide opportunities for financial success for them and their children.

My parents knew they would suffer difficulties, but they were optimistic that they could not only survive, but *thrive* if they worked hard enough. In between taking classes to learn English, raising two children, and pursuing the path to citizenship, they both went to school, at night, to earn college degrees from American universities. They hardly complained. The freedom, hope, safety, and opportunities for their daughters to have a better life far outweighed the cons. Because of that, we were encouraged to embrace America.

My sister and I eventually earned graduate degrees because we valued education and pursuing goals. In my early twenties, I decided to become a therapist. I wanted to empower others to discover their own strength and set goals for themselves. My parents had set this example for me, and becoming a therapist was my way of paying it forward as well as paying tribute to their legacy of hope and inspiration. I wanted my future clients to grow and learn to believe in themselves and internalise what my parents reminded me of daily: "Don't feel sorry for yourself; lift yourself up." This was always presented in a compassionate and gentle approach.

Training to become a licensed therapist was challenging. The coursework covered complex theories and conceptualizations of the human mind and psychological development. With each step I took toward the path of licensure, what got me through was remembering my mother's words: "It doesn't matter how long it takes. Take it one step at a time." After she died—while I was in graduate school—that would become my mantra as I moved forward through the internship phase, which was significantly more difficult.

Through my own trials and tribulations personally and professionally, I was finally able to get my footing and managed to become licensed. The day I passed my second and final exam, I burst into tears—how I wished that my deceased mother was

there to see what I had accomplished even as her words reso-
nated with me the whole time.

My training

Before I discuss the impact of CSJ on the training program, it is
important to describe its original form—the traditional training in which I and countless thousands at similar institutions
participated.

In professional therapy training, there are, as would be
expected, two main components comprising theoretical knowledge and practical skills. The focus of the program in the early
2000s was purely on helping the students to become therapists.
We learned models of treatment and theories dating back to
Freud. We studied human development from childhood through
the lifespan based on actual peer-reviewed research and studies.
In regular practical sessions, we were able to grasp how to trans-
late all these theories into practice. We learned to hold the balance between staying curious and wondering, without assumption, and the ability to gently challenge our clients when needed.

Most importantly of all, our practice sessions helped to
ground us in one of the fundamental principles of psychotherapy:
the client is the expert on their life—the therapist is merely the
guide rail that supports their growth.

However, there is more to working as a therapist than knowledge of theories and competence in skills. I remember one of my
professors commenting that only 60% of those who study clinical
psychology intending to become licensed psychotherapists will
actually reach that goal. He continued: "The reason for this attri-
tion rate is because the art of psychotherapy is not in memorizing
theory or interventions; it's in learning how to 'be' with your clients during the most painful, agonizing moments in their lives."

It took me two years into my internship to grasp his meaning.
It meant not having a solution for your client when you desperately

wanted to fix it for them. It meant reserving judgment when you didn't agree with a harmful decision they made. It meant supporting them through their process of self-discovery, even when you could see patterns of behaviour and decision-making that did not appear to serve them. It meant never acting as the authority figure or "expert" in their lives. It meant walking with them hand in hand through their journey, while gently guiding or challenging them to look deeper within. Ultimately, it meant trusting the process even when you didn't see "improvement". *Practising psychotherapy is an art, and this art requires deep self-awareness both in our own actions and when considering the state of others.*

Up until fairly recently, traditional therapy training has always placed a lot of emphasis on developing the required level of self-awareness. This training would endeavour to create an environment that provides the right balance of safety and challenge to support the trainee's self-development process. My original therapy training program was an exemplar of this tradition. The classroom modelled the anchor and foundation upon which effective treatment lies by creating a space of safety, respect, and positive regard. Mistakes were never pathologized. The students were provided space to be "wrong" and yet, still, they were met with respect and grace rather than punitive judgement or shame. We struggled with not having definitive answers or reaching a concrete destination in the therapy process. However, in the struggle, we learned that therapy is messy and rarely has concrete, measurable outcomes or clear margins.

We were encouraged to reflect on our need to "fix" and how that informed our practice of the art of therapy. Direct feedback from professors and other students was welcomed, even though, sometimes, it was an uncomfortable experience. If any discomfort arose for us, we had the opportunity to explore and identify its origins. Through roleplay, observers critiqued each other's body language, tone, and other nuanced behavior that had the potential to affect how a client experiences them. Even the act of giving and receiving feedback, no matter the reason, was a teachable moment on how to deliver feedback to clients.

This traditional training highlighted that the measure of a good therapist is directly linked to the capacity for self-reflection, empathy, and compassion more than the execution of interventions learned from a book. Furthermore, it was believed that these particular capacities correlate with the therapist's ability to hold space for their clients' reflection, sorrow, and pain.

Every aspect of the delivery of the program took into account the importance of nurturing the right conditions for students to engage in developing their own self-awareness. In addition, the students were required to participate in supervision groups and peer consultation groups, which created further opportunities to identify "blind spots" that might stall the growth process.

When I now reflect on my experience in this traditional therapy training program, I am aware of the determined efforts of all of the faculty to provide an environment where I was able to express myself authentically and engage with the complex, challenging process of self-development.

The issue of identity

When ruminating on traditional therapy teachings, it is worth noting, therefore, how teaching informed by CSJ will hold radically different perspectives on the nature of identity. This is important to understand because views on identity formation will have a very significant bearing on both the "what", as well as, the "how", the program is taught.

In CSJ-informed training, identity is highly politicized; the person is not viewed as an individual but rather as a member of an oppressed or oppressor group. As we will see later on in this chapter, this position leads to an unconducive environment for personal growth.

330

Identity is an essential element in traditional training; it is informed by classical therapy theories which assert that complexities of identity can never be reduced to one factor such as gender or race.[3] Further, identity and maturation are formed from many factors unique to the individual. This can be from their formative experiences as a child, the community in which they live, the meaning they attribute to their life experience, and messages absorbed from peers, colleagues, and family. And lastly, one must not forget that identity changes as the person grows and develops.

How CSJ became established in the therapy training program

In a very short period throughout my time teaching at the university, I had the deeply unsettling experience of observing a traditional therapy training program mutate into a different kind of therapy training entirely. Almost overnight, a training that delivered the knowledge, skills, and self-awareness required by a proficient therapist pivoted into a training designed to produce social justice activists. I found myself teaching on a program that facilitated bullying and censorship and promoted a narrow, fundamentalist view of what is to be a human being. Instead of teaching students to be a healing presence, we were training them to deliver moral re-education to vulnerable clients.

However, before I detail the consequences of the CSJ capture of my therapy training program, it is important to set this in a wider context. CSJ did not arrive out of the blue; there were both external and internal factors that are implicated in its encroachments which I indicate below. Other writers in this anthology have discussed how CSJ scholar–activists have infiltrated the professional bodies and institutions of therapy—we are now seeing how therapy is being harnessed to new political–ideological ends.[4] These moves have inevitably influenced the curriculum.

However, the particular university context of the training has also contributed to the radical changes in both the delivery and ethos of the training program. In particular, generic diversity, equity, and inclusion policies—adopted by nearly all higher education providers—impose a new moral directive that places constraints on the traditional professional therapy training practice.

In the case of the university where I worked, the mission statement includes a commitment to empowering students in "challenging the status quo and advancing social, environmental, and economic justice".[5] Consequently, the institution encourages trainee therapists to view themselves as a political activist rather than a professional skilled in facilitating individual growth and development.

All these factors contributed to the radical change I observed in our professional training programs. But there is one additional factor that, in my view, ensured the death knell of traditional training with its emphasis on producing self-aware practitioners. This was the arrival of "woke" students primed to disrupt and dismantle.

In the case of the psychotherapy program at my university, their arrival was not just the function of inevitable demographic change; it was also the result of a deliberate policy.[6] I can say this with certainty, as I was also on the admissions team at the school, so I had first-hand knowledge of the recruitment procedures.

As an admissions interviewer, our mandated questions for potential students revolved around activism and the candidate's understanding of systemic racism.[7] Students who didn't have all that knowledge were turned away and called "not self-aware enough" to succeed in our program. We were encouraged to accept more and more students of color so that the make-up of our program looked sufficiently diverse.

Needless to say, diversity of thought was not important, nor was it supported. The consequence of such a biased selection procedure resulted in cohorts containing a significant proportion of highly vocal activist students, and as I will be going on to detail, this negatively affected the dynamic of the classroom.

How this ideology is playing out in the training context

Once CSJ became established, the impact of this new ideology was felt in all aspects of the program. It changed not only what was taught but also how it was delivered. In this section, I want to give the reader a flavor of the resulting narrow-minded curriculum and hostile learning environment that transpired.

By its very nature, this ideology is the antithesis of what psychotherapists are traditionally trained to do. The subscribed narrative left little room for thoughtful and intelligent discourse.[8] Viewpoint diversity was strongly discouraged, and CSJ concepts such as microaggressions were accepted as uncontested facts.[9,10]

Critical Race Theory (CRT) became the required foundation for classes. In simple terms, CRT asserts that someone, based on their race, is either a privileged oppressor or a marginalized oppressed person.[11] Furthermore, racism is inherently deeply embedded and will never go away. We must either acknowledge privilege and make reparations where necessary or be told that we are marginalized by situations that are out of our control. Furthermore, we don't need to educate others about who they are because "by the color of my skin, you should already know what you've done to my people". When taking all of this into account, it makes me sad to say that we have reduced people to stereotypes; we have watered down the complexity of people's identities that effectively diminishes our common humanity and rich life experiences.

The insidious nature of this ideology contributed to a classroom of activists before anyone realized that the ground of the training program had shifted. It was like being hit by an avalanche with professors scurrying around desperate to change their syllabi and learning materials. Now, we had to present a political position that defined what "privileged" meant and encouraged the necessity of acknowledging and feeling shame for it.

Additionally, it seemed that the only acceptable solution to racism was to raise the underprivileged groups and mandate reparations for the pain caused by a system eradicated many decades ago. Even more troubling, the expectations of the students' performance were lowered in order to align with the perception that members of underprivileged groups were incapable of reaching academic excellence on their own.

The irony is that if the therapist uses a CSJ ideological lens to understand their client, they are in fact assuming, stereotyping, and labelling clients based on immutable characteristics and demographics. The client is reduced to a victim of a system that will never change. In our program, we were teaching our students the exact opposite of traditional therapy, which focuses on helping clients develop self-empowerment and write their own narratives, their own stories, and not be told what to think and believe.

The negative influence of CRT on the training program was exacerbated in the immediate aftermath of George Floyd's death. Students were allowed to skip class to join Black Lives Matter protests. The white students were encouraged to apologize to students of color and acknowledge how "whiteness" was the root cause of problems experienced by marginalized communities.

Then, because the school's mission rested on CRT ideology, the professors were constrained in any attempt to help the students work through their pain and confusion. Round table discussions would feature professors of color discussing their emotional pain due to rampant systemic racism. A white male professor told me, "We cannot comment because we're white. We have to listen to this discussion to understand how we've contributed to racism and victims' pain."

Needless to say, this relentless emphasis on the relationship between the oppressor and the oppressed pushed by a highly vocal group of activist students led to a hostile learning environment. Classroom debates nearly always devolved into arguments about who caused whom pain. All the teaching material was scrutinized in the light of power dynamics. It was frowned upon to use case studies that involved heterosexual white men and women. Instead, we were informed that we needed to choose examples with multiple dimensions of marginalized and disenfranchised characteristics. In essence, there was a hierarchy at work; certain groups were elevated, and others were dismissed as unworthy of attention.

On a daily basis, it was an uphill battle to focus the student group on learning conventional psychotherapy theory and practice. One day, I screened a Ted Talk featuring a new model of treatment for addiction—a particularly important issue for any trainee psychotherapist. The following class discussion lasted two hours. Frustratingly, rather than debating the clinical implications of the treatment model, the vocal activist students focused on the problematic ethnicity of the trainer in the video: they were "offended" and "felt harmed" because the Ted Talk speaker was white. This was just one example out of many instances of how CSJ has sent students down the wrong path. Constant redirecting and constant debate did not leave room for learning how to be a therapist.

CSJ ideology allowed the activist students to make absolutist moral judgments regarding people's experience of pain and disenfranchisement. These students were very quick to silence other perspectives which hold that most people are privileged in some ways but not in others. This diminished view of human complexity limited their understanding of privilege to the possession of immutable characteristics such as skin color and gender. I could see how this new lens imposed on all group discussions thereby creating animosity, shame, and depression. Students began to feel hopeless and pessimistic about the possibility of any change.

Given this hostile learning environment, it should be unsurprising that the more subtle and delicate aspects of teaching students to become good psychotherapists fell by the wayside. Furthermore, the relentless focus on CSJ rendered it impossible to create the right conditions for facilitating the students' self-development. For example, students' overall performance evaluation in class was based on a five-point rubric of achieved objectives, with one specifically stating that the student will "demonstrate awareness, sensitivity, and skills in working with individuals, groups, and communities from various cultural backgrounds and identities, and, in working to dismantle systems of marginalization, domination, and oppression".

As one of the main five objectives for each course, the CSJ element was deeply embedded in the course material and the assignments. In order to measure this, professors had to include assignments that incorporated exploration of marginalization and the dismantlement of oppressive systems. Time out of the classroom that should have been spent on explorative activities that promoted self-discovery and evolution as a therapist was, instead, spent on identifying how they personally contributed to the oppressor/oppressed systemic patriarchal structure and how this impacted the emotional well-being of entire populations.

Often, as an evaluator, I struggled because I never assigned projects that incorporated CSJ and it became increasingly more difficult to evaluate my students' work using our standard rubric. It simply had no place in the training of psychotherapists. As a curriculum developer, I designed course material for two brand-new workshops that I presented to the curriculum committee. Before I could receive official approval, they implored me to add CSJ-focused assignments. Eventually, I even started to receive feedback from students that the assignments in my class focused too much on internal reflection and self-discovery and not enough on identifying external social problems with proposed solutions.

As a teacher, my experience in this program was a heart-sinking one. It was almost as if I was peddling this ideology myself. Then, one day I woke up and it hit me: *I don't believe in what I am teaching or that I am required to teach it.*

Not long after I had left the school, one student, a white man, connected with me, saying, "This program was the most traumatizing period of my life." I fear that he was not alone in his assessment.

Conclusion

My experience has been unusual in that I have witnessed two versions of psychotherapy training at the same institution. This unique experience has given me an insider view of what happens to psychotherapy training when it is captured by a political ideology. Although my testimony is anecdotal, I strongly suspect that my observations would apply to professional therapy training more generally.

In my view, the impact of CSJ on psychotherapy training is nothing short of disastrous. Clients deserve properly trained therapists who are truly responsive to their needs. This isn't to say that our clients don't face real challenges due to race, gender, or other immutable characteristics, and I am not claiming that the world is always fair. But I am watching my profession begin to move far away from a nuanced understanding of those challenges to a deeply dangerous politicized practice, directly opposed to how therapists used to be trained.

Therapist trainers must model the qualities that we want our students to exhibit. One of these qualities would be courage. It is time to stand up and tell the truth about what is happening to our profession—our students and their future clients require this level of commitment and bravery.

Endnotes

[1] Decades of research has identified the quality of the therapeutic relationship as the key factor in the efficacy of counselling and psychotherapy. See the overview provided by Tori DeAngelis, "Better relationships with patients lead to better outcomes", *CE Corner,* 50 no.10 (2019: 38) accessed June 1, 2022, on the website for the American Psychological Association, https://www.apa.org/monitor/2019/11/ce-corner-relationships.

[2] See the recent example of Aaron Kindsvatter, formerly a professor of counseling at the University of Vermont, who made a series of videos protesting about the imposition of CRT on therapist training. Students campaigned to have him expelled. Accessed June 1, 2022, https://www.sevendaysvt.com/OffMessage/archives/2021/03/16/uvm-professors-viral-video-prompts-calls-for-his-resignation.

[3] Each therapy school has a particular theoretical perspective on identity development. However, Eric Erickson, one of the earliest psychological researchers, is regarded as having developed the standard for basic identity formation through life stages. For a simplified overview of his framework, see Saul McLeod, "Erik Erikson's Stages of Psychosocial Development", *Simply Psychology* (2018), accessed June 5, 2022, https://www.simplypsychology.org/Erik-Erikson.html#:~:text=The%20fifth%20stage%20of%20Erik,values%2C%20beliefs%2C%20and%20goals.

[4] It is important to note that these moves are not restricted to within the therapy field itself—activists are targeting licensure requirements. For example, the Michigan Licensing board (LARA) recently amended its licensure requirements based on recent changes to the state Public Health Code. Physicians and healthcare practitioners (including counselors) are now required to undergo "Implicit Bias Training" to become licensed, and must continue to receive Implicit Bias Training (1 hour) every year. Accessed on June 6, 2022, https://www.msms.org/About-MSMS/News-Media/new-implicit-bias-training-requirement. Strikingly, the State of Michigan currently has no requirements for continuing education for therapists. So, in this state, being trained in implicit bias is viewed as a priority rather than developing and enhancing therapeutic skills and knowledge.

[5] The introduction to the University of Antioch's mission statement concerning its core attributes demonstrates its emphasis on CSJ as follows: "Antioch University prides itself on its mission to provide 'learner-centered' education to empower students with the knowledge and skills to lead meaningful lives and *to advance social, economic, and environmental justice.* An Antioch education inspires our students to transform themselves, connect with others, and harness their tal-

ents to win victories for humanity. During their studies and throughout their careers, Antioch students actively reflect on their values, biases, and behaviors. In classroom communities and beyond they seek diverse perspectives and *confront dynamics of power, privilege, and oppression.* They engage with the complex, interconnected systems comprising our world, *challenging the status quo and advancing social, environmental, and economic justice.*" (Italics added). Accessed on June 20, 2022, https://www.antioch.edu/about/core-attributes.

[6] A recent survey of generational attitudes in the US indicates that younger people are significantly more likely to accept restrictions on free speech in order to protect perceived disadvantaged groups from harm. Eric Kaufman, "The Politics of the Culture Wars in Contemporary America", *The Manhattan Institute* (January 25, 2022), https://www.manhattan-institute.org/kaufmann-politics-culture-war-contemporary-america.

[7] The questions for admissions interviewers were internal documents and only accessible on the faculty's intranet; therefore, I am unable to make these available to the reader.

[8] See, for example, this discussion of intersectionality in therapy training by Val Thomas, "Disingenuous Pedagogy in Professional Counselling Training: Turning an Intersectional Lens into an Ideological Straitjacket,", *Critical Therapy Antidote* (2020), https://criticaltherapyantidote.org/2020/09/28/disingenuous-pedagogy-in-professional-counselling-training-turning-an-intersectional-lens-into-an-ideological-straitjacket.

[9] See the critique of the concept of microaggressions in the review of the evidence by Scott O. Lilienfeld, "Microaggressions: Strong Claims, Inadequate Evidence", *Perspectives on Psychological Science* 12, no.1 (January 2017): 143. https://doi.org/10.1177/1745691616659391.

[10] The key texts for the training program inevitably reflected the ideological bias of the teaching program and the professional bodies more generally. Examples include an accredited publication from the APA Division of Counseling Psychology by Lisa A. Goodman, Belle Liang, Janet E. Helms, Rachel E. Latta, Elizabeth Sparks and Sarah R. Weintraub, "Training Counseling Psychologists as Social Justice Agents: Feminist and Multicultural Principles in Action", *The Counseling Psychologist* 32, no 6 (2004):793-836.

Another example would be a more recent APA-approved book by M. E. Kite, K. A. Case, and W. R. Williams, W. R. (Eds.), *Navigating Difficult Moments in Teaching Diversity and Social Justice.* (American Psychological Association: Washington DC, 2021).

[11] Sarah E. Movius, "Critical Race Theory", Theoretical Models for Teaching

and Research, PB-PRESSBOOKS, accessed on November 9, 2022, https://opentext.wsu.edu/theoreticalmodelsforteachingandresearch/chapter/critical-race-theory/.

Chapter 21:

How Does the Therapy Field Move Forward?

by Val Thomas

Introduction

Counselling and psychotherapy, like other applied cultural practices, have reached a critical juncture. A profound crisis is happening in Western culture as it grapples with the arrival of a new worldview, one that is hostile to the fundamental principles informing Western democratic societies.

In the first chapter, it was made clear that, so far, the therapy field seems to be passively reflecting the mainstream; therapists are now expected to support social justice activism. It was argued that the stifling of any public debate or critique has allowed a political ideology to infiltrate the field; the chapters included in this book spell out the ramifications of this takeover for practitioners and their clients.

However, even if therapists become emboldened to challenge the cultural hegemony of Critical Social Justice (CSJ), the reality is that our professions, whether we like it or not, are going to change in response to these wider shifts in the collective. One thing—maybe the only thing—that can be predicted with any certainty is that these changes will be fundamental and structural.

Offering an informed critique of CSJ in relation to therapy is a very important first step; it is necessary but not sufficient. We need to be able to identify potential strategies for pushing back against the whole-scale dismantling of well-established and effective therapeutic practices.

This closing chapter, therefore, advocates for developing a groundswell of an informed public and professional opinion strong enough to defend the field. To that end, one particular rhetorical strategy is proposed: insisting that CSJ-driven therapeutic practices are explicitly named as such. All those who wish to preserve the healing ethos of counselling and psychotherapy can contribute to holding this boundary.

Background

To recap, CSJ is an authoritarian ideology that is in the process of diverting therapy from its proper concern with individual healing and repurposing it as a political practice focused on societal change. Instead of properly integrating the cultural aspect of human experience into clinical theory and practice, this collective dimension has just become the new site of reductionist and simplistic explanatory frameworks for human distress.[1]

What is urgently required is a means of interrupting this regressive move posing as a radically new development, in the hope that the counselling and psychotherapy disciplines can recentre the individual (or couple/family in systemic approaches) as both the locus and focus of therapy.

It is important to understand that CSJ theories not only change the focus of therapeutic practice but threaten to transform its very ground. As described in the first chapter, one particularly defining characteristic of the contemporary therapy field is its pluralistic nature. This pluralism evolved through the last decades of the 20th century and comprises many different perspectives on psychological distress and how to facilitate recovery, flourishing, and wellbeing. These approaches range from empirically grounded Cognitive Behavioural Therapy (CBT) to philosophically informed Existential Psychotherapy.[2]

From observing how CSJ takes over other arenas, it can be confidently predicted that this ideology will impose a reductive field-wide homogeneity achieved through problematising, and then dismantling, already-established effective therapies.[3] Determined practitioners and heterodox clinical theorists and trainers need to make a concerted effort to resist the illegitimate totalising claims of CSJ in the therapy field before it is too late. Efforts should be focused on ousting this antitherapeutic ideology from the wider territory. Firstly, though, it is important to understand the ethical and moral ground on which this battle can be fought.

In the first decade of the new millennium, there was a chance that the disciplines of counselling and psychotherapy could have taken steps to protect the integrity of the field. Voices were warning of the dangers that CSJ posed to the mental health professions.[4] If the therapy field had heeded them at the time, perhaps this virulent conflation of Critical Theory and postmodernism might have been halted in its tracks before it started to run amok.

One container could have been a CSJ therapy modality. This mode of assimilating new perspectives and positions has been a time-honoured tradition in counselling and psychotherapy. CSJ-driven therapy could have then taken its place alongside other modalities and been incorporated into the pluralistic field. This type of container would have preserved the heterodox characteristic of the therapy field currently under threat.

Unfortunately, as this CSJ ideology has become more deeply entrenched in wider society and has infiltrated professional institutions, that opportunity appears to have been lost.

However, even though CSJ can no longer be clearly contained within the bounds of a separate modality, we can still work towards establishing a boundary. Such a boundary rests on actively differentiating CSJ-driven therapy from the rest of the therapy field.

One of the sleight-of-hand rhetorical strategies that activists have made use of is to conflate CSJ-driven practice with generic counselling approaches. In other words, the labels of "counselling" and "psychotherapy" are now being applied to practices that are political rather than therapeutic (as would be traditionally under-stood). Everyone concerned about the direction therapy is taking needs to understand that there are solid grounds for pushing back against and exposing this bad-faith manoeuvre. These grounds can be encapsulated in the unequivocal ethical duty of counsellors and psychotherapists to be transparent about the nature and efficacy of the services they offer to potential clients. In the following sections, these two duties are spelled out in more detail.

Transparency

There is a strong moral and ethical imperative for identifying CSJ-driven practice as a particular type of politicised therapy. It goes without saying that clients have the right to know what type of service they are signing up for. All ethical codes of professional bodies include the principle of informed consent.[5]

Therapists associated with particular schools of therapy such as psychodynamic, humanistic, or Cognitive Behavioural Therapy (CBT) would be expected to be transparent about their approach and to make sure that their clients understand the type of treat-ment they will receive. As CSJ is not identified as a particular modality, there is no concomitant obligation to make its politi-cised approach to therapy clear to the consumer. As CSJ-driven perspectives encroach further into the counselling and psycho-therapy disciplines, more therapists are embracing this ideolog-ical worldview. This move is particularly evident in professional training institutions, so it is likely that a significant proportion of newly qualified practitioners will have been strongly encouraged to adopt CSJ-driven perspectives on therapeutic practice. Yet, the general public will not necessarily be able to discern which therapists have adopted this political view rather than practising a traditional form.

It should go without saying that consumers of therapeutic services need to be made aware if a therapist is going to primarily view their clients' difficulties through the prism of intersected identities, diagnose their problems in living as the consequence of societal oppression, and propose political activism as a treatment solution. Without this information, how can potential clients make an informed choice or go on to assess the suitability of the treatment they are receiving?

It is important to point out that this principle of transparency serves everyone—there will be individuals who would embrace a politically activist therapy and would therefore also benefit from a clear labelling of the services on offer. People who seek out therapy need to interview potential therapists and ask for clarification about their treatment approach; one useful question would be to ask how the therapist would explain the causes of their clients' problems. Therapists who have adopted a CSJ world view the source of difficulties as arising from oppressive societal conditions.

Evidence for efficacy

Another compelling argument for insisting that CSJ-driven therapy is distinguished from generic counselling approaches rests on the ethical requirement to provide clients with proven services.[6]

It took many years of intensive research programmes to be able to first establish, unequivocally, that talking therapies were effective, and then, later on, to tease out the factors operating in such complex processes which are implicated in successful outcomes.[7] In general, it takes a long time before therapy approaches and methods are accepted as proven. However, CSJ-driven clinical practice has not followed the usual developmental trajectory for a new therapy which would consist of an iterative process of refinements informed by rigorous testing, clinical observations, and resolving internal contradictions. And consequently, there is hardly any evidence for its effectiveness as a therapeutic approach. Additionally, claims that this is empirically supported rest on tangential evidence such as some research studies which indicate the improved efficacy of counsellors with multi-cultural competencies.[8]

In other words, the disciplines of counselling and psychotherapy are now opening themselves up to a radically new approach to therapy—one informed by a collectivist ideology—without raising any questions about its efficacy. This move represents a complete dereliction of the therapy profession's ethical duty to the clients they serve.

It is worth pausing, at this point, to state that it should be no surprise that a CSJ approach to therapy would sidestep such a fundamental requirement for proof of its therapeutic efficacy. One of the characteristics of this ideology is a particular stance toward the idea of empirical evidence. Its postmodern underpinnings imbue it with a distrust in science, which it would view as a discourse that upholds oppressive systems of power. Objective science is compared unfavourably with more subjective perspectives on the nature of truth—readers will, no doubt, be familiar with the oft-touted term "lived experience". Left to its own devices, CSJ would completely dispense with any requirement to empirically substantiate its practices.

The resistance to engaging with developing an evidence base is also informed by the Critical Theory component of CSJ. Critical Theory is political and tactical; its goal is to create more activists.[9] Any arena or discipline that it infiltrates will then be co-opted to these political ends, and rhetorical strategies will be deployed. In order to complete a successful takeover—or in its words to establish itself as the hegemony—the true intentions of CSJ will be disguised.

In the case of counselling and psychotherapy, there will be some passing reference to an empirical evidence base, but these appeals are usually bad-faith attempts to present themselves as similar in nature to established therapy practices. CSJ has no interest in researching the efficacy of its treatment approach, let alone in developing solid clinical theory and procedures; this is because it is not, primarily, a healing endeavour.

Arguably, even for its self-identified victim group members, it does not offer healing but instead amplifies feelings of anger and resentment. It is worth bearing in mind that Critical Theory distinguishes itself from other approaches to theory and knowledge; Critical Theory focuses on changing society, whereas traditional theories attempt to better understand the world.[10] This distinction helps to explain the radical difference between CSJ-driven therapy, with its disinterest in developing clinical knowledge, and the commitment to improving therapeutic methods evident in the rest of the field.

It is understandable, therefore, that attempting to name this CSJ-driven practice as a particular type of approach will be met with very fierce resistance. Once it is differentiated from the rest of the field, CSJ approaches become vulnerable to legitimate and persuasive critique. It is very important to hold this boundary because this is how its antitherapeutic nature can be more easily exposed.

Put simply, CSJ-driven therapy diagnoses the problems that clients bring to therapy as arising out of oppressive societal conditions and views all human interactions through the lens of power. Clients are encouraged to attribute all difficulties in their life to the internalisation of external forces; for example, depression would be caused by racism. In practice, this is an approach that consolidates the client's sense of victimhood and discounts their own agency in making productive changes in their life. I imagine that most people would view this as a counterintuitive approach to helping people. In fact, it contradicts the evidence that we have from psychology that shows an unequivocal correlation between increased agency and optimal functioning.[11] *In other words, CSJ-driven treatment approaches would appear to be working to weaken people's sense of self.*

Taken to its logical conclusion, vulnerable people who present for therapeutic interventions can be damaged by a CSJ approach. This is because the clinical space becomes, primarily, a site of moral re-education; the issues brought by the clients are relegated to lesser importance.

Clinical theorists who have embraced a CSJ perspective are now arguing for the therapist's duty to refocus the clinical work on developing critical consciousness in their clients.[12] Applying this thinking to white clients; in particular, a case is being made that, no matter what problem is being presented, the therapist needs to bring the client's attention to matters of race.[13] Such a move amounts to advocating for the imposition of a politicised agenda on the client.

Furthermore, we now have clear, real-world evidence of how this ideological approach can result in abusive practice. A good example is provided by the Edinburgh Rape Crisis Centre in the UK. It would be self-evident that vulnerable women in a distressed state after a sexual attack would want to see a female counsellor. The recently appointed transgender CEO thinks otherwise, stating that any clients who object to male-bodied counsellors are bigots who require moral re-education as part of their treatment.[14] This move again prioritises a political agenda over the therapeutic needs of a vulnerable individual.

I am strongly of the opinion that the current disciplines of counselling and psychotherapy are violating the basic ethical requirements of any profession by turning a blind eye to these abusive practices. It is incumbent upon practitioners, trainers, supervisors, and clinical theorists to honour their ethical commitments and strongly resist these incursions. Delivering a service and claiming it is therapeutic requires transparency and evidence; a clear boundary is urgently needed.

Holding the boundary

Holding the boundary—insisting that approaches to therapy are clearly labelled—and maintaining the commitment to a heterodox field that rests on proven therapeutic approaches requires concerted action.

One of the striking features of CSJ is its genius for rhetorical strategies. It is important to learn how to combat these. Furthermore, we must recognize that there are legions of lay people and professionals who are not convinced by CSJ. For any pushback to succeed, theoretical critiques of the tenets of CSJ-driven therapy need to be bolstered by common sense arguments that will resonate with the silent majority.

CSJ rhetorical strategies rely on getting the opponent onto the back foot. It is crucial to prevent oneself from being overpowered in this way. In the following discussion, we will look at two classic CSJ strategies that require attention: the destabilisation of categories and the weaponisation of problematics.

Let's start with the issue of categories. One of the principles informing postmodern philosophy is the blurring of boundaries; all established categories are viewed with suspicion as they are regarded as vehicles for systems of power.[15] Therefore, apart from the more cynical motives attributed earlier on to the project of conflating CSJ-driven therapy with generic therapy, postmodernism will instinctively resist the creation of boundaries. Furthermore, categories are to be dissolved and destabilised (readers will, no doubt, be familiar with how this has been applied to categories of sex and gender).[16] Any position that insists on distinguishing CSJ-driven therapy as a particular category of cultural political practice will engender strong opposition based on this principle. This resistance will not take the form of good faith arguments but rather the deployment of a now classic arsenal of weapons designed to shut down any debate.

The response to these attacks should be a refusal to be silenced and maintain a stand on the deeper irrefutable ground of the moral duty of the professions to be transparent about their services (as discussed earlier). Appeals to common sense can be used. Posing rhetorical questions is an effective strategy, such as: in what other profession would it be acceptable to expect someone to sign up for a service that is neither proven nor accurately labelled? It is also helpful to provide illustrations of where clear labelling is already viewed as obligatory within the field of therapy. One example would be therapists with particular religious commitments. Clients would be rightfully aggrieved if they signed up for a generic counselling service and then discovered that their problems were being diagnosed through a particular religious framework. Services that are clearly labelled—Christian counselling would be a good example here—would permit an informed choice. As CSJ-driven therapy is informed by a particular worldview, the obligation for clear labelling should also hold.

Second, CSJ activists will often resort to the weapon of problematics.[17] The therapy field has been particularly vulnerable to any attack that is based on the notion that knowledge and culture are socially constructed.[18]

As mentioned in the first chapter, by the turn of the millennium, the disciplines of counselling and psychotherapy had been paying increasing attention to the collective dimension of human experience, particularly the role that societal structures play in shaping people's lives.

In addition, there was a significant focus on the problematics of therapy—the limitations of theory and practice which originated within a 20th-century Western culture. Such critiques offered a helpful corrective, allowing the field to expand and assimilate other viewpoints. An example would be the later feminist critiques of classic psychoanalytic theory based on the view that Freud's understanding of women was limited by his historical and cultural experience.[19]

Critiques such as these stimulated debate and further developments in theory and practice, overall making an important contribution to the dynamism of the field. However, as the ideology of CSJ has encroached into the mainstream, it has created the conditions for more destructive applications of such critiques.

Once the therapy professions started to pivot, alongside mainstream culture, to accepting a new postmodern worldview, they became increasingly vulnerable to critiques informed by social constructionism. It is as if the river of problematics has burst its banks and is now flooding the whole territory. Now, instead of critiques being used to develop theory and practice—as in the previous example of feminist perspectives on psychoanalysis—problematics are being used to erode the ethos of traditional therapy. Generic ideologically motivated criticisms are levelled at therapy as a whole. A good example of this tendency would be the view endorsed by professional bodies such as the APA that psychology is systematically racist.[20] Once this narrative is established as the hegemony, it is easy to argue that psychologists should focus on changing systems. Radical activist scholars and clinical theorists can then advocate for imposing the clinician's agenda on the client.[21] This move, in effect, divorces clinical practice from its traditional client-centred ethos.

It is particularly important to counter these critiques; otherwise, a whole-scale demolition job will take place in the therapy field. One way of doing this is for everyone concerned by the direction in which therapy is travelling to name the destructive intent that informs this widespread recourse to problematics. When dealing with rhetorical strategies, the focus is on exposing the end goal rather than the actual contents of the argument.

To recap, an insistent focus on problem-detecting at the expense of a more balanced historical perspective on the development of theory and practice will prove ruinous. It is much easier to problematise therapy rather than undertake the challenging work of developing and testing new contributions to therapeutic practice.

Nevertheless, the pluralistic ethos of contemporary therapy is precious and hard-won. It operates as a bulwark against an authoritarian ideology intent on imposing a simplistic, one-dimensional collectivist worldview throughout the therapy field, one that reduces all human interactions to power relations and threatens to dismantle rich traditions of theory and practice. Therefore, rhetorical strategy in the defence of talking therapies needs to be harnessed to the goal of repositioning CSJ as only *one of several* competing explanations of human distress. Put more bluntly, CSJ, and, in particular, its core framework of intersectionality, needs to be brought down to size, not acting as an uncontested foundational worldview but just one of the many perspectives on the human condition.[22]

A caveat and a call

Having proffered some strategies for establishing and maintaining a boundary between CSJ-driven approaches and traditional established therapeutic practice, it is also important to be realistic. CSJ has now entrenched itself in the professional institutions of therapy; any pushback will be ferociously resisted.

Unless a strong internal resistance rapidly crystalises within the disciplines of counselling and psychotherapy, the most likely outcome will be the chaotic breakdown of the field itself. As CSJ moves through the therapy professions in its usual manner, dismantling, disrupting, decolonising, and problematising all that exists therein, it will hollow out the centre.[23] The foundations of the disciplines will be eroded and replaced with an obsessive pre-occupation with power relations. Likely, the new generations of therapists will not receive traditional schooling in the seminal theories generated by the originating geniuses of psychotherapy.[24] The counselling and psychotherapy disciplines will have less and less to do with healing, and instead just become one of the many cultural practices that are now operating to consolidate an ideological hold over the population.

Very soon, there may only be two possibilities: this politicised version of therapy and other pre-existing, more traditional approaches that are likely to be characterised and discredited as reactionary. Practitioners and clinical theorists who do not hold this new ideological worldview will be driven to the margins, go underground, or withdraw into private practice.

Therefore, in the midst of these difficult times, it is incumbent upon all of us to do what we can to help the therapy professions move through this crisis with minimal collateral damage. Everyone who rejects the lie that therapy should be a political practice can contribute to building up a swell of informed public and professional opinion. Everyone who joins a network or alliance can increase the pressure that can be brought to bear on the institutions. Academics, clinical theorists, and writers can collaborate to re-establish the ground of therapy and reconnect it with its traditional healing ethos. And all of us need to stand firm and insist that an obsessive preoccupation with power is damaging to everyone.

By pushing back against the illegitimate encroachments of politicised approaches to therapy, we will be helping to realign the therapy professions to a higher duty. In the previous century, counselling and psychotherapy operated as a corrective to the one-sidedness of culture, helping to loosen up overly rigid boundaries and repressions present in the society of those times. In a postmodern world, we are faced with the inverse: a destabilisation of categories and an indiscriminate erosion of boundaries. If the therapy field ceases to be just a passive reflection of mainstream society, and instead takes a stand for authenticity, clarity, and legitimate boundaries, it can help to stabilise a dangerously out-of-balance culture. By so doing, the disciplines of counselling and psychotherapy will be reconnecting with their original radical roots and re-establishing themselves as a force for moral good in society.

Conclusion

Finally, above all else, it is important to bear in mind the bigger picture. In the end, no matter how this crisis plays itself out, reality always has the last say. If CSJ does take over the therapy field, replacing a rich heritage with a monolithic, antitherapeutic culture, it will not be able to eliminate the spirit of healing, but new therapeutic practices will arise on the margins. Disillusioned practitioners will probably develop their own organisations and professional associations, replacing the old, weak legacy professional bodies and training institutions of the past. We can also be assured that CSJ-driven therapeutic practices will not survive the test of time. As its pretences to be a therapeutic enterprise are exposed in the cold light of day, the whole house of cards will inevitably and eventually collapse.

In these postmodern times, unanchored in reality and attached to simplistic reductive explanations, it has been fashionable to condemn our past forebears and reject the universality of the human condition. Yet, anyone who practises any form of healing knows that they are responding to a timeless vocational calling. We owe it to everyone before us in this lineage to stand for and uphold the dignity of the human spirit.

As we move through a great epochal shift into an unknown future, ancestral voices call out to us. Written in hieroglyphs on an ancient papyrus scroll over three millennia ago, the scribes remind us to hold on to what matters: "Great is the power of the human heart to love, to change, to make new ... Truth shall not pass away."[25]

Endnotes

[1] See the contemporary philosopher Ken Wilber's elegant AQAL frame-work, which lays out the four main dimensions (or "quadrants" of the individual's existence as individual/interior (the subjective contents of the mind), individual/exterior (the body), collective/interior (intersub-jectivity and culture), and collective/exterior (the structures of society). An overemphasis on one (or two) of these dimensions at the expense of the others is termed "quadrant reductionism". Thus, the earlier focus in psychology on biological explanation of human behaviour would be an example of one type of quadrant reductionism. The overemphasis on the collective dimensions of human experience would be a contemporary version—an inverse of the previous one. An accessible overview can be found in Ken Wilber (2007). *The integral vision: A very short introduc-tion to the revolutionary integral approach to life, God, the universe, and everything.* (Boulder, Colorado: Shambhala Publications, 2007).

[2] Existential Psychotherapy is informed by a philosophic approach to the human condition. It is believed that all individuals need to come to terms with the basic universal conditions of human existence. See Emmy van Deurzen, *Existential Psychotherapy and Counselling in Practice.* 3rd rev. edn, (London: Sage, 2012).

[3] Problematising is a focus for CSJ—all efforts are made to identify the ways in which present conditions do not meet an ideal. See the following definition and extended commentary by James Lindsay, "Problematize", *New Discourses*, accessed October 20, 2022, https://newdiscourses. com/tftw-problematize/.

[4] See Rogers H. Wright and Nicholas A. Cummings, eds., *Destructive Trends in Mental Health: The Well-intentioned Path to Harm* (New York: Rout-ledge, 2005).

[5] All professional therapy bodies will have clauses within their official ethical codes that relate to obtaining informed consent from the client to the therapeutic services offered. The following example is Clause 15 taken from *The UK Council for Psychotherapy Code of Ethics*, p3, issued in October 2019, https://www.psychotherapy.org.uk/media/bkjdm33f/ukcp-code-of-ethics-and-professional-practice-2019.pdf. "Confirm each client's consent to the specifics of the service you will offer, through a clear contract at the outset of therapy ... Help clients to understand the nature of any proposed therapy and its implications, what to expect, the risks involved, what is and is not being offered, and relevant alternative options."

6 All professional therapy bodies will attend to the requirement to use proven methods in their official ethical codes. The following example is Clause C.7.a taken from the American Counseling Association's Code of Ethics, p.10, issued in 2014, https://www.counseling.org/docs/default-source/ethics/2014-code-of-ethics.pdf?sfvrsn=2d58522c_4. "When providing services, counselors use techniques/procedures/modalities that are grounded in theory and/or have an empirical or scientific foundation."

7 For a good overview of the research evidence, see B. E. Wampold and Z. E. Imel, (2015). *The great psychotherapy debate: The evidence for what makes psychotherapy work* (2nd ed.). (New York: Routledge, 2015).

8 There has been significant interest in researching the relationship between counsellors' multicultural competencies and therapy outcomes. However, reviews of the research suggest that no firm conclusions can be drawn so far. See K. W. Tao, J. Owen, B. T. Pace, and Z. E. Imel. "A meta-analysis of multicultural competencies and psychotherapy process and outcome", *Journal of Counseling Psychology,* 62, no. 3 (2015): 337–350, https://doi.org/10.1037/cou0000086.

9 Max Horkheimer, "Traditional and Critical Theory" in P. Connerton (Ed.), *Critical Sociology Selected Readings* (Harmondsworth: Penguin,1976), pp. 206-224.

10 Ibid.

11 Ralf Schwarzer and Lisa Warner, "Perceived Self-Efficacy and its Relationship to Resilience", in *The Springer series on human exceptionality: Resilience in children, adolescents, and adults: Translating research into practice,* eds. S. Prince-Embury & D. H. Saklofske (New York: Springer, 2013), pp. 139-150.

12 "Critical Consciousness" is the ability to identify and then challenge societal structures of oppression.

13 In this example, the author presents a model (described in the abstract) "for how psychotherapists can bring up and work with the topics of race and racism during the course of therapy. The model includes ways for white therapists … to introduce the salience of race in the white client's life, and how to connect race and racism to the client's explicit goals for therapy". See David Drustrup, "Talking with white Clients about Race", *Journal of Health Service Psychology,* 47, (2021):63–72. NB: the use of lower case for white in this case is faithful to the original journal title. https://doi.org/10.1007/s42843-021-00037-2.

[14] In a transcript of a podcast, this CEO states the following: "But I think the other thing is that sexual violence happens to bigoted people as well." Her thoughts on what such "bigots" need in terms of their recovery are laid out and discussed at "The Real Crisis at Rape Crisis Scotland", For Women Scotland, accessed July 22, 2022, https://forwomen. scot/10/08/2021/the-real-crisis-at-rape-crisis-scotland/?fbclid=IwAR-2OrABjPJeKOlWwtcljhooWVC85E2f9WiVyFWlyVp5AatvBY9piFI25__A.

[15] See the overview by Helen Pluckrose and James Lindsay, "Postmodernism", in *Cynical Theories,* (Durham, NC: Pitchstone, 2020), pp. 21-43.

[16] See a very clear explanation of gender-identification ideology and its dissolution of biological sex categories in Helen Joyce, *Trans: When Ideology Meets Reality* (London: Oneworld, 2021).

[17] See endnote 3.

[18] Simply put, social constructionism is a theory of knowledge that posits what we hold to be true about the social world is not objective fact; instead, it is subjective and the product of our interaction with society. Kenneth Gergen and Mary Gergen, eds. *Social Construction: A Reader.* (London: SAGE, 2003).

[19] See Juliet Mitchell, *Psychoanalysis and Feminism with a new introduction.* (London: Penguin, 2000).

[20] See the APA resolution adopted on October 29, 2021, "Role of Psychology and APA in Dismantling Systemic Racism Against People of Color in U.S.", https://www.apa.org/about/policy/dismantling-systemic-racism.

[21] For example, see P. Grzanka, K. Gonzalez and L. Spanierman, "White Supremacy and Counseling Psychology: A Critical–Conceptual Framework," *The Counseling Psychologist* 47, no.4 (May 2019): 478-529. https://doi.org/10.1177/0011000019880843.

[22] A framework for understanding how different social identities intersect and create layers of disadvantage for the person. First laid out by Kimberlé Crenshaw in "Mapping the Margins: Intersectionality, Identity Politics, and Violence against Women of Color", in *Stanford Law Review.* 43 no 6 (July 1991): 1241–1299. https://doi.org/10.2307/1229039.

[23] Decolonisation here refers to the practice of critiquing the Eurocentric shaping of cultural practices and opening these practices up to include marginalised perspectives.

[24] For evidence that this process is well underway, see the independent report on the current state of training counselling psychologists in the UK. Carole Sherwood and Kirsty Miller, "The Politicisation of Clinical Psychology Training Courses in the UK", *Save Mental Health,*

accessed October 20, 2022, https://save-mental-health.com/train-ing-courses/.

[25] Quote taken from Normandi Ellis's sublime poetic rendering of the Papy-rus of Ani, a copy of the Egyptian Book of the Dead. Written in the 19th Dynasty of ancient Egypt, 1275-1250 BCE. Ellis, N. (trans.) *Awakening Osiris: The Egyptian Book of the Dead.* (Grand Rapids, MI: Phanes Press, 1988), p. 158.

Afterword

by Val Thomas

The brief for this book has been to focus on the professions of counselling and psychotherapy. However, these therapeutic practices are also situated in and shaped by a broader professional context.

This afterword provides an opportunity to widen the discussion and consider, albeit briefly, how allied professional fields have responded to Critical Social Justice (CSJ) and what light this can shed on the position of talking therapies.

Counselling and psychotherapy are "small fry" in terms of professional numbers and societal influence, so it would be instructive to look at what is happening in the much bigger fields of education and healthcare. The following discussion focuses on North America due to its dominant position in terms of size and influence and identifies some key points relevant to the existential threat posed by CSJ to the therapy professions.

The professional education context

The field of education is particularly relevant to counselling and psychotherapy mainly because professional therapy training usually takes place in a higher educational context.[1] Students will exit these programmes with an academic qualification often at master's level, which will be accredited by a university or equivalent educational standards board. This context inevitably shapes the way in which teachers/instructors and lecturers design and deliver the training of future generations of therapy practitioners.

The education professions have had the longest experience with CSJ, and recently the general public has started to awaken to the impact of this political ideology becoming mainstream in schools and colleges. Starting in 2016–17, news reports appeared showing angry mobs on university campuses attempting, often successfully, to de-platform speakers with whom they did not agree.

Three or four years later, home-schooling, due to COVID-19 restrictions, allowed parents to see the contents of their children's school curricula. Up until then, the general public had been unaware that a process of replacing a traditional understanding of education with a new politicised teaching approach had been happening almost imperceptibly for many years.

It is important to understand how this radical shift has occurred behind the scenes in the education system. In the early 1980s, radical education theorists, in particular Henry Giroux, helped to popularise the work of the Brazilian Marxist Paulo Freire, who believed that education must serve an emancipatory political goal.[2,3]

Over the next three decades, a new politicised approach to teaching called Critical Pedagogy began to supplant the previous traditional mainstream one (with its focus on knowledge and competence) in colleges of education.[4] This approach has one main objective—encouraging the student to embrace a particular political critique of society called "critical consciousness".[5] Put simply, what this means is that newly trained teachers started to populate the schools, and they began to teach their students to develop the ability to detect the operation of systems of oppression and how to counter them.

Additionally, over these decades, scholars created a large body of theoretical work developing applications of postmodernism and Critical Theory to education practice—one arena of application with particular relevance to therapy has been multicultural education. This scholarly work, in particular, has been highly influential in the development of radical approaches to multicultural competency in therapy.

As discussed in the first chapter, activist scholars who were informed by this ideological approach, such as Derald Wing Sue, were instrumental in supporting the therapy field's pivot from an individual focus to a collective worldview.[6] It is worth adding, at this point, that the dominant CSJ ideology in education has also affected the provision of counselling to school students. Unsurprisingly, the American Schools Counselor Association (ASCA) has committed itself to the politicisation of therapy and requires school counsellors to "embrace their roles as social justice advocates and change agents who examine and dismantle systems of oppression".[7]

But, let's now return to the higher education training context for professional therapy. Colleges of education do not only produce school teachers; they are also the main source for the training of university and college education managers.[8] During the last couple of decades, there has been a notable expansion of the bureaucratic departments in higher education, and the administrators employed there have been trained in the same political ideological approach as the school teachers.[9] These professionals have had more power in being able to impose generic CSJ policies and procedures—mandated diversity, equity, and inclusion trainings being the obvious example—across all faculties.

This combination of activist scholars and politicised bureaucrats has created an environment that supports the imposition of policies reflecting the ideological tenets of CSJ, including decolonising the curricula; microaggressions as uncontested facts;

centering the lived experience of the marginalised; and dismantling white supremacy.[10] Training programmes for counselling and psychotherapy would be hard-pressed to resist such an aggressively politicised educational context.

The professional healthcare context

Another very significant professional context is in healthcare. The relevance, in this case, is that counselling and psychotherapy are often viewed as ancillary or adjunct services to medical ones. Any significant changes in the way that society views healthcare will also affect the delivery of nonmedical services such as psychological therapy. Therapists working in agencies or within public or private healthcare systems will very often be members of multi-professional teams. Consequently, the model of healthcare embraced by the institution will inform the type of counselling or psychotherapy that is provided as an adjunct treatment.[11]

An example of where CSJ-driven medical policy (exacerbated by the zealotry of trans-activists) is creating particular constraints for therapists is in the treatment of gender dysphoria. The Tavistock Gender Identity Disorder Clinic (recently closed down) has faced legal challenges arising out of the consequences for patients due to its commitment to gender ideology—young former patients complained that they were not made fully aware of the long-term medical consequences of medical transition.[12] Unfortunately, a commitment to gender ideology positions Affirmation Therapy as the only acceptable psychological treatment. Therapists are thus prevented from exploring the client's dysphoria.[13]

Until relatively recently, the empirical base of medicine and nursing has been an effective barrier to the incursions of a radically different worldview which is anti-science and anti-reason. Furthermore, the huge advances in medical technology are evident to everyone. And yet, the heretofore uncontested biological ground of medicine is showing signs of erosion. Consider an example from *The New England Journal of Medicine,* widely regarded as one of the most prestigious scientific medical journals. In 2020, the journal published an article that argued for downgrading the importance of biological sex classification on birth certificates.[14] As yet, neither the journal's editors nor the paper's authors have responded formally to the tirade of opposition on social media pointing out the significance of sex concerning health and illness.[15]

The fact that such an article could be published in the first place is evidence that activists working within the healthcare professions are successfully employing the same strategy as we have seen in therapy—see Chapter 1—namely to change the mission of the professions through altering the narrative.

In the case of healthcare, the goal is to shift society away from an individual biological model of medicine and to embrace one that privileges the collective dimension. Any disparities in health outcomes between groups can then be explained as the result of unequal power relations between the majority and the "oppressed" groups. It is then an easy next step to advocate for a redistribution of medical services to compensate for historical oppression. This final move is the actual meaning of the concept of health equity. This, on the surface, is rather an innocuous-sounding term. However, it would allow for society-wide discriminatory health practices. In short, these are practices that could deliberately disadvantage patients who belong to the majority group.

Any objection that the above claim for activists' strategic ambitions is far-fetched can be countered by reading the policy documents published by the American Medical Association (AMA). Consider its recent official guidance on advancing health equity where it states unambiguously, "in this guide, dominant narratives (also called malignant narratives), particularly those about 'race', individualism, and meritocracy, as well as narratives surrounding medicine itself, limit our understanding of the root causes of health inequities. Dominant narratives create harm, undermining public health and the advancement of health equity; they must be named, disrupted, and corrected."[16]

Following this (using terms noted earlier in this chapter about education), the guide states that medical practitioners "must develop *a critical consciousness* of the root causes and structural drivers of health inequities in their communities" (italics added for emphasis).[17] The premier professional body of American medicine is making its CSJ-driven agenda perfectly clear—the ethic of healthcare practice is being re-engineered.

In addition to these rhetorical tactics, activists use another set of strategies that are familiar to the therapy professions—the use of bureaucratic and quasi-legal means to enforce practitioner compliance with the new collectivist ideological worldview. There is no space afforded in a short afterword to deal with this issue in any detail, but a couple of examples will suffice. Pro-equity and antiracist policies have been proliferating within the AMA recently, but the public might be disturbed by the authoritarian nature of some of the initiatives. For instance, in 2021, the AMA adopted guidelines that incorporated the American Academy of Paediatrics' proposal for setting up confidential reporting systems. These are designed to allow anyone to file an anonymous report if they perceive themselves to be on the receiving end of a microaggression or implicit bias.[18] It does not take much imagination to realise how such a one-sided reporting system would have a chilling effect on professionals and practitioners in any work environment.

Another opportunity for compliance is afforded by instituting new criteria for professional licensure and renewal. These criteria are not open to negotiation, so all practitioners have to comply in order to begin or continue practising. An example, just one of many, of harnessing criteria to ideology is a new rule announced by the Michigan Department of Licensing and Regulatory Affairs (LARA) that, effective from June 1, 2022, requires implicit bias training for medical licensure and renewal.[19] This move is concerning because there is poor and contradictory evidence for the efficacy of such training.[20] It demonstrates that, for the Michigan State government, the ideological coherence of the concept of implicit bias with CSJ trumps all other considerations.

Conclusion

Counselling and psychotherapy operate within a much larger professional context, and it is clear that a new radically different political ideology is undermining the traditional base of professions more generally. This process began in education decades ago and has started to move rapidly into healthcare since the turn of the millennium.

What happens in these wider arenas constrains therapy; it cannot hope to stand alone. The tactics employed by CSJ activists that have been applied to the therapy field are no different from the ones used in other professions. The particular combination of narrative reframing and the use of bureaucratic means to force professional compliance is a powerful one.

This afterword could end here with a realistic but bleak appraisal of the current state of counselling and psychotherapy caught inside a much wider professional sphere increasingly captured by CSJ ideology. However, there is a positive message to be gleaned from looking at the wider professional picture.

Education, in particular, is instructive, as it is further down the ideological path than other professions. As mentioned at the beginning, people have become aware of what is happening on college campuses and in schools. Parents especially have started to push back with determination and vigour, protesting against the excesses of gender ideology and Critical Race Theory praxis.[21] A swell of informed public opinion has generated legal moves to protect children from age-inappropriate teaching content.[22] An awakened general public is a powerful force.

Concerned professionals and practitioners can do what they can to work inside their professional spheres, but it looks as if some of the most effective levers can be applied outside the captured institutions. This is an important message here for the therapy professions.

It is possible that a similar grassroots pushback will happen in healthcare when people discover that health equity means preferential treatment for certain groups. And, turning to therapy, how likely is it that the general public will continue to embrace a profession which offers moral re-education instead of responding in an authentic healing way to the sheer complexity of the troubled human condition? I trust the instincts of the general public to resist such indoctrination.

It is our job to make the interior of the profession of therapy transparent to the outside world. We don't know where this is all headed, but in a time when the tectonic plates of the culture are shifting, the best strategy is clarity.

Endnotes

1   The great majority of professional counselling and psychotherapy trainings take place in universities. In the UK, there is a significant proportion
of programmes offered in other settings such as independent therapy
institutions. However, no matter where the training is delivered, the
ensuing therapy qualification will be accredited by a university.

2   Henry Giroux is a highly influential Canadian American education scholar
who is credited as one of the figures who helped lay the theoretical foundations of Critical Pedagogy.

3   Paulo Freire developed his radical political approach to education while
working with illiterate peasants in Brazil. The first of his books to be
translated into English remains one of the most cited works in education, *Pedagogy of the Oppressed*, (M. B. Ramos, Trans.), (New York: The
Seabury Press, 1970). However, it was Henry Giroux's championing of
Freire's later work, *The Politics of Education: Culture, power and liberation* (D. Macedo. Trans.), (Westport, CT: Bergin & Garvey, 1985), that
cemented his reputation in North America.

4   Critical Pedagogy means an approach to education informed by Critical
Theory. For a detailed account of the origins of this approach as well as a
broader discussion of the impact of Critical Theory and postmodernism
on education, see Isaac Gottesman, *The Critical Turn in Education: From
Marxist Critique to Poststructuralist Feminism to Critical Theories of Race*
(New York and London: Routledge, 2016).

5   Critical consciousness is the ability to recognize and analyse systems of
societal inequality and the commitment to take action to disrupt and
dismantle such systems. Cultivating critical consciousness is the general
aim of all the Critical Theories, no matter what their particular focus.

6   Derald Wing Sue is a professor of counselling psychology at Columbia
University and co-author with David Sue of the highly influential standard
text on multi-cultural competency, *Counseling the Culturally Diverse:
Theory and Practice* (9th edn.), (Hoboken, NJ: John Wiley & Sons, 2022).

7   The American School Counselor Association adopted its most recent
position on anti-racism in 2021. Accessed April 16, 2022, https://
www.schoolcounselor.org/Standards-Positions/Position-Statements/
ASCA-Position-Statements/The-School-Counselor-and-Anti-Racist-Prac-
tices.

8   Lyell Asher, "How Ed Schools Became a Menace to Higher Education",
Quillette, March 6, 2019, https://quillette.com/2019/03/06/how-ed-
schools-became-a-menace-to-higher-education/. His thesis is succinctly

summarised in a more recent video presentation, "Why Colleges are Becoming Cults", accessed April 20, 2022, https://www.youtube.com/watch?v=0hybqg81n-M.

9   In the US, colleges and universities have been gradually expanding their administrative functions for decades. Sector-wide, per-student spending on administration increased as much as 61% from 1993 to 2007. Recent data shows the trend continuing and also confirms that instructional teaching is not doing so well in comparison; from 2016 to 2018, colleges' per-student spending on instruction decreased by 0.7%, while per-student spending on administration increased by 1.4%. Erik Gross, "Administrative Bloat Meets the Coronavirus Pandemic", American Council of Trustees and Alumnae, June 2020, accessed April 20, 2022, https://www.goacta.org/2020/06/administrative-bloat-meets-the-coronavirus-pandemic/. This trend is also becoming apparent across European universities – see R. D. Baltaru and Y. N. Soysal, "Administrators in higher education: organizational expansion in a transforming institution", *High Educ* 76, August 2018, 213–229. https://doi.org/10.1007/s10734-017-0204-3.

10   Decolonising the curricula is not restricted to the humanities and social science faculties; it has also made inroads into the empirically based STEM departments. See this recent report about a prestigious UK university, Ewan Somerville, "'Decolonise' maths by subtracting white male viewpoint, urges Durham University", *Telegraph,* April 9, 2022, https://archive.ph/O0ltb.

11   Even though counsellors and psychotherapists working privately will have more autonomy, they will rarely be able to work completely outside the medical system. For example, most will accept client referrals from various institutional sources such as employee assistance programmes. These clients will usually have undergone a medical and psychological assessment which will identify goals for therapy and recommend treatment approaches.

12   See Peter Jenkins' detailed analysis of the legal and medical issues arising in the Tavistock case. "Calibrating Gillick in the age of the gender wars: Part 2 – the curious case of the Tavistock", *Critical Therapy Antidote,* January 2, 2022, https://criticaltherapyantidote.org/2022/01/02/calibrating-gillick-in-the-age-of-gender-wars-part-2-the-curious-case-of-the-tavistock/.

13   See Peter Jenkins' forensically detailed account of the way in which trans-activism working through the professional bodies in the UK has affected therapeutic practice with gender dysmorphia. "Through the

Looking Glass: Making sense of the MOU – Part 1" *Critical Therapy Antidote,* March 31, 2022, https://criticaltherapyantidote.org/2022/03/31/through-the-looking-glass-making-sense-of-the-mou-part-1/, and "Part 2", *Critical Therapy Antidote*, March 31, 2022, https://criticaltherapyantidote.org/2022/03/31/through-the-looking-glass-making-sense-of-the-mou-part-2/.

[14] M. Vadim, et al., "Failed Assignments — Rethinking Sex Designations on Birth Certificates", *N Engl J Med* 383, December 2020, 2399-2401, https://doi.org/10.1056/NEJMp2025974.

[15] See the discussion of the response to the NEJM article by Colin Wright, "On Sex and Gender, The New England Journal of Medicine Has Abandoned Its Scientific Mission", *Quillette*, December 23, 2020, https://quillette.com/2020/12/23/on-sex-and-gender-the-new-england-journal-of-medicine-has-abandoned-its-scientific-mission/.

[16] *Advancing Health Equity: A guide to language, narrative and concepts,* (American Medical Association, 2021), 4, https://www.ama-assn.org/system/files/ama-aamc-equity-guide.pdf.

[17] Ibid, p. 6.

[18] American Medical Association, Reference Committee on Amendments to Constitution and Bylaws, June 2021, https://www.ama-assn.org/system/files/2021-05/j21-handbook-addendum-ref-cmte-conby.pdf#page=106.

[19] "Governor Gretchen Whitmer and LARA Announce Adopted Training Requirement to Improve Equity Across Michigan's Health Care System", Michigan State Press Release, June 2021, https://www.michigan.gov/whitmer/news/press-releases/2021/06/01/governor-gretchen-whitmer-and-lara-announce-adopted-training-requirement-to-improve-equity-across-m.

[20] See the short digest written by Tiffany L. Green and Neo Hagiwara, "The Problem with Implicit Bias Training", *Scientific American,* August 28, 2020, https://www.scientificamerican.com/article/the-problem-with-implicit-bias-training/.

[21] News reports in the US media of angry parents confronting their children's schoolboards have become a very common occurrence. Grassroots organisations are springing up informed by effective tactical thinking, such as the guide issued by The Manhattan Institute, "Woke Schooling: A Toolkit for Concerned Parents", June 17, 2021, https://www.manhattan-institute.org/woke-schooling-toolkit-for-concerned-parents.

[22] The current governor of Florida, Ron DeSantis, is proving to be a staunch defender of traditional schooling. His recent bill is an example of a

swathe of recent legislation in states opposed to the excesses of Critical Pedagogy. "Governor Ron DeSantis Signs Historic Bill to Protect Parental Rights in Education", Florida State Press Release, March 28, 2022, https://www.flgov.com/2022/03/28/governor-ron-desantis-signs-historic-bill-to-protect-parental-rights-in-education/.